S0-AJA-434

The Collection Program in Schools

Library Science Text Series

Developing Library and Information Center Collections. 3d ed. By G. Edward Evans. 1995.

The Collection Program in Schools: Concepts, Practices, and Information Sources. 2d ed. By Phyllis J. Van Orden. 1995.

The Humanities: A Selective Guide to Information Sources. 4th ed. By Ron Blazek and Elizabeth Aversa. 1994.

The School Library Media Manager. By Blanche Woolls. 1994.

Systems Analysis for Librarians and Information Professionals. By Larry N. Osborne and Margaret Nakamura. 1994.

Information Sources in Science and Technology. 2d ed. By C. D. Hurt. 1994.

Introduction to Technical Services. 6th ed. By G. Edward Evans and Sandra M. Heft. 1994.

Library and Information Center Management. 4th ed. By Robert D. Stueart and Barbara B. Moran. 1993.

Introduction to Library Public Services. 5th ed. By G. Edward Evans, Anthony J. Amodeo, and Thomas L. Carter. 1992.

Introduction to Library Services. By Barbara E. Chernik. 1992.

Introduction to United States Government Information Sources. 4th ed. By Joe Morehead and Mary Fetzer. 1992.

Introduction to Cataloging and Classification. Bohdan S. Wynar. 8th ed. By Arlene G. Taylor. 1991.

Reference and Information Services: An Introduction. By Richard E. Bopp and Linda C. Smith, General Editors. 1991.

Immroth's Guide to the Library of Congress Classification. 4th ed. By Lois Mai Chan. 1990.

Library Instruction for Librarians. 2d rev. ed. By Anne F. Roberts and Susan G. Blandy. 1989.

The Social Sciences: A Cross-Disciplinary Guide to Selected Sources. By Nancy L. Herron, General Editor. 1989.

Audiovisual Technology Primer. By Albert J. Casciero and Raymond G. Roney. 1988.

Online Reference and Information Retrieval. 2d ed. By Roger C. Palmer. 1987.

Micrographics. 2d ed. By William Saffady. 1985.

Introduction to Library Automation. By James Rice. 1984.

The Library in Society. By A. Robert Rogers and Kathryn McChesney. 1984.

THE COLLECTION PROGRAM IN SCHOOLS

Concepts, Practices, and Information Sources

SECOND EDITION

Phyllis J. Van Orden

1995
LIBRARIES UNLIMITED, INC.
Englewood, Colorado

Copyright © 1995 Libraries Unlimited, Inc.
All Rights Reserved
Printed in the United States of America

No part of this publication may be reproduced, stored in a
retrieval system, or transmitted, in any form or by any means,
electronic, mechanical, photocopying, recording, or otherwise,
without the prior written permission of the publisher.

LIBRARIES UNLIMITED, INC.
P.O. Box 6633
Englewood, CO 80155-6633
1-800-237-6124

Library of Congress Cataloging-in-Publication Data

Van Orden, Phyllis.
   The collection program in schools : concepts, practices, and
information sources / Phyllis J. Van Orden. -- 2nd ed.
   xviii, 376p. 17x25 cm.
   Includes bibliographies and index.
   ISBN 1-56308-120-2 (hardbound ed.) -- ISBN 1-56308-334-5 (pbk.)
   1. School libraries--Collection development--United States.
I. Title.
Z675.S3V334   1995
025.2'1878--dc20   94-32233
                                                       CIP

CONTENTS

Part III

Administrative Concerns

Author's Comments

Writing a book can be a solitary or a collective experience. This book, like its predecessors, was both.[1] A recurring theme in each work is that one must know oneself. The solitary moments of writing gave me that opportunity. I hope the ideas presented in this book will create opportunities for readers to learn about themselves. So, in part, this work is dedicated to those who will carry out the ideas expressed in it.

Many individuals contributed to the ideas in this book. Colleagues across the country kindly gave of their time to react to ideas, to share their experiences with collections or with students in collection-development courses, and to offer specific recommendations for changes and updating. Students, teachers, administrators, and colleagues with whom I have worked also influenced the creation of this book. Some may recognize themselves, although their names have been changed. So, in part, this work is dedicated to the many individuals who participated in its creation, including the necessary detail work. I appreciate their interest, support, and encouragement. May our dialogue continue as we add new participants.

NOTES

[1]Phyllis J. Van Orden, *The Collection Program in Elementary and Middle Schools: Concepts, Practices, and Information Sources* (Littleton, CO: Libraries Unlimited, 1982); *The Collection Program in High Schools: Concepts, Practices, and Information Sources* (Littleton, CO: Libraries Unlimited, 1985); *The Collection Program in Schools: Concepts, Practices, and Information Sources* (Englewood, CO: Libraries Unlimited, 1988).

Introduction

Collection development can be an exciting challenge demanding special knowledge, skills, and positive attitudes. While the general principles and techniques of collection development can be applied to most library settings, the unique characteristics of each media program produce new and changing demands requiring flexibility and creativity. To help media specialists face these challenges, this work

describes the environment within which the collection exists;

presents principles, techniques, and common practices of collection development;

raises issues that affect all collections but that must be resolved in accordance with the goals and needs of a particular collection;

identifies sources of help, including documents, agencies, and associations; and

suggests approaches to handling a wide range of situations and demands on the collection.

This introductory text provides an overview of the processes and procedures associated with developing, maintaining, and evaluating a collection at the building level. The processes and procedures practiced in school library media centers are discussed in relation to educational theory and principles of collection development.

The book reflects the opinion that the collection is a key element of the media program, providing the means for meeting the informational and instructional needs of the school. To serve these needs, the collection must be considered a physical entity composed not only of its internal resources but also of the informational and instructional resources available through community resources, human resources, resource-sharing plans, and telecommunications. This work attempts to fill a void in the literature by bringing together concepts from curriculum theory, children's and adolescent literature, educational technology, and library science. The work reflects the concept that collection program activities interact in a cyclical pattern and proposes that the principles of collection development, selection, resource sharing, and acquisition be addressed as parts of a whole in a school's policy statement. Because of the importance of copyright, the school needs a separate policy relating to it.

This book is divided into three parts. Part 1 examines the media collection in relation to its educational setting and discusses general principles of collection development. This part of the book establishes the environmental framework, that is, the collection's external ties to educational and informational systems and its internal relationship to the media program. Chapter 1 presents an overview of the external and internal relationships of the media program. Chapter 2 examines six perspectives of the concept of collection on which the process of collection development is based. Chapter 3 identifies the activities involved in building and maintaining a collection. These principles provide the framework for the remaining chapters, which provide fuller discussions of each activity. Chapter 4 describes the basis for children's rights to access information, raises issues media specialists will encounter, identifies barriers to access, and identifies the media specialist's responsibilities. Scenarios of situations that media specialists face can be used to prompt discussion about how to handle such incidents. Chapter 5 describes the external environments that influence the collection and to which it must respond. Chapter 6 describes how policies and procedures address these relationships, outlines steps for developing policy statements, and identifies resources.

Part 2 moves from the theoretical aspects of part 1 to the practical considerations of materials selection. Chapter 7 identifies selection tools and suggests ways to involve teachers and students in the selection process. Chapter 8 identifies criteria that apply to all formats. Chapter 9 describes the characteristics of each format as well as its advantages, disadvantages, selection criteria, implications for collection development, and copyright considerations. Sources of information about each format are listed. The remaining chapters of this section identify criteria and sources of information about materials to meet specific needs. Chapter 10 discusses staff members' curricular and instructional needs. Chapter 11 identifies needs for multicultural and reference materials generated by the curriculum or by programs for preschoolers and kindergartners or for inner-city schools. Chapter 12 discusses criteria and resources for sharing literature with students, including poor and reluctant readers, on topics like personal and social development, personal interests, and individuals with disabilities.

Part 3 describes the operations involved in developing and managing a collection. Chapter 13 describes traditional acquisition activities and identifies resources to use in this process. Chapter 14 describes how resource-sharing plans and telecommunications are used to expand the resources available to students and teachers. The chapter identifies sources about how to use the Internet. Chapter 15 describes maintenance policies and procedures, inventory, and reevaluation of materials. It also offers a list of resources that can help media specialists carry out maintenance activities. Chapter 16 describes techniques for evaluating collections using collection-centered measures, use-centered measures, and simulated use studies. The chapter identifies selected standards and guidelines and resources to guide media specialists through the evaluation process. Chapter 17 discusses the issues and procedures involved in creating, shifting, and closing collections.

Lists of recommended readings and resources point readers to in-depth coverage of many of the processes and techniques described in the book. For example, students' rights and intellectual freedom are cornerstones of the media program and are worthy of far greater coverage than this book can provide. The recommended readings in chapter 4 provide in-depth treatment of these topics.

While recognizing the importance of bibliographic control, this work does not address the issues and operations involved in that process, nor does it address the circulation and housing of materials. An evaluative assessment of computer programs for managing collections is beyond the scope of this work.

This book is addressed to individuals preparing to work or presently working in school library media centers. While the examples are from public school library media programs, the principles, practices, techniques, and materials discussed also apply to parochial and independent schools. The focus is on the United States, but some resources for individuals working in Canada are included.

Many standard works cover various aspects of the school library media program. This work is not intended to duplicate those efforts; rather, the focus is on the collection. Many of the standard works are referenced in the text or are listed in appendix B.

Appendix A identifies agencies and associations of use to media specialists. Appendix B is a bibliography, and appendix C reprints three important statements about intellectual freedom.

NEW FEATURES

The new features of this edition reflect growing concerns about students' intellectual freedom, protection of intellectual property through implementing copyright regulations, acquiring information from sources outside the school, technological developments, meeting the needs of a multicultural society, and preserving materials in collections. Students' rights are examined in terms of First Amendment rights and possible barriers to intellectual and physical access to information. Scenarios of censorship situations serve as a basis for discussing how one can handle such situations. Sample wording for selection policies dealing with these issues are provided.

Suggestions are offered for developing copyright policies. The discussion about formats of materials in the collection has been expanded to include copyright regulations for each format. The section on formats, organized in one alphabetical list, is expanded to include CD-ROM, software, and interactive video. Increased attention is given to media specialists' responsibilities in working with vendors and producers.

A new chapter describes how media specialists are acquiring information upon demand from sources outside the school. The approaches include formal and informal resource-sharing plans involving networks and coordinated collection-development plans. The impact and use of telecommunications as an information-delivery system are highlighted. A list of recommended sources (print and electronic) identifies materials to help media specialists learn how to use the Internet.

With the growing concern about the state of collections and the decreasing levels of financial support, information about preventive maintenance and preservation of materials is included. Additional resources describing these processes are identified.

The reorganized and expanded chapter on evaluation covers collection-centered measures, use-centered measures, and simulated-use studies. Examples describe how these approaches are used in schools.

I

THE SETTING

Where is that green book I used for my report last year? Where can I find a picture of Saturn? This video says Pluto is 1,150 miles in diameter and the computerized encyclopedia says 1,430 miles. Which is correct?

Does this symbol mean I can get this title through interlibrary loan from the university library? Do you have a story that will make me cry? Don't we have any new horse stories? I've read all of these. Why don't we have any good recordings? Why isn't the computer accepting what I entered? How can I copy this map? Questions such as these bombard the media specialist as students seek information.

Teachers' voices enter the fray to make requests. *I need a bulletin board idea! Do you remember the poem I used for Martin Luther King's birthday last year? Will you show Marcus how to use the computer to make a chart for his report? One of my friends said his Spanish class used electronic mail to correspond with another Spanish class. Can we set up a similar experience for my class? What can I do to get Meaghan to read something besides dog stories? Sean and Heidi need help in making a videotape for their report. Can you arrange a teleconference lecture for me? I have five new Chaldean students. Do we have any materials they can use?*

How can a collection satisfy all of these requests? Collections that are responsive to users' needs result from the planning and care of dedicated media specialists—individuals who have thought about the purpose of their collections, what they ideally should be, and how they respond to the needs of the school and of the users. An effective collection cannot simply appear and endure unaltered; it must evolve, responding to changing demands. The following chapters describe the setting of the collection with the media program and suggest ways collections can meet the continuing challenges of its users.

CHAPTER 1

The Media Program and Its Environment

A MEDIA PROGRAM SCENARIO

An opening-day scene: You arrive in late August for the teacher-preparation days before students arrive for the new school year. As the new school library media specialist[1] at Gaver Elementary School, you are eager to learn about its curriculum, faculty, and students and to prepare the media program for the coming year. As you familiarize yourself with the collection, teachers arrive in the media center.

First to arrive is Valerie, a fifth-grade teacher who obviously has been planning for classes. She wants to arrange a series of meetings with you to discuss the resources and information-processing skills instruction she needs for her first two units, science and social studies. Valerie alternates subjects so students can concentrate on one at a time. The unit on light will cover the first four weeks and will be followed by four weeks on colonial America. To stimulate her pupils' curiosity, Valerie plans to have a science corner in her classroom, where she will display a variety of lenses, prisms, and other materials the children can explore before formal teaching begins. After presenting general information to the class, she will divide it into groups based on individual interests.

Valerie researched the characteristics of her class, so she knows the science corner needs books that can be read by children whose reading levels range from the second to the seventh grade. Recognizing that all children are not motivated to read, she wants materials that present the basic information in other formats—videodiscs, study prints, and software. As you talk with Valerie, you realize she knows the needs and abilities of her students and tries to provide a wide range of experiences for them using various media and teaching strategies.

Keyona, a kindergarten teacher, looks for study prints about the school environment to help the children feel at home in their new surroundings. She is interested in having some stories to read aloud when children become overly excited. Keyona also asks for your assistance in locating sound recordings for musical activities.

3

Carole, an experienced fourth-grade teacher, arrives with Jerome, a new teacher. Jerome, whose preparation was in secondary education, has been assigned a fifth-grade class. Carole tries to ease some of Jerome's anxieties and seeks your advice about materials that appeal to fifth-graders. In her own class, Carole likes to start the year by observing each child's interests. You watch her gather a variety of items: books on the care of pets, biographies of sports figures, a rock-specimen display, a kit for making puppets, maps of the moon, play scripts, craft magazines, recordings of homemade musical instruments, and some science fiction titles. Carole explains to Jerome that she places the materials around the classroom to attract children into groups with common interests.

At Kennedy High School your colleague Bob faces similar challenges. He meets Willie, who teaches five sections of American history. Although each of Willie's classes uses the same outline, he gives more independent assignments to the class for college-bound students. For the honors class Willie wants Bob to instruct students in how to prepare a pathfinder before they begin their online searches for their independent research papers. Students in three other sections will supplement the textbook by writing short biographical sketches. These students will need Bob's help in locating videos, books, and biographical reference materials. The remaining class is made up of students who read below grade level. For this group Willie needs visual and manipulative materials that will help him cover the prescribed content.

Next is Judy, chairperson of the English department, who wants to arrange a series of meetings with Bob to discuss the resources and information-processing skills instruction needed during her first two units. She asks Bob to introduce the older students in her research course to search strategies, including the use of CD-ROM databases. Judy plans to start the unit by showing videodiscs about how to take notes. She mentions that last year several English teachers wanted to use the videodiscs on the same day.

Dinora, another English teacher, joins the conversation in hearty agreement about the demand for the videodiscs. Dinora and Judy want ideas for encouraging expository writing. They ask Bob if he can recommend magazine covers, posters, or art prints that could be used as prompts for writing.

Carlos, another English teacher, joins the conversation; He needs ideas for motivating his students' interest in poetry. Does the media center have any recordings of popular music? Perhaps students could listen to them, read the lyrics, and discover poetry. Does Bob know any composers or lyricists who would perform for the class and describe how they create the lyrics?

Dieter, from the mathematics department, wants to know if the computer software he requested last spring has arrived. Will he be able to send students to the media center to use the programs?

Rodrigo, the guidance counselor, has been asked to talk to a community group about teenage pregnancy, substance abuse, and the increase in teenage suicide. The group wants to know how the community can help. Rodrigo asks Bob to help him create the presentation. Can visuals be made to display the facts?

These incidents, occurring in the first hour of opening day, represent only a few typical staff requests. They illustrate the day-to-day challenges media specialists encounter. They also show that the media program is not limited to activities within the media center itself. The media program (its administration, services, staff, facilities, and collection) is an integral facet of the entire school program and must be responsive to the needs of individuals, groups, and programs.

THE MEDIA PROGRAM'S ENVIRONMENT

The media program should be based on well-defined policies and procedures to make its resources, facilities, services, and personnel an integral part of the school's program. The collection, the major resource of the internal environment, interacts with the other components—including the facility, staff, and users—to form the media program.

Neither the collection nor the media program is an end in itself; both are means to achieve the educational goals of the school. The media program must also function as an integral part of other systems that form its external environment, as shown in figure 1.1 on page 6. The relationship of the media program to other systems, formal or informal, affects the program and its collection. At the most basic level, the media program is an integral part of the school in which it functions, reflecting the philosophy and goals of that school. The media program frequently is part of a district or system media program and is governed by policies established at the district or system level. The program is part of media programs within the state, sharing state-generated goals and guidelines. The program may be part of regional activities; for example, a regional center may provide electronic bulletin boards and other services. The media program is part of the professional activities and agencies at the national level. The individual media program is influenced by society's view of information and education. Finally, the program serves as an information link to the global community. These relationships, functioning as the external environment, affect the quality of the individual media program.

The Role of the Collection

The collection plays an important role in ensuring that the media program is integrated with the overall school program and in providing access to information within and outside the school. Most media specialists would agree that to meet the school's media needs effectively, the media program must

be an essential part of the total school program.

respond to the curricular and instructional needs of the school.

respond to the needs and interests of teachers, administrators, and other staff members.

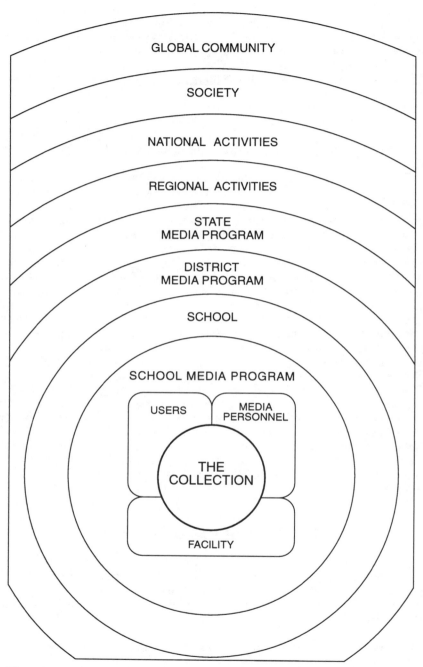

Fig. 1.1. The collection and its environment.

respond to the multicultural diversity of the student population, to the developmental level and learning styles of students, and to the needs of disabled individuals.

provide guidance in the use of and access to a full range of resources—print, nonprint, and electronic—with appropriate equipment.

cooperate with other institutions to provide the widest possible access to information. This may involve interlibrary loan, coordinated collection development, and other forms of resource sharing.

exemplify the total media concept, providing access to varied materials, necessary equipment, trained personnel, and resources housed inside and outside the media center.

have a staff that adequately plans and carries out the selection, maintenance, and evaluation of resources.

The media specialist is the individual responsible for seeing that these conditions exist and these functions take place.

The Role of the Media Specialist

The responsible media specialist supports the philosophy, goals, and objectives of the school within which the media program functions. This individual collaborates with teachers and administrators in the planning process to ensure that the media program is an integral part of the school program, manages the media program's operations, selects materials and other resources, and instructs students and teachers. The media specialist, who best understands the value of the media program, acts as its chief advocate by planning informational, instructional, consultative, and production services; evaluating the services and collection; and promoting the media program through publicity and public relations activities.

All members of the school faculty share responsibility for the media program. A media specialist cannot run an effective, integrated program alone. The media specialist's expertise and human relations skills are called upon to involve others in the program. The media specialist needs to work with teachers in curricular planning; teachers need to work with media specialists in planning and evaluating the media program.

Media specialists may find it difficult to involve administrators, teachers, and students in planning, implementing, and evaluating the media program. However, collection-related activities provide a range of opportunities for media specialists to involve everyone.

First, the media specialist should identify the characteristics of the users and the demands of the curriculum. What are the needs and interests of students and the teachers? Second, steps should be taken to involve administrators, teachers, and students in the development of policies. How can their needs and interests be reflected in policies? Third, an effort should be made to invite others to participate in the selection of materials for the collection. How can students, teachers, and administrators be involved in the process? Fourth, the media specialist facilitates inter-agency borrowing and lending of materials. Are students and teachers aware of resources available through other agencies? Are they familiar with the use of online databases or other forms of electronically delivered information? Do they understand the procedures for obtaining information located outside of the collection? Fifth, the effectiveness of a collection cannot be judged by the media specialist alone. Does the collection meet the needs of the students and teachers? Do the policies support the needs of the school? How can teachers, students, and administrators be involved in the evaluation of the collection, the materials, and the policies? Examples of techniques for involving others will be addressed as the collection program activities are examined.

The media specialist makes many decisions about the collection: what to add, what to access through resource sharing, what to remove. Others can help with these decisions. The media specialist must have an overview of the total program, take responsibility for the decisions, and manage a responsive collection while involving others in the planning and evaluation process.

SUMMARY

The media program is an entity with interacting components: users, materials, facilities, and environment. An effective media program is an essential part of the school program. The media program's external environment includes the school it serves and its district or system media program, media programs within the state, regional activities, national agencies and associations, global information sources, and society.

The media specialist is responsible for the effective functioning of the media program and for involving administrators, teachers, and students in the program. The collection program provides means by which the media specialist can involve others to implement a media program with an integral role in the school's program.

NOTES

[1]The term *school library media specialist* is the currently accepted title for this position. In this work it is shortened to *media specialist*. In like fashion, the term *media program* is used in place of *school library media program*.

BIBLIOGRAPHY

American Association of School Librarians and Association for Educational Communications and Technology. *Information Power: Guidelines for School Library Media Programs*. Chicago: American Library Association; Washington, DC: Association for Educational Communications and Technology, 1988.

Colorado Educational Media Association; Colorado Library Association; and Colorado Department of Education, State Library and Adult Education Office. *A Model*

Evaluation Form for School Library Media Specialists. Denver: Colorado Department of Education, 1991.

Connecticut. Board of Education. *A Guide to Program Development: Learning Resources & Technology.* Hartford, 1991.

Hopkins, Dianne McAfee, et al. *School Library Media Programs: A Resource and Planning Guide.* Bulletin no. 7368. Madison: Wisconsin Department of Public Instruction, 1987.

Utah. Office of Education. *A Master Plan for Utah's School Library Media Programs: Empowering Students to Function Effectively in an Information World.* Salt Lake City, 1991.

Washington Library Media Association Certification and Standards Committee and State of Washington Office of Superintendent of Public Instruction. *Information Power for Washington: Guidelines for School Library Media Programs.* Olympia: Office of Superintendent of Public Instruction, 1991.

CHAPTER 2

The Collection

Traditionally, the term *collection* described the resources, mainly print items, housed in a single room of a school. This room, called the library, contained some books, a few magazines, and perhaps a newspaper rack. A student or teacher searching for information went to this library—a collection confined to the printed matter within its walls. If Todd, a fifth-grade student, entered this library with a bird's nest, he could look for information about the nest in the encyclopedias and books about birds. If he could not find a picture of his nest, he probably would leave the library disappointed, unable to find out what kind of nest he had found.

In today's media center, Todd can compare his nest with those housed in the realia collection or illustrated in an electronic encyclopedia. If Todd wants to learn about the bird's habitat and migratory route, he can use an interactive video or correspond via electronic mail with a student in a county to which the bird migrates. If Todd wants to know more, the media specialist can help locate sources outside the school. Todd can use interlibrary loan to obtain materials from other libraries or the media specialist can arrange a loan of natural history museum materials.

Todd's older sister, Alexia, can use electronic tools to explore any number of research topics. She can use a modem to communicate with university researchers who are working on a local project or she can request a fax of the information. Searches today go beyond walls.

OVERLAPPING PERSPECTIVES OF THE COLLECTION

Today's wider access to information calls for a definition of the term *collection* that goes beyond four walls. How one defines *collection* influences how one makes materials available. To think of a collection as merely the holdings of an individual facility creates a limited view of what a collection can be. An analysis of several overlapping perspectives of the collection reveals a comprehensive definition. A collection

is a physical entity;

includes materials in print, visual, auditory, tactile, and electronic formats with associated equipment;

serves school goals and programs and meets users' informational, instructional, and personal requirements;

provides access to human and material resources in the local and global community;

provides access to information and materials from other library or information systems through interlibrary loan, resource sharing, and electronic access; and

is only one element of the media program.

The ways in which these perspectives overlap indicate their multifaceted external and internal relationships (see fig. 2.1).

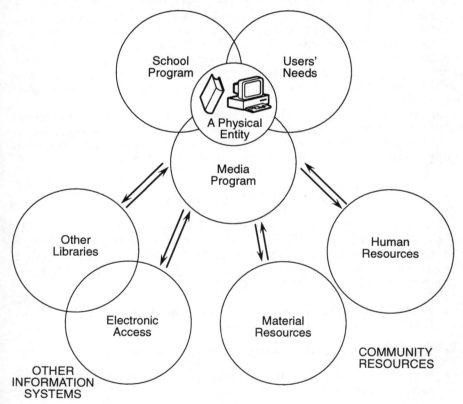

Fig. 2.1. Overlapping perspectives of the collection.

Accessibility and *availability* are key concepts in the definition of *collection*. When an item exists and can be located, it is accessible. When the item is actually at hand, it is available. Today, Todd, the budding ornithologist, may go to the media center's online catalog to find a wide range of resources. Todd knows that the items he needs are in the collection, and he finds them; at this point, the information is accessible. If, on the other hand, he learns he can go to the local science museum to obtain the information, the information is available. When Todd goes to the museum, he has access to the information there. Another student may obtain access to materials through interlibrary loan or use of a computerized database.

The interval between availability and accessibility can be crucial for the student with a limited attention span. It is also crucial for the classroom teacher whose students need information right now, not after they have moved on to a new subject. The media specialist's definition of collection and the resulting practices affect both accessibility and availability. In many media programs, use of a fax machine and electronic information systems are decreasing the time between an expressed need and the user's access to information.

The Americans with Disabilities Act requires all institutions serving the public to provide access to all people. Students with cognitive and perceptual disabilities will find audio, video, toys, and multimedia materials more useful than traditional formats. Deaf individuals may need captioned materials. Blind students will appreciate learning about the services offered by the National Library Service for the Blind and Physically Handicapped. Chapter 12 discusses ways the collection can meet the needs of disabled students.

Accessibility goes beyond physical access. Media specialists, as teachers and information providers, also are responsible for providing intellectual access. Helping students locate, access, select, and evaluate information are important elements in information-skills instruction.

PHYSICAL ENTITY

The collection is a physical entity; the individual items collectively create a whole. The value of a single item must be viewed in relation to other items in the collection as shown in figure 2.2. When deciding whether to add or withdraw a specific item, the item should be evaluated both as an entity and in relation to the collection:

- Is the same information in the collection, possibly in a different format?

- If so, do you need the information in this format?

- Is the same or a similar item quickly accessible through a resource-sharing network?

- Does this item uniquely fill a particular need?

Questions like these help identify the relationship of one item to another in the collection.

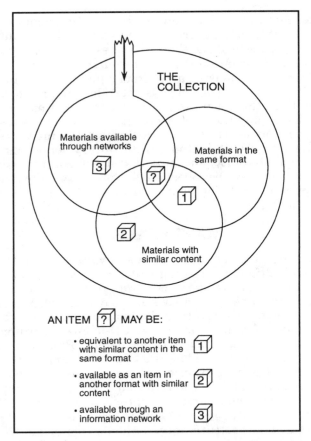

Fig. 2.2. Relationship of an item to the collection as a whole.

Schools that intershelve subject-related materials in various formats physically show how the individual items relate. If inadequate physical space or other limitations do not allow this integration, the user must rely on the catalog to reveal all potential information sources.

Centralized bibliographic control informs people of the locations of materials, whether in the media center or elsewhere on the school's campus. This approach to identifying the collection is particularly important in open schools or those with team teaching, where resources are housed in the area of highest use. In addition, centralized bibliographic control provides access to materials in departmental libraries throughout a campus. Centralized bibliographic control is not limited to materials; human resources can be made available through entries in the bibliographic record. Even teacher notes—for example, information about field trips—can be made available. All materials should be treated as information resources for the entire school and should be accessible to all potential users.

With access to information through resource sharing and electronic means, media centers are moving away from a philosophy of ownership to one of accessibility. The immediate physical collection provides a starting point for students as they begin to search for information. However, the physical collection is only the starting point. In the larger sense of accessibility, anything that users can obtain through the media center comprises the collection. (This includes interlibrary loan items.) In the broadest sense of availability, anything that users can find using tools in the media center comprises the collection. In this context, the collection as a physical entity provides a starting point for coordinated collection development.

MATERIALS

Considering the collection as materials in various formats recognizes that students with different learning styles comprehend information in different ways. Competent readers may find print materials most useful; individuals with aural or visual literacy skills may find audiovisual materials more appealing. Computer-literate individuals may prefer software, electronic encyclopedias, and information on CD-ROMs. Learning activities involving several individuals may call for games. Programmed texts or software may be the most effective format for practicing skills.

A wide range of learning experiences can be offered through a collection that includes materials in various formats. Of course, to support these materials, the collection must provide appropriate equipment. Figure 2.3 identifies some, but not all, formats found in school media centers. Collections also may include postcards; live animals; materials that support creative activity, including carpentry tools, easels, paints, printing presses, and puppets; braille materials; talking typewriters; clothing patterns; and calculators. The list is virtually endless, for people gather information in a variety of ways and from many sources.

The term *integrated* describes a collection that includes materials in a variety of formats selected to meet the information-seeking habits of its users. This variety can meet the learning styles of various students and teaching patterns, including small-group, large-group, and individualized instruction.

The media specialist must be familiar with each format's characteristics, advantages and disadvantages, compatibility with other formats, equipment needs, purposes, potential use, and copyright regulations. In evaluating formats, one considers the technical and physical characteristics of each item, the quality of content, potential use, and its relationship to other items in the collection.

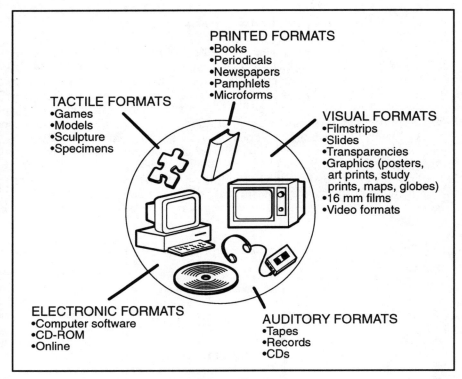

Fig. 2.3. Formats commonly found in collections.

PURPOSES

The collection may be considered in light of its purposes. First, the collection must support the school's goals and programs. Second, the collection must meet the informational, instructional, and personal needs of its users. These purposes often overlap; each has specific implications for collection activities.

School Goals and Program Needs

If the media program is to be an integral part of the school, the media specialist must learn about the school's programs and goals. To do this, the media specialist must become familiar with the school's philosophy; programs (curricular and noncurricular); people (administrators, teachers, students, staff, parents); and facility. Each of these elements has implications for planning, building, and evaluating the collection. Curriculum plans and teaching strategies must be studied and discussed. Does the school have programs for gifted students? For speech therapy, remedial reading, and career guidance? Does it offer short-term projects, such as an Earth Day program, or public relations projects? Does the school sponsor a student council, safety patrol, Latin club, drama club, or other group?

The implications of goals and programs for the collection can be analyzed by asking

- Does the collection need to house formats suitable for large groups and small groups?

- Is information to be subject-oriented or skill-oriented?

- Is there an emphasis on individualized study?

- What range of subjects and learning styles is represented in the school? Do advanced placement and remedial classes exist?

Information, Instructional, and Personal Needs

A collection comprises communication media designed to meet the informational, instructional, and personal needs of users. Materials may be designed to instruct, inform, or appeal to the interests of individual users.

Individuals use the collection for many reasons. Administrators require materials for in-service programs, publicity, and speeches. Teachers need professional information, including up-to-date ideas about teaching methods. Nonteaching personnel and caregivers use the professional collection to aid them in their work with students.

The student population exhibits a wide range of needs, abilities, and interests. Students' age, sex, interests, experiences, personality, learning style, and physical characteristics affect their use of materials. The media specialist needs to know the abilities and interests of each student. Some students develop high levels of proficiency in computing, reading, listening, or viewing skills, while others are sophisticated users of all types of media. Students from homes with video systems and microcomputers may be more familiar with a new technology than their teachers. Within one class, students' abilities in all skills may vary by many levels. For example, a sixth-grade class may include children reading from the second-grade through the eighth-grade level. In a high school, reading levels may range from second grade through college level.

Many other differences exist. Individuals with physical disabilities may require special materials. Recent immigrants may need the help of translators. Some students may be employed on a full-time or part-time basis. Other students may live alone, be responsible for younger members of their families, or be parents. All of these factors may affect which formats students find easiest or most convenient to use.

If the collection is to fulfill its purposes, materials must be evaluated in terms of the goals and purposes of the school and the needs and interests of the users. For example, materials that are in high demand should be readily available. Materials that are rarely requested, or whose use is not anticipated, may be obtained through interlibrary loans, networking, or other avenues to resource sharing.

ACCESS TO COMMUNITY RESOURCES

Another perspective of the collection is as a gateway providing access to the human and material resources of the community. Museums, businesses, industries, and local government agencies often encourage field trips or provide personnel to visit schools. For example, a natural food store's distribution of cookies made from kelp provides an effective learning experience about the resources of the sea.

In some cases, the media center staff visits the business to create a field trip on video. For example, a media center staff member might videotape a local newspaper's operations to prepare a class for a visit by an editor. The range of resources is limited only by a media specialist's imagination and the size of the community.

People are valuable information sources. People can provide career information, share travel slides, demonstrate hobbies or crafts, or relate local history. Many government officials, business people, and other members of the community make themselves available for student interviews. The school's occupational specialist can help identify such people.

Teleconferences and electronic mail are transforming the school's community and expanding its borders to the world and outer space. In 1992 elementary schoolchildren had the opportunity to interview an astronaut in orbit. The Internet offers myriad opportunities for students to expand their research beyond geographical boundaries (see chap. 14).

Integrating community resources expands the collection. Access can be provided through listings in the online catalog, in notebooks, or in information packets distributed to teachers. Such listings identify the participating institution or agency, a contact person, the resources and services offered, and the intended audience.

ACCESS TO RESOURCES FROM OTHER LIBRARIES OR INFORMATION SYSTEMS

Yet another perspective of the collection emphasizes resource sharing, or providing access to materials owned by other institutions. Many media programs share resources by participating in networks and coordinated collection development plans. In one school district with four high schools, each school has an area of collecting responsibility. The school with a strong music department collects in that area and has the district's only copy of Grove's *Dictionary of Music*. The second school collects social studies materials, the third science materials, and the fourth materials in the humanities. All four schools have basic collections in all areas but rely on the other schools for a wider selection of materials. In multitype library networks, schools may do major collecting in career education materials, video materials, professional materials, ethnic materials, and high interest/low vocabulary materials.

District Media Program Resources

Many building-level media programs (those designed to meet the needs of a single school) are units of a school district media program. Therefore, the district's goals and objectives apply to the building-level media program, and the district-level media program personnel and resources provide a wide range of services to the building-level program. The district may provide centralized purchasing and processing of materials. It may also provide a union list of the holdings of the entire school system, providing access to resources outside the school. Some districts are developing wide area networks (WANs) to provide building-level personnel with access to resources throughout the district.

Collections in the district media center often include items that supplement materials owned by individual schools. The district collections may include materials that are expensive or heavily used at limited intervals, museum items with curriculum value, and back-up equipment. They also may include video libraries, professional libraries, or materials examination collections. District-level collections may be used by all schools within the district. A description of the operations and services of a district media program are beyond the scope of this work. However, attention will be given to those aspects directly relating to the building-level media programs collections.

Resources Within the State

In the United States, education is the responsibility of each state. Each has a philosophy, goals, and objectives for its educational programs, including the media program. Media program consultants may be employed by either the state department of education or the state library. Some consultants distribute information or provide in-service educational programs or examination centers. For media specialists working without benefit of a district-level media program, the state media program consultant is a key contact. In addition to consultants, state educational agencies also offer recommendations and standards for the media program and collection, as well as other useful works for media specialists. (See appendix A for a list of state agencies and associations.)

In addition to providing guidance about the media program and collections, state agencies also are information resources. For example, some state agencies provide information about the state. Personnel may visit schools to talk to students about the environmental or economic concerns of the state. Finally, state agencies and associations often publish lists of resources available from the state.

Resources Within a Region

The media program and the media specialist have formal and informal relationships with groups and agencies within the county and regions of the state or nation. County-level professional associations provide programs and contacts useful to the media specialist. Some states have regional examination centers where the media specialist can personally evaluate materials and attend in-service programs.

Regional accrediting associations issue standards for schools. When a school seeks accreditation, the school's media specialists are involved in self-studies prepared before visits by association representatives. (See appendix A for a list of regional accrediting associations.)

Resources Throughout the Nation

Both the school and the media program have national affiliations that provide guidance and information. Two professional associations directly involved with media programs are the American Association of School Librarians (AASL), a division of the American Library Association, and the Association for Educational Communications and Technology (AECT). Their joint efforts led to the publication of *Information Power: Guidelines for School Library Media Programs* (1988). Each association offers other sources of information and assistance. Throughout this book, reference will be provided to documents or services these and other associations provide.

Resources Within Society

The school and the media program are units of the education and information systems of our society. Society's concerns in these areas influence the building-level media program. The following examples illustrate this relationship.

Society's concern about people with physical disabilities has spawned several pieces of legislation that affect school and media programs. In 1990 the Americans with Disabilities Act (ADA) mandated that public services and facilities be accessible to people with disabilities. The media specialist should assess whether the media center meets that mandate.

Another piece of legislation that directly affects the operation of the media center is the Copyright Act of 1976. Designed to balance the interests of authors and artists with the user's ability to access information, the law guides media specialists in carrying out their responsibilities.

Society expresses interests and concerns through various influential commission reports. One example is *What Work Requires of Schools* (U.S. Department of Labor, 1991), which outlines the views of the U.S. Department of Labor. Specific recommendations address skills needed for employment, acceptable levels of proficiency, and ways to assess proficiency. The recommendations of this and similar reports influence our educational programs. As media specialists, we need to be informed about these influences and anticipate their effect on the collection.

ELEMENT WITHIN THE MEDIA PROGRAM

Finally, the collection can be viewed as an element in the school's media program. From this perspective, the collection is a tool that supports the roles and activities of the media specialist. The media specialist's roles can be characterized as direct or indirect. The direct roles involve interaction with patrons; they include the professional services the specialist provides as teacher, instructional consultant, and information provider for students, teachers, staff, parents, and community members. The specialist's indirect roles provide the means for carrying out the direct roles. The media specialist serves as developer of collections and manager of the media program. Roles overlap; media specialists may be acting in several roles at the same time.

The media specialist's roles operate in a cyclical pattern as shown in figure 2.4. The direct roles are primarily user-oriented, involving direct interaction with the user. The indirect roles are primarily collection-oriented, including the development, control, and use of materials. The direct and indirect roles are interdependent. Acting as a teacher, instructional consultant, and information provider, the media specialist gains knowledge and information that is then used in making decisions about the collection.

As teachers, media specialists help students develop skills in critical thinking, computer literacy, research, and production. They promote reading, listening, and viewing activities and encourage students to continue to use resources for lifelong learning. Providing in-service activities for teachers and staff development opportunities is another part of this role. As teachers, media specialists work with caregivers in the community to promote reading and learning and to interpret the value of the media program.

As information providers, media specialists provide materials for students to consult and offer assistance in the identification, location, evaluation, and use of materials. They provide information-awareness services, compile bibliographies, and offer assistance with the use of online or CD-ROM databases. Also in their role as information providers, media specialists ensure that the media center's hours of operation are adequate for users, that the circulation system works effectively, and that the appropriate materials and equipment are available to facilitate use of the collection. Media

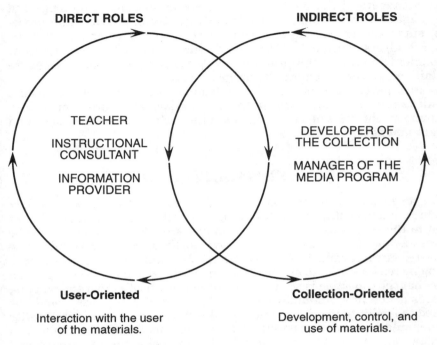

Fig. 2.4. Roles of the media specialist.

specialists are responsible for seeing that no element of the educational process is limited by a school's walls or its organizational demarcation.

As instructional consultants, media specialists work with teachers to develop and design instruction that makes use of existing and new technology. Using their knowledge of the curriculum, learners, and information technologies, media specialists can help administrators and faculty develop strategies to integrate the media center's resources with the school's curriculum.

In the role of collection developer, media specialists provide information sources to meet curricular needs and to satisfy the personal interests of students. To do this media specialists analyze the curriculum; develop policies and procedures; select and acquire materials; organize, maintain, and evaluate the collection; and produce materials. They provide teachers and other school staff with resources for teaching, professional materials, and access to internal and external information resources. They also provide appropriate materials for parents, other caregivers, and community members.

As managers of the media program, media specialists do long- and short-range planning; establish goals and objectives, policies, and procedures; supervise personnel; and work with advisory committees. They manage budgets; design facilities (maintaining an attractive, efficient environment); promote the program; evaluate the program; and ensure that daily operations promote the program's goals.

In any particular setting, the collection must support the media specialist's roles as teacher, consultant, and information provider. It also must support the roles of the media specialist as collection developer and program manager.

SUMMARY

The media specialist's perception of the collection affects how the media program functions within the school program. Thinking of the collection as limited to the materials contained within one area of the school limits the resources available to students and teachers. Extending the definition to include resources available throughout the building or from outside the building increases access to materials. A knowledgeable media specialist can ensure that the collection is an integral part of the school's program, meeting the needs of the program and its users. Policies and procedures should be designed to facilitate this integration. At the same time, there is the reality that one building cannot physically hold, nor financially afford, a collection comprising all the requested materials. At this point the knowledge and creativity of the media specialist come into play.

BIBLIOGRAPHY

American Association of School Librarians and Association for Educational Communications and Technology. *Information Power: Guidelines for School Library Media Programs*. Chicago: American Library Association; Washington, DC: Association for Educational Communications and Technology, 1988.

United States. Department of Labor. Secretary's Commission on Achieving Necessary Skills. *What Work Requires of Schools: A SCANS Report for America 2000*. Washington, DC, 1991.

Walling, Linda Lucas. "Granting Each Equal Access." *School Library Media Quarterly* 20, no. 4 (Summer 1992): 216-22.

CHAPTER 3

ThE CollEcTioN PROGRAM

The term *collection program* denotes the processes necessary to develop and maintain a collection. The media specialist carries out the program by

1. becoming knowledgeable about an existing collection or creating one;

2. becoming familiar with the community (that is, the external environment);

3. assessing the needs of the school's curriculum and other programs as well as the needs of the users;

4. establishing collection development policies and procedures (the overall plan);

5. creating the basis for selection (including policies and procedures to guide selection decisions);

6. identifying criteria for evaluating materials;

7. planning for and implementing the selection process: identifying and obtaining tools, arranging for personal examination of materials, and involving others in the decision making;

8. participating in resource sharing through networking and coordinated collection development;

9. establishing acquisition policies and procedures (that is, guides to obtaining materials);

10. setting up the maintenance program; and

11. evaluating the collection.

These activities draw on the information presented in the previous chapters and establish the framework for the remaining chapters of this book. The purpose of this chapter is to present an overview of the relationships among the processes involved, as illustrated in figure 3.1 on page 24. While the media specialist is the primary actor in the processes, he or she cannot control all the factors influencing collection activities. Constraints may be imposed by school or district programs, financial concerns, or the facility.

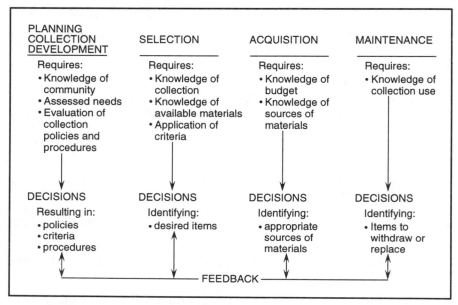

Fig. 3.1. Processes of the collection program.

COLLECTION PROGRAM ACTIVITIES

How the media specialist carries out collection activities determines how well the collection reflects the principles addressed in the perceptions outlined in chapter 2. Knowledge, skill, and sensitivity are required to systematically plan and carry out collection activities.

Learning About an Existing Collection or Creating a New One

If a collection is to serve as a communication and information base, the media specialist must know both the users' needs and the collection's available resources. Browsing is an easy way to learn about a collection. When walking through the collection, do you recognize titles and equipment? Are materials housed in unusual areas? Will students overlook them? Are materials housed behind unmarked cabinets or drawers? Put yourself in a student's position. Would you find those materials? Would the catalog help you? Test a few entries.

Are you familiar with the various formats? Are encyclopedias available in print, CD-ROM, online, and videodisc formats? What evidence do you see of access to electronically delivered information? Are connections to the LAN available throughout the school or only in the media center? Are there signs of distance-learning delivery systems, such as campus cable systems or satellites?

As you roam the collection, scan items new to you. Read tables of contents or book jackets to get a general sense of the books in the collection. Scan album jackets to see what recordings are available. Examine the teachers' guides to audiovisual materials to learn what subjects and formats are covered in the collection. Take note of the software manuals. Are there programs with which you are unfamiliar? Make notes about materials that are new to you. Also note areas that need a sign to make materials more accessible. Equipment should be housed in an area convenient to the materials that require it. Is there a ready reference area? Are these materials duplicated in the circulating collection?

Remember, the collection extends to materials outside the media center. Professional journals or other materials may be housed in the teachers' lounge or in department offices. Check other resources in the school. Is there a staffed career center that assumes responsibility for collecting vocational materials? Are there other departmental collections? These should be identified in the collection development policy. Does the catalog identify storage locations for resources throughout the school?

As you gather these first impressions, check the media center's procedure manual for explanation of unusual situations. Ten copies of a particular videotape may seem unusual, but the manual may state a good reason for having them. As the school year progresses and you become involved with teachers and students, you will soon become quite familiar with the collection.

If you face the task of creating a new collection, guidelines will help you get started. This challenging and exciting opportunity is discussed in chapter 17.

Knowing the Community

A basic consideration of all collection development activities is the relation of the media program to the school, to other educational or informational institutions and agencies, and to its external environment. The community—its geographical, political, economic, cultural, and social characteristics—influences the collection. Changes—in school objectives, in access to other collections, or in citizens' attitudes about education—affect decisions about the collection.

Today, the global community has become a resource. Through electronic bulletin boards, teachers talk with colleagues at other sites. Telefacsimile (fax) machines speed the delivery of an article for a student's report. Check to see whether your state has a network for media specialists, so you can share concerns and ideas with other professionals. On the national level media specialists share concerns through LM_NET.[1]

Assessing Needs

To ensure that the collection fulfills the informational and instructional needs of its users, the media specialist must identify those needs. Whom does the collection serve? What are their informational needs? What are the teachers' instructional needs? The media specialist can begin to answer these questions by researching the characteristics of the users, the preferred teaching methods, and the preferred size for learning groups. Two sources of statistical information are the automated circulation system and the logs for online and CD-ROM searches. Analysis of interlibrary loan requests identifies gaps in the collection. Knowledge of the existing collection, the school, the community, and assessed needs must all be considered in plans and policies that guide the development of the collection.

Establishing Collection Development Policies and Procedures

The plans and policies for collection development should reflect the short- and long-term goals of the library. Factors like audience demand, need, and expectation; the information world; fiscal plans; and the history of the collection must be integrated into the policies and plans. Attention to collection development assures selection—not merely accumulation—of materials.

Collection development policies guide acquisition, selection, and evaluation activities. They identify the goals and limitations of the collection, including the use of materials covered by the Copyright Act of 1976. Procedures guide methods of handling collection activities, including censorship challenges.

The differences between policies, which identify the reason for doing something, and procedures, which identify how to do it, are addressed in chapter 6.

Creating the Basis for Selection

The selection policy is only one element in the collection program policy; however, it may be the only existing policy. In October 1986, Wisconsin reported that only 66-75 percent of the Wisconsin school districts had materials selection policies. To address this situation and to ensure equal treatment for all students, Wisconsin adopted legislation to achieve nondiscrimination. The specific wording regarding library media states:

> PI 9.03 POLICIES (1) Each board shall develop policies prohibiting discrimination against pupils. The policies should include the following areas: . . . (e) an instructional and library media materials selection policy.[2]

Even if the school lacks a long-range development policy, a selection policy is necessary to guide the media specialist's day-to-day choice of new materials. Selection policies establish principles of selection that guide the collection toward the library's goals as outlined in the collection development policy. Selection procedures are the specific processes that carry out selection policies.

Identifying Criteria

Criteria, the standards by which items will be evaluated, are a major part of the selection policy. Criteria for assessing the item itself and its relation to the collection development policy must be established. Generally accepted criteria include literary quality, currency, accuracy of information, appeal and value to students, application within the curriculum, quality of presentation, and format. Criteria need to be established for specific formats and for materials to be used by specific types of users.

Planning and Implementing the Selection Process

Selection is the process of deciding whether an item will be a valuable addition to the collection. During this process, one keeps in mind set criteria and works within established policies. Personal examination and favorable reviews can provide the basis for selection decisions. Sources that provide reviews include selection tools, reviewing journals, and bibliographic essays. These are valuable references to consult during the selection process; they should be readily accessible.

To plan for the selection process, the media specialist should obtain bibliographic and selection tools. These resources will tell whether an item is available for purchase, rent, or loan. Materials should be secured for reviewing or previewing. Plan to involve teachers, administrators, and students in these processes.

Established criteria, policies, and procedures are not the sole factors influencing a media specialist's choices. One's selection skills, values, interests, and even prejudices influence selection decisions. To make sound selection decisions, the media specialist sets aside personal biases and makes objective choices. Self-awareness helps the media specialist know when to seek the opinion of others.

Resource Sharing

Networks created by multitype libraries sharing resources provide access to information services outside the collection. A school that participates in a network has access to a plethora of resources and services; however, participation carries with it certain responsibilities and, perhaps, financial obligations. If your school participates in a network, what are your collection responsibilities? Has your school been assigned the task of collecting specific subjects or formats? In a typical example, one school collects high interest/low vocabulary materials while another collects reference works about a specific subject. Or, the local public library or historical museum collects local history items while the school collects yearbooks. What materials, services, and financial obligations are included in the agreement? Networks offer cooperative purchasing programs, cataloging and processing, computerized databases, delivery systems, production services, examination centers, serials cooperatives, and resource sharing. If your school does not participate in a state network, learn how you can join.

Some facilities serve both the school and the public. Meeting the needs of patrons whose ages range from preschool to senior citizen creates advantages and disadvantages for the collection. A distinct advantage is the librarian's knowledge of the community, but a disadvantage is conflicting demands on the collection. Questions to be addressed include: How can such a conflict be most efficiently resolved? Should the collection be directed to the curricular and instructional needs of the students or toward the general informational and recreational needs of the public? Do separate budgets exist? Are materials for adults and children together? Policies and procedures statements should address these questions.

Establishing Acquisition Policies and Procedures

Acquisition, the process of obtaining materials, is a direct result of the collection development policies and the selection policies and procedures. Acquisition policies and procedures guide the implementation of selection decisions. These processes provide for adding material to the collection. Acquisition policies determine who will supply materials; acquisition procedures establish the process for obtaining the materials. Acquisition policies establish methods of determining the appropriate source for material, that is, the quickest and most economical source. Acquisition procedures establish the processes by which the media specialist orders, receives, and pays for the materials. Using the policies and procedures as a guide, the media specialist may choose to purchase materials from a jobber (a company that handles titles from several publishers), from the publisher, or from a local store. In like fashion, the policies guide the media specialist's choice of vendors for computer hardware and software.

Establishing a Maintenance Program

Collection maintenance is an important and often neglected function of the collection program. Decisions must be made concerning replacing, removing, mending, or rebinding and keeping magazines and other similar materials. Equipment must be kept in working condition. Are appropriate personal computers available so that patrons may use the software in the collection? Are there sufficient supplies of consumable items like projector bulbs and slide mounts so that they can be promptly replaced when needed? How will heavily used items be replaced? Must items be completely unusable before they are replaced? If so, will replacements be available when they are needed? Obviously, the media specialist must establish policies and procedures for maintenance activities.

Inventory time provides an excellent opportunity to systematically check the condition of all items, but the collection may not be inventoried frequently enough to spot the gradual deterioration of some items. Planning for the systematic maintenance of all materials is important in keeping the collection usable.

Establishing Plans for Evaluation

Both the collection and the policies and procedures governing its growth demand evaluation. Many questions need to be addressed. What factors determine the value of the collection? Value can be assessed quantitatively, that is, by the number of items in the collection, and qualitatively, for example, by how well the collection fulfills users' needs. A collection is an evolving entity that must be responsive to its environment; evaluation is the method by which media professionals assess a collection to determine whether it is responding effectively. Ideally, evaluation is a continuing process; however, daily routines often interfere. Evaluation of a collection is also complex. Planning is required to create an evaluation system that is both manageable and comprehensive, one that allows media specialists to respond to changes in the collection or its environment.

Interaction of the Activities

One can view collection development activities as a continuum in which one activity leads to and influences the others (see fig. 3.2, on page 30). Activities are not isolated; rather, their interaction is cyclical. Thus a change in one activity affects others.

The collection development policy establishes priorities that directly affect both selection and acquisition activities. When Fermi Middle School adopted a critical thinking approach to teaching science, the goal was to have students learn through observation, experimentation, and individual or group investigation, not through textbooks. The collection development policy was altered to reflect this change. If budgetary constraints prevent the collection from meeting all the demands of the new program and the other informational and instructional needs of the school, the revised collection policy may read, "Priority will be given to the purchase of materials that support the concepts and skills presented in the science curriculum."

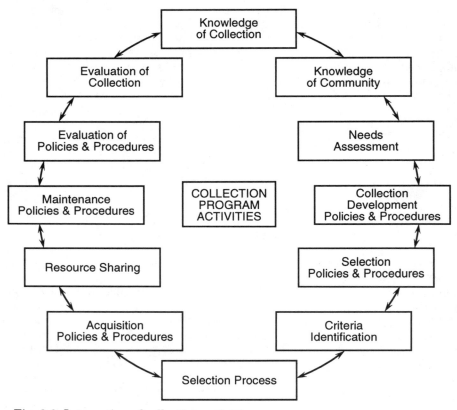

Fig. 3.2. Interaction of collection activities.

The media specialist should establish policies that provide guidance with flexibility to anticipate and meet changes. With the rapid developments in technology, the media specialist can expect new formats to be added to the collection. Appropriate selection criteria should be incorporated in the policy.

FACTORS THAT GOVERN COLLECTION ACTIVITIES

The media specialist is responsible for the development and implementation of the collection program. However, the media specialist cannot control all the factors that influence collection activities. The media program must operate within policies adopted by the board of education. The goals of the district and the school also must be met. The attendance districts established by the school board may change yearly and affect the composition of the student body or potential users of the collection. Legislation at the state or federal level may dictate requirements about the student population, the curriculum, and other school programs. Shifts in student population bring new demands on the collection and must be accommodated in the collection program.

District Media Programs

A building-level media program that is part of a district media program offers many advantages to the entry-level media specialist. The system's media program coordinator or director is someone to turn to for guidance. The district-level guidelines for media programs and the selection policy adopted by the governing body also aid the media specialist. The district-level media program may offer opportunities for the media specialist to examine new materials and invite teachers to exhibits and demonstrations at district-level media program meetings. District-level media programs offer many services to help establish and maintain the collection program.

Regional centers or intermediate school districts also provide personnel and services, including consultants or technicians, cooperative collections, examination centers, in-service programs, and clearinghouses for information about new technology.

Although such systems offer many benefits, they also may impose constraints on the school media program. An approved buying list generated by a districtwide committee may limit the range of titles that can be purchased. If you encounter this situation, learn the procedures for ordering items not on the list. In some systems, titles on specific subjects must be ordered at specified times. Typically, science materials are ordered in December, replacements in March, and so on. Although this practice is efficient for the processing operation, it severely constrains the collection program. Fermi Middle School's science curriculum changes would have had a difficult, if not impossible, task of fulfilling curriculum needs under such regulations.

Some school districts acquire materials via electronic systems, placing and tracking orders and asking questions using the jobber's CD-ROM and a modem.

Financial Support and Control

The institution's funding policies, including its policies regulating use of outside funding sources, impose constraints on the collection program. Accrediting agencies also may make budget demands. Media specialists operate within the limits set by budget allocations. In addition to the size of budget, the budgeting system used can affect collection activities. A traditional line-item budget establishes a flat amount for media program materials. Line-item budgets divided by format impose further restrictions. This type of funding can prevent the collection from responding to school programs and individual users. For example, funds designated for audiovisual materials cannot be used for books or magazines. Collection development is more successful when budgeting allows priorities to be based on program objectives and needs.

The school's position on the use of outside funding affects the collection. Some school districts opt not to use outside funds; others encourage media specialists to seek grants or endowments. Grants and endowments may specify materials to be purchased or may limit the type of use or user for whom materials may be purchased. For example, some funding may be used only for materials for student use.

Across the country, media specialists are facing the problem of how to fund automation projects. One question is, should monies designated for materials be used for electronic formats? If the answer is yes, for how long? The next question is, which electronic formats should be purchased? Are CD-ROMs more effective than online databases for teaching students how to conduct searches?

Some states have established networks and encouraged media specialists to participate in discussions of these topics. ACCESS PENNSYLVANIA, for example, encourages high-school media specialists to apply for funds to support the addition of automation to their programs. In addition, media specialists attend in-service programs designed to familiarize them with the network and its purposes and uses.

At some point in your career as a media specialist, a school official will inform you that a large sum of money earmarked for materials for special uses must be spent within seven to ten days. This situation does not encourage thoughtful planning or selection but is typical of outside funding announcements. Try to stay alert to sources of outside funding to learn what they will fund and when the funding will occur. A file of materials currently being considered for purchase is essential in these situations.

Budget control and authorization of purchases are sensitive issues for the media specialist. A salesperson may visit the principal, who controls the budget, and promote a package deal that sounds like a bargain. If the principal buys the package without consulting the media specialist, the principal may learn after the purchase that (1) the collection already contains these materials, (2) the materials do not meet any needs of the collection, or (3) the materials require equipment not available in the school. Establish professional rapport with principals and purchasing agents to avoid such problems.

School Facilities

Limitations of the physical facilities or the physical plant can create constraints on the collection. Adjustable lighting will be needed to accommodate the use of a wide range of formats. The lack of safe electrical outlets limits the use of media. If the media center serves a multistory building, equipment should be available on each level. As information delivery systems change, spatial accommodations and equipment needs will change. Other changes may be generated by new usage patterns, for example after-school programs or programs for preschoolers. As media centers change from print to electronic collections, less shelving space is needed but more work stations are required. Curricular changes, such as an emphasis on critical thinking skills, require different modes of delivery and a wide range of materials to meet individual learning styles. The flexibility of the facility influences the use of resources.

Many items in the collection (such as picture books, large study prints, or art prints) require specialized storage units. When evaluating materials, consider how and where they will be stored and used. Will sound from printers interfere with other activities? How many terminals will be needed? Having a LAN ensures multiple use of materials.

SUMMARY

At the most basic level, media specialists cannot make information accessible unless they know it exists. The importance of knowing the collection increases as you learn about the users and their needs. Poetry books, art works, and picture books that deal with mathematical concepts may be overlooked if you or the mathematics teacher consider only the items classified in the 500 section.

To ensure that information is accessible, policies and procedures must be altered to meet changing needs. However, media specialists must consider all the demands on the collection when initiating changes. The Fermi Middle School media center staff faced an awkward and demanding situation when the new science curriculum was implemented. Materials in the collection were inadequate to support both the new curriculum and the needs of individual users. As a result, circulation of science materials had to be limited to teachers; this was difficult to explain to the students but necessary to support school priorities. Even the maintenance policy was affected. For two years the priority for mending and repairing went to science-oriented materials. Titles dealing with science were removed from the collection only when the information in them was inaccurate or out-dated.

How did the situation affect requests from teachers for materials on other subjects? The whole language curriculum called for a wide range of materials and multiple copies of stories students were reading. The program required many titles written for the third- through ninth-grade reading levels. These needs could not be adequately met.

Such situations illustrate the danger of overreacting to an immediate problem at the expense of the collection as a whole. Changes in one program activity have an impact on other program activities. Media specialists must take care that the collection responds well to all of the demands on it.

NOTES

[1]To join LM_NET on the Internet, contact Peter Milbury at pmilbur@eis.calstate.edu or Mike Eisenberg at mike@suvm.syr.edu.

[2]"District Materials Selection Policy Mandated," *Channel DLS: Wisconsin Division for Library Services* 22, no. 2 (October 1986): 1.

CHAPTER 4

Issues and Responsibilities

Media specialists continually call on decision-making skills while building a collection. Each decision reflects personal perceptions of the characteristics of collections, views about the responsibilities of a selector, and philosophical positions on issues. For example, the materials selected reflect the media specialist's stance on intellectual freedom and students' rights. The media specialist's stance on these and other issues consciously or unconsciously influence decisions about the collection. To explore these critical issues, this chapter examines the questions

- How does the concept of intellectual freedom apply to children[1] and young people?

- Should there be limits on students' rights to read, view, and listen? Who has the right to impose those limits?

These issues are complex and can arise within a variety of contexts: social, ethical, economic, political, religious, psychological, or in regard to pornography.

To help the media specialist explore his or her own perceptions about the characteristics of the collection and views of selection responsibility, the following questions should be considered:

- What is a balanced collection? Is balance a legitimate goal?

- Should all sides of issues be represented in the collection?

- Should popular materials have priority over materials with greater literary value?

- What barriers to access exist?

- What professional responsibilities do media specialists have?

The issues are not new. The opinions of society and of the profession are constantly scrutinized. This chapter presents various viewpoints. Media specialists need to reflect on the opinions expressed here and by the writers of the recommended readings listed at the end of the chapter. You, the media specialist, must know yourself. Where do you stand on the issues? At the end of this chapter are scenarios involving intellectual freedom and students' rights. As you study them, bear in mind the very real possibility that you may one day face such situations.

INTELLECTUAL FREEDOM
AND CENSORSHIP

The information you make available and accessible to students reflects the value you place on intellectual freedom and students' rights.

First Amendment Rights

In the United States, the First Amendment serves as the basis of intellectual rights. A child's intellectual rights can be viewed as legal rights and ethical rights. The application of the First Amendment to children generally arises in matters dealing with public education, particularly in court cases concerning censorship.

Intellectual freedom is the basis of the First Amendment's three major sections: freedom of religion, freedom of expression, and freedom of association. These three rights have been the topic of controversy and court cases. Although the U.S. Supreme Court has taken a dim view of restrictions based on content, it does allow the government, when it has legitimate reasons, to restrict the time, place, or manner of expression. Schools may limit speech by prohibiting the use of vulgar or obscene language in school activities. In like fashion, the government may limit freedom of association (by which one expresses views alone or in association with others, perhaps by demonstrating against the government). For example, the government may require permits from groups that wish to demonstrate.

Consider the implications of the First Amendment's guarantee of freedom of expression. This section guarantees freedom of speech and of the press. It extends the scope of intellectual freedom to all ideas, not only those of a religious nature. David Moshman reminds us that, "These clauses refer most directly to the expression of ideas. It is clear, however, that one cannot *express* ideas unless one *has* ideas, and that one cannot *have* ideas unless one *forms* them. Thus the right to form and hold beliefs is implicit in the right to express them."[2]

Accepting this interpretation of the First Amendment influences how you view a student's right to speak in an open assembly or to write a piece for a high school newspaper. Moshman's interpretation also provides a basis for teaching critical-thinking skills.

Application to Children

How does the First Amendment apply to children? Moshman describes its relevance in terms of five aspects of constitutional interpretation: text, intent, constitutional theory, precedent, and values. As in other areas of constitutional law, there is no clear-cut answer; the five aspects do not fully support each other.

First, according to Moshman, the text of the First Amendment makes no distinction between children and adults; there is no indication that the amendment applies only to adults. Second, the authors of the amendment intended it to apply to people and persons in general. (One could argue that the authors of the Constitution were referring only to white males. The Fourteenth Amendment includes women and nonwhites but does not mention children.) However, constitutional theory, the third test, finds nothing in the amendment to suggest that the word *people* refers only to those of voting age. Moshman's fourth test of the amendment, precedent, is inconclusive. "Application of the First Amendment to children is at best highly complex and multifaceted and at worst mutually contradictory."[3] Fifth, in terms of values, Moshman argues that

> to limit intellectual freedom based on limited rationality is to restrict the development of rationality itself. Ethical considerations, then, suggest that children have a vital stake in the First Amendment and that society as a whole has a compelling interest in including them within its scope.[4]

Indeed, Moshman goes so far to say that First Amendment rights are more important to children than to adults.

> When one denies an adult access to diverse ideas, one is restricting available input; when one denies such access to a child, however, one is also restricting development of the ability to coordinate differing views. When one denies an adult free expression, one is denying the opportunity to communicate; when one denies free expression to a child, however, one is also restricting development of the ability to form one's own ideas. In short, in denying First Amendment rights to a child, one is restricting not merely the present exercise of those rights but also the further development of precisely those intellectual competencies that make the First Amendment meaningful. Contrary to the suggestion that children have little at stake, it appears that as future adults they may have more to lose than present adults from governmental restriction of their intellectual freedom.[5]

Legal and Moral Implications

Moshman proposes that the First Amendment has both legal and moral implications. The first five principles listed in figure 4.1, on page 38, limit government action, reflecting the common view that the First Amendment places restrictions on all levels of government, including public schools, but not on individuals acting in nongovernmental capacities, such as parents or private schools. The sixth principle listed in figure 4.1 limits the extent to which childhood status may be used to limit application of the first five principles. Moshman's moral principles exceed the language of the Constitution; they restate children's First Amendment rights in language that addresses the child rather than the government.

Intellectual Rights of Children

Legal Rights

Free Expression—Government may not control a child's right to form or express ideas.

Freedom of Nonexpression—Government may not require a child to adopt or express belief in a particular idea.

Inculcation—Government may inculcate ideas only when a legitimate purpose, such as to produce educated citizens, exists.

Freedom of Access—Government may not restrict children's access to ideas and sources of information.

Free Exercise of Religion—Government may not restrict children from acting according to their religious beliefs.

Distinction of Child from Adult—Limiting First Amendment rights must be based on compelling reasons by showing that harm would occur because the children in question are less competent than the typical adult.

Moral Rights

Free Expression II—A child has the right to form, express, and communicate ideas.

Freedom of Nonexpression II—A child has the right to choose not to adopt or express belief in particular ideas.

Inculcation II—Children have the right not to be indoctrinated and to be subject to inculcation only when there is a legitimate reason.

Freedom of Access II—Individuals responsible for children's development have an obligation to provide access to diverse sources of information and to diverse opinions and perspectives.

Free Exercise of Religion II—Children have a right to act according to their religious beliefs unless such actions would be harmful or illegal.

Distinction of Child from Adult II—Restrictions on children's intellectual rights should be based on the individual child's circumstances and intellectual limitations.

Right to Education—Children have the right to the type of environment that will facilitate their intellectual development to the extent of their intellectual limitations.

Fig. 4.1. Rights guaranteed by the First Amendment. Based on David Moshman, "Children's Intellectual Rights: A First Amendment Analysis," in *Children's Intellectual Rights*, ed. David Moshman, New Directions for Child Development series, no. 33 (San Francisco: Jossey-Bass, 1986), 27.

Court Decisions

How do First Amendment rights apply to children? As one example, Moshman examines these rights in the context of censorship cases involving school libraries. He notes that schools must make choices; they cannot use every text or stock every book in the library. Selections should, however, be made in accord with educationally relevant, written criteria aimed at providing as wide a variety of views and ideas as students can handle (Principle 3). Removals should follow carefully designed procedures in which these criteria are carefully applied (Principle 4) and claims of harm based on alleged lack of cognitive competence are seriously scrutinized (Principle 6). (Principles here refer to the numbered list in figure 4.1.)[6]

How have the courts interpreted children's rights? The classic court case for children's First Amendment rights is *Tinker v Des Moines* (1969). This is the first time the Supreme Court declared a government action unconstitutional because it violated minors' rights to freedom of expression. The Supreme Court said

> School officials do not possess absolute authority over their students. Students in school as well as out of school are "persons" under our Constitution. They are possessed of fundamental rights which the State must respect, just as they themselves must respect their obligations to the State.[7]

According to Moshman, *Tinker*

> clarified that children have First Amendment rights not simply because government respect for their intellectual freedoms is in the best interests of their parents, their teachers, the educational system, or society as a whole, but more fundamentally, because they are persons under the Constitution.[8]

This action creates a balance to maximally protect both liberty and learning. School officials may maintain order but do not possess absolute authority over their students. However, confusion exists in the courts about what this means and how far it extends. Edward B. Jenkinson reminds us that, in the courts' responses to cases involving censorship of school materials,

> human beings preside in the courts, and human beings do not agree on all matters. Thus it is not surprising that the courts have not been uniform in their decisions involving the removal of books and other teaching materials from public school classrooms and libraries. The courts do tend to agree that they prefer not to become involved in debates over educational objectives and practices, leaving such matters to school boards, unless they believe that specific constitutional rights have been violated. But when they do become involved, their decisions are not always predictable.[9]

Tinker and other cases ensure children the rights to know and to read. Jenkinson quotes attorney Julia R. Bradley:

> A student's right to read, and thus to have available in a school library a full range of materials which reflect differing literary

studies, and differing social, political, and religious views, is a variant of a constitutional doctrine described as the "right to receive information."[10]

Figure 4.2 highlights court decisions about intellectual freedom that affect children.

President's Council, District 25 v. Community School Board No. 25 (New York City), 457 F.2d (2nd Cir. 1972), 409 U.S. 998 (1972).
First case to consider whether a school board could remove books from the school library. Judge Mulligan declared the board, as statutorily empowered to operate the school, is the body responsible for selection and can remove books.

Minarcini v. Strongville City School District, 541 F.2d 577 (6th Cir. 1976). Circuit Court Judge Edwards stated:
A library is a storehouse of knowledge. When created for a public school it is an important privilege created by the state for the benefit of students in the school. That privilege is not subject to being withdrawn by succeeding school boards, whose members might desire to "winnow" the library for books the content of which occasioned their displeasure or disapproval.

Right to Read Defense Committee v. School Committee of the City of Chelsea, 454 F. Suppl. 703 (D. Mass. 1978).
Arguing that the complainant could not remove a book, in whole or in part, in accordance with standard library procedures.

Bicknell v. Vergennes Union High School Board, 475 F. Suppl. 615 (D. Vt. 1979), 638 F.2d 438 (2nd Cir. 1980).
After the librarian and students protested the board's removal of *The Wanderer* and *Dog Day Afternoon* from the library, a freeze on new acquisitions, and the board's policy to screen all major acquisitions, the courts ruled that the right of professional personnel under that policy "to freely select" materials for the collection are explicitly limited by the phrase "in accordance with Board policy."

Board of Education, Island Trees Union Free School District No. 26 v. Pico, 457 U.S. 853 (1982).
After a politically conservative organization informed it about objectionable titles, the school board appointed a review committee, which recommended retaining five books, restricting two, and removing two. (The committee made no recommendation for one title.) The board voted to remove all but one title. In a 5-4 vote, the Supreme Court upheld the student's challenge. The Court suggested decisions based on educational suitability would be upheld when a regular system of review with standardized guidelines were in place and condemned politically motivated removals.

Fig. 4.2. Court decisions about intellectual freedom.

Keep these cases in mind as you read about the development of policies (chapter 6) or as you review your school's policies. Are you comfortable with the language in view of these court cases?

The Media Specialist As Protector or Advocate

Librarians tend to take one of two positions in response to the question "What intellectual rights do children have?" One position assumes that adults know what is best for children, what will harm them, what information they need, and how their needs should be met. The other position assumes an open stance, perceiving children as capable of defining both their information needs and their resource needs. The first position strives to protect students from themselves, from others, and from ideas. The second, the youth advocate, strives to help students identify, retrieve, and use information. While protectors create barriers for students, advocates remove barriers.[11] Dianne McAfee Hopkins shares the view that "the school library media specialist should assume the role of an advocate for youth, rather than a protector of youth."[12]

Censorship

What is the difference between selection and censorship? After all, selection is by nature exclusive. In choosing among materials to include in the collection, the media specialist excludes the materials not chosen. And, as we have seen, media specialists' choices are colored by their personal values and commitments to such issues as intellectual freedom. Selection and censorship can be differentiated. Selection is a process of choosing among materials. The choices are relative as one item is compared with others. In choosing materials, the media specialist strives to give each item fair consideration and makes a concerted effort to suppress personal biases. In censorship an individual or group attempts to impose its values on others by limiting the availability of one or more items. By examining several definitions of selection and censorship, one can see how censorship creates barriers to intellectual freedom and how selection can promote intellectual freedom. Lester Asheim compares selection and censorship in this way: "Selection begins with presumption in favor of liberty of thought, whereas censorship begins with a presumption in favor of thought control."[13] Asheim perceives selection as democratic, censorship as authoritarian, and reminds us that "it is the librarian's responsibility as a representative of the public in a democratic society, to be a selector and to resist censorship."[14]

Henry Reichman also describes the differences between selection and censorship.

> In general, selection is carried out by trained professionals, familiar with the wide variety of available choices and guided by a clear graph of the educational purposes to be fulfilled. . . . By contrast, the censor's judgment is that of the individual, and it is most

frequently based on criteria that are inherently personal and often intolerant. . . . Where the censor seeks reasons to *exclude* materials, those engaged in the process of selection look for ways to *include* the widest possible variety of . . . library materials. . . . Censorship responds to diversity with suppression; the selection process seeks instead to familiarize students with the breadth of available images and information, while simultaneously erecting essential guideposts for the development of truly independent thought.[15]

Table 4.1 contrasts selection and censorship.

Table 4.1.
Characteristics of Censors and Selectors

CENSORS	SELECTORS
Censors look for items to exclude.	Selectors apply criteria as they compare materials and choose to include items.
Censors search for what they want to discard.	Selectors examine materials, looking for that which best presents their educational objectives.
Censors judge a book on the basis of a few passages they dislike.	Selectors judge the book as a whole.
Censors rely on the reviews of other censors to get rid of books.	Selectors rely on reviews published in professional journals.
Censors want the collection to include only books that represent their point of view.	Selectors look for books that represent a variety of points of view.
Censors look outside the book for reasons to reject it, for example, the author's religion or politics.	Selectors judge the book on its own merits.

Based on Edward B. Jenkinson, *The Schoolbook Protest Movement: 40 Questions & Answers* (Bloomington, IN: Phi Delta Kappa Educational Foundation, 1986), 21.

Complaints About Materials

The American Library Association's Intellectual Freedom Committee offers the following definitions for various levels of inquiry and challenge to materials in the collection:

Expression of Concern—An inquiry that has judgmental overtones

Oral Complaint—An oral challenge to the presence and/or appropriateness of the materials in question

Written Complaint—A formal, written complaint filed with the institution (library, school, etc.), challenging the presence and/or appropriateness of specific material

Public Attack—A publicly disseminated statement challenging the value of the materials presented to the media and/or others outside the institutional organization in order to gain public support for further action

Censorship—A change in the access status of material, based on the content of the work and made by a governing authority or its representatives, including: exclusion, restriction, removal, or age/grade level changes.[16]

Two studies conducted in the 1980s reveal patterns of challenges. Dianne McAfee Hopkins studied U.S. high schools that experienced challenges between 1986 and 1989. She found that of 4,736 schools, 64.1 percent (3,036 schools) reported no challenges and 35.9 percent (1,700 schools) reported one or more challenges.[17] For the period September 1982 to August 1984, David Jenkinson studied 6,644 public and private schools at all levels and 73 public libraries located in the Canadian province of Manitoba. He found approximately 25 percent of all school libraries and 40 percent of all public libraries experienced at least one challenge during that time. One school faced seven challenges.[18]

Recent reports suggest an increase in the number of challenges. According to Judith F. Krug, director of the American Library Association Office of Intellectual Freedom, the office received more than 700 requests for assistance or reports of censorship during 1993.[19] That figure takes on greater significance in light of the common belief that only 20 percent of all school censorship efforts are reported in the media.

According to the *Intellectual Freedom Manual*, intellectual freedom

requires the fulfillment of two essential conditions: first, that all individuals have the right to hold any belief on any subject and to convey ideas in any form the individual believes appropriate; second, that society makes an equal commitment to the right of unrestricted access to information and ideas regardless of the communication medium used, the content of the work, and the viewpoints of both the author and receiver of information.[20]

If either freedom of expression or freedom of access to ideas is stifled, then intellectual freedom does not exist. Ironically, commitment to intellectual freedom obligates media specialists to safeguard the rights of censors. On the one hand, media specialists recognize the right to unrestricted access to information; on the other hand, media specialists recognize the right to protest.

Who Are Censors?

The list of those who initiate challenges is long. Individuals include parents and other members of students' families, teachers, students, principals and other school administrators, school support staff, community members, library media supervisors, library support staff, and even librarians. Groups include school boards, local government officials, and organized groups of individuals who share political or religious beliefs. Reichman reminds us that:

> The word "Censor" often evokes the mental picture of an irrational, belligerent individual. In most instances, however, it is a sincerely concerned parent or citizen interested in the future of education who complains about curricular or library materials. Complainants may not have a broad knowledge of literature or of the principles of intellectual freedom, but their motives in questioning the use of educational materials are seldom unusual. Complainants may honestly believe that certain materials will corrupt children and adolescents, offend the sensitive or unwary reader, or undermine basic values and beliefs.[21]

Both Hopkins and Jenkinson found that the majority of challenges involved printed works of fiction. Authors whose books were challenged include Judy Blume, Stephen King, Jean M. Auel, Norma Klein, Harry Mazer, Shel Silverstein, and Paul Zindel. Individual titles challenged 10 or more times during the period of the Hopkins study included *Forever* by Judy Blume (13 times), *Go Ask Alice* (10 times) and *The Chocolate War* by Robert Cormier (10 times), and *Clan of the Cave Bear* by Jean M. Auel (10 times).[22] Respondents in the Hopkins study reported challenges to magazines as well, including *Rolling Stone, Sports Illustrated, Seventeen, Glamour, Health, Hot Rod,* and *Mad Magazine.*[23]

Common objections to materials include sexuality, profanity, obscenity, morality, witchcraft, nudity, the occult, and violence. Less frequently cited reasons included incest, mental illness, and slavery. Censors cited family values and the immaturity of students as reasons for challenging the materials.

Results of Challenges

What happened to the challenged materials? Hopkins found that more than half of the challenged items were retained on open shelves during the period of the challenges.[24] Following the challenges, 52.3 percent of the challenged materials were retained; the remaining 47.7 percent were restricted or removed.[25] Table 4.2 lists Hopkins's other findings regarding retention.

Table 4.2.
Significant Findings of the Hopkins Study

Independent Variable	Dependent Variable
Retention by region (South)	Lowest level of retention rate
Challenges involving board approved policies compared with no policy or other types of policies	Higher retention rate
Assistance received within the district	Higher retention rate
Schools with larger enrollments	Higher retention rate
Support of school principals	Higher retention rate
Support of teachers in the school	Higher retention rate
Assistance received outside the district	Higher retention rate
Parent-initiated challenges (rather than challenges initiated by principals or superintendents)	Higher retention rate
Written complaints (rather than oral complaints)	Higher retention rate

Based on Dianne McAfee Hopkins, *Factors Influencing the Outcome of Challenges to Materials in Secondary School Libraries: Report of a National Study* (Madison: University of Wisconsin-Madison, School of Library and Information Studies, 1991), chap. 7, p. 1.

Hopkins identified several factors that influenced whether challenged materials were retained, removed, or restricted.

In terms of initiator, challenges initiated by superintendents and principals were more likely to have material removed. When principals were initiators, the material was also more likely to be restricted. . . . Parent-initiated challenges were more likely to result in retention and less likely to result in restriction.[26]

The reports by Hopkins and Jenkinson indicate the importance of working with teachers, principals, and the local media to encourage their support of intellectual freedom. Local authors can aid in these efforts.

Two examples illustrate how individual media specialists handle controversy. Linda Douglas, who was responsible for a collection that served elementary and junior high students, faced this dilemma: "How could our library serve the needs of the mature junior high reader and yet protect the younger readers from subject matter and language inappropriate for them?"[27] Joined by the junior high English teachers, she selected 50 appropriate titles for the mature readers and set out to

> read and familiarize ourselves with as many of these books as possible and to identify those titles that should be restricted from general circulation to the upper elementary grades. These restricted titles were marked with a blue Signal Dot on the book card. All of the new titles were placed in the YA [young adult] section.[28]

Parents signed permission slips for their children to use the marked materials.

Contrast that position with Elyse Clark's, who was required under protest to enforce a school board restriction on five Judy Blume titles.

> A large sign under Blume's books reads, "These books may not be checked out without parent's permission, by order of the Hanover School Board." Yet students question me. They still show me other books, such as the *Unabridged Dictionary*, which contains the same words which were taken out of context from Blume's books. How do I respond? Do I ignore the student? Ignore the book? Report the dictionary to the school board? Where is the librarian's duty in matters of this kind?
>
> . . .
>
> I feel my job now entails something of the role of police officer. . . . The atmosphere of freedom in our library has been replaced by one of moderate tension and confusion. Students reading the titles are skeptical about adults who are so threatened by these books. I can't estimate how many students won't be able to read the books because their parents don't care enough to sign the permission forms, or because they don't want to be singled out. For many students, it's too much of a hassle to bother with the forms. . . . The chill factor has extended to the present and future ordering of new books. . . . The way is paved for continued infringements on academic freedom, not only for librarians, but for teachers and students as well.[29]

Preemptive Censorship

Not only are selection decisions a matter of concern, but so are the actual policies guiding such decisions. A case in point is the Racine Unified School District in Wisconsin, which in 1986 was censured by the Wisconsin Library Association for internal censorship of library materials. This action followed a series of events: The Wisconsin Library Association received a letter from a school librarian alleging censorship in the district. The Intellectual Freedom Committee requested information from the president of the school board, discussed the "authoritarian, negative tone" of the school district's policy, and conducted a formal inquiry. The investigation was a first for the Wisconsin Library Association. The investigation not only revealed that the school district administration did indeed abridge the principles of intellectual freedom but also revealed that "the policy seemed to be designed to anticipate and to weed out orders for controversial materials rather than to encourage sound principles of selection."[30] The school board's policy recommended that requests for materials of a "highly controversial nature" be referred to the public library, local bookstores, or newsstands.[31]

A number of professional groups have issued statements about people's rights. Appendix C presents nationally endorsed statements supporting intellectual freedom and the student's right to information. In addition, a number of organizations offer support and assistance (see chap. 6).

ACCESS TO INFORMATION

Access to information involves both intellectual and physical access. Intellectual access addresses students' rights to hear, read, and view information; to receive ideas; to express ideas; and to develop skills to receive, examine, analyze, synthesize, evaluate, and use information. Physical access refers to an environment that permits the unimpeded location and retrieval of information. This involves provision of adequate media center staff; access to the media center during and after regular school hours; provision of a broad range of resources to meet the needs of students in terms of learning styles and linguistic and cultural diversity; use of interlibrary loan; and access to computerized information networks or databases. The media specialist's commitment to intellectual freedom influences the extent of intellectual access provided. The media specialist's commitment to intellectual access and sensitivity to individuals' needs influence the extent of physical access provided. Commitment to intellectual and physical access affect the media specialist's response to collection issues.

Intellectual Access and Balance

Intellectual access embraces many issues, most of which center on balance in the collection. Pressing questions regarding balance in the collection are: Should materials in the collection represent all sides of issues? and Should selection be based on demand (popularity), quality (literary merit), or both?

Objectivity Versus Presenting All Views

A balanced collection can be defined as one that contains materials that represent all sides of various issues. Advocates of this position express the belief that young people should learn to gather and evaluate information; they believe these skills are necessary to preserve democracy. Opponents argue that students need to be directed or guided to materials selected by adults to reflect the adults' beliefs and values.

Another debate centers on whether any controversial subject can be objectively presented. Would oversimplification and generalization result? Attempting to be objective may put constraints on the writer who is well informed about an issue and cares about the outcome. Authors attempting to present both sides may become bogged down in phrases like "some experts believe." Fortunately, many writers achieve objectivity while stimulating curiosity.

A more realistic goal of collection development is to maintain objectivity by including works that present differing views. Some students may not be aware that there are a range of viewpoints on a particular subject. To help the student who stops at the first source of information, media specialists should encourage students to seek a wide range of information.

When examining materials about controversial subjects, consider not only content but presentation. Excluding relevant facts is only one way to slant information. Word choice and connotations, use of visuals, vocal inflection, or filming techniques may be used to elicit emotional responses. For example, videos about alcohol, driving, and sex may include frightening scenes.

One benefit of a balanced collection containing many diverse viewpoints is that there will be materials on hand to counter criticism of controversial works. For example, one can anticipate questions about contemporary works about creation science, sexuality, birth control, and homosexuality. One response to critics is to refer them to works that present a different perspective on adolescents' problems. To address this situation, some media specialists select some works that reflect traditional, conservative, or various religious views.

Popularity Versus Literary Merit

To achieve balance within a collection, media specialists must grapple with the conflict between popular appeal and literary value. At one end of this spectrum is a collection that includes only popular items lacking literary merit. At the other end is a collection that contains classic works of no interest or relevance to young people. Proponents on both sides argue vehemently, generating lively debate in conversations and in print. Some say that appeal is more important than quality; others promote the role of libraries in preserving and providing quality materials.

The issue of demand selection versus literary selection cuts across the boundaries of content, format, reading level—and intellectual freedom. Should the media specialist purchase popular material that contains racial, ethnic, or sexual stereotypes? Should one buy heavily in visual materials and software because "no one reads anymore"?

Some people argue that if children do not find items they want in the media center, they leave with a negative attitude about libraries that endures for life. Others argue that media specialists' professional responsibility is to motivate young people by exposing them to materials that will aid the development of their literary and aesthetic tastes. Some people argue that responding to readers' requests encourage reading. Their position is that children will reach a saturation point with series and then turn to media specialists for recommendations. Others argue that limited budgets demand that media specialists encourage readers to explore worthy works that are less advertised.

An ongoing debate centers on the inclusion of series titles from "fiction factories," where hired writers complete a prepared character and plot outline (formula writing). The debate, active since the 1920s, when the series in question were Nancy Drew and Hardy Boys, is a prime example of the demand versus quality issue. A similar debate centers on the widely advertised, paperback young adult romance series displayed in mall bookstores. Will the collection include the Sewing Girls or Sweet Valley High series? On what basis will series be selected?

The issues concerning series apply to other materials as well. Comics, materials from the popular culture, and materials based on popular television programs are a few examples. Should comics be in the collection? On what basis? Are there differences in value among *Peanuts*, *Mad Magazine*, and *Wonder Woman*? Are these materials more or less valuable than graphic novels or nonfiction presented in comic-book form?

Some media centers' selection policy refer to the Code of the Comics Magazine Association of America (see appendix A) as a guide to whether the violence portrayed is unacceptable. Those who say comics have a place in the collection call for clear guidelines for selection beyond those established in the code. These criteria address the visual art, social values, potential use for language development, and quality of the story.

Barriers to Access

Common barriers to access include inequality of access; fiscal limitations; physical limitations of materials, equipment, and individuals; design of resources, such as interactive retrieval systems; attitudes and practices regarding reference service and interlibrary loan services; and censorship.

Computer-Based Information

We are increasingly aware of inequality in accessing computer-based information. These inequalities result from such factors as

- girls are less computer literate than boys;

- software is designed to appeal boys, not girls;

- wealthy school districts continue to own more computers than less wealthy ones;

- the gap between rich and poor schools is widening;

- in affluent communities students are learning to direct the computer, while in less affluent communities students are learning to do as the computer directs; and

- schools without media specialists may have the equipment but lack staff with the ability to use it.

Delia Neuman recommends actions to meet the challenge, including

- look for software that appeals to girls;

- provide adaptive input and output devices designed for the disabled (for example, guarded keyboards for the physically impaired and large-print monitors for the visually impaired);

- assure equitable scheduling; and

- look for biases in the curriculum and uses of technology.

Noting that long-term, widespread solutions to the problems must await national political attention, Neuman encourages media specialists to seek grants from both the public and private sectors.[32]

Fiscal Limitations

Budgetary constraints limit available resources, including personnel. Lack of a replacement policy encourages media specialists to hold onto out-of-date materials. Media specialists who automate circulation and cataloging systems or expand software and online services without outside funding have fewer funds for books and audiovisual materials.

Physical Limitations

Physical barriers to access limit the use of resources and the individuals who can use them. The physical environment of the media center can create limitations: lack of seating and work space, shelving beyond the reach of individuals, lack of electrical outlets for equipment, or insufficient number of terminals. (Provisions for individuals with disabilities will be discussed in chapter 12.) Barriers created by administrative decisions include–rigid schedules, limited hours for use, restrictive circulation and interlibrary loan practices, and pass systems. Inappropriate or missing catalog subject headings also can inhibit access to resources.

Design of or Lack of Resources

Another aspect of access is the effectiveness of interactive information-retrieval systems for children. Frances F. Jacobson calls for an evaluation of exactly how these systems are used by children; such research will reveal whether software is properly designed. Researchers are just beginning to report the typical search patterns and strategies that young people use and the cognitive processes that must be understood to design age-appropriate system interfaces.[33] Jacobson describes the challenge:

> There are clearly many issues to be explored in evaluating information retrieval systems in youth services. Until recently, designers seem to have assumed that products initially developed for adults also would meet the needs of children and young adults. But unlike paper-based systems, electronic systems are fluid in nature. They *can* be adapted and modified; they also can be developed specifically for targeted user groups. Researchers and practitioners have a unique opportunity to influence this process by communicating their concerns to product developers. Certainly, the potential for truly responsive systems is worth the effort.[34]

Publishers, producers, and vendors can benefit from media specialists alerting them to areas in which materials or improvements are needed. Regional associations can collect comments and suggestions or sponsor a workshop on this topic at a conference.

Professional Responsibilities

As professionals, media specialists' responsibilities for intellectual freedom and access extend to collection activities other than selection. As selectors, media specialists need to be aware of their own biases. As managers of the collection, they need to ensure adequate funds to support the collection. As respecters of the creative contributions of authors, illustrators, and producers, media specialists need to ensure that copyright practices are enforced. In each of these areas, commitment to intellectual freedom and balance in the collection come into play.

Selection

Knowing one's self is an important prerequisite for selection. Media specialists should be aware of their own biases and preferences so that personal prejudices do not inadvertently affect selection decisions. A media specialist with a strong belief in higher education may be tempted to purchase more college-oriented materials than those for vocational courses. A media specialist who advocates online searching as a major teaching tool may be overzealous in budgeting for this area. A media specialist whose hobby is cinema may push film making or videotaping. College preparatory materials, online databases, and film making are worthy components of the media program, and a media specialist's interests can be a creative and exciting influence on the media center; however, the media specialist's personal interests should not unduly influence selection decisions.

Are you an active conservationist? Will your position on such issues cloud your evaluation of materials presenting different views? If you are an advocate of the feminist movement, will your sensitivity to the treatment of women dominate your evaluation of materials? Will you be equally sensitive to the treatment of racial or ethnic groups?

When you next visit a media center, examine the collection. Can you detect any bias on the selector's part? Does this indicate the need for involvement of others in selection?

One purpose of the collection is to fulfill the needs of all individuals in the school. If you sense that your personal views may be outweighing your professional judgment, seek other people's opinions.

Funding

A media specialist's professional responsibilities include obtaining funding that will support and strengthen a collection. This may mean presenting facts about the collection, noting its condition, anticipating replacement costs using the formulas in *Information Power,*[35] informing funders of the average costs of materials, deciding how much of the budget should go to the introduction of automation, or seeking outside funding through grants. Soliciting free materials, for example, review copies from journals or publishers, is not selection, it is begging. To use Lillian N. Gerhardt's words, seeking monies to buy books is fundraising, which enables selection, but "Pleading for free books is called panhandling, mooching, or beggary. Since beggars can't be choosers, librarians who beg free books can't really be selectors. That's not only unethical, it's worse. Forfeiting selection responsibility is professional suicide."[36] Gerhardt's remarks were triggered by the *School Library Journal* staff's impression that requests for review copies had quadrupled during the last five years.

Gerhardt learned that publishers also experienced increasing requests for free books.

Copyright

As respecters of creative contributions, media specialists have a responsibility to ensure that copyright laws are honored. These professional responsibilities include educating teachers and students about the copyright laws, placing a copyright notice near copy machines, identifying copyrighted materials, and monitoring use of copyrighted materials. (Chapter 9 describes copyright regulations for various formats.)

SCENARIOS

Think about how you would handle the following situations based on Edward B. Jenkinson's *The Schoolbook Protest Movement: 40 Questions & Answers.*[37]

1. A board member removes books from a high school media center because a citizen said the books were objectionable. Neither the citizen nor the board member have read the books in question.

2. A media center staff uses a black pen to block out the word *crap*, whenever he finds it in a book. Another staff member uses razor blades or scissors to remove words and passages.

3. When you are checking in materials, you discover a book with pages glued together.

4. You learn a district administrator commissioned an artist to put shorts on the little boy who wanders around naked in Maurice Sendak's *In the Night Kitchen.*

5. A school board member admits that she checked out materials she did not like, failed to return them, and sends you a check to cover the cost.

6. You discover that many books are missing. Through quiet investigation and observation you discover that the principal is removing any book that a citizen objects to.

7. You learn about publishers who, in response to protests, have told authors to avoid writing about certain objectionable ideas.

8. You realize one of your coworkers is not ordering titles that have been challenged elsewhere.

Other examples can be found in *Academic Freedom to Teach and to Learn: Every Teacher's Issue*[38] (National Education Association, 1990).

SUMMARY

The definition of *child* is at best vague and evolving. Society in general, and librarians in particular, are beginning to address the rights of children, but existing barriers must be removed to provide children with intellectual and physical access to information. One final thought from David Moshman: "Childhood status in itself should never be a basis for denial of personhood"[39] and one from Theodore Geisel (Dr. Seuss): "As Horton the elephant says, . . . after all, a person's a person, no matter how small."[40]

Your position on intellectual freedom and students' rights will be reflected in your practices as a selector and the resources you make available to students. As you reflect on these issues and the concepts of balance and objectivity, what is your philosophy of collection development?

NOTES

[1]For purposes of this discussion, the terms *children*, *young people*, and *students* refer to individuals under the age of 18.

[2]David Moshman, "Editor's Notes," in *Children's Intellectual Rights*, ed. by David Moshman, New Directions for Child Development series, no. 33 (San Francisco: Jossey-Bass, 1986): 4.

[3]David Moshman, *Children, Education, and the First Amendment: A Psychological Analysis* (Lincoln: University of Nebraska Press, 1989), 27.

[4]Moshman, *Children, Education*, 28.

[5]David Moshman, "Children's Intellectual Rights: A First Amendment Analysis" in *Children's Intellectual Rights*, ed. by David Moshman, New Directions for Child Development series, no. 33 (San Francisco: Jossey-Bass, 1986), 33.

[6]Moshman, "Children's Intellectual Rights," 35.

[7]*Tinker v Des Moines Independent Community School District*, 393 U.S. 503 (1969).

[8]Moshman, *Children, Education*, 13.

[9]Edward B. Jenkinson, *The Schoolbook Protest Movement: 40 Questions & Answers* (Bloomington, IN: Phi Delta Kappa Educational Foundation, 1986), 31.

[10]Jenkinson, *Schoolbook Protest*, 27.

[11]Frances M. McDonald, "Information Access for Youth: Issues and Concerns," *Library Trends* 37, no. 1 (Summer 1988): 30.

[12]Dianne McAfee Hopkins, "School Library Media Centers and Intellectual Freedom," in *Intellectual Freedom Manual*, 4th ed., comp. by American Library Association, Office for Intellectual Freedom (Chicago: American Library Association, 1992), 156.

[13]Lester Asheim, "The Public Library Meets the Censor," *Texas Library Journal* 55, no. 2 (1979): 46.

[14]Asheim, "Public Library," 46-47.

[15]Henry Reichman, *Censorship and Selection: Issues and Answers for Schools* (Chicago: American Library Association; Arlington, VA: American Association of School Administrators, 1993), 6.

[16]American Library Association, Office of Intellectual Freedom, comp., *Intellectual Freedom Manual*, 4th ed. (Chicago: American Library Association, 1992), 65.

[17]Dianne McAfee Hopkins, *Factors Influencing the Outcome of Challenges to Materials in Secondary School Libraries: Report of a National Study* (Madison: University of Wisconsin-Madison, School of Library and Information Studies, 1991), chap. 8, p. 1.

[18]David Jenkinson, "Censorship Iceberg: Results of a Survey of Challenges in Public and School Libraries," *Canadian Library Journal* 43 (February 1986): 8.

[19]American Library Association, Public Information Office, *Fact Sheet* (Chicago, 1944).

[20]American Library Association, *Intellectual Freedom Manual*, ix.

[21]Reichman, *Censorship and Selection,* 14-15.

[22]Hopkins, *Factors Influencing*, chap. 4, p. 23.

[23]Hopkins, *Factors Influencing*, chap. 4, p. 20.

[24]Hopkins, *Factors Influencing*, chap. 4, p. 26.

[25]Hopkins, *Factors Influencing*, chap. 4, p. 40.

[26]Hopkins, *Factors Influencing*, chap. 5, p. 52.

[27]Linda Douglas, "An Ounce of Prevention: Before the Censor Knocks," *Ohio Media Spectrum* (Spring 1985): 41-42.

[28]Douglas, "An Ounce of Prevention," 41-42.

[29]Elyse Clark, "A Slow, Subtle Exercise in Censorship," *School Library Journal* 32, no. 7 (March 1986): 96.

[30]Alan M. Tollefson, "Censored & Censured: Racine Unified School District vs. Wisconsin Library Association," *School Library Journal* 33, no. 7 (March 1987): 108, 110.

[31]Tollefson, "Censored & Censured," 112.

[32]Delia Neuman, "Beyond the Chip: A Model for Fostering Equity," *School Library Media Quarterly* 18, no. 3 (Spring 1990): 158-64.

[33]Frances F. Jacobson, "Information Retrieval Systems and Youth: A Review of Recent Literature," Focus on Technology column, *Journal of Youth Services in Libraries* 5, no. 1 (Fall 1991): 109.

[34]Jacobson, "Information Retrieval Systems," 112.

[35]American Association of School Librarians and Association for Educational Communications and Technology, *Information Power: Guidelines for School Library*

Media Programs (Chicago: American Library Association; Washington, DC: Association for Educational Communications and Technology, 1988).

[36]Lillian N. Gerhardt, "Choosing vs. Begging," *School Library Journal* 38, no. 10 (October 1992): 4.

[37]Jenkinson, *Schoolbook Protest*, 17-19.

[38]Anna S. Ochoa, ed., *Academic Freedom to Teach and to Learn: Every Teacher's Issue*, NEA Aspects of Learning series (Washington, DC: National Education Association, 1990).

[39]Moshman, *Children, Education*, 33.

[40]Theodore Geisel (Dr. Seuss), *Horton Hears a Who!* (New York: Random House, 1954).

BIBLIOGRAPHY

American Association of School Librarians and Association for Educational Communications and Technology. *Information Power: Guidelines for School Library Media Programs.* Chicago: American Library Association; Washington, DC: Association for Educational Communications and Technology, 1988.

American Library Association. Office for Intellectual Freedom, comp. *Intellectual Freedom Manual,* 4th ed. Chicago: American Library Association, 1992.

Asheim, Lester. "The Public Library Meets the Censor." *Texas Library Journal* 55, no. 2 (1979): 44-48.

Clark, Elyse. "A Slow, Subtle Exercise in Censorship." *School Library Journal* 32, no. 7 (1986): 93-96.

Douglas, Linda. "An Ounce of Prevention: Before the Censor Knocks." *Ohio Media Spectrum* (1988): 93-96.

Gerhardt, Lillian N. "Choosing vs. Begging." *School Library Journal* 38, no. 10 (October 1992): 4.

Hopkins, Dianne McAfee. "Challenges to Materials in Secondary School Library Media Centers: Results of a National Study." *Journal of Youth Services in Libraries* 4 (Winter 1991): 131-40.

———. "A Conceptual Model of Factors Influencing Outcome of Challenges to Library Materials in Secondary School Settings." *Library Quarterly* 63, no. 1 (1993): 40-72.

———. *Factors Influencing the Outcome of Challenges to Materials in Secondary School Libraries: Report of a National Study.* Madison: University of Wisconsin-Madison, School of Library and Information Studies, 1991.

———. "Perspectives of Secondary Library Media Specialists About Material Challenges." *School Library Media Quarterly* 21, no. 1 (Fall 1992): 15-24.

———. "Put It in Writing: What You Should Know about Challenges to School Library Materials." *School Library Journal* 39, no. 1 (January 1993): 26-30.

———. "Toward a Conceptual Model of Factors Influencing the Outcome of Challenges to Library Materials in School Settings." *Library and Information Science Research* 11 (1989): 247-71.

Jacobson, Frances F. "Information Retrieval Systems and Youth: A Review of Recent Literature." Focus on Technology column. *Journal of Youth Services in Libraries* 5, no. 1 (Fall 1991): 109-13.

Jenkinson, David. "Censorship Iceberg: Results of a Survey of Challenges in Public and School Libraries." *Canadian Library Journal* 43 (February 1986): 7-21.

Jenkinson, Edward B. *The Schoolbook Protest Movement: 40 Questions & Answers.* Bloomington, IN: Phi Delta Kappa Educational Foundation, 1986.

McDonald, Frances M. "Information Access for Youth: Issues and Concerns." *Library Trends* 37, no. 1 (Summer 1988): 28-42.

Moshman, David. *Children, Education, and the First Amendment: A Psychological Analysis.* Lincoln: University of Nebraska Press, 1989.

———. "Children's Intellectual Rights: A First Amendment Analysis," pages 27-38 in *Children's Intellectual Rights*, ed. by David Moshman. New Directions for Child Development series, no. 33. San Francisco: Jossey-Bass, 1986.

Neuman, Delia. "Beyond the Chip : A Model for Fostering Equity." *School Library Media Quarterly* 18, no. 3 (Spring 1990): 158-64.

Ochoa, Anna S., ed. *Academic Freedom to Teach and to Learn: Every Teacher's Issue.* NEA Aspects of Learning series. Washington, DC: National Education Association, 1990.

Reichman, Henry. *Censorship and Selection: Issues and Answers for Schools.* Chicago: American Library Association; Arlington, VA: American Association of School Administrators, 1993.

Tollefson, Alan M. "Censored & Censured: Racine Unified School District vs. Wisconsin Library Association." *School Library Journal* 33, no. 7 (March 1987): 108-12.

RECOMMENDED READINGS

Censorship

American Library Association. Young Adult Services Division. Intellectual Freedom Committee. *Hit List: Frequently Challenged Young Adult Titles: References to Defend Them.* Chicago, 1989.
For each of 20 titles, this work provides bibliographic information; a descriptive annotation identifying controversial features; examples of challenges; and a list of reviews, articles, and recommended reading lists in which the titles are included.

Burress, Lee. *Battle of the Books: Literary Censorship in the Public Schools, 1950-1985.* Metuchen, NJ: Scarecrow Press, 1989.

DelFattore, Joan. *What Johnny Shouldn't Read: Textbook Censorship in America.* New Haven: Yale University Press, 1992.

Hentoff, Nat. *Free Speech for Me—But Not for Thee: How the American Left and Right Relentlessly Censor Each Other.* New York: HarperCollins, 1992.

Karolides, Nicholas J.; Lee Burress; and John M. Kean. *Censored Books: Critical Viewpoints.* Metuchen, NJ: Scarecrow Press, 1993.
Discusses individual titles.

McDonald, Frances Beck; Matthew Stark; and William Roath. *A Report of a Survey on Censorship in Public School Libraries and Public Libraries in Minnesota 1993.* Minneapolis: Minnesota Civil Liberties Union, 1993.

Peck, Richard. "The Great Library-Shelf Witch Hunt." *Booklist* 88, no. 9 (January 1, 1992): 816-817.

Pico, Steven. "An Introduction to Censorship." *School Library Media Quarterly* 18, no. 2 (Winter 1990): 84-87.

Volz, Edward J. "You Can't Play That: A Selective Chronology of Banned Music: 1850-1991." *School Library Journal* 37, no. 7 (July 1991): 16-18.

West, Mark I. *Trust Your Children: Voices Against Censorship in Children's Literature.* New York: Neal-Schuman, 1988.
Interviews with authors and publishers whose books have been censored and with five anticensorship activists.

Comics and Teen Romances

Krashen, Stephen. *The Power of Reading: Insights from the Research.* Englewood, CO: Libraries Unlimited, 1993.
See especially the section on light reading, pages 46-65.

Copyright

Reed, Mary Hutchings. *The Copyright Primer for Librarians and Educators.* Chicago: American Library Association; Washington, DC: National Education Association, 1987.

Demand Selection Versus Quality Selection

Genco, Barbara A.; Eleanor K. MacDonald; and Betsy Hearne. "Juggling Popularity and Quality." *School Library Journal* 37, no. 3 (March 1991): 115-19.

Intellectual Freedom

Bosmajian, Haig A., ed. *The Freedom to Read.* The First Amendment in the Classroom Series, no. 1. New York: Neal-Schuman, 1987.

Harer, John B. *Intellectual Freedom: A Reference Handbook.* Contemporary World Issues series. Santa Barbara, CA: ABC-Clio, 1992.

Students' Rights

Guggenheim, Martin. *The Rights of Young People: The Basic ACLU Guide to a Person's Rights.* New York: Bantam Books, 1985.

Price, Janet R. *The Rights of Students: The Basic ACLU Guide to a Student's Rights,* 3d ed. Carbondale: Southern Illinois University Press, 1988.

CHAPTER 5

ThE CollECTiON's ExTERNAL ENViRONMENT

The collection is not an isolated entity. It is one component of the media program within a school which is in a district and a state. The school also functions within the local community it serves. Relationships among these components of the environment influence the collection program. For instance, financial support for educational programs may reflect society's attitudes about the quality of education or a slow economy. How a community values information sources also can be a factor.

THE COMMUNITY

To understand the importance of the external environment to the collection program, one must recognize the give-and-take nature of the relationship. The collection will attract a certain number of outside users—institutions and people outside the school—and the collection must offer those users the information they need. On the other hand, the outside environment has much to offer the school collection. Online databases and electronic networks provide access to myriad external information sources in the community and beyond.

Educational administrators and community officials are often responsible for establishing the directions, limitations, and strategies under which the media specialist will be working. Their goals and attitudes about education and information will support or challenge the media specialist's views. Their actions will influence the financial support and selection policies of the collection program.

If you do not know the decision makers and their goals or attitudes, you will find it difficult to communicate with them or to offer them useful services. Your daily contacts within the school and the local community offer opportunities to discover needs, receive requests, recognize attitudes, and offer services. How well do you know the policy makers at the district and state level? These people establish policies that affect your environmental structures: budget, programs, and operational activities. Use your initial visit to the district and school to observe these environmental structures.

Learning About the Community

Beyond the school grounds lies a group of businesses, offices, factories, and residences full of people who have self-interests in the activities of the school program—the local community. The term *local community* has two meanings. The first refers to the area that surrounds the physical site occupied by the school, including adjacent institutions, agencies, businesses, and residences. A second interpretation relates to the area where the students live. The latter may be identical to the first setting or students may be transported to the school from a broader area.

How do you learn about the community? Generally, the seven best sources are the school district, the Chamber of Commerce, news media, government agencies, service and civic clubs, local census data, and the public library. These sources can provide maps, surveys, brochures, community profiles, lists of local activities, and projections for future population shifts. They can lead you to other information sources, such as planning commissions or historical societies. If the public library surveyed the community's information needs, their findings will be of interest. Is the local public or university library a United States government documents depository? Such libraries will have the United States census data for your community. The summary of characteristics should include the items identified in figure 5.1 on page 62.

Demographics

How does this profile help the media specialist with the collection? The demographics can provide useful guidance. You may find a community of young families, which are more likely to support educational programs than a community of retirees. The educational level of the population may be another clue to the willingness of citizens to financially support schools.

Remember, neighborhoods in large districts differ drastically. You may find pockets of support—or opposition—in the various neighborhoods.

Census data about racial, ethnic, and language backgrounds indicate types of materials needed in the collection. Staff members who serve as translators can be a source of information about students' needs. Another source of help are groups organized to serve diverse populations, such as a Hispanic Council, who may be responsible for helping locate tutors to mentor young Hispanics. For example, if children come from Cuban families, you will want to have Spanish-language materials. You also may want to incorporate Cuban folklore that parallels literature familiar to American children. In communities with refugees and immigrants, you also will need materials that help the indigenous young people and teachers understand the new members of their community.

Stability of the population also affects the collection. A community without an influx of young families may face a decline in student population leading to closing or consolidating schools. If you are in a school with migrant families, you may need to emphasize materials in less permanent

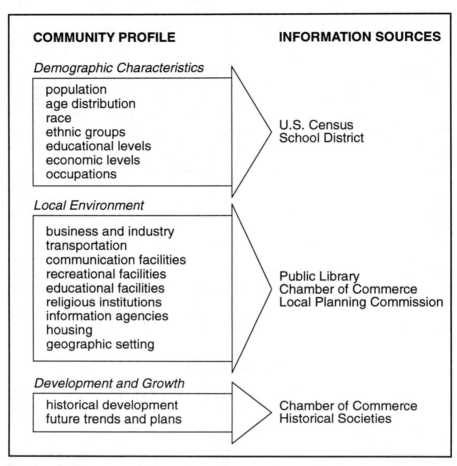

Fig. 5.1. Information about the community.

formats. Children of inner-city factory workers or migrant farm workers may spend only a few weeks at your school. A migrant family's decision to move may happen suddenly. In this situation, it may be better to select mostly paperback books and not fret about the loss of materials.

Students' Personal Lives

Even the students' home conditions affect their use of materials. Are there students in your school who support themselves and pay the rent on an apartment? Are there students who hold full-time jobs to maintain cars or trucks, which are their primary concern? The latter group may seek auto repair or career guidance materials. How many students have children of their own?

How many look after younger siblings? Responsibilities such as these may leave limited time for schooling, even for highly motivated students.

We also need to recognize that some students move among several cultures in any given day. They get up, go to school, go to work, go home, constantly reacting as each of these cultural environments places different demands upon them. Some students, unable to cope with the regular school setting, may temporarily attend an alternative school. When they are ready to return to regular school, the adults who worked with them can help the school staff understand their needs and interests. Other students may be heavily involved in sports, music or other performing arts, or have other interests that call for discipline and heavy time commitments. These demands affect the time they have to use the media center.

The effect of students' home environments can be shown through the lives of two elementary school children. Kayla, a third-grader, is responsible for seeing that her five-year-old brother and three-year-old sister are fed, clothed, and supervised. She is a good reader and likes to read aloud to her younger charges, as well as to the children of another family who share the same apartment. Kayla was only permitted to take out two books overnight. The media specialist felt that it was unfair to ask Kayla to keep track of books for a longer period. It placed an additional burden on this very responsible child. Kayla happily renewed her books or took out new ones each morning, giving her an opportunity to receive encouragement and personal attention from the media staff.

Contrast Kayla's experience with that of Stephanie, whose home has a live-in housekeeper. Stephanie flatly demanded materials—then left them wherever she pleased when she was ready to move on to another activity. Until Stephanie's mother volunteered to work in the media center, she did not realize how conditioned her children were to having someone wait on them and pick up after them. She also realized that many children lacked the resources available to her own children. For example, Stephanie and her siblings each had their own computer.

In some homes, parents' convictions affect their children's use of materials. For example, some parents do not approve of their children using films, videos, or fiction.

Community Opportunities and Constraints

The community's layout affects students' mobility and thereby influences demands on the collection. To map a student's mobility, look at your community's transportation patterns. How easily can children get to the public library or other information agencies? Limiting factors may include the absence of mass transit, pedestrian walks, or bike trails. Betty J. Morris recommends drawing a simple map of the community and locating on it the various community resources and the school and public bus routes as well as other modes of transportation.[1] The children who attend Gaver Elementary School have to cross two major highways to reach the public library. For the students dependent on bicycle transportation, their school's media center was their only source of materials for instructional or recreational use. The school library cooperated with the public library in bringing the summer reading program to these students.

The location of the community, its climate, and its recreational patterns also make demands on the collection. You will soon learn whether students are active in 4-H clubs, Scout troops, or other activities. Schools in areas where skiing, snowmobiling, or surfing are regular activities need appropriate materials in the collection.

Many communities support recreational and educational programs. Young people may regularly attend functions at museums, zoological gardens, art institutes, and concert halls. These interests result in demands on the collection. If the community planetarium is open to the students, the collection will need stronger astronomy resources than one in a community without this facility.

Other Libraries

Your most valuable ally may be the public library's children and young adult specialists. Questions you will want to explore are: What services do libraries and other information agencies offer to students? Is there a branch library near your school, or do the students use a bookmobile? Do school and public libraries offer cooperative programs or services? Can you borrow public library materials for classroom use? If so, for how long? Has the school established a procedure for alerting the public library of forthcoming assignments? Do the two library systems share selection policies or plan collections jointly?

You can ask if the libraries have jointly applied for grant funds. One example is the DeForest Public Library (Wisconsin) which cooperates with the public schools in a project funded through a Library Services Construction Act (LSCA) grant. The monies provide materials and activities for cognitively, emotionally, and physically challenged children and young adults. The materials include children's classics in alternative formats including videos, books on cassette, and books with sign language translations. Cognitively disabled middle and high school students help assemble kits of learning activities for families and act for the library's preschooler story hours.[2]

Visit local community colleges, colleges, and university libraries. Their collections probably include reference works and other bibliographic tools too expensive for the school collection. The resources may be identified by using networked information services available through searching a library's computerized catalog.

Bringing the Community into the School

The school media center's relationship with the community is reciprocal. Just as the media center has much to offer the community, so the community has much to offer the media center—in terms of both information and human resources.

Organizations As Resources

Each community has a wide range of cooperative organizations and individuals who provide educational experiences. Typical examples are accountants, airports, cemeteries, city halls, junkyards, mental health workers, nurses, taxicab drivers, tree surgeons, and zoos. A guide to community resources is a helpful reminder of the vast range of resources within the community. Electronic bulletin boards may list local community activities or announce the meetings of hobby groups.

Students and teachers can gain access to community resources through use of the school's online public catalog (OPAC), which lists holdings of collections throughout the community. The OPAC may include entries for community resources, such as options for field trips. A sample entry for a health food store might be organized like figure 5.2.

Green Acres Natural Food Store [organization resource] / Ms. Eatright, owner. — Our Town (112 Liveoak Ave., 99999) : Phone 555-5555, 9:00 a.m.-4:00 p.m.

Audience level: 4th-7th grades.
  Summary: Ms. Eatright will visit classes to discuss natural foods. Students can visit the store in groups of 12 for an hour tour that includes sampling foods. The store can supply cookies made from kelp for science units on foods from the sea.
  Available every day except Saturday and Sunday.

  1. Food, Natural. 2. Seafood. 3. Stores, Retail.
  I. Eatright, Ms.

Fig. 5.2. Bibliographic record for organization resource. Cataloging according to *AACR2* by Doris H. Clack, professor of cataloging at Florida State University, Tallahassee.

The visit described in figure 5.2 included a science-related activity about food from the sea. As a reminder of the visit, each participant received a cookie made from kelp. Such entries could also include preferred time and/or dates for field trips; resource people available at the site; time needed to travel to the location; types of experiences; charges; presence of eating facilities and restrooms; rules concerning the use of cameras, tape recorders, and video cameras; and the availability of preparation materials for use before the visit, such as a slide presentation or a video tape. Before planning field trips you will want to consult your district's policy about use of community resources and any restraints such as a limit on the amount of school time allotted for field trips. Helpful ideas for planning educational experiences around field trips appear in Mary D. Lankford's *Successful Field Trips* (ABC-Clio, 1992). She offers many practical suggestions for arranging field trips, preparing students for the experience, and post-field trip activities.

Community Members As Resources

Another valuable resource are individuals within the community. Human resources also can be listed on the OPAC. You may be looking for people with travel experiences, hobbies, collections, talents, or occupations. Other individuals can serve as role model examples, such as a stay-at home father or a female construction worker. Individuals can be identified through speakers' bureaus, extension agencies, and directories of local artists, authors, and illustrators.

Like organizations or materials, human resources can be listed in the OPAC. A sample entry might include items similar to those in figure 5.3. The entry could include cost, time needed to arrange for a program, whether the individual can best be interviewed in the classroom or at the work place, and the appropriate audience. The mortician described in figure 5.3, for example, might tell tenth-graders about the personal characteristics a mortician needs and tell eleventh-graders about the educational requirements of the profession or the problems of operating a business.

Smith, Jacob.
  Mortuary science as a career [human resource] :
oral presentation / Jacob Smith. — Contact at the
Pleasantview Funeral Home : Phone 222-2222, 10:00 a.m.-
5:00 p.m.

Audience level: 10th-12th grades.
  Summary: Mr. Smith describes academic requirements,
educational costs, admissions procedures, and the
advantages and disadvantages of work as a mortician.

  1. Undertakers and undertaking —Vocational guidance —
Addresses and essays. 2. Professions. I. Title

Fig. 5.3. Bibliographic record for human resource. Cataloging according to *AACR2* by Doris H. Clack, professor of cataloging at Florida State University, Tallahassee.

Other Community Resources

In addition to the traditional uses of organization and human resources—field trips and guest speakers—information can be found in other ways. Students can gather oral history by interviewing senior members of the community, and recording their reminiscences. For example, at Kennedy High School, Wilma's American History class visited the Salvation Army's "Golden Agers" group to interview the members about the Great Depression and Prohibition. The students heard about the experiences of real "rum-runners" who had traveled back and forth between Canada and the United States. The students were enthusiastic about their experience.

Younger students also can collect oral histories, beginning with questions that interest them, such as "What did you do for fun if you didn't have computer games?" Oral histories can be valuable resources for the historical section of the media collection. Students in Connie's fourth-grade class interviewed their parents and grandparents as part of a state library project to gather the history of small communities. Using data sheets prepared by the historical archives section of the state library, the children asked their parents how long they had lived in the community, why they had moved there, and how far this was from their previous home. When possible, children interviewed their grandparents, asking them the same set of questions. Each child kept one copy of the report; the other became part of the archives collection. A similar type of project could be initiated through a local historical society.

These examples represent only a few of the educational experiences available in any given community. As you get to know local community people, ask for their suggestions. Individuals at the school district and state level will doubtless have many ideas, but don't overlook the suggestions of your neighbors, students, parents, and everyone else you meet. The school staff should not be overlooked: for example, the school custodian or cook may have valuable experiences to share.

THE SCHOOL DISTRICT

A community's attitudes about and expectations of education are inevitably translated into policies of the school district. Awareness of the district's priorities can alert the media specialist to demands that may be placed on the collection. If the school board emphasizes basic education, be prepared to relate the collection to that approach; if the district emphasizes computer literacy, be prepared to meet that priority. If a curriculum area is to be reviewed, become involved. These fundamental decisions can be made by administrators, board members, teachers, or media personnel, but it is best if they are made by a committee representing a combination of these.

School Board and Administrators

Attending or listening to school board meetings allows the media specialist to see how the members interact and how they approach the issues. Find out the positions the board members have taken on matters concerning media program. Keep in mind that many school board policies directly or indirectly affect the media program.

Some states and districts require that advisory committees comprised of students, faculty, and community members to advise the media specialist on policies, operations, priorities for purchase of materials, and selection. Advisory committees also can:

strengthen the media program and in turn strengthen the school's overall instructional program;

promote positive relationships among media personnel, teachers, students and administrators;

provide a line of communication between the school and community; and

assist in maintaining a balanced collection of resources and equipment.[3]

As a media specialist, you will benefit from the contributions of such groups, gaining strong support for the media program and identifying individuals who can help with public relations efforts.

The district's administrative hierarchy affects communication and decision-making. Learn what types of decisions are made at the district and regional levels, along with those made at the individual school level. Is school-based management the pattern? Where do media personnel fit into the organization chart? Where do special projects staff—perhaps those funded by state or federal programs—fit into the organization chart? Determine how you can participate in the decision-making process.

In a large district with a central media supervisor, the school-level media specialist may have little direct contact with other district personnel; however, in many districts this is not true. Be assertive about establishing good lines of communication. When the central administrative staff visits your building to look into other matters, be sure to meet them. Establishing contact with administrators may be useful, for example, you may one day need to ask the curriculum coordinator for resources that will help teachers.

Teachers' Organizations or Unions

The districtwide teacher organization or union also can serve the media program. Are media specialists represented on the negotiating team? What media concerns are considered? Does the contract make provisions for the media staff, collections, or production facilities? Does the contract address intellectual freedom or spell out who should be involved in selection of materials? Media specialists should not overlook the mutual concerns they share with teachers about environmental conditions and access to materials. Teacher's groups "watchdog" legislation and convey relevant information to local districts.

One way you can become involved is to alert the union president to your willingness to serve on committees involving curriculum matters. These volunteer efforts have many benefits. They help you to learn more about curriculum matters, and they help you make useful contacts. For example, when a censorship case came up in one school district, a media specialist who was chairperson of the Instructional Development Council and was able to use her committee contacts—parents, board members, students, teachers, and the curriculum director—to resolve the matter.

District Services

A district's public information office can help you track down information or publicize your needs to the community. Their staff will have contacts with people in the local mass media and can guide you to those who can help. Staff can also help to involve the public in development of policies.

Ask about the district media program. Its history will reveal important clues to the level and consistency of support for media personnel. Decisions at this level also determine the focus of both your services and the collection. In schools with site-based management, the planning and direction, including hiring, evaluation, and budget will be handled at the building level. In other situations, these activities may be handled by the district media program personnel. Regardless of the situation, it is important to learn about the services offered through the district level program.

Typical functions of district-level media programs include planning and administration, staff development, and services. Planning and administration activities may include designing facilities, developing selection policies, interpreting the media program to the community through public information systems, coordinating federal projects, and requesting funds. Staff-development activities include orientation of new media specialists, consultative services, and in-service opportunities. Services include central ordering and processing, examination collections, producing materials, assisting in developing basic collections, delivery services, and maintenance of media and equipment.

Before you are hired, you may be interviewed by the media supervisor or district media coordinator. When talking with them and other district staff members, a number of questions should be raised. How is the district media program administered? Is the district coordinator or supervisor part of the central administrative staff? What services are offered by the district media center? With what cooperative programs is the district involved? Do coordinated collection development programs exist within or outside the district? Is there a district-wide manual or policy handbook? Are consultant services provided? What roles do the district media personnel play in deciding budgets? Are in-service programs provided for media personnel? What types of support are there for integrating emerging technologies into the building programs? By learning answers to these questions, you can identify the magnitude of your responsibilities and identify the services you can expect from the district.

Another group of questions relates to how materials are selected and made accessible to students and teachers. In some states the media program's advisory committee plays a strong role in the selection process. Your state may mandate the creation of such a body. Are selection committees appointed on a district-level basis, rather than at the building level? How does one become a member of the district selection committee? If an "approved list" is used for purchasing, how you can purchase items not on that list? Are there delivery services between buildings and the district center? Is the school district involved in networking at the local, regional, or multistate levels and in a multitype-library situation? What interlibrary loan procedures have been established? The answers to this set of questions reveal the control you have over selection decisions and the ease with which you can borrow materials from other collections. In examining these relationships, you can learn how much you and the collection can or must depend upon the district organization.

THE REGION AND STATE

At the regional or intermediate level media program, one will find functions similar to those described for the district level. Consultant services, cooperative programs among schools within one or more districts, staff development programs, examination collections, production, telecommunication delivery systems, and publications are a few examples of their services. Where is the regional center? How does one learn about their services? How do they differ from the district media program?

Another crucial relationship is that between school and state. School goals and objectives reflect broad guidelines developed by the state. Frequently, legislators encourage certain educational goals. For example, the Statutory Citation of the Texas Education Code, 11:36: Library Standards reads:

(a) The State Board of Education shall establish regulations for accreditation of schools that establish standards for library services and personnel. The standards shall include:

    (1) minimum standards for employment of librarians and other library personnel;

    (2) acquisition and maintenance of library materials; and

    (3) the operation and development of learning resource programs for each school district in this state.[4]

The rule for the preceding citation reads:

(c) The district shall provide a cataloged and centrally located collection of materials that is available to faculty members and students to support instruction and learning in the essential curriculum elements and to satisfy individual interests.[5]

and describes the following minimum requirements for the collection:

(A) Books—10 books per Average Daily Attendance (ADA) or 1,500 books total, whichever is greater; effective September 1, 1993, 10 books per ADA or 2,000 books total, whichever is greater. On single campuses with ADA over 3,000, eight books per ADA.

(B) Audiovisual items—items may include filmstrips, slides, transparencies, study prints, pictures, sound recordings, maps, globes, kits, microforms, games, single concept films, 16-mm films, audio and video tapes, and microcomputer software, in a total of at least two items per ADA; and

(C) If a district participates in the media services of the regional education service center, the district is required to provide one audiovisual item per student.

(D) Equipment—appropriate equipment for use of the materials.

(E) Inappropriate, worn, and/or obsolete materials and equipment shall be systemically weeded from the collection.[6]

The Connecticut guidelines emphasize the unique characteristics of schools noting

there will be many and varied definitions of what constitutes a *quality collection*. This flexibility, however, must be balanced by the responsibility of all schools to provide a *foundation collection* of materials and equipment. This collection represents the minimum number of items that must exist to cover the diverse subject areas, formats, reading levels, reference and leisure needs of a comprehensive, developmentally appropriate educational program. Certain quantities of resources and equipment must be considered in providing learning resources and technology services.[7]

Neither quality nor quantity can be considered in isolation from the other. Quality collections, according to parameters developed and recommended by the Connecticut State Department of Education, are:

• adequate in size, currency, breadth, depth and diversity of format to enable students to complete classroom assignments and explore areas of personal interest;

• rich in materials that support cultural awareness;

- responsive to the general educational and specific curriculum philosophies, goals and objectives established by the local board of education;
- appropriate to the ages and/or grade levels of the students in the school, for special needs students and for the gifted and talented;
- varied in presentation format to provide for students with diverse learning styles;
- acquired in accordance with a selection policy approved by the local board of education;
- listed in a centralized union catalog; and
- easily accessible.[8]

The term *foundation collection* is also used in the Wisconsin guidelines, which read

A *foundation* collection of excellent current materials is needed in each school building, regardless of enrollment or grade levels served, in order to

- insure equal educational opportunity;
- support general reference services;
- encourage use of resource materials to satisfy general information and leisure reading needs; and
- provide basic support for instructional units.

Additional materials will be needed as schools develop fully integrated library media programs.[9]

The guidelines address the need

to insure that the collection meets the needs of all learners in a school, including those with physical, mental, emotional, and/or learning disabilities; those with special talents; and those from different backgrounds or socioeconomic groups within society.[10]

In Wisconsin, resources are available through cooperative educational service agencies, cooperative agreements with other libraries, and use of the statewide data base (WISCAT).

Similar legislation may exist in your state. Your district supervisor or the state-level school media supervisor/consultant can provide this information. The latter position may be in the state department of education (or public instruction) or in the state library. Your state media association also can provide information about efforts to change legislation.

Many state consultants or media associations produce publications. For example, the *Pennsylvania Guidelines for School Library Media Programs*

(State Library of Pennsylvania, 1987) includes facts about school libraries in that state and offers helpful suggestions on a wide range of topics.

Typically, state boards of education or offices of public instruction

- develop standards and guidelines for school library media programs in the state;

- provide consultant and in-service activities for school districts;

- promote equal opportunities for all students to access school library media programs and services in the state;

- coordinate school library media programs with other educational activities in the state;

- assist in design and developing the integration of school library media programs in the instructional program;

- administer federal and state funds to facilitate development of school library media programs;

- disseminate information about school library media programs;

- encourage development of long range plans for effective school library media programs integrated with the instructional program and using state-of-the-art technology;

- help to monitor and evaluate school library media programs;

- provide leadership in promoting intellectual freedom;

- identify and promote research about school library media programs; and

- promote cooperative arrangements among school, public, academic, and special libraries.

A number of states have developed technology plans. In some cases funds are specified per student, in other situations schools apply through a grant proposal. The funds may be designated for hiring engineers as consultants on wiring, for acquiring equipment and facilities, or for in-service activities. In states with school-based management, media specialists need to be involved in the decision making.

Michigan's technology plan identifies five major themes, including restructuring schools using technology to meet changing expectations; developing statewide telecommunication systems for teaching, learning, and communications; professional development for the learning community; technology investments for the future; copyright and fair use implications.[11] The plan offers 22 recommendations. Among them are

- A computer network should be established that is accessible by all educational institutions, including K-12 classroom teachers.[12]

- At a minimum, every building at an educational institution, including teacher preparation programs, should be equipped with a computer network, fiber optics, cable access, and a dual-band, steerable satellite dish.

- At a minimum, every classroom at an educational institution, including teacher preparation programs, should be equipped with a telephone line, computer, videodisc player, videocassette recorder, and television/monitor.

- At a minimum, the state's library media centers and programs should be equipped with the same technology tools as a classroom, incorporating automated circulation and card catalog system.

. . .

- Educational agencies should be informed about the copyright law and monitor their use of copyrighted materials to ensure compliance with the law.[13]

The document provides direction for those responsible for the educational program within the state. Its implementation is "dependent on available funds, coordination with other state initiatives, or passage of new legislation."[14] and calls for seeking funds and making linkages with private and public sectors.

The state consultant and the association are two contact points for up-to-date information about services, programs, legislation, and standards. Your involvement in these activities is an essential part of your professional role.

SUMMARY

Media specialists can help bring the community to the school. As you explore the resources of any community you will find individuals and groups interested in sharing with students. Contacting members of the community also provides an opportunity to learn about the community itself and how the members of that community view education. Students will benefit from your knowledge of ways to access information from other agencies.

The community, your school district, and the professional association offer many opportunities for participation. As you engage in these activities you will learn who makes decisions that affect the collection and how you can be involved with those decisions or help influence them.

NOTES

[1]Betty J. Morris with John T. Gillespie and Diana L. Spirt, *Administering the School Library Media Center* (New Providence, NJ: R. R. Bowker, 1992), 257.

[2]"Meeting Service Needs of Special Users Is 1993-94 Goal," *Channel DLS: Wisconsin Division for Library Services* 29, no. 4 (December 1993): 5.

[3]North Carolina Department of Public Instruction, Division of Media and Technology Services, *Learning Connections: Guidelines for Media and Technology Programs* (Raleigh, 1992), A-1.

[4]TEA [Texas Education Agency]/Curriculum Development/Library Media, *19 TAX Chapter 63, Student Services* April 1991, unpaged.

[5]TEA, *19 TAX*.

[6]TEA, *19 TAX*.

[7]Connecticut, Board of Education, *A Guide to Program Development in Learning Resources and Technology* (Hartford, 1991), 30.

[8]Connecticut, Board of Education, 30-31.

[9]Dianne McAfee Hopkins, *School Library Media Programs: A Resource and Planning Guide* (Madison, WI: Wisconsin Department of Public Instruction, 1987), 8.

[10]Hopkins, *School Library Media Programs*, 9.

[11]Michigan, Board of Education, *Michigan's State Technology Plan 1992-1997* (Lansing, n.d.), ii.

[12]Michigan, Board of Education, iii.

[13]Michigan, Board of Education, iv.

[14]Michigan, Board of Education, iv.

BIBLIOGRAPHY

Connecticut. Board of Education. *A Guide to Program Development in Learning Resources & Technology*. Hartford, 1991.

Hopkins, Dianne McAfee. *School Library Media Programs: A Resource and Planning Guide*. Madison, WI: Wisconsin Department of Public Instruction, 1987.

Lankford, Mary D. *Successful Field Trips*. Santa Barbara, CA: ABC-Clio, 1992.

Maryland. Department of Education. *Building Library Media Collections: Analysis of Client Groups*. Baltimore, n.d.

———. *Standards for School Library Media Programs in Maryland*. Baltimore, n.d.

"Meeting Service Needs of Special Users Is 1993-94 Goal." *Channel DLS: Wisconsin Division for Library Services* 29, no. 4 (December 1993): 3-9.

Michigan. Board of Education. *Michigan's State Technology Plan 1992-1997*. Lansing, n.d.

Morris, Betty J., with John T. Gillespie and Diana L. Spirt. *Administering the School Library Media Center*. New Providence, NJ: R. R. Bowker, 1992.

North Carolina. Department of Public Instruction. Division of Media and Technology Services. *Learning Connections: Guidelines for Media and Technology Programs*. Raleigh, 1992.

Pennsylvania Guidelines for School Library Media Programs. Harrisburg, PA: State Library of Pennsylvania, 1989.

Texas Education Agency. *School Library Media Centers*. Austin, 1992.

Washington Library Media Association Certification and Standards Committee and State of Washington Office of Superintendent of Public Instruction. *Information Power for Washington: Guidelines for School Library Media Programs*. Olympia: Office of Superintendent of Public Instruction, 1991.

CHAPTER 6

Policies and Procedures

How can media specialists ensure that the collection reflects the goals of the media program and the school? One major task of media specialists is to think through and articulate the answers to the "why, what, how, and by whom" questions involved in the creation and maintenance of a collection. By establishing policies and procedures, media specialists assign selection responsibility, facilitate quality selection decisions, protect intellectual freedom, and ensure fair use of copyrighted materials.

DIFFERENCES BETWEEN POLICY STATEMENTS AND PROCEDURE STATEMENTS

Policy statements and procedure statements guide the activities of the collection program. Figure 6.1, on page 78, illustrates the fundamental differences between policies and procedures. Policies explain why the collection exists, thus establishing the basis for all the collection program activities, and delineate what will be in the collection, thus defining its scope. Procedure statements explain how policies will be put into practice and identify who is responsible for implementation. Policies need to be in place before procedure statements are written.

Policy statements should be issued separately from procedure statements. The two should be distinguishable. Many policy statements comprise both policies and procedures without differentiating their functions.

Policy statements tend to be of a general nature, stating the ideal goals while allowing for flexibility and change. Procedures direct the implementation of policies and should be concrete and measurable. They define objectives and tasks or processes to attain the policy goal. An example of the two types of statements can illustrate their different functions. A policy statement may read: "Materials reflect the pluralistic character and culture of American society." A procedure statement stemming from that policy may read: "Specialized selection tools, such as *Multicultural Review* (Greenwood Publishing Group, 1992-) will be used to identify recommended titles." This is very specific, and it should be revised regularly so the selection tools specified provide current information about availability and cost. The need to update procedures on a regular basis is one argument for issuing the two statements separately.

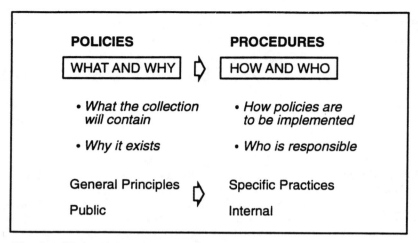

Fig. 6.1. How policies and procedures differ.

Examine documents entitled "collection policy," "selection policy," or "materials policy" to see whether policies and procedures are properly distinguished.

- Does the statement address the purpose of the collection: why it exists? (a policy)

- Does the statement identify what types of materials will be included or what authority is responsible for the collection? (a policy)

- Does the statement explain why materials will be added or withdrawn from the collection? (a policy)

- Does the statement explain how the collection will be created? (a procedure)

- Does the statement explain who (students, teachers) will be involved in the selection process? (a policy)

- Does the statement explain how teachers, administrators, and students will be involved in the selection process? (a procedure)

You probably will find policies and procedures in the same document. The inclusion of both statements in a document entitled "policy" can be confusing and creates a need for more frequent updating than is necessary when policies and procedures are in separate documents.

Think of policy statements as public documents. The collection policy states the media program's goals, communicates the purpose of the collection, and establishes general principles for collection. The selection policy identifies who is responsible for selection, establishes criteria to guide the selection of materials, and takes a stance on intellectual freedom. The procedure statements are the media center's internal document; they guide the day-to-day operations. In its most practical context, one might consider the procedures statement as a job manual or employee guide. Many authors frequently do not distinguish between the two.

VALUE OF WRITTEN POLICY STATEMENTS AND PROCEDURE STATEMENTS

Policy statements and procedure statements provide direction and guidance for the decisions made in carrying out the collection program activities. A written policy statement is more effective than an unwritten one for directing media specialists' activities or for explaining their actions to others. This guidance is the chief internal reason for having a *written* policy statement and a *written* procedure statement. The *Intellectual Freedom Manual* addresses this point.

> First, it [a written policy] encourages stability and continuity in the library's operations. Library staff members may come and go but the procedures manual, kept up-to-date, of course, will help assure smooth transitions when organization or staff changes occur. Second, ambiguity and confusion are far less likely to result if a library's procedures are in writing.[1]

This passage combines policies and procedures while describing their differences. Written policy statements and procedure statements can guide the internal operations of the media center.

A written policy statement explains to others why materials are in the collection. This is especially important when someone challenges materials. Without a written policy, challenged materials may be judged by headlines in the local media rather than the professional judgment of educators.

Dianne McAfee Hopkins, in a study of schools serving seventh grade through twelfth grades that faced challenges, reported

> The majority of respondents, i.e., 72.1%, report having a written board approved policy for the selection of materials. These policies were largely approved in the 1980s. It was found that board approved written policies result in the retention of materials more than schools reporting no policy, informal policy, or a written but not board-approved policy. It was also found that when the policy was followed, materials had a greater likelihood of retention than when the policy was not used.[2]

David Jenkinson, in an earlier study, reported greater retention rates in school libraries with policies than in schools without policies.[3] Having a policy, however, was not synonymous with adhering to it. One teacher-librarian in an urban elementary school remarked, "Very often the policy for challenged material is not followed because it's easier just to do what the parents want."[4] Both Jenkinson and Hopkins documented the failure to use existing policies during a challenge process.

Of the 720 schools in Hopkins's study, 95 had informal policies, 70 had written but not approved policies, 519 had written and approved policies, and 36 did not have a policy.[5] A reason frequently given for the lack of a written policy was the time it takes to develop one. This constraint hardly outweighs the value of a written policy. Consider the expenditure of time against the benefits:

- Promotion of collection development principles that reflect institutional goals and user needs and outline the scope and coverage of the collection.

- Delineation of the responsibilities of participating individuals and the limits of their responsibilities.

- Establishment of general principles for selection decisions, for example, guidance for consistency in material selection.

- Justification for inclusion of materials in the collection, for example, defense of selection decisions for materials that may be challenged.

- Selection through application of clearly detailed criteria to ensure better and more useful items for the collection.

- Involvement of others in the process, which enhances public relations and understanding of the purpose of the collection.

- Provision of readily accessible information for all school personnel—teachers, librarians, principals, supervisors, superintendents, and members of the governing board—about the specific selection ideals of the district.

- The community's increased confidence in its schools based on knowledge of the thorough and reasoned philosophies and procedures underlying the selection of materials.

- Provision of information needed for budget preparation and allocation.

- Documentation of cooperative programs in resource sharing.

- Identification of areas suitable for interlibrary loans.

As you consider this responsibility, think about Lillian N. Gerhardt's observation:

> Writing policy and procedures is not difficult. Identifying support to get them approved is harder. Then ensuring that they are carried out is the hardest part and the loneliest. But, if there were no risks or strains involved, librarianship would not be a profession.[6]

Required Policy Statements

Many states require school districts to have selection policies. For example, Wisconsin requires each school board to develop written policies and procedures to disallow discrimination against students.[7] Chapter PI9, of the Wisconsin Administrative Code specifies that library media selection and evaluation policies must contain language prohibiting discrimination. Suggested wording to meet this requirement is

> The School District shall not discriminate in the selection and evaluation of instructional and library materials on the basis of sex, race, national origin, ancestry, creed, pregnancy, marital or parental status, sexual orientation or physical, mental, emotional or learning disability.[8]

Another example is Minnesota, which identifies the range of resources in a collection and the need to select them according to an adopted selection policy. Minnesota State Board Rule (3500.0710) Library Media Program (1989) reads

> Subpart 3. *Resources*. There shall be provided for the Curriculum of the school, up-to-date resources and the necessary equipment and technological systems to use these resources. The resources shall include a variety of formats, such as books, periodicals, and projected and electronic resources, selected according to a school board adopted selection policy.[9]

Other states have similar mandates for selection policies and for procedures for reconsideration of challenged materials. Contact the state department of education or department of public instruction for information about such mandates.

Experienced school personnel can provide insight about the community and experiences with school policy development. Local, regional, and state professional associations are additional sources of information.

TYPES OF POLICIES

The problems created by a combined policy and procedure statement become increasingly complicated when three types of policies are combined in one document, usually called a selection policy. So-called selection policies often include policies and procedures relating to: collection development, selection, and acquisitions. Using the term *selection policy* for this combined document is misleading because selection policies address individual materials, not the collection as a whole.

The *Guide for Written Collection Policy Statements* (American Library Association, 1989) defines collection development as "the process of planning, building and maintaining a library's information resources in a cost efficient and user-relevant manner."[10] The collection-development policy provides a broad overview of the needs and priorities of users and reflects the goals of the media program and school. It offers guidance for decisions regarding the procurement of materials on certain subjects and identifies the depth of coverage. The collection-development policy provides the framework for the selection policy. The acquisition policy reflects both the collection-development policy and the selection policy.

The selection policy identifies the criteria for evaluating materials and assigns responsibility for selection decisions. An individual item under consideration must meet not only the criteria identified in the selection policy but also the needs and priorities established in the collection-development policy. The selection policy establishes who is responsible for selection decisions and who participates in that process.

The acquisition policy addresses the most efficient and cost-effective process for obtaining materials. This policy reflects both collection-development and selection policies. The acquisition policy establishes the conditions under which materials will be obtained though a jobber, a distributor, or by direct order. For example, if one needs a selected item immediately, the policy justifies direct ordering or local purchasing. Acquisition policies also address whether the media program will participate in resource sharing through exchange programs, including interlibrary loan and coordinated collection-development plans.

Combined Policy Statements

All three types of policies may be combined in one document called the collection plan. Many policy statements found in schools today emphasize selection policies, failing to recognize the importance of the collection development and acquisitions functions. A combination of the three statements in one document does not diminish the importance of the selection policy but emphasizes that selection decisions about individual items should consider the collection as a whole. Labels for these documents vary from media center to media center. Whatever its title, a policy should define the direction of the collection and guide the selection and acquisition processes.

ELEMENTS OF A COLLECTION POLICY

Collection policies must be designed to reflect the goals and needs of the individual media program and its institution. To be effective and responsive to these specific goals and needs, policy statements must be created at both the district and school level.

The inclusion and organization of the elements of the collection policy must be determined by the local group responsible for creating the policy statement. The diversity of building-level educational programs and the changing needs of users limit the effectiveness of adopting another school's policy statement. However, it is prudent to examine model policy statements from various sources. Examining model policy statements can prevent omissions, provide guidance for the outline, and offer suggestions for wording. This chapter provides general outlines of some policies and lists sources of model policy statements.

In this chapter's example, the *procedures* for reconsidering challenged materials appear in a policy document for use by the public. The rationale for this recommendation, which defies the argument for writing separate policy statements and procedures statements and making only policy statements available to the public, is the fact that procedures for reconsideration involve the public.

The first outline presented in this chapter is a combined policy focusing on collection development, selection, and acquisition. It includes (I) introduction, (II) general collection management and development policies, (III) selection policy, (IV) conspectus approach (detailed analysis of special areas), (V) policies for acquisition, (VI) evaluation of the collection, (VII) policies and procedures for reconsideration of challenged materials, and (VIII) copyright policy. To encourage the use of standardized terminology, this model conforms to *Guide for Written Collection Policy Statements* combined with information from *Intellectual Freedom Manual*.[11]

I. Introduction

The introduction to the collection policy statement establishes the authority, foundation, scope, and uses of the document.

A. *Purpose of and reasons for the document, how the policy was developed and by whom, and provision for reviewing the policy on a regular basis.* The policy should identify the governing body of the district as legally responsible for the selection of materials and should give the date the governing body adopts the policy. Part of the introduction to a policy might read:

> The _____ School Board hereby declares it is the policy of the _____ District to provide a wide range of instructional materials on all levels of difficulty, with diversity of appeal, and the presentation of different points of view and to allow the review of allegedly inappropriate instructional materials through established procedures.[12]

This sentence alerts the reader to several key considerations. It establishes the responsibility of the board, the criteria for selection, and the means to question materials in the collection. Policies should be reviewed by legal counsel before the board endorsement.

B. *Intended audience (staff and / or public).*

C. *School's and media center's philosophy, mission, goals statement.* The latter section identifies the philosophy and goals of the institution and the media program, creating a theoretical foundation on which the more practical sections are built. Much of the information included in this section is gleaned from other school documents or gathered through an analysis of the community.

D. *The media program's stance on intellectual freedom.* Many schools endorse documents like the "Library Bill of Rights"[13] and other professional statements about intellectual freedom (see appendix C).

E. *The location(s) of the collection throughout the school.*

II. General Collection Management and Development Policies

A. *Clientele to be served.* This statement identifies students, teachers, staff, and others who will use the collection.

B. *General subject boundaries.* This statement describes factors affecting the subject coverage, for example, limiting coverage to subjects within the curriculum or expanding coverage to subjects useful in extra-curricular programs. The definition of the scope of the collection explains whether (1) all instructional materials, including textbooks, or (2) all materials under the bibliographic control of the media center are part of the collection.

C. *Kinds of programs or user needs supported.* This statement addresses the specific types of coverage in the collection. The collection may include instructional, informational, and recreational materials as well as materials supporting particular teaching methods, student organizations, and user groups, including individuals with special needs.

D. *General priorities and limitations governing selection.* This section provides an overview of the selection policy.

1. *Sources of funds designated for the collection program.* A statement should specify the role of external institutions in providing funds or materials. Is the collection the sole source of materials to meet the needs of the school? Are instructional materials bought with separate funds? Are funds available from sources outside the regular budget?

2. *Forms of materials to be collected or excluded.* This statement identifies which formats are in the collection. For example, only microform materials on a particular subject may be included. Textbooks may be excluded.

3. *Languages and geographical areas collected or excluded.* A statement should specify foreign-language materials or special geographic areas (for example, city or county publications) included in the collection. Policies for schools serving Spanish-speaking students will differ from policies for schools that teach Spanish as a second language. Even if a school does not offer foreign-language classes, this statement should list appropriate language materials. For example, a statement might limit materials to English and Spanish languages.

4. *Other exclusions.* State other conditions or factors that will exclude materials from the collection.

5. *Duplication of materials.* This general statement describes the circumstances under which duplicate materials may be obtained.

6. *Participation in resource-sharing plans, such as networks, inter-library loan, and coordinated collection development.* This section identifies the resource-sharing programs in which the school participates and identifies the school's responsibilities in those programs. Responsibilities for participation in coordinated collection development should be identified. For example, the district professional collection serves the needs of all teachers within the district; individual schools assigned specific journals share them among the network's libraries. In addition, interlibrary loan arrangements are described in this section.

E. *Other policies appropriate to the general management of the collection.* Additional statements could address local authors' publications; multiple copies; formats (print, CD-ROM, or online) for reference works; government publications; acquisition procedures affecting collection policies (standing orders, approval plans, blanket orders, gifts, or exchanges); expensive purchases; and replacements.

III. Selection Policy

A. *Responsibility for selection.*

1. *Delegation of responsibility to professional staff.* This statement clearly identifies the governing body's legal responsibility for selection and that body's delegation of this responsibility to certified library media personnel. This statement delineates who will make selection decisions and their responsibilities. If the policy applies to all instructional materials, this statement should distinguish between those responsible for text materials and those responsible for media-program materials.

2. *Identification of participants in the selection process.* This statement identifies the role and level of involvement of teachers, students, administrators, staff, and community members in the selection process. A statement regarding advisory committees of teachers, students, and community members is appropriate for this section. Questions to be addressed include: Will selection be done by a committee, by use of approved lists, or by media specialists working independently? How is responsibility delegated?

B. *Selection criteria.* This section lists general criteria that apply to all materials under consideration, plus criteria that apply to materials about specific subjects, for specific users, and in specific formats. Criteria commonly used include technical qualities; literary qualities; qualifications of the authors or producers; controversial issues (for example, sex, profanity, cultural pluralism, political ideologies, or religious beliefs); and intended use (for example, textbooks, supplementary classroom materials, free materials, and replacements). Criteria are discussed in chapters 7 through 12.

If reviews are a factor in the selection decision, then a statement might read: "Select and replace items found in standard recommended lists." It might go on to say, "Select only those items that have been favorably reviewed in at least two review sources" or "Do not select anything that has received a negative review."[14] Before adding a statement about recommended lists or a minimum number of reviews, consider its impact. Should the selection decision be based on knowledge of the curriculum, the users, and the collection, or should it be constrained by a reviewer's opinion? With clearly defined priorities and selection criteria, a statement calling for reliance on reviews may limit the acquisition of appropriate materials.

C. *Other situations.* This section addresses other situations relating to selection. Can teachers expect that materials will be procured solely on their recommendations? How much information or justification must they submit before an item will be purchased? Will the principal be allowed to make selection decisions without consulting the media specialist? Criteria for equipment also should be established.

IV. Conspectus Approach
(Detailed Analysis of Subject Areas)

As media specialists participate in the conspectus approach to resource sharing, they become involved in the detailed analysis of the collection appropriate to the particular plan (see chap. 14).

The conspectus approach involves an examination of the collection and acquisition practices. Collections are analyzed in terms of Current Collecting Intensity (CCI) and Desired Collecting Intensity (DCI) or Collection Goal (CG) (that is, the funds and staff needed to achieve the collection's mission). Level of collection intensity can be applied for each subject, type of user, and program. Typically a range within the Dewey classification scheme (for example, 800, 810, or 820) is used. The levels of collection intensity (or priorities) derive from the *Guide for Written Collection Policy Statements.*

Table 6.1 defines a number of conspectus levels, from minimal to comprehensive. If at first these definitions appear irrelevant to media programs, consider their use in setting priorities. In a school with a revised science curriculum, the priority for science materials is higher than the priority for materials collected at minimal or basic levels. (It is unlikely that schools will collect at research or comprehensive levels. These terms are included in table 6.1 to illustrate the distinctions among conspectus levels and the use of standard terminology.) Media specialists using the conspectus approach may use a more extensive version of the levels established by the coordinating agency.

Table 6.1.
Conspectus Levels

Code	Conspectus Level	Definition
0	Out of scope	The collection excludes this subject.
The media center will have no materials on this subject.		
1	Minimal level	The collection includes selected current basic titles on this subject.
The media center will have a few works on a subject, such as art appreciation, even though the subject is not a part of the curriculum.		
2	Basic level	The collection includes selected introductory and reference materials, access to appropriate bibliographic databases, and a few key periodicals.
This is the common collection intensity for subjects in media center collections.		
3	Study or instructional level	The collection includes basic works in appropriate formats on a subject, representative journals, access to appropriate machine-readable data files, reference works, and basic bibliographies.
For the hypothetical Fermi Middle School's new science curriculum, this level of intensity was sought, and all other subjects were collected at a lower level.		
4	Research level	The collection includes the major published and source materials required for research.
This level could apply to a district collection supporting a specific research program.		
5	Comprehensive level	The collection is exhaustive in coverage and includes all significant works.
The collection of school publications, for example, programs, yearbooks, and student newspapers, could be at this level.		

Based on *Guide for Written Collection Policy Statements* (Chicago: American Library Association, 1989) and *Pacific Northwest Collection Assessment Manual* (Fred Meyer Charitable Trust, 1986).

To assign accurate collection intensity levels, the existing collection and the current levels of collecting must be analyzed and compared with collection goals.

V. Policies for Acquisition

This section addresses the process for obtaining materials. A general statement may read, "All materials will be obtained from the most cost-effective and efficient source. Preference will be given to jobber services that can supply at least 80 percent of an order within 60 days." The same statement may continue, "When materials are needed sooner than a jobber can deliver, the media specialist may purchase appropriate materials from a local source." This exception allows the media specialist to obtain materials quickly under special circumstances.

The policy may state, "Magazines will be acquired through the services of a subscription agency, except titles obtained through institutional memberships in professional associations or titles that can be obtained only directly from the publisher." The acquisition policy also should address how other types of materials, such as videotapes or pamphlets, are to be obtained from a specified source or in a particular manner.

VI. Evaluation of the Collection

Continual evaluation of the collection ensures that it will meet established collection levels. Evaluations should result in removal of deteriorated or obsolete materials. The policy statement establishes the criteria for reevaluation; addresses the scope, frequency, and purpose of evaluation; and establishes disposal policies. An accompanying procedures manual outlines the steps for disposing of materials. The terms *reevaluation*, *deacquisition*, *weeding*, *discarding*, and *deselection* describe the same process.

VII. Policies and Procedures for Dealing with Challenged Materials

This section of the document provides directions for handling complaints, focusing the complainant's attention on the principles of intellectual freedom rather than on the material itself.

A school district may include policies and procedures for dealing with challenged materials in the collection policy, in the selection policy, or in a separate policy that is referenced in the collection and selection policies. Because of the importance of this policy, for the purposes of this book a separate section is devoted to it (see pages 97-101). However, the elements of the challenged materials policy remain the same, whether the policy stands alone or is incorporated in the collection policy.

VIII. Copyright Policy

The school's copyright policy guides the use of materials by students, teachers, and media center staff. Related procedures (provided in a separate document) establish how copyright compliance will be managed. The policy places the burden of litigation on the individual responsible for the illegal actions.

A. *The governing body's intent to comply with the U.S. Copyright Act of 1976 (Title 17, U.S. Code, Sect. 101, et seq.).*

B. *The conditions under which copyrighted works may be copied.*

C. *The location of the procedures.*

D. *A statement identifying who is responsible for implementing the policy and keeping records.*

Media centers are required to post copyright warning notices near all copying equipment and to place a copyright warning notice on the first page of copied materials. Media specialists should assume that they are responsible for educating teachers and students about copyright law and for monitoring use of copyrighted materials.

DEVELOPING SELECTION POLICY STATEMENTS

Policy statements, particularly selection policies, are rarely the product of an individual. The media specialist has a professional responsibility to develop and review policies, involving teachers, administrators, students, and citizens in the process. The media specialist can use this opportunity to explain the media center's role in the educational process and the importance of intellectual freedom. The community representatives can contribute, as

> writers or media people will bring their special interests to bear; a public health nurse will be able to speak to the need for health and human development materials in the collection; parents will share their knowledge of the community and its concerns; students will provide a voice from that quarter; and a lawyer will give advice on drawing up the document and procedures.[15]

A major benefit of a statement written by a committee is the members' advocacy and support of the principles on which the policy is based.

If your district does not have a policy, assume the professional responsibility of alerting your administrator and the governing body to the need for a policy. If a policy exists, but has fallen out of use, encourage a review of the policy. Ask the director of the district media program to coordinate the formulation of a district media-selection policy. If you are the only certified media specialist in a one school district, you will be responsible for starting the process of creating a working policy. As you work with others, remind them that

The library media specialist understands that her/his role is not to personally approve of or believe in every item that is in the library media collection, but to recognize the role of applying sound criteria to selection as well as the value of differing viewpoints on subjects of interest.[16]

Remind the school board about the purposes of a materials selection policy and the procedures for handling challenges. An adopted policy and reconsideration statement

provides a public document to help parents and citizens understand the purposes and standards of the selection of materials;

promotes intellectual freedom by recognizing the value of information in a variety of formats;

provides equal access to resources for all students;

establishes a climate in which criteria guide the collection development activities;

interprets the selection process to the school and community;

provides a method to handle challenges; and

provides guidance and protection for all involved in the selection and use of materials.

Steps in Policy Development

The policy-development process begins with the governing body as it

1. decides to establish and adopt a selection policy.

2. appoints an ad hoc committee composed of representatives of the school community. These representatives might include parents, students, certified media specialists, administrators, and individuals from other libraries or educational agencies. If the policy is to cover all instructional materials, including textbooks, then subject specialists should be included on the committee.

3. charges the committee with the responsibility of developing a selection policy and establishing a deadline for presenting a draft of the policy statement. General guidelines should be provided to the committee to facilitate its work.

4. studies the draft before discussion with the committee.

5. solicits discussion and suggestions from legal counsel, from personnel within the school (such as department heads or curriculum

committees), and from groups, such as parent-teacher associations and the teachers' association.

6. conducts a closing review of the committee's recommendations and the comments expressed by others who studied the draft.

7. adopts a formal written statement as the approved selection policy of the district or local education agency.

8. provides for implementation of the newly adopted policy. This involves disseminating the policy to all staff members involved in the evaluation, selection, and use of the materials covered in the policy. A meeting or in-service program could familiarize the staff with the policy so they can respond to any inquiries about it. Media personnel and teachers are likely to be the individuals who receive requests that materials be reconsidered.

9. disseminates the policy to the community. Plan school and community activities to make people aware of the importance of the freedom to read, speak, view, listen, evaluate, and learn.

10. establishes periodic evaluation and revision of the policy. Reviews should be scheduled on a regular basis of intervals of one to three years.

11. formally adopts changes. Dates of the original adoption and sequential revisions recorded on the document are helpful indicators of the history of the document.

Figure 6.2 (on page 92) is a graphic representation of the process.

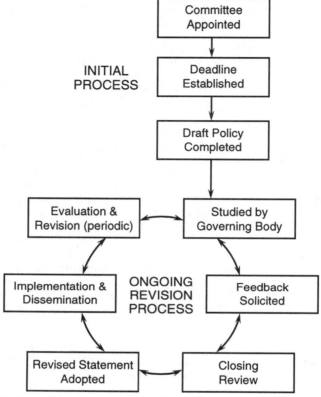

Fig. 6.2. Process of policy formation and revision.

ELEMENTS OF A SELECTION POLICY

This discussion focuses on the elements of the selection policy, not procedures for selection.

I. Statement of Philosophy

This brief statement presents the school district's values and beliefs. Reference may be made to the school's mission and goals statement, or language from relevant documents may be included. The statement may address how the educational resources help the school achieve its goals.

Other statements in this section may refer to the First Amendment's protection of students' rights to access information to read, listen, view, and evaluate. Another sentence may state the school or school board's responsibility to provide a wide range of educational resources.

Sample phrases in this section start with "the Board of [school district's name] shall provide," "will provide," or "is committed to facilitating teaching and learning by providing"

- materials for students and teachers;
- resources of varying levels of difficulty, diversity of appeal, and various points of view; and
- materials that will help students develop critical-thinking skills and aesthetic appreciation.

Other statements may refer to the needs of a democratic society or the nature of a pluralistic society.

II. Selection Objectives

This section translates the school district's philosophy and goals into collection objectives. The statements show how the collection helps the school meet its goals. Objectives address what materials will be in the collection, or the rationale for using a variety of resources in the school, and how the materials will be judged for educational suitability for their use by students and teachers. Examples of main objective statements are

To make available to faculty and students a collection of materials that will enrich and support the curriculum and meet the educational needs of the students and faculty served.[17]

or

The primary objectives of professional selection shall be to provide the curriculum with a variety of materials. Selection shall represent a variety of attitudes and the points of view of many religious, cultural, ethnic, and social groupings within the community, shall demonstrate artistic value and/or factual authority, and shall be selected as valuable in stimulating intellectual, ethical, and aesthetic growth in our young people.[18]

A statement identifying the materials covered in the policy might read

Media center materials are defined as all electronic, print, and nonprint resources, excluding textbooks, used by students and teachers for the District's educational program.

The combination of materials definition, main objective, board delegation, and sub-objectives are found in the Irving (Texas) Independent School District *Policies and Procedures Manual*, which reads

In this policy, "instructional resources" refers to textbooks, library acquisitions, supplemental materials for classroom use, and any other material used for formal or informal teaching and learning purposes. The primary objective of instructional resources are to deliver, support, enrich, and assist in implementing the District's educational program.

The board generally shall rely on its professional staff to select and acquire instructional resources that:

1. Enrich and support the curriculum, taking into consideration students' varied interests, abilities, learning styles, and maturity levels.

2. Stimulate growth in factual knowledge, literary appreciation, aesthetic values, and societal standards.

3. Present various sides of controversial issues so that students have an opportunity to develop, under guidance, skills in critical analysis and in making informed judgments in their daily lives.

4. Represent many religious, ethnic, and cultural groups and their contributions to the national heritage and world community.[19]

Another statement of objectives could express the belief that students need ideas beyond those presented in textbooks. Other phrases commonly found in objective statements include

- represent the breadth of the curriculum.

- wide range of the best materials available on appropriate levels of difficulty.

- resources to support various styles of teaching materials that allow students to analyze, synthesize, evaluate, and use information effectively.

- provide resources for students with particular physical disabilities and other special educational needs.

III. Responsibility for Selection

An important element of the selection policy is statements about who is responsible for selection decisions. These statements usually acknowledge that the school board is legally responsible and delegates to media specialists the authority to select. The term *media specialists* may be defined as "professional, certified personnel, employed by the district."

The responsibilities of the board may be described in terms of the operations of the school, policy making, and the determination of the use of monies. The Minnesota Coalition Against Censorship recommends, "In some school districts, it might be valuable to indicate that the role of the principal is supervising the process, not actually performing the selection."[20]

This section also identifies who may make suggestions but states the media specialist is the individual responsible for the final evaluation and selection. In states with mandated advisory committees, that body's role in selection should be identified. Other individuals who may be mentioned in this section include administrators, supervisors, faculty, other professional personnel, students, parents, and community representatives.

IV. Selection Criteria

This section generally consists of two or more parts. The first is a list of general criteria that apply to all materials and relates to the district or school goals articulated in section I. A statement that these criteria apply to all materials, including gifts and loans, can eliminate the need to write a separate section about such materials.

The second part addresses criteria for specific categories of materials, users, treatment of sensitive issues, and formats. These more specific criteria may be treated separately in the procedures guidelines due to the changes in topics of concern or changes in the technologies or presentations involved.

A. *General Criteria.* Chapter 8 identifies general selection criteria that could be highlighted in this general section. Following are examples of wording:

- relevant to today's world.
- represent artistic, historic, and literary qualities.
- reflect the problems, aspirations, attitudes, and ideals of society.
- contribute to the objectives of the instructional program.
- are consistent with and support the general educational goals of the state and district.
- appropriate for the age, ability level, learning style, and social and emotional development of the intended user.
- appropriate for the subject area.
- meet quality standards in terms of content, format, and presentation.
- help students gain an awareness of our pluralistic society.
- motivate students to examine their own attitudes, to understand their rights, duties, and responsibilities as citizens, and to make informed judgments in their daily lives.
- be selected for their strengths rather than rejected for their weaknesses.
- reputation and significance of the author, producer and publisher.

- validity, currency, and appropriateness of material.
- contribution the material makes or breadth of representative viewpoints on controversial issues.
- high degree of potential user appeal.
- value commensurate with cost and/or need.
- integrity.
- does not represent a personal bias.

B. *Specific Selection Criteria.* Criteria for picture books, fiction, nonfiction, topics like racism and sexism, multicultural materials, and specific formats are included in this part. Additional sections may deal with online services and television news services. (See chapters 8-12 for specific criteria that may be included.)

V. Position on Intellectual Freedom

In this section, the policy addresses the importance of access to information. The wording may indicate that the board endorses actual professional statements, such as the "Library Bill of Rights," or the wording may state that the district supports the concepts or values in one or more documents. In either case, the referenced documents should be attached to the policy. See appendix C for reprints of commonly used professional statements. Wording of this section might read:

The Board of Education of [name of school district] supports the principles of intellectual freedom inherent in the First Amendment of the Constitution of the United States as expressed in official statements of professional associations. These include [identify statements] and form a part of this policy.

VI. Other Elements

Other elements found in selection policies include statements about potentially controversial subjects and the role of reviewing and selection tools in the selection process. The group developing the policy will want to consider the advantages and limitations of including such statements.

Traditionally, selection policies have attempted to justify inclusion of potentially controversial topics by issuing statements about the variety of approaches sought in the collection on subjects dealing with religious, political, and social points of views. That position should be weighed against the position taken by the Minnesota Coalition Against Censorship's observation that

By their nature, resources about ideologies, religion, and sex will be considered by some persons to be biased. The identification of areas for special consideration creates a risk that considerations other than educational suitability, appropriateness, and other adopted criteria will be used. We do not recommend special considerations, rather adopted criteria should be applied equally to all resources.[21]

Some policies list specific selection sources that will be used to locate two or more favorable reviews before the item will be considered for selection. There are several disadvantages to this practice. A specific list may not be comprehensive or may not identify sources actually used. This creates a problem if a certain item is not reviewed in any of the cited sources. The problem is exacerbated if the title is purchased anyway and later is challenged. The Minnesota Coalition Against Censorship points out other problems.

This requirement limits the teachers and media specialists and should not be included in policies. While selection aids are useful in helping teachers and media specialists identify titles to be considered for purchase, using reviews as a criteria for selection focuses on the review, rather than the professional judgment of the teachers and media specialists. There are several reasons why a review should not be considered a criteria for selection. Published reviews are necessarily general and are written for both school and public librarians. Resources of local or regional interest are not usually reviewed in national selection aids. Reviews do not address educational needs in specific school districts. Whether selection results from a review or actual examination of the resource, professional judgment should be the focus, not lists of acceptable selection aids.[22]

Keep copies of both the selection policy and procedures for handling challenged materials in the circulation area. Put a copy of both documents in the media center's policies and procedures handbook.

ELEMENTS OF POLICIES AND PROCEDURES FOR DEALING WITH CHALLENGED MATERIALS

This policy document provides directions for handling complaints, focusing the complainant's attention on the principles of intellectual freedom rather than on the material itself. Generally speaking, policies and procedures should be separate documents (policies for the public, procedures for internal use), but in this case, both policies and procedures should be combined in a single document for the public's use. Sharing this information in a forthright manner can alleviate some of the tension that can occur in this situation. To ensure that all challenges, whether internal or external, are treated in the same manner, each individual's complaint should be treated according to the school board's adopted procedure. The American Association of School Librarians notes that this procedure provides for

> a hearing with appropriate action while defending the principles of freedom of information, the student's right to access of materials, and the professional responsibility and integrity of the certified library/media personnel . . . . In the event instructional materials are questioned, the principles of intellectual freedom should be defended rather than the materials.[23]

Hopkins recommends that media specialists

> Examine your district's materials selection policy carefully. Is the wording inclusive enough to show that challenges initiated by administrators, teachers, and other school personnel are to be included in reconsideration steps outlined in the policy? If not, contact your state library or media association and/or LMC consultants at the Department of Public Instruction/Education. Seek a critique of the current policy as well as sample policies to review.[24]

She observes that, when challenges are submitted in writing, they are more likely to be handled with due process and the materials are more likely to remain on the shelves.[25]

The Wisconsin Department of Public Instruction offers the following advice:

> When an expression of concern or a complaint occurs, the person expressing concern should be treated with respect. The public has the right to request that material be reviewed. Inquiries should not be taken personally; reactions should not be defensive.[26]

Without a collection-development policy, or even a selection policy as a statement of principles and the basis for selection decision, the media specialist would very likely feel that, indeed, the inquiry was personal.

Advantages of including procedures for handling complaints in the written statement are identified by *Intellectual Freedom Manual.*

> First, knowing the response is ready and that there is a procedure to be followed, the librarian will be relieved of much of the initial panic which inevitably strikes when confronted by an outspoken and, perhaps, irate library patron. Also important, the complaint form asks the complainants to state their objections in logical, unemotional terms, thereby allowing the librarian to evaluate the merits of the objections. In addition, the form benefits the complainant. When citizens with a complaint are asked to follow an established procedure for lodging their complaint, they feel

assured that they are being properly heard and that their objections will be considered.[27]

In summary, the advantages of having the procedures in place are:

1. Complainants are reassured their comments will be heard. This recognizes the rights of individuals to express their grievances.

2. The media specialist knows the procedure is in place and can use it to turn what may be an emotional situation into one where the complainants objections are stated in logical terms.

3. The procedures should be designed to provide a timely and fair review of challenges resources. The complainants know what will happen.

I. Statement of Philosophy

To focus attention on intellectual freedom in this policy, rather than on materials or personnel, many libraries reproduce national statements, such as the "Library Bill of Rights," which have been endorsed by the school board.

II. Handling Complaints

Other items to be included in this policy are statements establishing procedural details.

A. *Who may register a complaint*: a U.S. citizen, resident of the community, teacher, student, administrator, or member of the board of education.

B. *Who should be notified when a complaint is received.*

C. *Whether complaints must be in writing.*

D. *A form for the complainant to complete* (see fig. 6.3 on page 100).

E. *Procedures for handling a complaint when the complainant is unwilling to fill out the form.*

F. *A committee to consider the complaint.* This item addresses the questions Which groups or authorities should be represented on it? How long will their terms be? How is voting to be handled? Under what guidelines will it operate? Is there a specified time period for consideration of any one complaint? Who is responsible for informing the complainant of the processing of the complaint and final action? To whom should the committee report its decision? The New York State guidelines offer this advice:

It is recommended that the report be submitted to the Board of Education directly rather than to establish a hierarchy of appeal from principal to superintendent to the Board of Education. The longer the issue remains in question, the more potential exists for creating additional tensions.[28]

STATEMENT OF CONCERN ABOUT
LIBRARY/MEDIA CENTER RESOURCES

Name _____ Date _____

Address _____

City_____State_____ Zip _____Phone _____

1. Resource on which you are commenting:

_____ Book   _____Audiovisual Resource

_____ Magazine   _____Content of Library Program

_____ Newspaper   _____Other

2. What brought this title to your attention?

3. Please comment on the resource as a whole as well as being specific on those matters which concern you. (Use other side if needed). Comment:

Optional:

4. What resource(s) do you suggest to provide additional information on this topic?

Return this form to: (identify media specialist, principal, or superintendent).

Fig. 6.3. Sample complaint form. Based on American Library Association, Office for Intellectual Freedom, comp., *Intellectual Freedom Manual*, 4th ed. (Chicago: American Library Association, 1992), 217.

G. *How challenged materials are to be handled during this process.* Do they remain in use or are they removed? An argument for keeping materials available is that intellectual freedom is being challenged, not specific materials.

H. *Whether any item can be reconsidered more than once within a specified time period.*

I. *Whether an explanation of the final action should be reported in writing to the complainant.*

J. *Procedures for appealing the committee's decision.* Display a copy of the complaint form and identify who has authorized its use—the media specialist, principal, superintendent, board of education, or other—and to whom to return the form.

Both the complaint form and the process for handling complaints should be designed to encourage constructive dialogue. The review committee should be a standing one consisting of members who are informed about the policies and procedures and prepared to handle their responsibilities. This facilitates the process, supports the idea that this is an established routine, and avoids the tensions that can occur if such situations are treated as unusual incidents. There is, perhaps, no other area in which interpersonal skills, commitment to intellectual freedom, and sound knowledge impact a situation.

OTHER MODEL POLICIES AND GUIDES

Examples of model policies or wording for policies can be found in a variety of sources. The following list provides a sampling of these sources and indicates the types of agencies and associations that can provide guidance in policy development.

American Association of School Librarians. Intellectual Freedom Committee. *Intellectual Freedom and the School Library Media Program: Documents and Resources.* Chicago: American Library Association, 1989. ISBN 0-8389-7357-4. $15. Available from American Library Association, Order Department, 50 E. Huron Street, Chicago, IL 60611; 800-545-2433.

Includes reprints of American Library Association policies, intellectual freedom statements from other professional organizations, state intellectual freedom statements, guidelines for policies and procedures, and resources.

American Library Association. Office for Intellectual Freedom, comp. *Intellectual Freedom Manual,* 4th ed. Chicago: American Library Association, 1992. 282p. ISBN:0-8389-3412-9. $25. Available from American Library Association, Order Department, 50 E. Huron Street, Chicago, IL 60611; 800-545-2433. ALA Order Code 3412-9-0051.

Includes the wording and history of the "Library Bill of Rights" and interpretative documents; "The Freedom to Read" statement and related policies; essays on intellectual freedom; guidelines for developing a "Materials Selection Program" and "Handling Complaints"; information about assistance from the American Library Association; and suggestions for working with others in the area of intellectual freedom.

California Department of Education. *Suggested Copyright Policy and Guidelines for California's School Districts*. Sacramento, 1991. 13p. $3. Available from California Department of Education, Bureau of Publications, Sales Unit, P.O. Box 271, Sacramento, CA 95812-0271.

Provides a model policy, identifies guidelines for use of specific types of copyrighted materials, and includes sample forms for requesting to use copyrighted materials.

Craft, Anne Hale. "Handling Censorship Incidents in Positive Ways." Pages 61-91 in *School Library Media Annual*, vol. 8. Edited by Jane B. Smith. Englewood, CO: Libraries Unlimited, 1988. ISBN 0-87287-635-7. o.p.

Offers practical advice and reprints a copy of the "Instructional Materials Selection and Appeal Procedures, Gwinnett County (Georgia) Public Schools."

Folke, Carolyn Winters. *Dealing with Selection and Censorship: A Brief Handbook for Wisconsin Schools*. Bulletin no. 92152. Madison: Wisconsin Department of Public Instruction, Bureau of Instructional Media and Technology, 1991. 34p. Available from Wisconsin Department of Public Instruction, Bureau of Instructional Media and Technology, P.O. Box 7841, Madison, WI 53707-7841; 800-267-9221.

Includes guidelines for developing school district policies and procedures, selected bibliography, Wisconsin statutes, statements on intellectual freedom, and sources of assistance.

Minnesota Coalition Against Censorship. *Selection Policies and Reevaluation Procedures: A Workbook*. Stillwater: Minnesota Educational Media Organization, 1991. 34p. $8. Available from Minnesota Educational Media Organization, 408 Quarry Lane, Stillwater, MN 55082. Send check payable to MEMO.

Includes sample wording for various sections of the selection policy, using wording from existing policies. Identifies and reprints professional association documents supporting intellectual freedom.

National School Boards Association. *Censorship: Managing the Controversy*. Alexandria, VA: National School Boards Association, 1989. 88p. ISBN 0-88364-143-7. $20 plus $3.75 shipping and handling. Available from NSBA, 1680 Duke St., Alexandria, VA 22314; 703-838-6722.

Although the focus is on textbooks, this guide offers practical suggestions for documents and handling of complainants.

Ochoa, Anna S., ed. *Academic Freedom to Teach and to Learn: Every Teacher's Issue*. NEA Aspects of Learning series. Washington, DC: National Education Association, 1990. 135p. ISBN 0-8106-3006-0. Available from NEA, P.O. Box 509, West Haven, CT 06516; 800-229-4200 or 203-934-2669.

Includes scenarios for teachers to analyze, offers practical suggestions for handling complaints, and offers guidelines for conducting an open hearing on a complaint.

Scholtz, James C. *Video Policies and Procedures for Libraries*. Santa Barbara, CA: ABC-Clio, 1991. 265p. ISBN 0-8743-6582-1. $45. Available from ABC-Clio, P.O. Box 1911, Santa Barbara, CA 93116-1911; 800-422-2546 or 805-968-1911.
Includes guidelines and sample wording for policies and sample forms for reconsideration.

Vlcek, Charles W. *Adoptable Copyright Policy: Copyright Policy and Manuals Designed for Adoption by Schools, Colleges & Universities*. Washington, DC: Copyright Information Services, 1992. 116p. ISBN 0-89240-064-1. $27.95 for members of the Association for Educational Communications and Technology, $34.95 for nonmembers (plus $3.00 for shipping and handling on all orders). Disk version with site license based on FTE: less than 5,000, $150; 5,001-10,000, $300; 10,001 and more, $500. Available from: Association for Educational Communications and Technology, 1025 Vermont Avenue, NW, Suite 820, Washington, DC 20005.
Provides copyright policy; an adoptable faculty copyright manual consisting of an overview, application of the law to specific media, copyright management, copyright quick guide, and obtaining permission; an adoptable student copyright manual; and addresses that may be needed in seeking copyright permission.

Additional organizations offering information or assistance in censorship disputes include the American Association of School Administrators, American Association of University Women, American Civil Liberties Union, American Federation of Teachers, Association of American Publishers, Freedom to Read Foundation, International Reading Association, National Coalition Against Censorship, National Conference of Christians and Jews, National Congress of Parents and Teachers, National Council of Teachers of English, National Education Association, National School Boards Association, and People for the American Way. Their addresses are provided in appendix A.
Finally, to obtain more information, consult professional colleagues in nearby school districts and colleagues in professional associations.

SUMMARY

Written and formally adopted policy statements and procedure statements guide collection development, aid in selection decisions, assign responsibilities, guide acquisition practices, and ensure compliance with copyright law. These documents also aid in the protection of intellectual freedom by establishing policies and procedures for dealing with requests for reconsideration of materials.
The collection development policy provides the broad overview of needs and priorities based on the media program's goals and offers guidance for decisions regarding the procurement of materials. The selection policy establishes criteria by which materials are evaluated and explains how

selection decisions are made. The acquisition policy addresses the most efficient process for obtaining materials.

In practice, elements of the collection-program policy may be established at the district level rather than at the building level. However, the sections pertaining to a specific school's collection (such as the analysis of instructional objectives, the detailed analysis of subject areas and format collection and criteria for selection, and the evaluation of the collection) must describe the needs of the individual building's collection.

If your school district has adopted either an overall collection-development policy or just a selection policy, you will need to be familiar with it. Do the district policies reflect the goals of your school or the needs of your collection? Is your principal aware of the policy and its implications? When was the last time the governing body studied the policy? Do additional guidelines need to be developed for your school to cover the collection development and selection activities? Policies need to "be reviewed at intervals to verify that existing collection goals are being met and to insure that changes in defined goals and user needs are recognized."[29]

The involvement of many diverse participants in developing policies is important to assure students the right to read, speak, view, listen, evaluate, and learn. An adopted procedure for receiving and handling complaints recognizes the rights of individuals to challenge school practices. The media specialist has a professional responsibility to ensure that policies are developed and reviewed. The governing body has a responsibility to develop policies and ensure their implementation. Models and policies from other school districts can be examined, but each school district needs to develop policies tailored to its situation. Education associations and agencies provide other examples, offer guidelines for their development, and provide support when complaints are registered.

NOTES

[1]American Library Association, Office of Intellectual Freedom, comp. *Intellectual Freedom Manual*, 4th ed. (Chicago: American Library Association, 1992), 205.

[2]Dianne McAfee Hopkins, *Factors Influencing the Outcome of Challenges to Materials in Secondary School Libraries: Report of a National Study* (Madison: University of Wisconsin-Madison, School of Library and Information Studies, 1991), chap. 8, p. 3.

[3]David Jenkinson, "Censorship Iceberg: Results of a Survey of Challenges in Public and School Libraries," *Canadian Library Journal* 43 (February 1986): 11.

[4]Jenkinson, "Censorship Iceberg," 12.

[5]Hopkins, *Factors Influencing*, chap. 4, p. 29.

[6]Lillian N. Gerhardt, "Matters of Policy," *School Library Journal* 39, no. 1 (January 1993): 4.

[7]Carolyn Winters Folke, *Dealing with Selection and Censorship: A Brief Handbook for Wisconsin Schools*, Bulletin no. 92152 (Madison: Wisconsin Department of Public Instruction, Bureau of Instructional Media and Technology, 1991), 15.

[8]Folke, *Dealing with Selection*, 5.

[9]Minnesota State Board Rule (3500.0710) (1989).

[10]Bonita Bryant, ed., *Guide for Written Collection Policy Statements, Collection Management and Development Guides*, no. 3 (Chicago: American Library Association, 1989), 21.

[11]American Library Association, *Intellectual Freedom Manual*.

[12]American Association of School Librarians, "Policies and Procedures for Selection of Instructional Materials," *School Media Quarterly* 5 (1977): 111.

[13]American Library Association, *Intellectual Freedom Manual*, 3.

[14]G. Edward Evans, *Developing Library Collections*, 2d ed. (Littleton, CO: Libraries Unlimited, 1987): 131.

[15]Larry Amey, "Pyramid Power: The Teacher-Librarian and Censorship," *Emergency Librarian* 16, no. 1 (September-October 1988): 18.

[16]Dianne McAfee Hopkins, "The School Library Media Specialist: Dealing with Complaints About Materials," *Catholic Library World* 56, no. 4 (November 1984): 173.

[17]American Library Association, *Intellectual Freedom Manual*, 211.

[18]Media Services Department, *Library School Media Center Handbook* (Dallas, TX: Dallas Independent School District, 1993), 4.3.

[19]Mary D. Lankford and Deborah Chaney, "Policies and Procedures Manual," (Irving, TX: Irving Independent School District), 1993.

[20]Minnesota Coalition Against Censorship, *Selection Policies* (Stillwater: Minnesota Educational Media Organization, 1991), 17.

[21]Minnesota Coalition Against Censorship, *Selection Policies*, 32.

[22]Minnesota Coalition Against Censorship, *Selection Policies*, 23.

[23]American Association of School Librarians, "Policies and Procedures," 110-11.

[24]Dianne McAfee Hopkins, "Put It in Writing: What You Should Know About Challenges to Materials," *School Library Journal* 39, no. 1 (January 1993): 29.

[25]Hopkins, "Put It in Writing," 29.

[26]Folke, *Dealing with Selection and Censorship*, 8.

[27]American Library Association, *Intellectual Freedom Manual*, 215.

[28]University of the State of New York, State Education Department, Bureau of School Libraries, *Selection Guidelines: School Library Resources, Textbooks, Instructional Materials* (Albany: University of the State of New York, n.d.), 8.

[29]Bryant, *Guide for Written Collection Policy Statements*, 4.

BIBLIOGRAPHY

American Association of School Librarians. "Policies and Procedures for Selection of Instructional Materials." *School Media Quarterly* 5 (1977): 109-16. Reprinted in *Intellectual Freedom Manual*. Available as a reprint from American Library Association Office of Intellectual Freedom.

American Association of School Librarians and Association for Educational Communications and Technology. *Information Power: Guidelines for School Library Media Programs*. Chicago: American Library Association; Washington, DC: Association for Educational Communications and Technology, 1988.

American Library Association. Office of Intellectual Freedom, comp. *Intellectual Freedom Manual*, 4th ed. Chicago: American Library Association, 1992.

Amey, Larry. "Pyramid Power: The Teacher-Librarian and Censorship." *Emergency Librarian* 16, no. 1 (September-October 1988): 15-20.

Bryant, Bonita, ed. *Guide for Written Collection Policy Statements*. Collection Management and Development Guides, no. 3. Chicago: American Library Association, 1989.

California Library Association. Intellectual Freedom Committee. *California Intellectual Freedom Manual: A Manual for California Librarians*. Sacramento: California Library Association, 1992.

Callison, Daniel. "The Evolution of School Library Collection Development Policies, 1975-1995." *School Library Media Quarterly* 19, no. 1 (Fall 1990): 27-34.

Evans, G. Edward. *Developing Library Collections*, 2d ed. Littleton, CO: Libraries Unlimited, 1987.

Folke, Carolyn Winters. *Dealing with Selection and Censorship: A Brief Handbook for Wisconsin Schools*. Bulletin no. 92152. Madison: Wisconsin Department of Public Instruction, Bureau of Instructional Media and Technology, 1991.

Gerhardt, Lillian N. "Matters of Policy." *School Library Journal* 39, no. 1 (January 1993): 4.

Hopkins, Dianne McAfee. "Challenges to Materials in Secondary School Library Media Centers: Results of a National Study." *Journal of Youth Services in Libraries* 4 (Winter 1991): 131-40.

———. *Factors Influencing the Outcome of Challenges to Materials in Secondary School Libraries: Report of a National Study*. Madison: University of Wisconsin-Madison, School of Library and Information Studies, 1991.

———. "Put It in Writing: What You Should Know About Challenges to School Library Materials." *School Library Journal* 39, no. 1 (January 1993): 26-30.

———. "The School Library Media Specialist: Dealing with Complaints About Materials." *Catholic Library World* 56, no. 4 (November 1984): 172-74.

Jenkinson, David. "Censorship Iceberg: Results of a Survey of Challenges in Public and School Libraries." *Canadian Library Journal* 43 (February 1986): 7-21.

Karpisek, Marian. *Policymaking for School Library Media Programs*. Chicago: American Library Association, 1989.

Kemp, Betty, ed. *School Library and Media Center Acquisitions Policies and Procedures*, 2d ed. Phoenix, AZ: Oryx Press, 1986.

Lankford, Mary D., and Deborah Chaney. "Policies and Procedures Manual." Irving, TX: Irving Independent School District, 1993.

Media Services Department. *Library Media Center Handbook*. Dallas, TX: Dallas Independent School District, 1993.

Minnesota Coalition Against Censorship. *Selection Policies and Reevaluation Procedures: A Workbook*. Stillwater: Minnesota Educational Media Organization, 1991.

Reed, Mary Hutchings. *The Copyright Primer for Librarians and Educators*. Chicago: American Library Association; Washington, DC: National Education Association, 1987.

Scholtz, James C. *Developing and Maintaining Video Collections in Libraries*. Santa Barbara, CA: ABC-Clio, 1989.

"Selection of Learning Resources: A Policy Statement." *Emergency Librarian* 12 (September-October 1984): 23-24, 26.

Texas Education Agency. *School Library Media Centers*. Austin, 1985.

University of the State of New York. State Education Department. Bureau of School Libraries. *Selection Guidelines: School Library Resources, Textbooks, Instructional Material*. Albany, n.d.

Vlcek, Charles W. *Adoptable Copyright Policy: Copyright Policy and Manuals Designed for Adoption by Schools, Colleges & Universities*. Washington, DC: Copyright Information Services, 1992.

II

SELECTION OF MATERIALS

Selection sounds like a simple task, but it has broad implications for the quality of education offered in an individual school. The needs of one person or program often conflict with those of another. For example, in one tenth-grade social studies class, students collect data, analyze it, and draw conclusions. The teacher wants materials that collectively present different opinions about topics. In another tenth-grade social studies class, however, students need structured information with constant reinforcement. For these students, open-ended presentations are confusing. The two classes need the same content presented in different ways. Without sufficient materials of both types, the desired learning experience is not possible.

Wide-ranging needs coupled with limited resources result in conflict. The collection policy identifies the collection's priorities and offers selection guidelines. The media specialist has an item in hand and needs to make a decision. Who can use it and when might they use it? How will they use it? Does it duplicate materials already in the collection? Factors like these must be weighed when making selection decisions.

If the media specialist does not know the teaching methods used, the school program goals, and the needs and interests of students, funds may be spent for items that are shelf-sitters. If the media specialist does not know the materials in the collection, selection decisions can lead to duplication. Without knowing what materials are available, items of limited value may be selected. It is disheartening to purchase an item and then learn about a better one.

The burden of selection is not the media specialist's alone; teachers, administrators, and students can participate in the decision-making process. However, the media specialist, as the one individual who knows the collection and the needs of the school, is ultimately responsible for making wise selection decisions.

CHAPTER 7

Selection Procedures

In choosing materials, a media specialist plans and carries out certain activities that culminate with selection decisions. These activities include identifying and assessing evaluative information about materials; arranging for examination of materials through preview sessions, exhibits, and visits to examination centers; and providing ways to involve others in the process. These steps lead to the direct acquisition of materials or obtaining materials and information through resource sharing and electronic means.

OVERVIEW OF THE
SELECTION PROCESS

Selection is the process of deciding what materials are to be added to the collection. Potential materials can be identified through many sources. Administrators, teachers, and students request specific items or types of materials. Items in the collection wear out, are lost, or need replacing. The media specialist learns about new materials by reading reviews, seeing publisher's announcements, and previewing materials. People may donate materials to the collection.

Suggestions and requests for materials to be purchased should be recorded in a consideration file. The media specialist should record as much bibliographic and purchasing information about the item as can be obtained at this stage, including the identifying source or person who requested it. The next step is to check if the item already is in the collection or is on order. Some media specialists file a copy of the order slip in the card catalog by title entry to simplify this procedure. Others with automated catalogs enter the title into the record with a notation that the work is on order.

Once an item is fully identified, a decision must be made whether to include it or exclude it from the collection This selection decision is based on several considerations, including collection policy; budget; selection criteria regarding content, format, and use; and immediacy of need. After the decision has been made to purchase the item, the record for the item is moved from the consideration file to the "to order" file. The actions following this step comprise the acquisition process.

SOURCES OF INFORMATION
ABOUT MATERIALS

The opening-day scene in chapter 1 reveals many requests for materials. Are there recommended videodiscs that present general information about light for Valerie's class? Where do you find music activity records for Keyona's kindergarten children? Which play scripts, science fiction titles, and biographies of sports figures are appropriate for Connie's fourth-grade class? Is there a videotape that Rodrigo can use for his talk to the community group? Is there software for note taking? Which posters or art prints will stimulate students to write? Does the collection include visual and manipulative materials for Willie's American history class? Will any of the popular music recordings be useful for Dieter's poetry unit? To fulfill these requests, the media specialist must investigate

- specific formats—art prints, posters, books, software, recordings, videodiscs, and videotapes.

- user groups (audiences)—kindergarten children, fourth-graders, college-bound students, individuals reading below grade level, and adult members of a community group.

- subjects—light, teenage pregnancies, American history, and English.

- literary forms and genres—plays, science fiction, and poetry.

This analysis indicates the broad coverage needed in sources of information about materials.

Bibliographic Tools

Bibliographic tools are a basic source of information about the availability of materials, their cost, and whether they are recommended. Two types of bibliographies are useful. *Trade bibliographies*, such as *Books in Print* (R. R. Bowker, 1948-) and *Canadian Books in Print* (University of Toronto Press, 1975-), provide information about the availability of materials. *Selection tools*, such as *Senior High School Library Catalog* (H. W. Wilson, 1992) and *Elementary School Library Collection* (Brodart, annual), evaluate materials and may include purchasing information.

When considering a bibliography for use or purchase, read the introduction and examine several entries. This will answer the following questions about the work:

- Purpose of the bibliography: Is your need met by that purpose?

- Directions for use: Are the directions adequate? Are sample entries with explanations given?

- Format: Is the bibliography available in print, CD-ROM, or other formats?

- Extent of coverage: Does it include information about a variety of formats? Does it provide information for many items, or is coverage limited? Does it include materials for a wide range of audiences, preschool through adult? What periods of publication and production are included?

- Method for collecting the information and who is responsible: Who wrote the annotations? What are the writers' qualifications? Are the reviews signed?

- Criteria for inclusion: On what basis are items included? Are the criteria stated? Is the selection policy provided?

- Information provided and form of entry: Is the information clearly presented? Are symbols and abbreviations used? Symbols may indicate levels of recommendation, reviewing sources, interest level, readability, and type of media. What ordering and bibliographic information is given? Are the annotations descriptive or evaluative? Are all items recommended equally? Are items recommended for specific situations, uses, or audiences? Are comparisons made with other titles or formats? Are materials included only when they have received favorable reviews in other tools?

- Organization of entries: Are the indexes necessary to locate an item? Do cross-references help you locate related items? Are there indexes that provide access by author, title, series title, audience, level, subject, and analytics (sections of materials)?

- Date of publication: Is the compiler's closing date provided? How often is the bibliography revised or cumulated? Are supplements provided? What time lag exists between compiling the information and the publication or issuing of the bibliography?

- Special features: Does the bibliography include directories for sources of the materials included? Does the work include appendixes? If yes, about what?

- Cost.

Selection Tools

Selection tools are bibliographies that include an evaluative or critical annotation for each item, providing

- recommendations;

- bibliographic information for each item;

- purchasing information;

- access to entries by author, title, subject, format, and even audience approaches to aid in locating recommended materials; and

- analytical indexes, appendixes, or other special features useful in helping students and teachers locate portions of works that may be in the school's collection.

For example, analytical entries in the indexes to *Children's Catalog* (H. W. Wilson, 1991) and *Senior High School Library Catalog* are useful for locating materials about specific subjects and individuals.

Where should these tools be housed? Are they the media specialist's property, shelved in the media center office, or are they publicized and housed for maximum accessibility to all users? The multiple uses of these resources should be considered when justifying their cost and when deciding where to shelve them.

Selection tools exist in a variety of formats: books, reviewing periodicals, and bibliographic essays.

Books

Commonly used general selection tools that appear in book format are the H. W. Wilson series that includes *Children's Catalog, Junior High School Library Catalog, Senior High School Library Catalog*; and Brodart's *Elementary School Library Collection*. In 1994, *Elementary School Library Collection* became available in both print and CD-ROM formats.

The lead time required to produce these books creates a time gap between the publication of the last item reviewed and the publication date of the bibliography. As a result, books are not as current as reviewing journals. A careful reading of the introduction can provide clues as to whether a new title was not recommended or was not received in time for review in that edition of the book.

Book-format selection tools provide a means of checking recommendations for titles that have been available for 12 months or more. These selection tools are especially useful for checking to see whether titles listed in the teacher's edition of textbooks are recommended. Other book-format selection tools list recommended materials for specific subjects or audiences. (See chapters 11 and 12 and appendixes A and B.)

Elizabeth Ann Poe, Barbara G. Samuels, and Betty Carter observe that, "book lists are all too often seen as compilations of subjective recommendations, when in fact they are the product of rigorous selection policies. To eliminate this perception, selectors must share their processes and policies with their audiences."[1]

Reviewing Journals

Reviewing journals evaluate currently published and produced materials. There is a wide range of these journals, each with some unique and valuable feature. Reviewing journals are produced by commercial firms, professional associations, education agencies, and other publishers; generally, they are written for a specific audience, such as media personnel or classroom teachers. The coverage of materials reviewed by journals may be limited by (1) format: print materials, audiovisual materials, software, text, and instructional materials; (2) potential users: children in grades K-6, junior high school students, preschoolers through adult, young adult; (3) subject: all materials that may be in a media collection or materials on a specific subject; and (4) from a particular perspective, such as *Multicultural Review: Dedicated to a Better Understanding of Ethnic, Racial and Religious Diversity* (1992-).

Reviews may be written by journal staff members or by professionals in the field. Signed reviews can provide clues to the reviewer's position or background. Reviewing journals also may include articles, directories, or columns of interest to media personnel.

The selection policies annually printed in *Booklist* and *School Library Journal* help potential purchasers understand the basis for judgments in reviews. Clearly explained symbols, like those used in *Bulletin of the Center for Children's Books*, can quickly clue the user to the recommendation.

What do media specialists look for in reviews? Janie Schomberg writes,

> I need and expect a lot from reviews. First, book reviews should be descriptive, objective statements about plot, characters, theme, and illustrations. Second, I expect book reviews to have an evaluative statement including comparison of the title being reviewed to similar titles and literature in general. Third, the potential appeal, curricular use, and possible controversial aspects of the title need to be addressed to fully inform me as a potential selector.[2]

Problems media specialists face in using the reviewing journals include time lag between publication and review; lack of access to reviewing journals for specific subjects; and limited coverage of audiovisual, software, and electronic resources.

There are legitimate reasons why journals may not review a specific title. One journal will not review a work unless the work can be reviewed within a specific time after its publication. The reader of that journal cannot be sure whether an item was received too late to be reviewed, was outside the journal's scope, or failed to meet another criterion. Time gaps among various journals' reviews of a work may be caused by each journal's policies and procedures. For example, testing material in the field is an advantage but adds time to the process.

The value of the assessments can vary in quality or in applicability to a specific collection. Note the position and geographic location of the reviewer to decide whether his or her situation is similar to yours. The journal *Appraisal* offers a unique feature. Items are reviewed by both a librarian and a subject specialist. Comparing reviews can offer more insightful information about the item than can be obtained from a single reviewer.

Trying to locate two or more reviews of a current title can be frustrating. Often, the problem is caused by the limited number of items reviewed and by the time lag between reviews. Table 7.1 shows the number of reviews (including both books and nonprint materials) published annually by the major reviewing journals.

Table 7.1.
Number of Items Reviewed by Major Reviewing Publications

Journals	Books Juvenile 1992	1993	Young Adult 1992	1993	Nonprint Materials 1992	1993
Booklist	2,647	2,696*	891		1,083	1,193
Bulletin of the Center for Children's Books	772	729				
Horn Book Guide	3,200	3,750*	600			
Horn Book Magazine	400	500	75			
Publishers Weekly	1,300	1,513				
School Library Journal	3,120	3,256	360	366	1,000	

*Includes young adult.

Extracted from *The Bowker Annual Library & Book Trade Almanac*, 38th ed. (New Providence, NJ: R. R. Bowker, 1993), 514; and *The Bowker Annual Library & Book Trade Almanac*, 39th ed. (New Providence, NJ: R. R. Bowker, 1994), 550.

Locating reviews for audiovisual materials, software, and online databases is a challenge. These materials are reviewed less extensively than books. No one journal reviews all the formats found in media center collections. A sampling of journals that review more than one format is displayed in Table 7.2 on page 117.

Table 7.2.
Reviewing Journals' Coverage by Format

Reviewing Journals – Coverage of Formats										
Title	books	CD-ROM	computer software	films	filmstrips	online databases	periodicals	recordings	slides	videos
AV Guide			•							•
Book Report	•	•		•	•					•
Booklist	•		•							•
Catholic Library World	•		•	•	•					•
Choice	•		•	•	•			•	•	•
CM, A Reviewing Journal of Canadian Materials for Young People	•									•
Curriculum Review			•	•	•					•
Emergency Librarian	•						•	•		
Kliatt Young Adult	•		•							
Library Journal	•							•		•
Library Talk	•		•	•	•					•
Media and Methods	•		•	•	•				•	•
Reviewing Librarian	•							•		
School Libraries in Canada	•	•		•						•
School Library Journal	•		•	•	•			•	•	•
VOYA	•			•					•	•
Wilson Library Bulletin	•	•	•				•	•		•

Legend:
- books
- CD-ROM
- computer software
- films
- filmstrips
- online databases
- periodicals
- recordings
- slides
- videos

Cumulated indexes in the journals can be helpful in the search for reviews, but a more comprehensive approach to review indexing can be found in tools like *Book Review Index*, *Book Review Digest*, or *Media Review Digest*. *Book Review Index* is available online (DIALOG file 137). *Book*

Review Digest is available on WilsonDisc. The cost of such tools may require that they be shared by all media centers in the district.

Bibliographic Essays

Bibliographic essays that describe and recommend materials about a particular subject or theme, or for a particular use or audience, can be found in journals like *School Library Journal*. These essays can be very helpful, but they demand careful analysis. The reader does not know whether the writer simply overlooked an omitted item or whether the writer deliberately omitted it. Usually, bibliographic essays focus on a specific component of an item and do not provide an overall assessment of the material.

Relying on Reviewing Media

Media specialists use reviewing media regularly. If there is no selection committee, the entire burden of selection rests with the media specialist. To examine every item published or produced within a given year would be a staggering task.

Remember that reviews reflect the writer's opinion based on her or his knowledge of materials and students. Whether your evaluation involves personal examination of items or reliance on reviews, some materials will, for one reason or another, remain unused or be inappropriate. Consider these situations learning experiences. Schomberg observes, "there seems to be no way to avoid the occasional 'lemon'. . . . Selection of materials based upon reviews cannot be expected to be successful 100% of the time."[3]

Charles W. Vlcek and Raymond V. Wiman warn,

> While a particular title may be given a poor professional review, it may be the only material available or the material that best meets a client's need. It is the client who is going to use the material, and his or her evaluation should be given more weight than that of the professional reviewer. However, if favorably reviewed materials can be found that meet the client's needs, then they should be given higher priority for purchase consideration.[4]

On the other hand, Betty J. Morris argues,

> Although a first hand evaluation is not feasible for all media purchases, it is still the most preferable method to assure that the media suit the needs of the school community. The reviewing sources that are available for many materials (for example, library books) are of sufficient quantity and quality that to ignore these sources in favor of local reviewing not only wastes time and duplicates effort but also fails to utilize the expertise of the knowledgeable critics and subject specialists who review in these publications.[5]

Your decision whether to use reviews, involve others in personal examination of materials, or use a combination of methods reflects a number of factors. The expense, in terms of time and money, for selection tools, for subscribing to reviewing journals, and for arranging previews must be weighed against the opportunity to help teachers and students become knowledgeable about materials and their potential use.

Other Sources of Information

Information about materials also can be obtained from publishers, producers, distributors, and wholesalers. The information may be in catalogs, flyers, or other announcements; it is not evaluative.

PERSONAL EXAMINATION

There are many ways to obtain materials for personal examination; however, the most practical ways include visits by sales representatives, formal previewing arrangements, and visits to examination centers and conferences.

Previewing

Previewing is one of the most efficient ways to examine materials personally prior to purchases. This is the practice of borrowing materials from an examination center, a producer, distributor, or jobber for a specific time for the purpose of evaluation. As Vlcek and Wiman warn

> There are a lot of 'dogs' produced that are made to look good in advertising brochures, but advertising does not improve a poor production. How can one know that the content fits needs or that the technical quality meets standards unless the material is evaluated? While evaluating and previewing materials is time-consuming it is time well spent. . . .
>
> Most distributors have "on approval" plans available to enable the purchaser to order materials and return them if they do not meet client content needs and technical or quality standards.[6]

Materials commonly evaluated through preview arrangements include video formats, laser discs, and software. Previewing is an effective way to involve students and teachers in the selection process. Review groups of teachers, administrators, and students may be organized by subject area or grade level. In his review of research, Daniel Callison observes one of the arguments for involving students is that "teachers and students tend to agree on software they do not like, but disagree on software they favor; students tend to favor simulation-formatted programs, while teachers tend to favor tutorials that match established lesson plans."[7]

If a committee is evaluating materials on a specific subject, make arrangements with several companies so their materials can be examined at the same time. When arranging previewing sessions, however, consider the needs and limitations of the committee. Viewing too many versions of the same subject or same format can be fatiguing. Planning can prevent such situations.

An advantage of having the media specialist make the preview arrangements is the avoidance of several teachers requesting the same item for preview within a given school year. Media specialists should establish a previewing plan with the school administrator. This should ensure that the media specialist serves as a clearinghouse, asking all groups participating in previewing to provide evaluations of the materials and arranging for other evaluation sessions.

Previewing is not a free way to supplement the collection, nor should several teachers within one building request the same item for examination at different times. The media specialist is responsible for returning previewing materials in good condition within the specified time. Check the policy of the company from whom you are considering purchases. Requesting materials you are seriously considering for purchase and planning for their systematic evaluation is an excellent way to make informed selection decisions.

Exhibits

Both teachers and media specialists appreciate the opportunity to examine materials first-hand. Some school districts arrange for exhibits of new materials in a central location during the pre-opening school activities. These exhibits allow media specialists and teachers to compare a wide range of materials, including software, on the same subject. If your school district sponsors such exhibits, invite teachers to examine the materials with you. In this way, you can learn how teachers would use the materials, and they can learn about similar materials in the collection. As you watch demonstrations of newer materials and equipment, you can identify which teachers are interested in learning more about them. Exhibits at conferences also provide an opportunity to join teachers in examining materials.

Examination Centers

Another way to personally evaluate materials is to visit an examination center. These centers may serve district, intermediate, regional, or state levels; they may be housed in the district media center, at a university, or in a state agency. Some centers house materials ranging from curricular and instructional materials to trade books, software, CD-ROMs, and interactive video. Other centers or clearinghouses focus on materials for specific users or specific formats. Examination centers, such as the Children's Book Council, provide newsletters and other information.[8]

Clearinghouses, such as the California Computer Software Clearinghouse, offer guidelines for the selection of the materials.

INVOLVING OTHERS IN SELECTION

The idea that teachers, students, and administrators should be involved in making selection decisions is not new, but its practice is not as common as one would expect. Common ways to involve others in the process include

- routing bibliographies to teachers and administrators;

- routing reviewing journals to teachers;

- attending faculty, departmental, or grade-level meetings to learn about curriculum changes and to discuss future purchases;

- conducting interest inventories with students;

- involving teachers, administrators, and students in the selection decision-making process.

Advisory committees are another way to involve others. Teachers, community members, and students may be members of the advisory committee. The committee can play a variety of roles. In some districts, the advisory committee's responsibilities are limited to policy issues and to establishing priorities for acquisition. In other districts, the advisory committee may be involved in the selection process or in helping to make decisions about which materials should be removed or replaced.

Teachers

Teachers bring to the selection process knowledge of their specializations, teaching methods, students, and instructional needs. They can provide opportunities to test materials in the classroom and encourage students to evaluate materials.

Shomberg describes the situation at her school,

> One of the keys to becoming informed about the curriculum is involving the teachers in the [selection] process. The staff at Leal is a group of very dedicated, knowledgeable teachers who know and care a great deal about teaching/learning materials. They are continually on the lookout for potential library materials through their own involvement in conferences, workshops, coursework, and constant use of the two public libraries that serve our communities, and they are bookstore fanatics. The teachers at Leal recommend materials to me on a regular basis through informal verbal exchanges as well as more formal recommendation forms and

requests. The professional review journals that are subscribed to through the school library media center are also routed, by request, to many teachers in the building who regularly read and mark reviews for my consideration.[9]

Plan to acquaint teachers with the collection. Explain to them or involve them in developing the criteria to be used in the selection process and have reviews available for reference. During these sessions you will find yourself providing in-service education on how to evaluate materials. As you work with the group, you are helping individuals develop their critical skills. In addition, you are developing more active users of the media center, users who will support media center budget requests.

With proper preparation, teachers can contribute a great deal to the selection process; however, some problems must be anticipated. Any group made up of people with diverse views will experience conflict. Jealousies may occur over who is serving on the committee.

When you ask teachers or department chairpersons to make suggestions or to participate on selection committees, some may respond that they don't have time or do not view the center as having teaching materials in their area of specialization. They may be expressing feelings of inadequacy about their knowledge of materials. Others may say that selection is your responsibility, not theirs. On the other hand, when approached for their expertise, either as subject specialists or as effective users of materials, many teachers will be glad to participate.

The best way to gain cooperation is to sincerely seek others' opinions, act on them, and inform the individuals of the results. Remember, teachers are busy and may lose interest if you do not accept their recommendations. If you are unable to purchase a specific item they recommended, explain why. When the requested item arrives, notify the person who recommended the material and explain where it will be housed.

As you work with selection committees, record the reasons for decisions. Forms listing criteria with places, names of the evaluators, and their ratings can simplify record keeping. Holding this information on file can prevent duplication of effort; it is easy to forget which items already have been evaluated. The record also provides accountability when a decision is challenged. Ideally, one form should cover all types of materials (see fig. 7.1). In practice, however, it may be easier to develop separate forms for different formats.

Media specialists have found various ways to involve teachers. In one high school, a social studies teacher suggested establishing an endowment to create funding for unbudgeted or unexpected purchases. After the contract was drawn, teachers were invited to be charter members. Later, community members and classes were invited to participate. As the practice continued, people thought of the fund as an appropriate place to contribute memorial funds or other gifts.

```
┌─────────────────────────────────────────────────────────────────┐
│                   MATERIALS EVALUATION FORM                       │
```

MATERIALS EVALUATION FORM

Title _____ Author/Producer _____

Edition _____ Series Title _____

Publisher/Distributor _____ Place _____ Date_____

Format: _____

Appropriate Users (circle): P K 1 2 3 4 5 6 7 8 9 10 11 12 Adult

Curriculum Uses Include:

Information Uses Include:

Personal Uses Include:

CRITERIA	RATING				WHY? Comments
	Poor	Fair	Good	Superior	
Authoritativeness					
Accuracy or Credibility					
Organization					
Appropriateness of Content					
Aesthetic Quality					
Technical Quality					
Overall Rating					

Recommendation: ☐ Add 1 copy   ☐ Add___copies   ☐ Do not recommend
                ☐ Uncertain Why?_____

Evaluator(s):_____

Evaluation test group:_____

Date: _____

Fig. 7.1. Sample evaluation form.

When the interest from the endowment reached $1,500, a committee was appointed to identify appropriate categories for purchases. Because the collection was weak in software, several programs of interest to various departments were exhibited. The media specialist invited department chairpersons and faculty to attend a demonstration of the software. The group made their selections and prioritized them. When the materials were received, the individuals were notified. Because all the funds were not used for these purchases, the media specialist took three of the department chairpersons to the district media center for a demonstration of other computer programs.

Another media specialist, Janet, uses a variety of techniques to involve faculty members in selection decisions. She consistently informs individuals when the materials they suggested arrive. In this case, a portion of the budget is reserved to purchase materials recommended by new teachers. Janet tries to purchase the items within a week, so new teachers know their suggestions are taken seriously. This practice gives her an opportunity to meet each new teacher and to share information about the collection. Janet encourages all teachers and administrators to make suggestions about materials they see at conferences or learn about through in-service programs. When new materials arrive, she displays them in the teacher's lounge or in the departmental areas. She uses a sign to ask teachers to indicate which materials they like or whether other materials should be obtained. When special funding becomes available for purchases, Janet notifies teachers, giving them a deadline for submitting their suggestions.

For the principal and assistant principals, Janet circles reviews in journals and asks if they would like to see the items. Teachers and administrators are encouraged to mark reviews and advertisements of materials they would like to see. Every year at the first faculty meeting, teachers are encouraged to look for materials that should be added to the collection. Teachers are reminded that ideas may come from in-service programs, course work, professional meetings, and professional reading. When the media staff know that teachers will be attending professional meetings, they ask the teachers to look for specific types of materials. As the teachers suggest specific items, notes are made to record which teacher suggested which item. Teachers are notified whether the item was purchased, when it is received, and where it is displayed.

In Janet's school, students do independent projects and research papers. She asks teachers which papers received good grades in order to identify papers in which the content met the teacher's expectations. This assessment gives a clue to the quality of the citations. Then Janet checks the students' bibliographies to identify items that students found in other libraries. Those items are considered for purchase.

Janet encourages community members to participate in school activities. When exhibits, book fairs, or demonstrations are arranged, Janet encourages the faculty, students, and community to attend. The response by parents has been favorable and has led to donations.

Another media specialist who serves a very large high school with buildings on a campus plan, carries a clipboard so she can readily make notes as she talks with teachers. She also notifies teachers what action has been taken on their requests.

Students

Students can participate in some of the selection activities that primarily involve teachers, but there are additional ways to involve students. When a sales representative brought Spanish materials to Janet's media center, she took the representative to an area where Spanish-speaking students were working and asked them whether the school should purchase the materials. They identified items they thought were particularly useful as well as some they thought were poorly presented or of limited use or appeal.

In Janet's high school, tenth- to twelfth-grade students are required to take English. With the cooperation of the English teachers, Janet visits each English class near the end of the year. She starts the session by asking, "In what subject areas did you have difficulty finding materials?" Janet may present the budget, showing sources of funds and how they are spent. She points out how the students who work contribute to these funding sources. She also takes a printout of missing materials and estimates of the replacement cost.

Two issues frequently arise during these sessions. The first is the reading level of materials. Poor and reluctant readers complain about the difficult materials and about materials they consider too technical. More able students complain about the simple materials that do not cover subjects in sufficient detail. The second issue relates to format. Students who are computer-literate and competent searchers want more materials on CD-ROM or more access to online sources. Students who are visually oriented prefer materials on interactive videodiscs.

At the close of the discussion, Janet distributes 3-by-5-inch cards on which students are asked to answer three questions anonymously. First, What are all of their criticisms of the media center, its services, and its staff. Second, How do they suggest improving that situation? Third, What does the collection need and what do students want? Janet reminds the students that materials can include periodicals, recordings, newspapers, books, videos, software, online services, and CD-ROM. If they do not know specific titles, they can suggest subject areas.

The discussion often leads to problem solving, and Janet tries to follow up within a day on specific suggestions for improvements so students know they were heard. One complaint involved the inconvenience of having to walk the entire length of the media center to return materials to the circulation desk. The suggested solution was to put a plastic laundry basket at a stairway near the heaviest traveled corridor. When items were returned, staff could easily spot and retrieve them. Fortunately, Janet's concern that other students might take the materials without checking them out did not occur.

Janet's budgeting strategy—she holds a reserve of $500 for items students request—allowed her to follow up another student's suggestion. Erik had an avid interest in collecting baseball cards, but found few sources of information about the subject in the media center. Janet spotted a useful title in a local bookstore and purchased it. After it was processed, she prepared the book for circulation and took it to Erik's English class, where she announced she had it ready for him. Such efforts on Janet's part let students know that their suggestions are important. Erik's classmates felt free to make other requests. Such practices may seem impractical, but the idea of seeking suggestions and following up on them can be applied in a variety of ways.

At one high school, the media specialist sets aside $350 for the purchase of popular recordings. A student committee evaluates the suggestions from the student body and then recommends specific items for purchase. When the recordings or discs arrive, announcements on the school's daily televised morning program let students know the items are available.

Schools ask students to give brief reviews or announcements about new materials over the public-address system, through the daily television broadcast, on the school's electronic bulletin board, or in the student newspaper.

If someone in your community reviews materials for the local newspaper or for professional journals, they may welcome students' reactions to the materials. The district media center may have titles that students may review. Through these experiences students learn how to evaluate materials and may find titles they want to suggest for the collection. Even children in the first and second grade can begin to learn about the selection process. When groups of young children come to the media center to select materials for their classrooms, ask them the following questions: Do all your classmates share your interests? Are there children who like more pictures in their books? Are there times when you want something to read quickly? Are there children in your class who prefer facts over stories? Didn't Natasha get a new puppy? Do you think she would like this videotape about taking care of a puppy? These questions help children begin to think critically about the materials they use.

Students involved in the selection process can help alert others to materials and opportunities in the media center. A classmate's recommendation often carries more weight, certainly more appeal, than the same recommendation from an adult. These examples highlight a few ways to involve students in the selection process and point out the advantages, insights, and excitement that can be generated so easily.

SUMMARY

The selection process calls for professional knowledge and judgment about materials and the sources that review them. The media specialist must be a knowledgeable consumer of the review sources: selection tools, reviewing journals, and bibliographic essays.

Careful planning, initiative, and interpersonal skills are needed to effectively involve others in the selection process. Collective evaluation of materials through personal examination and group discussion can increase the knowledgeable use of the media center's collection.

NOTES

[1]Elizabeth Ann Poe, Barbara G. Samuels, and Betty Carter, "Twenty-Five Years of Research in Young Adult Literature: Past Perspectives and Future Directions," *Journal of Youth Services in Libraries* 7, no. 1 (Fall 1993): 67.

[2]Janie Schomberg, "Tools of the Trade: School Library Media Specialists, Reviews, and Collection Development," in *Evaluating Children's Books: A Critical Look: Aesthetic, Social, and Political Aspects of Analyzing and Using Children's Books*, ed. by Betsy Hearne and Roger Sutton (Urbana-Champaign, IL: University of Illinois, Graduate School of Library and Information Science, 1993), 41.

[3]Schomberg, "Tools of the Trade," 42.

[4]Charles W. Vlcek, and Raymond V. Wiman, *Managing Media Services: Theory and Practice* (Englewood, CO: Libraries Unlimited, 1989), 82.

[5]Betty J. Morris, with John T. Gillespie and Diana L. Spirt, *Administering the School Library Media Center*, 3d ed. (New Providence, NJ: R. R. Bowker, 1992), 260-61.

[6]Vlcek and Wiman, *Managing Media Services*, 82.

[7]Daniel Callison, "A Review of the Research Related to School Library Media Collections: Part I," *School Library Media Quarterly* 19, no. 1 (Fall 1990): 61.

[8]The Children's Book Council, Inc., is located at 568 Broadway, New York, NY 10012; 212-966-1990. To receive the *CBC Features* (newsletter) and information about Book Week and other activities, there is a one-time handling charge of $45. Send check or money order, name, and complete mailing address to The Children's Book Council, Order Center, 350 Scotland Road, Orange, NJ 07050.

[9]Schomberg, "Tools of the Trade," 40.

BIBLIOGRAPHY

Callison, Daniel. "A Review of the Research Related to School Library Media Collections: Part I." *School Library Media Quarterly* 19, no. 1 (Fall 1990): 57-62.

Hearne, Betsy, and Roger Sutton, eds. *Evaluating Children's Books: A Critical Look: Aesthetic, Social, and Political Aspects of Analyzing and Using Children's Books*. Urbana-Champaign, IL: University of Illinois, Graduate School of Library and Information Science, 1993.

Morris, Betty J., with John T. Gillespie and Diana L. Spirt. *Administering the School Library Media Center*, 3d ed. New Providence, NJ: R. R. Bowker, 1992.

Poe, Elizabeth Ann; Barbara G. Samuels; and Betty Carter. "Twenty-Five Years of Research in Young Adult Literature: Past Perspectives and Future Directions." *Journal of Youth Services in Libraries* 7, no. 1 (Fall 1993): 65-73.

Vlcek, Charles W., and Raymond V. Wiman. *Managing Media Services: Theory and Practice*. Englewood, CO: Libraries Unlimited, 1989.

CHAPTER 8

GENERAl SElECTION CRiTERiA

Selection is a complex decision-making process, not a simple, gut-level "I-like-this" response. Responsible collection development requires that broad considerations govern the evaluation and choice of a single item. The media specialist is responsible for the collection as an entity and for the individual items. The reasons for choosing a specific item must be based on your evaluation of the item and its relationship to the collection. Justification for the choice of an item should be formulated from an assessment of its contribution to the fulfillment of the policies and goals of the collection program.

Selection decisions require the evaluator to judge materials against given criteria. However, many selection decisions are subjective. Criteria must be established to guide decisions and lend consistency to this activity. These criteria can be used to evaluate content, physical form, or potential value of materials to users or programs. All criteria must be considered in the final decision to select an item for the collection. This chapter describes general criteria that may be applied to all types of materials, criteria related to intellectual content and its presentation, physical form, and equipment. Later chapters discuss criteria for specific formats; specific subjects; and for instructional, informational, and personal needs.

INTELLECTUAL CONTENT AND ITS PRESENTATION

When making selection decisions, the basic criterion is quality. Fundamental questions are: Is the format appropriate for the content? and Does the presentation effectively address the needs of the user? When evaluating an item's presentation, consider what is the idea (intellectual content), how is the idea presented, and does the medium used provide the most suitable treatment for the idea? Analysis of these questions provides the framework for this chapter. The criteria provided are guides, not absolutes. The collection, the users, resource-sharing plans, and outside resources influence the applicability of each criterion to specific items.

How can one evaluate the idea, or intellectual content, of a work? Criteria can include (1) authority; (2) appropriateness of content to users; (3) scope; (4) accuracy; (5) treatment; (6) arrangement and organization; (7) literary quality; (8) materials available on the subject; (9) durability of information; (10) reputation of author, artist, or producer; (11) special features; and (12) value to the collection.

Authority

The basis for the criterion of authority addresses the qualifications and abilities of the people who created the work. Authority can be judged by considering the qualifications of the author or director, the quality and acceptance of other works by the same person, and the dependability of the publisher or producer. Does this work meet the standards expected from this person or organization?

Appropriateness of Content to Users

Appropriateness of content focuses on the content in relation to its intended use and audience. The concepts must be presented at the users' developmental level. In other words, is the presentation geared to the maturity and interest level of the intended users? Whether the content is factual or imaginative, it should not be presented in a condescending manner, nor should it supersede the user's capacity to understand. An item should be appropriate for the students who will use it, not to some arbitrary standard established by adults.

Scope

Scope refers to the overall purpose and depth of coverage of the content. Examine the introduction or the teacher's guide to an item to learn the intended purpose and coverage. Evaluate whether the stated purpose meets a need of the collection and, if so, whether the material fulfills its purpose. When the content of the item being considered duplicates content in the collection, consider whether the item being considered presents content from a unique perspective. If it does, it may be a valuable addition to broaden the scope of the collection.

Accuracy

Information presented in materials should be accurate. Opinions should be distinguished from facts and, as much as possible, should be impartially presented. Accuracy is often linked to timeliness, or how recently an item was published or produced, especially in technological subjects where changes occur rapidly. Check with a subject area specialist, if necessary, to be sure the information is timely. Remember, however, that a recent publication date does not necessarily show that material is current or accurate.

Treatment

The treatment or presentation style can affect the potential value of an item. It must be appropriate for the subject and use. In the best items, the presentation catches and holds the user's attention, draws on a typical experience, and stimulates further learning or creativity. Are signs (pictures, visuals) and symbols (words, abstractions) necessary to the content and helpful to the user? Are graphics, color, and sound integral to the presentation?

Are the presentations free of racial or sexual stereotyping? Do materials reflect our multicultural society? Is the information accessible to those who may have physical limitations?

Does the user control the rate and sequence of the content presentation? With electronic information, can the user easily enter, use, and exit the program? Are on-screen instructions user-friendly? Do prompts and help screens provide clear directions? Is there an introductory or practice program?

The treatment of an item must be appropriate to the situation in which it will be used. Some materials require an adult to guide the student's use of material; other materials require use of a teacher's guide to present the information fully. Treatment may present very practical limitations. For example, is the length appropriate to class periods as generally scheduled? The use of a 60-minute video may be problematic if the longest possible viewing period is 55 minutes.

Arrangement and Organization

Presentation of the material in terms of sequence and development of ideas influences comprehension. Content should develop logically, flowing from one section to another, emphasizing important elements. Does the arrangement of information facilitate its use? A chronologically arranged work may present difficulties for users searching for specific information if there is no subject index. A summary or review of major points will help the user understand the organization of the work and find needed information.

Literary Merit

The artistic effect literature serves is another area of evaluation. What theme or idea is the author trying to present? The theme should be presented in a coherent manner and be relevant to the child's real or imaginary world. Organization of plot, setting, characterization, and style should be consistent. Is the user's interest captured early? The plot should develop logically. Does the story have a beginning, a middle, and an end? Are changes and developments plausible but not predictable? Does the description of the time and place evoke a clear and credible setting? The characters' actions should be convincing. Is the style or genre appropriate to the theme? Do the words and syntax create a mood or help to convey ideas? Is the point of view appropriate? What is the total effect of the work?

One component should not stand out from the others, except for emphasis, creating a unity of literary elements.

Materials Available on the Subject

In selecting materials to fill a need for a particular subject, program, or user, availability may outweigh other criteria. This occurs frequently with current events, such as the election of a new president. Biographical information may be needed immediately, and there are few, if any, materials available for younger students. By the end of a president's first four-year term, there is a wide range of titles and formats from which to select but fewer requests from users.

Durability of Information

The lasting value of information often relates to the scarcity of materials. The idea or subject may be stable or may change rapidly (such as political boundaries, fashions, or automobiles). Thus the subject presented and the information about it may change. An automobile assembly line today may be similar to one 10 years ago, but the automobiles, materials, and processes have changed. For rapidly changing subjects, less expensive formats may be preferred to more expensive formats, so replacements can be obtained more economically. As an example, for countries where political boundaries are rapidly changing, one may want to use news clippings until the situation stabilizes and materials that meet other criteria are available.

Reputation of Author, Artist, or Producer

Particular creators—authors, artists, or producers—and specific titles enjoy widespread reputations as essential to the education of students. For example, the classics are a staple of the collection. Does a work being evaluated exemplify the contributions of its creator? If a particular work falls into this category, purchase it and make plans to introduce it to students. This is an area in which a paperback collection might be considered.

Instructional Design

Materials designed for clearly defined instructional objectives should meet the expectations of the learner or teacher. Does the material encourage problem solving and creativity? Does it promote understanding of ideas? Will users have the necessary capabilities (reading ability, vocabulary level, and computational skills) to learn from the material? Will the presentation arouse and motivate interest? Is evidence of field tests provided? Does the presentation stimulate interaction? With electronic materials, do menus or icons always allow direct access to specific parts of the program? Is the screen well designed? Are instructions clear? Is there an effective use of color, text, sound, and graphics? Is clearly presented documentation provided? Are there suitable instructional support materials, such as hotlines, newsletters, and guides?

Special Features

Information or features that are peripheral to the main content of a work may be of value to the collection. Distinctive characteristics—maps, charts, graphs, other illustrations, and glossaries—can be used as reference materials. A record album may contain biographical information about the composer or performer; the teacher's guide may offer suggestions for follow-up activities or contain a bibliography of related materials. Is the information accurately and completely indexed? These special features can be a decisive factor in selection decisions that are less than clear-cut.

Value to the Collection

After evaluating the specific qualities of the item, the media specialist needs to consider it in relation to the collection. Does the item meet needs of the school program or the users? Can it be used for more than one purpose? Who are the likely users? How often would the item be used? Could the item be used by an individual for informational or recreational purposes or by a teacher in an instructional situation? Is the item readily available through interlibrary loan?

Other Considerations

Series

Each item within a series must be judged independently in terms of its value and known needs. Books in a series may be written by different authors, but all authors may not be equally skilled. If the entire series is written by one author, is that individual knowledgeable about all subjects presented in the series? Even an author of fiction may be unable to sustain the interest of the reader throughout a series. Can the works be used independently, or is sequential use required?

Cost

The price of an item and the expense involved in obtaining it can strongly influence the selection decision. Is the item within the budget specifications? Is a less expensive but satisfactory substitute available?

If the material requires new equipment, peripherals, and supplies, the price of these must be considered. Are there periodic enhancements? What do they cost? Will purchasing the new equipment make use of other materials in the collection easier? The item should receive enough use to justify its cost.

PHYSICAL FORM

Although content is one basis on which to evaluate an item, the packaging of the information, or its physical form, also must be evaluated. The quality of the content can be weakened if it is not presented through the appropriate medium. How does one decide which medium presents the content most effectively? This may appear to be a simple question; it is not. One of the primary criteria to be evaluated is the compatibility of content and format. In speaking of Michelangelo's *David*, Lillian B. Wehmeyer suggests that

> had a reader never seen the sculpture (or its model or photo), a purely verbal description, without visuals, would not likely enable him to envision more than a vague image. Just as the David must be seen, so must Beethoven's Ninth Symphony be heard, corduroy be touched, lilacs be smelled, or wonton be tasted before a learner can begin to understand them.[1]

Technical Quality

The physical characteristics of the item must be judged independently and collectively. Are illustrations and photographs clear and eye-catching? Is there a reason for soft-focus effects? Is the balance of illustrations to text appropriate to the content and prospective user?

Do colors express the theme or message? Are line, shape, and texture used effectively? Do use of sound, visual materials, and narrative help focus attention? Is there a balance of music, narration, and dialog? Are sound elements synchronized? Is the speech clear and effectively paced? Is the sound clearly audible?

Are film techniques, such as close-ups, animation, or flashbacks used to focus attention or reveal information? Are mobility of subjects, expressiveness of presenters, multiple camera work, resolution, and clarity used effectively? Is the result a smooth presentation with appropriate pacing, rhythm, length of sequences, and special effects?

The appearance of the type can be expressive and provide clarity. Typeface used in projected images, such as transparencies, should project clearly, and be suitable for various audiences.

Is software menu- or command-driven? Are there different levels of commands? Does it allow searching using Boolean logic, keywords, subjects, or truncation? Does the documentation or manual clearly explain how to use the software?

Aesthetic Quality

Both the external design and the presentation of the content need to be aesthetically pleasing: separate aspects combining to form an aesthetic whole. Is the item attractively packaged? Book jackets and album covers should appeal to the potential user. Does the design avoid colors that are difficult for colorblind people to see?

Safety and Health Considerations

Safety and health features are particularly important when selecting tactile materials, but they should be considered for all materials. Is the item constructed of nonflammable materials? Can an item be cleaned? Realia present a challenge in terms of cleanliness. What can you do with a piece of salt from the Great Salt Lake that probably will be licked by 905 of the 1,000 students in the school? Materials with movable parts pose problems, possibly with loss of integral parts. Models and kits may have parts that can cut fingers or be swallowed. Architectural models may collapse. Live animals can create health and safety problems.

Other Considerations

Is the material to be used by an individual or a group? The potential number of simultaneous users must be considered in selection decisions. For groups, using a videotape based on a book might be preferable to using the actual book. The variety of uses for the material also should be considered. For motivation, games and live specimens invite participation. Films bring distant places to the user more dramatically than a map but less effectively than electronic communication. Videotapes or photographs of the moon landing, or even a piece of the moon, have more impact than reading a text or viewing a filmstrip. If creativity is to be encouraged, a programmed text may be limiting. For example, programmed software can introduce a student to the basic principles of computer programming but may limit the creativity of a student who has reached an advanced level.

Users' personal preferences, when they can be discerned, should be considered. Will the viewer who first saw a telecast find a print version of the content equally acceptable? Will the person who first read a book appreciate the videotaped version? A television newscast may be preferred to a radio broadcast or a newspaper account. Does electronic access motivate students more than manual searches?

Translating a work from one medium to another can affect the treatment of the subject and the impact of the message. Verbal language differs from visual language. This difference can result in two seemingly unrelated works, ostensibly drawn from the same content.

Ease of use, storage, and maintenance are also important selection criteria. Can the item be used easily by an individual student or a group? Will work stations permit use of electronic media by several individuals simultaneously? Does the material require special storage? Is the item durable? Can it be easily replaced or repaired? Does the item include more than one part, such as a kit that may include print and nonprint materials? Must all the items be used together? If a single item or part is lost, can the remaining parts be used? Can missing items, such as game parts, be replaced locally? Can they be purchased separately? These practical criteria can be just as important as aesthetic considerations.

EQUIPMENT

Many materials found in media collections require equipment for use. Without proper equipment and conditions, such as dark rooms or rear-view projection, film can not be used effectively.

One of the first considerations in evaluating an equipment purchase is whether the equipment will be used enough, in the short or long term, to justify the purchase. If the item is not purchased, what will be the impact on the program? Will teachers be unable to use materials they want to use? If use of the equipment is limited to a single teacher and class working only in one subject area, is there sufficient justification for purchase? For some items, short-term rental may be a better alternative.

Ease of Use

Complex equipment discourages use. In any case, proper conditions and facilities should be provided. Projection areas should have permanently mounted screens and adjustable light controls. Are rear screen units needed? Multiple outlets will be needed in the area where the equipment will be used.

Examine the equipment, keeping in mind the potential users. What level of manual dexterity is needed to operate the equipment? How many steps are involved to run the equipment? Does the equipment have many controls? How operator-proof is the equipment? Does the equipment operate efficiently with minimum delay? Can parts be easily removed and possibly misplaced or lost? How much time is needed to teach students and faculty to use the equipment? Does each piece of equipment come with visual instructions? Are the directions complete, clear, and easy to follow? Are automatic operations dependable? Is there an option for manual or remote control? Are shut-off or cooling-down features automatic? Is configuration for peripherals, networks, and teacher options, such as sound and record keeping, easy to use and well documented?

Physical properties of the equipment can deter use. Are strong materials used in the construction of the equipment? Durability is a key criterion. Have established safety specifications been met? Does the size, weight, or design of the equipment require that it be used and stored in one location? Can the equipment be moved on a cart? If equipment is used in a two-story building, is it too heavy or bulky to carry up stairs? Equipment that circulates needs to be lightweight and compact. If equipment is circulated to students' homes, the equipment needs to be weatherproof, and carrying cases must be provided. Are there straps or handles that aid in moving the equipment? The straps and handles should be strong enough to withstand the weight of the item carried any distance.

Performance, Compatibility, and Versatility

Equipment should operate efficiently and consistently at a high level of performance. Poor quality projection or sound reproduction can negate the technical quality of materials so carefully sought in selection. What is the quality of mechanical construction? The noise or light from the equipment should not interfere with its use. Is the equipment subject to overheating? Evaluations of equipment performance can be found in *Library Technology Reports* and *Consumer Reports*.

Equipment needs to be compatible with other equipment in the collection. Can the item under consideration be used with existing equipment and computer systems? Is special hardware or software needed? Is its use limited to materials produced by the manufacturer?

Equipment that can be used in a variety of ways may be desirable. Can the equipment be used by an individual or a group? Can it be used with more than one medium? If attachments or adapters are needed to achieve versatility, how easily can the peripherals be used? Will users need special training?

Safety

Safety features demand consideration, especially when young children will use equipment. Rough or protruding edges should be avoided. Is the equipment balanced so that it will not topple easily? Users should be protected from potentially dangerous components, such as a fan or heated element, and electrical connections should be suitably covered and grounded. If the equipment generates heat or fumes, adequate ventilation is necessary. The item should carry the Underwriters Laboratory (UL) or Canadian Standards Association (CSA) seal.

Maintenance and Service

The equipment should be built to withstand hard use, but plan for regular maintenance and service. What conditions are covered in warranties or guarantees? Can minor repairs or parts replacement be handled quickly and easily? Does the distributor or manufacturer deliver, unpack, and test the new equipment? Does the manufacturer offer in-service training on operating or repairing the equipment? The district or school may have a staff person assigned to do repairs. Some distributors and manufacturers provide on-the-spot repairs, while others require that the item be sent to a factory. Does the manufacturer, vendor, or repair center provide replacement or rental while the equipment is being serviced?

Reliability of Dealer, Vendor, Publisher, and Manufacturer

The reputations of the distributor, manufacturer, and vendor are important. Is the manufacturer known for honoring warranties? Is delivery prompt? Are requests for assistance handled efficiently? Do they have outlets near the school? Is support service provided through telephone hotlines, toll-free numbers, backups, preview opportunities, updates, refunds, replacements, and electronic mail? Are the support and service hours convenient? Do they provide demonstration or in-service programs for teachers? Are they willing to negotiate licensing agreements?

Cost

Quality should be weighed over cost, but budget constraints must be considered. Does a competitor offer a similar, less expensive item? Does the lower price represent less quality in terms of performance standards, warranties, or service? Are trade-ins allowed? Should the equipment be leased or purchased?

Is a dedicated machine necessary? Can the facilities support the equipment? Are special furniture or telecommunications circuits necessary? Will the equipment under review require different replacement parts than items already in the collection or additional in-service training to operate it? Will time be needed to train teachers and students to use the equipment? How much maintenance and cleaning will staff need to do? Will special technical training be necessary for minor adjustments?

Sources of Information

Photographs of and specifications for equipment can be found in the annual *Equipment Directory of Audio-Visual, Computer and Video Products* (International Communications Industries Association, 1984-).

SUMMARY

Selection is a subjective activity for which the media specialist is responsible and, therefore, accountable. To fulfill this responsibility, the media specialist must ensure that the collection, as an entity, fulfills its purposes of meeting both the school's goals and instructional, informational, and user needs. To this end the media specialist must judge the value of individual items to the collection. Although selection decisions may be subjective, the media specialist should be able to justify the choice of any item.

A basic criterion for evaluating any material is the impact of its intellectual content. What additional information or new dimensions in presentation will that item add to the collection? Will it appeal to the users?

Another criterion is the appropriateness of the medium to the message. Are the purpose and use of the content promoted or hindered by the form in which the message is delivered?

These are the two basic criteria for judging all potential purchases. Additional criteria specific to various formats, uses, and needs also must be considered.

NOTES

[1]Lillian B. Wehmeyer, "Media and Learning: Present and Future, Part I: Present," *Catholic Library World* 50 (1987): 150.

BIBLIOGRAPHY

California Instructional Video Clearinghouse and California Computer Software Clearinghouse. *1991 Guidelines for CD-ROM in California Schools*. Modesto, CA: California Instructional Video Clearinghouse, 1991.

————. *1991 Guidelines for Computer Software in California Schools*. Modesto, CA: California Instructional Video Clearinghouse, 1991.

————. *1991 Guidelines for Computer-Interactive Videodisc in California Schools*. Modesto, CA: California Instructional Video Clearinghouse, 1991.

Carter, Betty, and Richard F. Abrahamson. *Nonfiction for Young Adults from Delight to Wisdom*. Phoenix, AZ: Oryx Press, 1990.

Donelson, Kenneth L., and Alleen Pace Nilsen. *Literature for Today's Young Adults*. New York: HarperCollins, 1993.

Heinich, Robert; Michael Molenda; and James Russell. *Instructional Media and the New Technologies of Instruction*, 4th ed. New York: Macmillan, 1993.

Huck, Charlotte S. *Children's Literature in the Elementary School*, 5th ed. Fort Worth, TX: Harcourt Brace Jovanovich College Publishers, 1993.

Natke, Nora Jane. "Emerging Technologies in Resource Sharing and Document Delivery." Focus on Technology column. *Journal of Youth Services in Libraries* 5, no. 2 (Winter 1992): 189-92.

Sutherland, Zena, et al. *Children and Books*, 8th ed. New York: HarperCollins, 1990.

Wehmeyer, Lillian B. "Media and Learning: Present and Future, Part I: Present." *Catholic Library World* 50 (1978): 150-52.

CHAPTER 9

CRITERIA by FORMAT

People acquire knowledge through their senses: seeing, hearing, touching, tasting, and smelling. The unique qualities of each format suggest criteria to use in the selection process. This chapter focuses on the characteristics of the different formats and how they should be considered in selection decisions. The formats are arranged in alphabetical order. Each description includes: physical characteristics, advantages, disadvantages, selection criteria, implications for collection development, copyright considerations, and specific bibliographic information and reviewing sources for that format. For bibliographic tools identifying the availability of more than one format, see chapter 13. For selection tools, see chapter 7. For addresses of private and public organizations, see appendix A. For bibliographic information about books and journals, see appendix B. See also this chapter's bibliography.

Although this chapter concentrates on format criteria, the decision to select an item involves an evaluation of all of its various components as well as its value to the collection. Who will use the item? Under what circumstances will it be used? Does it fulfill a unique need? Selection decisions must take into account the physical item, its content, potential use, and appeal.

Art Prints *See* Graphics

Audio Cards *See* Recordings

Books

Hardback and paperback books share similar characteristics but can fulfill different needs. Variations in size and typeface can affect potential use; layout, graphics, and photographs can enrich a text.

Advantages

1. Books are usually designed for individual users.

2. The user can set the pace and stop in the process to recheck information or reread a section.

3. The table of contents and index can provide ready access to information contained in a book.

4. Books are portable and inexpensive.

Disadvantages

1. Use of colored artwork or photography, while adding to appeal or clarity of text, increases the cost of a book.

2. Movement is difficult to illustrate on the printed page.

3. Use with large groups is impractical, except for "Big Books."

4. Contact with books is a personal, internal experience; interaction and feedback for the learner are difficult to achieve except in programmed texts.

Selection Criteria for Hardbacks and Paperbacks

1. Is the shape and weight of the book appropriate for the intended audience?

2. How opaque is the paper? A young or disadvantaged reader may be confused by print that shows through the page.

3. Is the typeface suitable for the intended audience?

4. Is the spacing between words and between lines adequate for the young or reluctant reader?

5. Is the book jacket attractive? Does it reflect the content of the book?

6. Are the illustrations placed within the text where they can be used easily, or are they bound together in an inconvenient location? Are they appropriate for the potential user?

7. Is the medium used for illustrations (for example, line drawings, watercolor, or block prints) appropriate to the setting and mood of the story?

8. Do the page layouts and color add appeal and clarity to the text?

9. When a readability formula, such as Fry or Spache, is applied, is the text appropriate for the intended audience?

Additional Criteria for Hardbacks

1. Are the bindings durable and covers washable? Are reinforced bindings available for titles that will be used by very young children or for titles that will be frequently circulated?

2. Will the hardcover books lie flat when open?

Implications for Collection Development

While selections should cover a wide range of subjects and genres, the reading and maturity levels of students also should be considered. Additional copies of popular books should be ordered; paperbacks are an inexpensive way to meet these demands. A paperback book may appeal to some users more than the same title in hardback.

Copyright Considerations

Print materials, as described in the copyright law, are books, periodicals, pamphlets, newspapers, and similar items. A teacher may make a single copy of a chapter in a book, a short story, short essay, short poem, chart, graph, diagram, cartoon, or picture to use in teaching. For multiple copies the limit is 250 words for poetry and 2,500 words for articles, stories, essays, and picture books, with further limitations on each. A copyright warning notice should appear on each copy of a work. Creation of anthologies, compilations, and collective works are prohibited.

Sources of Information

In addition to the reviewing sources identified in Chapter 7, reviews can be found in *The ALAN Review* (Assembly on Literature for Adolescents, National Council of Teachers of English, 1979-), *Appraisal: Science Books for Young People* (Children's Science Books Review Committee, 1967-), *Bookbird* (International Institute for Children's Literature and Reading Research, and International Board on Books for Young People, 1963-), *Bulletin of the Center for Children's Books* (University of Illinois Press, 1958-), *Children's Catalog* (H. W. Wilson, 1991), *Fiction Catalog* (H. W. Wilson, 1991), *Kirkus Reviews* (Kirkus Service, 1985-), *The Junior High School Library Catalog* (6th ed., H. W. Wilson, 1990), *KLIATT Young Adult Paperback Book Guide* (the *Guide*, 1967-), *Publishers Weekly* (R. R. Bowker, 1872-), and *Senior High School Library Catalog* (14th ed., H. W. Wilson, 1992).

To locate reviews, one can use *Book Review Digest* (H. W. Wilson, 1905-), *Book Review Index* (Gale Research, 1965-), and *Children's Book Review Index* (Gale Research, 1976-).

Information about the availability and cost of books can be found in the Bowker publications *American Book Publishing Record* (1960-), *Books in Print* (1948-), *Subject Guide to Books in Print*, *Children's Books in Print*, *Subject*

Guide to Children's Books in Print, Forthcoming Books, Forthcoming Children's Books, Large Type Books in Print, Books in Print with Book Reviews Plus (on CD-ROM), *Books in Print Plus* (on CD-ROM), *Publishers Trade List Annual*, and *Paperback or Paperbound Books in Print. Bowker's Children's Reference Plus* (on CD-ROM) includes children's titles from other Bowker products, including *Ulrich's International Periodicals Directory, Words on Cassette, Bowker's Complete Video Directory*, periodicals, and bibliographies.

Cartoons *See* Graphics

Cassette Tapes *See* Recordings

CDs *See* Recordings

CD-ROM

Compact disc-read only memory (CD-ROM) can provide access to very large quantities of textual information at relatively low cost. Graphics, sound, software, and other nontext items can mix with text. This format is used for encyclopedias, reference sources, databases, multimedia products, interactive books, games, music, Online Public Access Catalogs (OPACs), computer software, clip art, and graphics.

Advantages

1. A single CD-ROM can store the equivalent of 1,000 books.

2. With a good index, information retrieval is flexible and, with no online charges, use is inexpensive.

3. Use of CD-ROMs helps students learn search strategies before going online, thus saving online charges.

4. CD-ROM discs are small, lightweight, and portable.

5. CD-ROM discs are durable, resistant to fingerprints, and the laser beam reader does not come into direct contact with the disc.

6. More titles are becoming available.

7. Text downloaded from the CD-ROM is ready for word processing or other manipulation.

Disadvantages

1. A CD-ROM player is required.

2. To read the screen requires turning on the computer and CD-ROM player. In some cases, a certain sequence of turning on various pieces of equipment must be followed.

3. Different CD-ROM discs require different retrieval software.

4. Access is slower than on hard drives.

5. Capacity is limited compared to online databases.

6. Information cannot be updated or changed in any way.

7. Use is limited to one student or small group at a time.

Selection Criteria

For a fuller discussion about CD-ROM, see *Guide to Selecting and Acquiring CD-ROMs, Software, and Other Electronic Publications* (American Library Association, 1994). Criteria for CD-ROM and software are similar (see the discussion of software, pages 167-70). Additional questions to consider are:

1. How frequently is the CD-ROM updated?

2. Does the cost of the subscription include the update?

3. Is there an annual fee?

4. Are on-screen tutorials provided?

Implications for Collection Development

Will a bundled package of applications rather than individual ones suit your purposes? Is software on the CD-ROM scaled down or full versions? Do you have a machine dedicated for CD-ROM use?

Plan procedures to establish (1) time limits for individual student use of a CD-ROM workstation, (2) the number of printouts allowed and whether there will be a fee, (3) security for discs, and (4) whether each disc will have a dedicated machine.

Sources of Information

Besides the reviewing sources identified in chapter 7, recommended CD-ROMs can be found in *CD-ROM Collection Builder's Toolkit: The Complete Handbook of Tools for Evaluating CD-ROMs* (Pemberton Press, 1990) and *CD-ROM Software, Dataware, and Hardware: Evaluation, Selection, and Installation* (Libraries Unlimited, 1991).

Charts *See* Graphics

Closed-Circuit Television *See* Video

Databases, Online *See* Online Databases

Diagrams *See* Graphics

Dioramas *See* Models

Films

Films add motion and sound to presentation of information. The format options (black and white, color, silent, sound) provide alternatives that can help to meet the needs of individual users or groups.

Advantages

1. Special visual effects can be produced to encourage learning; examples include compression or extension of time, multiple images on one screen, distortions and illusions, and smooth transitions from one scene to the next.

2. Films can be used with front- and rear-screen projection for individual or group use.

3. Content is locked into a fixed sequence.

Disadvantages

1. A film's usefulness is limited by the timeliness of its content and the extent of its physical deterioration. Care must be take to prevent breakage; films must be cleaned regularly. Film maintenance involves considerable time and cost. This has implications for staffing and scheduling.

2. If films are rented, materials may need to be reserved as long as six months before the date of use.

3. Ready access to information is difficult.

4. Video formats and equipment are less costly.

Selection Criteria

1. Are content and treatment available in a less expensive format?

2. How often will the film be used and by how many people?

3. Are technical qualities, such as photography, sound, editing, and acting, handled in effective, imaginative, and appealing ways?

4. Is the content well organized, imaginative, interesting, and appropriate for the subject and audience?

5. Will the film affect attitudes, build appreciation, develop critical-thinking skills or entertain?

Implications for Collection Development

Increased availability of titles on video parallels the proliferation of video equipment in schools. Although each format (film and video) has unique qualities, having the appropriate equipment available and the ease of its use are factors that will strongly influence a media specialist's decision regarding which format to purchase. Often, video and film collections are maintained at the district level, and individual building users can borrow from the district collections. Plans must be in place for smooth operation in such situations.

Copyright Considerations

Copying or altering an entire film, including preview prints, is an infringement of copyright laws.

Sources of Information

Many selection sources and bibliographic tools review both 16-mm and video versions of a title. See the sources identified in chapters 7 and 13.

Filmstrips

Filmstrips (35-mm) may be black-and-white or color, silent or with sound. The material and equipment can be used by individuals or groups, often in fully lit rooms.

Advantages

1. Filmstrips can be shown on individual viewers or projected for large groups.

2. They are small and easy to store and distribute.

3. The fixed sequence of the frames ensures that visuals will not be lost or shown out of order. Manual operation allows the instructor to control the speed of the presentation and to point out critical items while holding a single frame on the screen.

4. Sound tracks can be operated manually or automatically with proper equipment.

Disadvantages

1. The fixed sequence does not allow flexibility in presentation.

2. With each showing, the film is subject to physical damage, such as scratches or ripped sprocket holes.

3. Today's students and teachers seem to have little interest in this format.

Selection Criteria

1. Is the treatment designed for self- or teacher-directed presentation?

2. Is the length appropriate for the purpose and audience?

3. Are the captions well written and easily readable?

4. Is sound synchronization manual or automatic?

Collection Implications

Available equipment and users' preferences influence whether filmstrips should be purchased with cassettes or disc recordings. Filmstrips that are packaged in containers the size and shape of books can be intershelved with other materials.

Copyright Considerations

Copying filmstrips or transferring them to another format requires written permission from the producer or publisher.

Sources of Information

Sources listed in chapters 7 and 13 cover filmstrips.

Games

A game is a simplified model of a real-life situation. It provides students an opportunity to participate in a variety of roles and events. Games encourage participation, but the number of players may be limited. Players must operate within rules covering the sequence and structure of their actions, as well as a time limit. Some games require using a computer or other equipment. Games available for use with computers tend to be designed for specific hardware and cannot be used with incompatible equipment from other manufacturers.

Advantages

1. Participants become involved in solving problems.

2. Games simulate a realistic environment, encouraging greater participation than other media.

3. Participation usually generates a high degree of interest.

4. Students receive immediate feedback.

5. Some games contribute to affective learning by motivating and supporting learning and attitudinal changes.

Disadvantages

1. Games can be time-consuming, lasting up to several days. The intense involvement in a problem-solving situation is often incompatible with school schedules.

2. The limited number of players can create problems if others want to be involved.

3. Games can distort the social situation they attempt to simulate through omitted details or creator bias.

4. Some experienced teachers are not as aware of the learning value of games as are younger colleagues.

Selection Criteria

1. Is the packaging designed to control parts? Can lost pieces be replaced locally?

2. Are the items durable?

3. Are the directions clear?

4. Are the content, reading level, time requirements, and required dexterity appropriate for the intended audience?

5. Does the game require a computer? Will it run on the media center's equipment?

6. Is the game too costly or elaborate for its intended use?

Implications for Collection Development

Commercially produced and locally developed games should be considered for inclusion in the collection. They serve many uses: educational purposes, practice of manipulative skills, opportunities for interacting with others, and relaxation.

Sources of Information

Booklist occasionally reviews games, as does *Elementary School Library Collection.* For a fuller discussion about video games, see *Guide to Selecting and Acquiring CD-ROMs, Software, and Other Electronic Publications* (American Library Association, 1994).

Graphic Materials

Graphics are nonmoving, opaque, visual materials that provide information through verbal images, such as tables, and visual images, such as drawings. These materials include posters, graphs, charts, tables, diagrams, cartoons, art prints, study prints, drawings, and photographs.

Posters relate a single specific message or idea and should be selected for their clarity of design and attractiveness.

Graphs illustrate the relationship of numerical data. Four major types of graphs are line graphs, which present data on a simple continuous line in relation to a horizontal and vertical grid; bar graphs, which show relationships through use of proportional bars; circle or pie graphs, which show relationships as percentages of a whole; and pictographs or picture graphs, in which symbols present information.

Charts include tables and diagrams to present classified or analyzed data. Tables list or tabulate data, usually in numerical form. Diagrams show relationships between components, such as in a process or device.

Cartoons are stylized drawings, often in series, that tell a story or quickly make a point. The symbols used in political and satirical cartoons may need to be explained to students.

Pictures include flat prints, art prints (reproductions of art works), and study prints. Study prints may have drawings or photographs on one or both sides, with accompanying text or a guide book.

Advantages

1. Graphic materials are inexpensive and widely available.

2. Physical detail can be illustrated with X-rays, electronic microscope photographs, and enlarged drawings.

3. Carefully selected pictures can help to prevent or correct students' misconceptions.

4. Graphic materials are easy to use, and some are easy to produce.

Disadvantages

1. Sizes and distances are often distorted.

2. Lack of color or poor quality may limit proper interpretation.

3. Students need to develop visual literacy in order to use these materials effectively.

4. The size of the material must be large enough for all members of a group to see the same detail.

5. Motion cannot be simulated, only suggested.

6. If an opaque projector is used, the room must be completely darkened.

7. Today, students prefer presentations created by more recently developed technologies.

Selection Criteria

1. Is the information presented in a precise manner?

2. Are less important elements deemphasized or omitted?

3. Is there unity of presentation? Are the basic artistic principles of balance and harmony observed?

4. Is the lettering clear and legible?

5. Is the size large enough for the intended audience?

6. Does an art print give an accurate reproduction of the original work's color and detail?

7. Are the framing and mounting durable?

8. Are there sufficient individual pictures in a series to show a sequence of information?

Implications for Collection Development

If you anticipate that the text on the reverse of a study print will need to be displayed, consider ordering two copies of the print. The teacher's guide to the series also may provide the text on the reverse of a study print.

Circulating graphics, especially for home use, should be laminated, mounted, or protected in some way. Special storage units may be needed so students can examine the materials without damaging them.

Copyright Considerations

Charts, graphs, diagrams, drawings, cartoons, and pictures that are not individually copyrighted can be copied in multiples at the rate of one per book or periodical.

Sources of Information

The catalogs of art museums, art galleries, or reproduction distributors provide ordering information, and many serve as visual reference works. One example is the National Gallery of Art's *Color Reproductions Catalog*, which describes postcards, plaques, and reprints from the gallery's collection. Prints are reviewed in *Booklist*, *Elementary School Library Collection*, and *School Library Journal*.

Interactive Video *See* Video

Kits

Kits contain a variety of formats in one package. The materials may be preselected to present information in a fixed sequence for use by an individual; they may be designed for user self-evaluation. Other kits and packages are less structured, such as a collection of related materials that can be used singly or in any combination by an individual or group.

Advantages

1. Various formats relating to a specific subject are combined into one package.

2. Programmed kits are designed to bring all users to the same level of development.

3. Kits that include sound recordings of accompanying text materials can help the learner who has difficulty reading.

Disadvantages

1. One kit may include material designed for several grade levels.

2. Some kits may include materials that duplicate items in the collection.

3. Kits may be very expensive.

Selection Criteria

1. Does the kit create a unified whole? Is there a relationship among its parts?

2. Is special equipment needed to use the materials included in the collection?

3. Does each item in the kit meet the criteria for that format?

4. Is the kit difficult to use?

5. Are the directions clear? Is adult guidance needed?

6. Does the kit fulfill a unique purpose not met by other materials in the collection?

7. Is there room to store the kit?

Implications for Collection Development

Kits should be selected on the basis of their potential use and appeal; they can be created from materials existing within the collection.

Sources of Information

Kits are reviewed in *Booklist, Curriculum Review, Elementary School Library Collection*, and *School Library Journal*.

Magazines *See* Periodicals and Newspapers

Maps and Globes

Materials included are flat maps, wall maps, and globes. When a map is published in a book, evaluate it in light of criteria here and on pages 139-42.

Advantages

1. Maps can provide a wide range of information: place locations and spellings; significant surface features; distances between places; and scientific, social, cultural, political, historical, literary, and economic data.

2. Wall maps can be studied by groups.

3. Outline maps or globes that are not labeled encourage students to learn the names, shapes, and locations of political and topographical features.

4. Maps are readily available at a wide range of prices.

Disadvantages

1. If a group of students is to examine the same detail in a map, multiple copies or a transparency may be needed.

2. Cartographic details, especially those on geographic, scientific, or political topics, are quickly outdated.

Selection Criteria

1. Is the map aesthetically pleasing? Does the color code help the user interpret the information?

2. Is the depth of detail suitable for the intended audience?

3. Is the map legible? Are symbols representational and clearly designed? Are printed markings of a size and type suitable to a particular map?

4. Is the item durable? Has plasticized or cloth-backed paper been used?

5. Is the surface nonglare?

6. Do the details obscure essential information?

Implications for Collection Development

The collection should include maps of various size to meet the different needs of individuals and groups. Simple neighborhood, community, and state maps should be available to students, as should more complex geographic, political, and literary maps. Maps should be easily accessible; those used frequently should be reinforced or protected.

Sources of Information

Catalogs of map and globe publishers are the easiest to use and least expensive sources of information about the availability of this medium. Federal and state agencies, chambers of commerce, and travel agencies are common sources of highway and historical maps. Reviews are scarce.

Microforms

Microforms include microfilm (reel), microcards, and microfiche (a sheet of microfilm). Storage of magazines and newspapers requires less space with these formats.

Advantages

1. A microform copy of a title is less expensive than the paper version.

2. Microforms can be converted to hard copy with proper equipment.

3. Primary source materials can be protected and stored.

Disadvantages

1. The cost of equipment needed to use a small collection of microforms outweighs the low cost of the microforms.

2. Many users spend more time trying to locate specific sections of the material than they do when using hard copy.

3. These formats have less user appeal than identical content in other formats.

Selection Criteria

1. Does the collection contain the equipment needed to view the specific type of microform being considered?

2. Does the material meet the criteria for its equivalent print formats? Is the reproduction clear?

3. Is the equipment easy to use?

4. The choice of negative or positive reproduction should be based on the equipment available and the users' preferences.

Implications for Collection Development

Newspapers and magazines may be easier to store in microforms, but hardback books may be easier to use than microform copies. Some media specialists find that subscribing to the microfilm edition of a newspaper like *The New York Times* is more economical and efficient than subscribing to the paper edition. If a collection includes professional materials and the proper equipment is available, microform documents, such as those from the ERIC Clearinghouse on Information Resources, can be obtained and stored at a lower cost. Consideration should be given to equipment that can project both microcards and microfiche if both formats are in the collection.

Copyright Considerations

If the original work is copyrighted, copies can be made following the rules applying to the format of the original work.

Sources of Information

For reviews see *Microform Review* (Microform Review, 1972-); for available titles see *Guide to Microforms in Print: Author / Title* (Meckler, 1975-).

Mock-Ups *See* Models

Models

Models, dioramas, and mock-ups are representations of real things. A model is a three-dimensional representation of an object and may be smaller or larger than the real object. Cut-away models show the inside of an object. Dioramas provide an impression of depth, with realistic replicas of objects placed in the foreground against a painted backdrop. Mock-ups stress important elements of the object.

Advantages

1. These formats offer a sense of depth, thickness, height, and width.

2. They can reduce or enlarge objects to an observable size.

3. They can simplify complex objects.

4. The model and mock-up can be disassembled and reassembled to show relationships among parts.

Disadvantages

1. The size of models may limit their use with a group.

2. Some models are difficult to reassemble.

3. Loose parts are easy to misplace or lose.

Selection Criteria

1. Are size relationships of the part to the whole accurately portrayed?

2. Are parts clearly labeled?

3. Are color and composition used to stress important features?

4. Will the construction withstand handling?

Implications for Collection Development

The size of many of these materials creates storage and distribution problems. Packaging models for circulation also may be difficult. Materials produced by staff and students may lack the durability needed for permanent inclusion in the collection.

Sources of Information

Bibliographic and review information is not readily available. Suppliers of scientific equipment, such as Ward's Scientific Establishment, list their products in catalogs.

Newspapers *See* Periodicals and Newspapers

Online Databases

Online databases provide electronic access to information through the use of a computer with a modem connected to a telephone line. Four types of databases are

- full text: includes all the information available for a certain record. Examples: encyclopedias, novels, magazine articles, or entire newspapers.

- bibliographic: provides citations and may include abstracts. Example: magazine index.

- directory: provides a list of information. Example: faculty and staff directory.

- numeric: contains numbers. Example: population and census figures.

Advantages

1. Provide rapid access to large quantities of information.

2. Information is current.

3. Users can locate all the information in a one-step process.

4. Searches can be modified during the process.

5. As users become proficient searchers, cost-effectiveness increases.

6. Immediate feedback lets users know whether information is available and whether their search strategy was too narrow or too broad.

7. Provide complete citations.

8. Bibliographies are easy to generate.

9. Search strategies can be saved. This can help the user who is interrupted during the search.

Disadvantages

1. All the subjects in the curriculum may not be included.

2. Users need training in search strategies.

3. Users need training in filtering and selecting information.

4. Users need training in interpreting the bibliographic information.

5. Teachers and media specialists may be unable to quickly determine if students are downloading information without analyzing it, evaluating it, or synthesizing information from several sources.

6. Teachers may need assistance in designing assignments that call for evaluation of information, rather than merely locating x number of sources on a topic.

7. Materials cited may not be available locally, and interlibrary loan requests may increase.

8. Information generated earlier than 1970 may not be included, limiting historical searches.

9. Full-text information may not include graphics from the original work.

10. Monographs are not covered as adequately as periodical articles and newspapers.

11. Downtime and malfunctions frustrate users.

Selection Criteria

1. Is the intellectual level and reading level appropriate for the intended users?

2. Will the disciplines covered in the database be used?

3. How is the database indexed? Can searches be conducted using title, author, or keywords?

4. Can the database be searched using words not considered subject descriptors (that is, free text searching)?

5. Can the searcher use Boolean logic, connecting search terms with *and*, *or*, and *not*?

6. Are cross-references provided?

7. How frequently is the database updated? Is this appropriate for curriculum needs?

8. How accurate is the information?

9. What years are covered in the database?

10. What services does the vendor offer? These can include offline printing, training, and help with problems.

11. How clear is the documentation? Does the documentation include sample screens and other aids?

12. Is there a print version? Is the online search time less than the time required to search the print version?

13. Is the screen easy to read? Do directions or icons distract the user?

14. Are practice files available? Is free time for practice searches provided?

15. What are the sources of the information on the database? What criteria or standards were used in creating the database?

Implications for Collection Development

Basic questions arise when making the decision to subscribe to and use an online service. Costs may include an annual fee, a per-search fee, a per-hour fee, update fees, and fees for other services. Sufficient equipment will be needed to accommodate the users: Should you lease or purchase the equipment? Licensing agreements identify constraints and limits on use. When you sign such agreements, you agree to the conditions the vendor imposes. Agreements with vendors can affect use. Interlibrary loan requests increase as searchers identify resources not available in the media center. Periodical collections may need to be expanded to support requests for articles cited. Future funding concerns may necessitate the formation of resource-sharing plans to accommodate the increase in requests for resources not owned by the media center.

Copyright

License agreements usually define what the publisher considers to be fair use of the product. Limitations may include the amount of information that can be downloaded or the number of users who may access the service at the same time.

Sources of Information

In-depth reviews are found in *Online: The Magazine of Online Information Systems* (Online, Inc., 1977-) and *Database: The Magazine of Database Reference and Review* (Online, Inc., 1978-). Both carry articles about database and use search aids. *Online & CD-ROM Review* (Learned Information, Inc., 1977-) provides lists of new databases.

Further information about selecting, using, and managing databases is described in *Online Searching Goes to School* (Oryx Press, 1989), *Selection and Evaluation of Electronic Resources* (Libraries Unlimited, 1994), and *Guide to Selecting and Acquiring CD-ROMs, Software, and Other Electronic Publications* (American Library Association, 1994).

Pamphlets

Pamphlets are multiple-page printed materials that are frequently housed in the vertical file rather than shelved as books. Local, state, and national governments as well as associations or businesses publish them. Pamphlets and other vertical-file materials can provide a wealth of current and special treatments of timely subjects. Government documents frequently provide concise and up-do-date information about a topic, although the vocabulary may be beyond the elementary school student's comprehension.

Advantages

1. Pamphlets are inexpensive or free. Duplicate copies can be readily obtained for topics of high interest.

2. Often, information found in pamphlets is more current than that found in other print media, except magazines and newspapers.

3. Pamphlets can provide a variety of viewpoints on a subject.

4. Pamphlets often discuss subjects unavailable elsewhere in the collection. Their treatment is usually brief, focusing on a specific subject.

Disadvantages

1. Because of their size and format, pamphlets are easily misfiled.

2. The flimsy construction of pamphlets limits repeated use.

Selection Criteria

1. Because many pamphlets are sponsored by groups or businesses, the extent of advertising must be considered. Does advertising dominate the presentation and distract from or distort the information?

2. Regardless of whether the item contains advertising, is the message presented without bias and propaganda? Pamphlets presenting various viewpoints may be needed for specific instructional units. Does the viewpoint interfere with objectivity?

3. Is the information already provided elsewhere in the collection?

Implications for Collection Development

Pamphlets are an inexpensive way to provide balanced information on controversial issues. Materials should be readily accessible and reviewed periodically for timeliness. Because many pamphlets are undated, media specialists find it helpful to date them as they are filed. This simplifies the reevaluation process.

Sources of Information

The Vertical File and Its Alternatives: A Handbook (Libraries Unlimited, 1992) offers advice about the acquisition, processing, and management of materials and identifies the wide range of sources. *U.S. Government Publications for the School Library Media Center* (2d ed., Libraries Unlimited, 1991) provides a wide-ranging list of available materials. *Guide to Popular*

U.S. Government Publications (2d ed., Libraries Unlimited, 1990) covers 2,500 publications.

Other lists appear in *Changing Times* (Kiplinger Washington Agency, 1941-), *The Consumer Information Catalog* (Consumer Information Center, General Services Administration, 1977-), *Good Housekeeping* (Hearst, 1885-), *Government Periodical and Subscription Services* (Superintendent of Documents, 1960-), *Government Reference Books: A Biennial Guide to U.S. Government Publications* (Libraries Unlimited, 1970-), *Monthly Catalog of United States Government Publications* (U.S. Government Printing Office, 1895-), *New Books: Publications for Sale by the Government Printing Office* (U.S. Government Printing Office, 1982-), *U.S. Government Books* (U.S. Government Printing Office, 1982-), *Using Government Documents: A How-To-Do-It Manual for School Librarians* (Neal-Schuman, 1992), and *Vertical File Index: A Subject and Title Index to Selected Pamphlet Materials* (H. W. Wilson, 1955-).

Periodicals and Newspapers

There are two types of periodicals and newspapers: general, such as *Time* and *Ranger Rick's Nature Magazine,* and instructional, such as *Scholastic Sprint* or *Literary Cavalcade.*

Advantages

1. Periodicals offer short stories, participatory activities for young users, and extensive illustrations.

2. Some periodicals solicit contributions of writing or illustrations from students.

3. Many periodicals suggest activities that adults can use with students.

Disadvantages

1. Circulation controls are difficult to establish. Many magazines on popular topics disappear from collections when students take them or teachers borrow them for a "great" bulletin board pattern.

2. When a large number of children are involved, reader-participation activities (such as fill in the blanks, connect the dots, or puzzles) need to be copied or laminated so they can be used more than once. Copying is subject to copyright restrictions.

3. Storage space that provides easy access to several volumes of a journal may be difficult or expensive to provide.

4. If fold-outs and cut-outs, such as calendars or photographs of sport figures or animals, are removed from periodicals, portions of the text may be eliminated.

5. The amount and quality of advertisements in journals may detract from their usefulness.

6. Storage can be a problem.

Selection Criteria

1. Is the content of interest to students and teachers?

2. Are subjects treated clearly in a well-organized manner?

3. Are the illustrations pertinent and adequately reproduced?

4. Is the format appropriate for the purpose of the magazine and the intended audience?

5. Are large-print items needed by any users?

6. Is the journal indexed? Commonly used indexes include *Children's Magazine Guide: Subject Index to Children's Magazines* (R. R. Bowker, 1948); *Abridged Readers' Guide to Periodical Literature* (H. W. Wilson, 1935-); *Readers' Guide to Periodical Literature* (H. W. Wilson, 1900-); *Canadian Periodical Index* (Info Globe, 1986-); online indexes, such as CARL's UnCover; and CD-ROM indexes, such as EBSCO's *Magazine Articles Summaries* (*MAS*).

Implications for Collection Development

Local, state, national, and international newspapers should be represented in the collection. If classes subscribe to instructional newspapers, the media specialist may find it useful to have a copy of the teacher's edition in the media center. The length of time periodicals are kept will depend on patterns of use and availability of storage facilities. A common practice is to acquire microform editions for items needed after five years and to either clip the others for the vertical file or discard them.

Copyright Considerations

A chart, graph, diagram, cartoon, picture, or article can be copied from a periodical or newspaper for use by a teacher. Word limits for multiple copies for classroom use are 250 words for poetry, 2,500 words for articles. A copyright warning notice should appear on each copy. Creation of anthologies, compilations, and collective works are prohibited.

Sources of Information

Magazines for Children: A Guide for Parents, Teachers, and Librarians (2d ed., American Library Association, 1991) offers evaluative comments about 90 magazines of interest to children through age 14 and provides information about editions for the blind. *Magazines for Young People: A Children's Magazine Guide, Companion Volume* (2d ed., R. R. Bowker, 1991) evaluates more than 1,100 magazines. *Serials Review* (Pierian Press, 1986-) is the major reviewing source for this medium.

Posters *See* Graphics

Radio Broadcasting, Educational

Electronic signals transmitted over AM and FM radio frequencies provide communication for geographically dispersed populations. Two major sources of educational radio programs are radio stations and National Public Radio (NPR).

Advantages

1. Radio provides information to persons in areas that lack satellites for video transmission or access to the electronic media.

2. Radio delivers standard messages over large geographical areas.

3. It is less expensive to operate than a television studio.

4. It is an effective and flexible medium for combining music and speech for storytelling programs.

Disadvantages

1. Because broadcast schedules are established by the broadcaster, classroom schedules may need to be adjusted to make use of a desired program.

2. It may be difficult to create or find a setting in which large groups can listen to a program.

3. If prerecorded materials are available, the cost is difficult to justify.

Selection Criteria

1. Is this the only source of the information?

2. Do teacher's guides, program guides, and announcements provide information to facilitate a program's use?

Implications for Collection Development

Information about forthcoming programs should be provided.

Copyright Concerns

The local radio station or NPR affiliate can provide copyright information about their programs.

Sources of Information

Daily programming or series broadcast guides can alert you to forth-coming programs of interest. Ask your local radio station or NPR affiliate about other services it offers.

Recordings

Audio formats commonly found in schools include cassette tapes, phonograph records, compact discs, and audio cards. Each format requires appropriate equipment.

Advantages

1. Recordings are portable and easy to use.

2. A wide range of content is available.

3. Equipment is fairly easy to use and relatively inexpensive.

4. Music and sound effects can create moods or draw attention to specific information.

5. Use can be easily scheduled.

6. Information is locked into a fixed sequence. Easy retrieval can be achieved through use of bands on discs or counters on tapes.

7. Most students are familiar with the equipment.

8. Compact discs retain superb sounds for hundreds of playings.

Disadvantages

1. People can become bored when listening for an extended period.

2. Different equipment is needed to accommodate the variety of tape speeds and track arrangements.

3. Use with large groups requires amplifiers.

4. Compact discs and cassettes are easier to steal than vinyl discs.

5. Cassette cases break easily. Have a supply of empty cases on hand.

Selection Criteria

1. Does narration begin with attention-getting words to capture the listener's attention? Are keywords or key statements emphasized to help the listener? Are the sentences short and simple?

2. Is the sound free of distortion?

3. Are the length and quality of the performance appropriate to the intended audience?

4. Do labels give enough information to distinguish one item from another? Do labels give playback information?

5. Are tapes and discs compatible with available equipment?

6. Is equipment easy to use and portable?

7. Does the equipment ensure accurate, high-quality reproduction?

8. If the recording is based on a book, is the recording true to the original? Is the reader an interesting person? Is the reader competent?

9. Are the accompanying materials, such as a teacher's guide, of high quality?

Implications for Collection Development

Provision should be made for individual and group use of music, documentaries, narrations, and drill masters. Storage for discs should be easily accessible and prevent warping. Cassettes are easier to store than discs. However, compact discs are less likely to be damaged in circulation than cassettes or vinyl discs. Compact discs require less care than vinyl discs.

Copyright Concerns

Reproducing musical recordings or converting them to another format requires written permission.

Sources of Information

Recommendations for recordings appear in *The New Penguin Guide to Compact Discs and Cassettes* (Viking Penguin, 1990), *Schwann Opus* (Schwann, 1949-), and *Words on Cassette* (R. R. Bowker, annual).

In addition to the sources described in chapter 13, recordings are listed in *Schwann Spectrum* (Schwann, 1949-) and in radio station catalogs, such as *The Audio Store Catalog* (Wisconsin Public Radio).

Realia *See* Specimens

Records, Phonograph *See* Recordings

Sculpture

Sculpture and sculpture reproductions add another means for learning through touch and for developing aesthetic tastes.

Advantages

1. Sculpture reproductions are becoming more readily available and are fairly inexpensive.

2. The use of sculpture is not limited to art study but can be used in social science, mathematics, language arts, science, and other subject areas.

3. Displaying the pieces about the media center can enhance the room's atmosphere and solve a storage problem.

Disadvantages

1. An item may be too small to be used by a group.

2. Storage may pose a problem.

3. The size and weight of some pieces may make circulation awkward.

Selection Criteria

1. Is the item made of durable material to withstand the touching that sculpture invites and which is necessary to fully appreciate the work?

2. Are reproductions true to the originals?

Implications for Collection Development

The range of subjects should reflect the various areas of the curriculum as well as interests of the students.

Sources of Information

Many museums, such as the Metropolitan Museum of Art, and some commercial firms make reproductions of sculptures. You will probably find examples on display at state and national conferences. Request museum catalogs.

Slides

Two types of slides are commonly found in media collections: (1) two-by-two-inch slides used in projectors with trays, carousels, or cartridges, on slide sorters, or in individual viewers and (2) microslides of biological specimens used with a microprojector.

Advantages

1. Color visuals can be produced economically.

2. Their size permits compact packaging and storage with ease of distribution and circulation.

3. Instructors can adapt sequencing and can edit according to their needs.

4. Sound can be ordered or can be added with the proper equipment.

5. Microslides permit an entire class to view microscopic materials, rather than requiring each student to have a microscope.

6. Slides can be projected for an indefinite time to accommodate discussion.

Disadvantages

1. Single slides are difficult to access rapidly.

2. Although slides can be processed or duplicated inexpensively, this takes time and depends on the quality and speed of local laboratory services. Fast service is often available but at substantially higher costs. Copyright restrictions apply.

Selection Criteria

1. Are art slides faithful to the original?

2. Are mountings durable?

3. Is there continuity to the set of slides?

4. Are content and length of presentation appropriate for the intended purpose and audience?

Implications for Collection Development

Effective group use of slides may require projectors with remote-control features and lenses of appropriate focal length. Ensure that slide storage and display units are compatible with the collection's equipment. Student- and teacher-produced slides should meet the criteria used for purchased items.

Copyright Considerations

Copying slide sets in their entirety, altering a program, or transferring a program to another format requires written permission. Copying a few slides is permitted when fair-use criteria are met.

Sources of Information

Slide Buyer's Guide: An International Directory of Slide Sources for Art and Architecture (6th ed., Libraries Unlimited, 1990) identifies companies, museums, and institutions that sell, rent, or exchange slides.

Software

Computer software and courseware (instructional software) are available through educational institutes and consortia, commercial vendors, software companies, and textbook publishers.

Advantages

1. Software and courseware can be used for creative problem-solving, drill and practice, testing, recreation, and guidance.

2. Individual and self-paced interaction are special instructional features of these systems. Programs can provide the reinforcement and stimulation needed by students who have learning disabilities.

3. Programs with branching allow the student with correct answers to move into more difficult questions, while allowing those who need to review and repeat responses the opportunity to do so.

4. These systems allow rapid information retrieval.

5. They provide instant calculations in programs where concept building is more important than mathematical manipulation.

6. Use of computers can be a highly motivating experience for disabled, gifted, and average learners, thus bringing diverse groups to the media center.

Disadvantages

1. Teachers who are not trained to use computers may be reluctant to use them in teaching.

2. Lack of compatibility of software and equipment can limit use.

3. Ignorance of special features of computers and poor programming can lead to improper use of the medium to teach material that could be taught more effectively using programmed instruction or other techniques. An extreme example of this is a program that is, in essence, an electronic page turner.

4. There are more software programs designed to appeal to boys than to girls.

Selection Criteria

A chief consideration is the compatibility of software and equipment.

1. Is the content more appropriate for presentation on a computer than on other instructional media?

2. Is the program designed to run on the user's computer? The computer's brand, model, memory size, operating system, storage format, display technology (monitor and graphics system), and accessories (mouse, game paddles, etc.) must be considered.

3. Is the computer's disk operating system compatible with the software program?

4. Does the user control the rate and sequence of the content presentation (unless timing is an integral part of the program)?

5. Can the user enter, use, and exit the program with relative ease and independence?

6. Are the responses or feedback to answers—both correct and incorrect—appropriate?

7. Is the software designed to lead students to correct answers or remedial instruction when assistance is needed?

8. Are on-screen instructions clear and easily understood?

9. Are the student guides and work sheets, the teacher guide, and technical information adequate and comprehensive?

10. Is the documentation clear and carefully indexed?

11. Does the program require the learner to be familiar with special terms or symbols related to computers?

Implications for Collection Development

What will be the scope of the software collection? Which strategies will be included: tutorial, drill and practice, simulation, entertainment, or problem solving? Will teacher's opinions be sought in deciding priorities among these strategies?

Copyright Considerations

Generally, one archival or back-up copy of each program is permitted. When students and teachers have access to software, warning notices about software copying should be posted. If your school has a LAN (local area network) or WAN (wide area network), obtain a license to use software on the network.

Sources of Information

For a fuller discussion about software, see *Guide to Selecting and Acquiring CD-ROMs, Software, and Other Electronic Publications* (American Library Association, 1994). In addition to the reviewing sources noted in chapter 7, reviews and recommendations can be found in *Compute* (Computer Publications, 1979-); *The Computing Teacher: Journal of the International Society for Technology in Education* (International Council for Computers in Education, 1979-); *Digest of Software Reviews: Education* (School and Home Courseware, 1983-); *The Education Software Selector (TESS)* (Teachers College Press, 1984-); *Electronic Learning* (Scholastic, 1981-); *Only the Best: The Annual Guide to Highest-Rated Educational Software, Preschool-Grade 12* (R. R. Bowker, 1989-); *Software Reviews on File* (Facts on File, 1985-); and *Technology & Learning* (Peter Li, 1980-).

Availability information can be found in *Software Encyclopedia* (R. R. Bowker, 1985-), *Software Information! For Apple II Computers* (Black Box, 1990), and *Swift's Directory of Educational Software for the IBM PC* (Sterling Swift, 1982-).

For a discussion of the software industry, evaluation forms to use in selecting software packages, and guides to inexpensive and free software, see *Microcomputer Software Sources: A Guide for Buyers, Librarians, Programmers, Businesspeople, and Educators* (Libraries Unlimited, 1990).

Specimens

Specimens include real objects, such as artifacts, stamps, postcards, plants, and animals, which may be preserved or imbedded in plastic. Specimens carry a special impact because they bring the real world into the hands of inquisitive users.

Advantages

1. Specimens can be handled and closely examined by students.

2. Some specimens, such as stamps and postcards, can be acquired inexpensively from a wide range of sources, including the students themselves.

3. Live specimens may be borrowed from or handled by staff of local zoos, museums, and breeders.

4. The handling and care of live specimens has many benefits for students and can provide an area of lively interest in the media center, especially at elementary schools.

5. Fragrant specimens, such as plants and cocoa beans, provide means for young people to learn through smell.

Disadvantages

1. Glass containers can be easily dropped and broken.

2. Some items may be too fragile or too small for more than one person to use at a time. Other items, such as birds' nests and stuffed animals, are hard to keep clean.

3. Live specimens need proper care: aquariums, terrariums, or cages may be needed, and special growing conditions may need to be simulated.

4. Live specimens are most successful in media enters where adults share the students' appreciation of plants, fish, reptiles, and animals. Are you prepared to find the snake that slipped out of someone's hand or to track down the hamster scurrying in and out of the shelving units?

5. Live specimens need care when school is not in session. Sometimes, arrangements for students to take specimens home over vacations can be made.

Selection Criteria

1. Is there a display area where specimens can be observed by several students at a time?

2. Are you or is someone else willing and available to take care of the live specimens?

3. Are the specimens safe to handle?

Implications for Collection Development

Avoid duplicating materials found in other parts of the school, such as the science laboratory.

Sources of Information

Journals like *Science and Children* have articles about the use of specimens and sometimes review these materials. Scientific supply houses, such as Ward's Natural Science Establishment, Denoyer-Geppert, and Hubbard Scientific Company, sell specimens and storage units. Local museums, zoos, and botanical gardens may loan materials to schools and provide speakers or visual programs about the materials.

Study Prints *See* Graphics

Tables *See* Graphics

Tape Recordings *See* Recordings

Textbooks and Related Materials

Instructional systems encompass a broad range of materials designed to meet stated instructional objectives. Materials include textbooks (basic and supplementary), work books, and multimedia packages (kits). These materials have been developed by commercial companies, school districts, and educational agencies. Textbooks may be used as chief sources of information or as supplementary information sources.

Advantages

1. Instruction is in a fixed sequence but can be reorganized by the instructor.

2. The table of contents and index provide rapid access to information.

3. Each student may have a copy.

4. The teacher's editions offer suggestions for related materials and activities.

5. Textbooks are field-tested, and the results of those tests can be requested and evaluated.

6. Users can move at their own pace.

Disadvantages

1. Adoption of textbooks often implies they will be used over a number of years.

2. Textbooks can limit a teacher's creativity.

3. Textbooks may encourage rote learning rather than stimulate exploration.

4. The content to be covered can be imposed by the limitations of the text.

5. A textbook's bibliographies may be out-of-print or fail to reflect appropriate resources in the collection.

Selection Criteria

The selection of textbooks or other instructional systems is usually done by teachers in consultation with media specialists. In some situations, the media specialist may not be involved, but the criteria presented here provide basic information necessary for selection. A media specialist may want to purchase a single copy of particular text for its information, even though it is not used in the classroom.

1. Is the content accurate and objective?

2. Does the content represent a broad spectrum of viewpoints on a given topic?

3. Are the visual materials keyed to the text?

4. Are bibliographies up-to-date? Do they include a wide range of formats?

5. Is the treatment appropriate for the intended purpose and audience?

6. Is the arrangement chronological or systematic?

7. Is the presentation free of racial or sexual stereotyping?

8. Is the type clear, and are the pages uncrowded?

Implications for Collection Development

In some schools, media specialists are responsible for the organization, storage, distribution, and inventory of textbooks. Whether or not you have this responsibility, you need to be aware of the content, the materials recommended in the bibliographies, and the potential use of textbooks as information sources.

Copyright Concerns

Work books, exercises, test booklets and other consumable works may not be copied.

Sources of Information

Textbooks and related teaching materials, such as charts and work books, are listed in *El-Hi Textbooks and Serials in Print* (R. R. Bowker, 1985-). Reviews can be found in *Curriculum Review* (Curriculum Advisory Service, 1960-) and the journals of professional teacher associations, such as *Reading Teacher* (International Reading Association, 1957-).

Toys

As with games, toys, such as blocks, puzzles, and construction materials, allow students opportunities to develop coordination and to learn through touch, manipulation, and sight.

Advantages

1. Play is a way of exploring natural laws and relationships.

2. Toys can be used to develop perceptual motor skills.

3. Dolls or stuffed animals can be used to develop affective skills.

4. Toys can be used by individuals or groups.

5. Toys are inexpensive and can be made locally.

174 / Criteria by Format

Disadvantages

1. Directions and parts may be lost.

2. The various shapes of toys can create storage problems.

3. Safety requirements must be observed.

4. Some toys can be used by a limited number of people.

Selection Criteria

1. Can the child play with the toy independently, or is adult guidance needed?

2. Has the user's developmental stage been considered in the selection?

3. Is color used to guide the use of the toy, or is it mere decoration?

4. Is the toy constructed of solid materials?

5. How fragile is the toy?

6. Can it be used without all of its parts? Can replacement parts be purchased or made in-house?

7. Is the material nonflammable?

8. Can the toy be washed or cleaned?

Implications for Collection Development

Selection should be based on knowledge of the developmental needs of children served. You may need to provide duplicate items so that the same toy can be used by more than one student or can be used in the media center and also circulated.

Sources of Information

The Consumer Products Safety Commission lists toys considered unsafe for children.

Transparencies

Transparencies are single sheets of acetate or plastic bearing visual or verbal information that may be used in multiple sets as overlays. They are shown to large groups using an overhead projector. Some books and reference materials use transparencies as overlays on illustrations to demonstrate relationships or sequence.

Advantages

1. The instructor or presenter can face the audience in a lighted room, thus facilitating interpersonal exchange and note taking.

2. The user can quickly edit, sequence, and review the presentation.

3. The presenter can write on the transparency while it is being projected or can use a pencil-sized pointer.

4. Local production is relatively inexpensive and can be accomplished with minimum skill.

5. Overlays can be used to add information to a base visual.

6. Within certain limits, motion can be simulated.

7. The equipment is simple to operate and involves little maintenance, except bulb replacement.

Disadvantages

1. Storage and circulation of transparencies may be more complex than with slides.

2. Multicolor transparencies may be more expensive than 35-mm slides.

3. A special tilted screen may be needed to avoid a distorted visual image.

4. Unless equipment is properly positioned, it may obstruct the view of the screen.

5. There is a lack of standardization in size and packaging of transparencies.

6. Complex overlays may create problems during presentations.

Selection Criteria

1. Does the subject lend itself to transparency rather than poster, mounted picture, slide, or other medium?

2. Is the lettering clear?

3. Is the information uncluttered?

4. Is the mounting secure?

5. Is the set logically sequenced and organized?

6. Is the transparency clearly labeled?

7. Are overlays easily manipulated?

Implications for Collection Development

In schools where teachers use the lecture method, more overhead projectors are needed than in schools where individualized instruction is given. In schools where many teachers and students use overhead projectors during the same time period, each classroom should have its own overhead projector. Production of transparencies by students or teachers requires materials, equipment, and work areas.

Sources of Information

See chapters 7 and 13.

Video

Video materials include materials transmitted by broadcast television, those transmitted within a closed-circuit television system, videotapes, and videodiscs. Broadcast programs bring to viewers people, places, and events they would not otherwise see. Teleconferencing allows interaction among presenters and viewers, for example, the elementary school students who interviewed astronauts during a flight. Live, interactive television presentations add immediacy.

Young people enter school as experienced television consumers. The school can capitalize on students' background while helping them to become more critical viewers. At the same time, students' exposure to television, or excessive use by teachers, can cause inattentiveness and passivity.

Videodiscs, which are the size of a 33-rpm record, are read by a laser beam. Videodisc readers can randomly search any segment and instantaneously access it. Videodisc programs provide three types of interactivity: (1) videodisc players used with or without a computer connection, (2) videodisc players used with a computer program within the videodisc, and (3) videodisc players connected to a computer controlled by software. Videodisc programs include movies; documentaries; interactive tutorials; instructional games; multimedia libraries of interrelated information from video clips, still frames, sound, maps, text, and graphics; visual databases; and simulations.

Advantages

1. Many of the visual effects used in filmmaking to enhance presentations can be used in the production of video.

2. As in films, the content and sequence of the program is locked in, but if it is recorded, the program can be stopped or replayed.

3. Systems can be created to allow simultaneous viewing in more than one location in the school.

4. Videocassette are easy to store, maintain, and use without damage.

5. The format is familiar to users.

6. Videodiscs provide fast and precise access to frames and segments.

7. Videodiscs can hold a still frame with no damage.

8. Videodiscs have two audio tracks, so that stereo sound or two separate tracks can be heard.

9. Videodiscs, unlike videotapes and videocassettes, cannot be erased.

10. Interactive videos can be used by individuals or small groups of two to five people.

Disadvantages

1. Small monitors limit the size of the audience, unless multiple monitors or video-projector systems are provided.

2. Compatible equipment is necessary.

3. On videodiscs, motion sequences are limited to 30 minutes, less than a videotape's capacity.

4. Videodiscs can be intentionally damaged.

5. Interactive videodiscs may be expensive.

Selection Criteria

1. Does the telecast make use of the full range of television production techniques, or is it a filmed lecture?

2. Selection criteria for films can apply (see pages 144-45).

3. Is the original case protective? Is it oversized, or does it contain another cassette or additional material, and will this cause shelving and circulation difficulties? Does the outside information accurately, attractively, and effectively advertise the contents? Is the title the same on the case, cassette, and title frame?

4. Does the interactive video provide multiple interactive paths?

Implications for Collection Development

This format has become popular because of its ease of use and the range of selections. When selecting video materials for the collection, media specialists face the question whether to buy, lease, or rent. Like other formats, video media should be previewed. When evaluating materials that originally appeared as films or filmstrips, consider the appropriateness of the format. Is the video merely a copy of the filmstrip? Videos produced by students, teachers, and staff—if they meet the selection criteria—should be retained in collection.

Receiving and playback equipment should be chosen for ease of use and durability.

Copyright Considerations

Copying or altering an entire video requires written permission. Off-air recordings may be retained for no more than 45 calendar days; then they must be erased. They may be shown to a class twice within 10 teaching days, and the copy should include the copyright notice.

Sources of Information

Study guides to forthcoming broadcasts are available from a number of sources, including the networks. General information is found in *TV Guide* and local television listings. State and regional public broadcasting stations frequently have announcements or newsletters for the school audience. *C-SPAN Newsletter* includes programming schedules and articles of interest to teachers.

Reviews are covered in *The Video Librarian* (Randy Pitman, 1986-) and *The Video Rating Guide for Libraries*, (ABC-Clio, 1990-). Recommended videos are listed in *Best Videos for Children and Young Adults: A Core Collection for Libraries* (ABC-Clio, 1990) and *Recommended Videos for Schools* (ABC-Clio, 1991). *The Video Source Book* (National Video Clearinghouse, 1979-) describes more than 125,000 programs available on videocassette, videodisc, and videotape. For a fuller discussion about videotapes and videodiscs, see *Guide to Selecting and Acquiring CD-ROMs, Software, and Other Electronic Publications* (American Library Association, 1994).

Films and videocassette also can be obtained through federal offices, such as the National Audiovisual Center and the National Gallery of Art. Nonprofit agencies that sell or rent videos include: the Agency for Instructional

Technology (AIT), which coordinates cooperative instructional television projects in the United States and Canada; Children's Television Workshop, which produces and distributes programming and television-related materials, including the well-known *Sesame Street*; and PBS Video, Public Broadcasting Service.

SUMMARY

When selecting materials, consider who will use the materials, what formats they prefer, how they will use the materials, and whether appropriate equipment is available. Few collections will include every format described. Some materials may be outside the scope of a school's collection policy; others may not be suitable for a particular group of users.

Advances in technology will bring new formats to the market. As new materials and formats appear, consider their relevance to the collection. Does a new format meet needs not met by earlier formats? Will the new format offer enough subject coverage to justify purchasing the necessary equipment? Does the new format add a dimension to content unavailable in other media? If not, it may not be a good investment. Further developments will bring new materials to the media center if they are truly advantageous and if the products are selected and implemented with the user in mind.

BIBLIOGRAPHY

Barron, Ann E., and Gary W. Orwig. *New Technologies for Education: A Beginner's Guide*. Englewood, CO: Libraries Unlimited, 1993.

Bosch, Stephen; Patricia Promis; and Chris Sugnet. *Guide to Selecting and Acquiring CD-ROMs, Software, and Other Electronic Publications*. Acquisition Guidelines no. 9. Chicago: American Library Association, 1994.

California Instructional Video Clearinghouse and California Computer Software Clearinghouse. *1991 Guidelines for CD-ROM in California Schools*. Modesto, CA: Clearinghouse, 1991.

———. *1991 Guidelines for Computer-Interactive Videodisc in California Schools*. Modesto, CA: Clearinghouse, 1991.

———. *1991 Guidelines for Computer Software in California Schools*. Modesto, CA: Clearinghouse, 1991.

Costa, Betty; Marie Costa; and Larry Costa. *A Micro Handbook for Small Libraries and Media Centers*, 3d ed. Englewood, CO: Libraries Unlimited, 1991.

Crawford, Walt. *Current Technologies in the Library*. Boston: G. K. Hall, 1988.

Dickinson, Gail K. *Selection and Evaluation of Electronic Resources*. Englewood, CO: Libraries Unlimited, 1994.

Ellison, John W., and Patricia Ann Coty, eds. *Nonbook Media: Collection Management and User Services*. Chicago: American Library Association, 1987.

Epler, Doris M. *Online Searching Goes to School*. Phoenix, AZ: Oryx Press, 1989.

Heinich, Robert; Michael Molenda; and James D. Russell. *Instructional Media and the New Technologies of Instruction*, 4th ed. New York: Macmillan, 1993.

Huck, Charlotte S.; Susan Hepler; and Janet Hickman. *Children's Literature in the Elementary School*, 5th ed. Fort Worth, TX: Harcourt Brace Jovanovich College Publishers, 1993.

Reed, Mary Hutchings. *The Copyright Primer for Librarians and Educators*. Chicago: American Library Association; Washington, DC: National Education Association, 1987.

Reynolds, Angus, and Ronald H. Anderson. *Selecting and Developing Media for Instruction*, 3d ed. New York: Van Nostrand Reinhold, 1992.

Richey, Ginny, and Kathryn Tuten-Puckett. "Toys Promote Learning in the Early Literacy Skills Project at Monroe County Public Library." *Indiana Libraries* 82 (1989): 64-70.

Scholtz, James C. *Developing and Maintaining Video Collections in Libraries*. Santa Barbara, CA: ABC-Clio, 1989.

Sitter, Clara L. *The Vertical File and Its Alternatives: A Handbook*. Englewood, CO: Libraries Unlimited, 1992.

Sorge, Dennis H.; John P. Campbell; and James D. Russell. "Evaluating Interactive Video: Software and Hardware." *TechTrends* 38, no. 3 (April/May 1993): 19-26.

Stewart, Linda. "Picking CD-ROMs for Public Use." *American Libraries* 18, no. 9 (October 1989): 738-40.

Stewart, Linda; Katherine S. Chiang; and Bill Coons. *Public Access CD-ROMs in Libraries: Case Studies*. Westport, CT: Meckler, 1990.

Sutherland, Zena, and May Hill Arbuthnot. *Children and Books*, 8th ed. New York: HarperCollins, 1991.

Swisher, Robert; Linda D. Pye; Bettie Estes-Rickner; and Malena Merriam. "Magazine Collections in Elementary School Library Media Centers." *School Library Journal* 37, no. 11 (November 1991): 40-43.

Vlcek, Charles W. *Adoptable Copyright Policy: Copyright Policy and Manuals Designed for Adoption by Schools, Colleges & Universities*. Washington, DC: Association for Educational Communications and Technology, 1992.

Vlcek, Charles W., and Raymond V. Wiman. *Managing Media Services: Theory and Practice*. Englewood, CO: Libraries Unlimited, 1989.

CHAPTER 10

MEETING CURRICULAR AND INSTRUCTIONAL NEEDS

A major purpose of the collection is to support school programs. The variety of instructional programs and practices in a school creates diverse demands upon its media collection. To be well versed about instructional programs, the media specialist must understand the school's approaches to education, be familiar with the curriculum plans, and be knowledgeable about the purposes and demands of the teaching models used.

The selection of teaching models reflects an individual's view of education. Each model depends on a teaching support system of human and material resources. The underlying principles of a particular teaching model provide the basis for selecting material resources with appropriate content and formats.

The curriculum in two schools may be identical, but the teaching models may not be similar. This overview will help you identify teaching models in your school. Some questions to explore are

- Does the school have a unified approach to the educational process?

- How are the teaching methods similar?

- Do some teachers prefer one method over another?

- Are specific methods recommended in the curriculum plans, or do teachers have freedom to choose their own methods?

As you work with teachers and other staff members, acquaint yourself with their attitudes, programs, and needs. This insight will help you plan the most appropriate services and media collection. This chapter focuses on the instructional program and the needs of the professional staff. Chapter 11 emphasizes subject-oriented needs. Chapter 12 will focus on needs of specific groups and individuals.

APPROACHES TO EDUCATION

People hold various opinions about the purpose of educating children. Society values different goals for education at different times. Two national documents illustrate different goals. *National Goals for Education* (U.S. Department of Education, 1990) resulted from the 1990 nation's governors conference. Lauro F. Cavazo, then secretary of education, states the purpose of the meeting was to "establish national education goals that focused on results, accountability, and flexibility in the use of federal education resources."[1] *What Work Requires of Schools* (U.S. Department of Labor, 1991) was created by the Secretary of Labor's Commission on Achieving Necessary Skills.

National Education Goals states that, by the year 2000,

1. All children in America will start school ready to learn.

2. The high school graduation rate will increase to at least 90 percent.

3. American students will leave grades four, eight, and twelve having demonstrated competency in challenging subject matter, including English, mathematics, science, history, and geography; and every school in America will ensure that all students learn to use their minds well, so they may be prepared for responsible citizenship, further learning, and productive employment in our modern economy.

4. U.S. students will be first in the world in science and mathematics achievement.

5. Every adult American will be literate and will possess the knowledge and skills necessary to compete in a global economy and exercise the rights and responsibilities of citizenship.

6. Every school in America will be free of drugs and violence and will offer a disciplined environment conducive to learning.[2]

In attempting to achieve these goals, individual states are developing strategies for restructuring their educational systems. Media centers, recognizing their commitment to these goals, are offering a wide range of services, including

1. activities, services, and materials for preschoolers;

2. a wide range of materials to meet the interests, subjects, and learning styles of students, especially those at risk;

3. programming, collections, services for multicultural experiences;

4. learning experiences so students can develop competency in accessing, processing, and evaluation of information;

5. equitable access to technology for students regardless of economic status, intellectual ability, or sex.[3]

This brief list suggests implications for collections in terms of potential users, materials, and experiences students should have. The parents of young children create another audience, as the goals address the need for parents to be involved in the child's educational experience.

In contrast, *What Work Requires of Schools* focuses on the competencies, skills, and personal qualities needed for solid job performance. The competencies are

1. Identifies, organizes, plans, and allocates resources, including time, money, material, facilities, and human resources.

2. Works with others as a member of a team, teaches others new skills, exercises leadership, negotiates, and works with people from diverse backgrounds.

3. Acquires and uses information, including acquiring, evaluating, organizing, maintaining, interpreting, communicating, and using computers to process information.

4. Understands complex interrelationships, including understanding systems, monitoring and correcting performance, and improving or designing systems.

5. Works with a variety of technologies, including selecting, applying, maintaining, and troubleshooting.[4]

These competencies build on a three-part foundation of skills and personal qualities, which are

1. Basic skills in reading, writing, arithmetic, mathematics, speaking, and listening.

2. Thinking skills of thinking creatively, making decisions, solving problems, seeing things in the mind's eye, knowing how to learn, and reasoning.

3. Personal qualities of individual responsibility, self-esteem, sociability, self-management, and integrity.[5]

Both documents identify citizenship as important. *What Work Requires* focuses on the competencies, skills, and personal qualities to hold a job, whether a clerk or an engineer. *National Goals* interprets citizenship to mean being self-disciplined, participating in the democratic process as a voting citizen, and engaging in volunteer efforts for the community's benefit. The two positions are complementary. Both approaches call for continued learning, productive employment, and being literate.

In the past philosophies shifted from a focus on basic education (reading, writing, arithmetic) to an emphasis on critical thinking. Both philosophical positions can exist within one school. While the principal and teachers may emphasize critical thinking, others may call for improvement of the basics.

The faculty of Kennedy High School agree that basic education is an important goal; they differ on how to achieve that goal. Several teachers prefer curriculum plans that detail teaching strategies and prescribe learning activities. Others prefer group investigation built on students' problem-solving abilities. The school's statement of goals may not reflect each teacher's individual approach to education. Knowing how teachers view education can help the media specialist work with them. This chapter describes three perspectives of education: academic, personal, and social (see table 10.1). All three may exist in one school. Although each perspective emphasizes a specific approach to instruction, each perspective can draw on the others.

Table 10.1.
Perspectives of Education

Mission	Role of Student	Role of Teacher	Role of Support System
Academic			
Teach academic skills and techniques	Master information	Act as instructional manager	Provide materials developed by disciplines
	Master methods of inquiry		Provide wide range of materials and equipment
	Develop intellectual skills		
Personal			
Develop personal capacity of individuals	Develop interests and abilities	Help students help themselves	Provide space for small-group activities
			Provide materials of interest to students
Social			
Improve students' relations with peers and society	Participate in group problem-solving activities	Assign and guide group activities	Provide materials on social issues
			Provide access to community resources

Depending on its basic approach to education, a high school may teach the same general subject, for example, economics, in a number of ways. Classes emphasizing academic disciplines may stress economic theory to develop students' analytical skills. If personal development is emphasized, economics may focus on the application of economic principles to one's personal life. Classes emphasizing the social approach may have students address the impact of the economy on the community. This simple example shows that, although primary emphasis can vary, the content and skills may be similar. Knowing the characteristics and implications of the three perspectives helps the media specialist anticipate demands on the collection.

Academic Perspective

The academic approach emphasizes academic skills and an intellectual world view. Scholar's ideas and techniques provide the focus for teaching. Students (1) develop proficiency with technical and symbolic systems, for example, the technical language of biology; (2) master knowledge of a selected discipline, for example, geography; (3) master major concepts from the disciplines through the study of related fields, for example, social studies, or specific disciplines, such as physics; (4) acquire a discipline's modes of inquiry, for example, the scientific method; and (5) gain an understanding of broad philosophical schools or problems, for example, aesthetics or ethics.

The goal of academic education is to improve students' abilities to master information. Instructional programs may be designed to develop problem-solving abilities or mastery of concepts or information. Although social relationships and development of the individual are important, they are achieved through emphasis on the intellectual function.

The teacher's role is that of an instructional manager, emphasizing symbolic proficiency, or that of a trainer, emphasizing the knowledge or mode of inquiry of a discipline. Teachers may approach instruction through the inductive, deductive, or guided-discovery methods. Under the inductive method, teachers lead students through the process of inquiry. Students collect and analyze data and are led to form concepts. In the deductive method, teachers present materials as a framework for students to master subject matter. In the guided-discovery method, the teacher leads the student progressively through a series of tasks representing intellectual processes.

Research tools developed by social scientists, such as interview guides and statistical models, acquaint students with these models of analysis. The community serves as a source of data. Students use the tools to collect oral history or to study local government or ecology. Other learning activities take place in laboratory centers equipped with appropriate tools.

In a school emphasizing the academic approach, the media center should have suitable, appropriately equipped spaces and laboratory areas for small groups to work. The collection should cover the disciplines and information about how scholars carry out scientific or academic inquiry and the tools they use. One should find in the collection the usual information sources and formats as well as materials and equipment that students can use in their investigations. For example, circulating tape recorders would facilitate the collection of oral history. Scientific and mathematics equipment also may be needed.

Personal Perspective

This approach recognizes the unique character of each human being and seeks to develop the individual's personal potential. The program emphasizes the individual. The instructional programs are designed to help students achieve self-understanding and formulate or recognize their goals. The underlying premise is, as the individual's motivation for learning develops, the student will be encouraged to seek knowledge and gain mastery of academic content and skills.

Students develop one or more of the following objectives: feelings of adequacy and openness, productive-thinking capacity, personal meaning, problem-solving abilities, aesthetic appreciation, or motivation to achieve.

The teacher's role is to help students teach themselves. The premise is that students are competent to direct themselves. The teacher brings new ideas and interpersonal situations to students, but the students generate their own education with the help of the counselor, teacher, and fellow students.

The students engage in independent inquiry and creative problem solving, respond to aesthetically stimulating experiences, or react to programs designed to motivate self-improvement or the desire for knowledge and skills.

The support system requires quiet places where the teacher-counselor can have private conferences with the student. In addition, space is needed for small-group activities.

The media center needs a wide range of subjects presented at different levels and formats so students can teach themselves. Students may interact with artists, musicians, writers, or scientists who teach on a part-time basis. Students may choose short courses on subjects of interest, enroll in specialized courses through long-distance learning, use laboratory materials, or create materials in a studio or shop. Lists of community and human resources must be available. The media specialist must know each student, be involved in his or her development, and bring resources and students together.

Social Perspective

The social approach to education emphasizes improving the students' relations with people, society, and culture. Students learn to work cooperatively to identify and solve problems, whether academic or social. This approach has the following objectives: (1) develop the student's cooperative problem-solving capacity (democratic-scientific approach, political and social activism); (2) develop the student's economic independence; (3) introduce the student to his or her culture and transmit the cultural heritage; (4) Improve the student's social behavior, increasing affiliation and decreasing alienation; and (5) develop the student's awareness of self as an international citizen.

Both interpersonal (group) skills and academic-inquiry skills can be emphasized to achieve these objectives. Personal development also is important. Although emphasizing social relations, the program promotes development of the mind and the self while learning academic subjects.

The teacher's role is that of group leader, trying to facilitate the student's relation with groups, society, and culture.

In a school focusing on social behavior, materials that provide opportunities for students to interact with others are certainly needed. Games and interactive videos provide such opportunities.

THE CURRICULUM

A school achieves its purposes through its educational program, the curriculum. Typical elements in a curriculum plan include a statement of goals and objectives, the content to be covered, the organization (or sequencing) of that content, teaching strategies designed to meet the objectives or organizational requirements, and a program for evaluation. Curriculum plans may emphasize one or more of these elements. Each element of the curriculum plan has implications for the media program and its collection.

Examine the curriculum plans for your school. This may be a time-consuming task, for curriculum plans vary in scope, and there may be plans for all subject areas. Some plans are comprehensive, covering all educational programs. Others cover specific subjects or specific learning situations.

Curriculum plans may be general or may give very specific directives to teachers. The general approach outlines the broad tasks of the school and identifies the teacher's responsibility. More specific curricula prescribe when, how, to whom, with what, and under what conditions the teacher is to function. The more specific curricula may offer more direct practical information for the media specialist than the general curriculum. However, both plans will be helpful guides to the types of materials to be included in the collection.

An analysis of the curriculum plan can indicate the content or subject matter to be covered, when it will be covered, to what depth, and how it will be presented. If several classes will be simultaneously studying the same unit, the collection will need duplicate copies of specific materials. Otherwise, the media specialist can work with teachers to decide whether certain units can be taught at different times of the year. The curriculum plan may indicate why a unit is recommended for a specific time and whether altering its sequence would be detrimental to the learning process.

Curriculum Materials Digest (Association for Supervision and Curriculum, 1985-) provides a list of school publications, for example, curriculum guides, units, and work materials. Reviews of commercially developed curricula and instructional materials can be found in *Curriculum Review* (Curriculum Advisory Service, 1960-), which also runs a column about free or inexpensive materials.

TEACHING MODELS

Bruce Joyce, Marsha Weil, and Beverly Shower, in *Models for Teaching* (Allyn & Bacon, 1992), describe four families of teaching models: social, information-processing, personal, and behavioral. Each has a unique orientation to the ways people learn. Although each family emphasizes a specific approach to instruction, each draws on the others.

The social family stresses the individual's relationships to other individuals and to society. Examples include cooperative group learning, role playing, and jurisprudential inquiry. Priorities include developing the individual's ability to relate to others, to engage in democratic processes, and to work productively in society.

The information-processing family is best suited to the academic mission of the school. The teaching models include concept attainment, inductive thinking, inquiry training, and mnemonics. These models develop the student's ability to acquire and organize data, sense problems, solve problems, and generate concepts. This orientation is characterized by teaching ideas and techniques from the parent disciplines.

Teachers emphasizing the personal perspective use models oriented to the individual and the development of the self. Examples within this family include nondirective teaching and enhancing self-concept. The premise is that individuals who have a productive relationship with their environment and consider themselves capable will have richer interpersonal relations and more effective information-processing capabilities.

The behavioral family of models is based on social learning theory (behavior modification, behavior theory, and cybernetics). Examples within this family include contingency management, mastery learning or direct instruction, and self-training. A common characteristic is the breakdown of learning tasks into small, sequenced behaviors. Facts, concepts, skills, reduction of anxiety, and relaxation can be taught using this model.

The discussion that follows does not attempt to cover all of the models described in *Models for Teaching* but instead highlights various demands on the collection. Each model makes different demands on the collection. No example of a model from the personal family of teaching models will be used; their support system relies more heavily on people than on materials.

Support Systems for Teaching Models

Joyce, Weil, and Shower's concept of the support system necessary to implement each model has important implications for media specialists.

What are the additional requirements of the model beyond the *usual* human skills, capacities and technical facilities? . . . Suppose a model postulates that students should teach themselves, with the roles of teachers limited to consultation and facilitation. What support is necessary? Certainly a classroom filled only with textbooks would be limited in perspective. Rather, support in the form of books, films, self-instructional systems, and travel arrangements is necessary, or the model will be empty.[6]

This concept of support involves the media specialist directly in the teaching process. Understanding teaching methods is necessary to communicate effectively with administrators about the implications of teaching models for the media program and the collection. This also serves to make the media program an integral factor in the educational process.

Teachers may use several teaching models to achieve results. Diversity also occurs as teachers and administrators personally interpret the selected models. Table 10.2 identifies characteristics of the models.

Table 10.2.
Characteristics of Teaching Models

Teaching Model	Role of Student	Role of Teacher	Role of Support System
Group investigation	Solves problems	Academic counselor, consultant, friendly	Provide wide range of resources Provide access to expert opinion and to information outside the school
Advance organizers	Integrates old and new information	Lecturer, explainer, presenter	Provide data-rich, well-organized materials
Simulation model	Learns simple or complex tasks	Demonstrate, provide feedback, or proctor	Provide materials that can break down content into small tasks and provide immediate feedback

Group Investigation Model

This approach recognizes the student as a social being, one who cares about social order and classroom culture. The teacher builds on the students' energy to create the social order, thus "Group investigation attempts to combine in one teaching strategy the form and dynamics of the democratic process with the process of academic inquiry."[7]

To achieve this goal, the classroom's social system is democratic. The teacher suggests a problem to stimulate inquiry. Students identify and formulate the problem, then seek solutions through hands-on activities. Students learn by examining their experience to formulate new interpretations of principles and concepts.[8]

The process follows six phases:

1. Encounter puzzling situations (planned or unplanned).

2. Explore reactions to the situation.

3. Formulate study task and organize for study.

4. Independent and group work.

5. Analyze progress and process.

6. Recycle activity.[9]

The teacher functions as academic counselor, consultant, and friendly critic, guiding the group experience at three levels: problem solving, task management, and group management. The teacher provides minimal structure. The atmosphere is one of reason and negotiation.

A world history class might consider the evidence for a textbook statement about the development of nationalism in Western Europe; a government class might examine the generalization that society depends on an accepted system of law. As students explore such statements, they need information from media resources, expert opinions, and sources outside of the school.

This model needs an extensive support system that is responsive to students' needs. Joyce, Weil, and Showers observe that

> The school needs to be equipped with a first-class library that provides information and opinion through a wide variety of media; it should also be able to provide access to outside resources as well. Children should be encouraged to investigate and to contact resource people beyond the school walls. One reason cooperative inquiry of this sort has been relatively rare is that the support systems were not adequate to maintain the level of inquiry.[10]

The media specialist faces a challenge in this situation. Constraints may come from limitations on when or how materials can be purchased, lack of access to other information sources, or lack of directories or other means to contact experts. On the other hand, the teacher who chooses this model is usually a resourceful person who will seek the media specialist's assistance. Unlike other models that require fewer external resources, this model provides an opportunity to work closely with teachers and students. The media specialist involved in this type of situation may get caught up in the stimulation of the experience, responding to this teacher's needs before those of other teachers who use models less dependent on resources. This is not a case of responding to the squeaky wheel but rather to a genuine need for information.

Other implications for the collection may seem obvious. A wide range of current materials must be available for students. Community and human resources will receive heavy use. Materials must be readily accessible, or the inquiry will be delayed and the sense of curiosity dampened. Access to electronic mail and pamphlets can supplement the use of newspapers, magazines, and videotapes to present various views on a subject. Materials that distinguish between fact and opinion reinforce this type of learning. The media specialist will need to help the students locate, retrieve, select, evaluate, and apply information.

Advance Organizers Model

The goal of this model, which belongs to the information-processing family, is to explain, integrate, and interrelate material to be learned with previously learned material. The social system within this model is highly structured. The teacher is a lecturer, explainer, or presenter, who controls both the social and intellectual systems. The experience begins with the teacher clarifying the aim of the lesson, presenting and exploring the organizer (a major concept or proposition of a discipline), and eliciting the learner's prior knowledge and experience that is relevant to the learning task and organizer. This phase requires conceptually well organized materials that are rich in data. In the second phase, the presentation of the learning task or material, the media specialist may help the teacher prepare materials that will help the teacher clarify the aim of the lesson and display the major concepts. In phase two, the teacher and media specialist may work together to identify and evaluate films and other materials that present the specific content. In the third phase, strengthening cognitive organization, materials soliciting response from students will be sought. This is perhaps the most traditional, familiar approach for most media specialists.

Simulation Model

The simulation model, which belongs to the behavioral family, applies to simple and complex skills, including psychomotor skills, problem-solving strategies, and interpersonal skills. Four phases in the process are orientation overview of the simulation, participant training, simulation operations with feedback and evaluation, and participant debriefing. The social system within this model is structured by the teacher's selection of materials and direction of the simulation. The teacher may explain the theory and demonstrate the skill or may use media, such as videos or programmed learning materials. With highly structured materials, the teacher's involvement may be limited to that of facilitator, maintaining a nonevaluative but supportive attitude. Instructional systems may be simple, teacher-made games or specifically designed simulations like driving a car or navigating an airplane.

STAFF MEMBERS' NEEDS

Staff members include individuals with teaching responsibilities as well as those who work with children in other ways: administrators, guidance counselors, social workers, nurses, speech therapists, aides, secretaries, technical staff, and others. The portion of the collection that is designated to fulfill these individuals' needs is usually called the professional collection. Parents and other community members also may use this collection. (Resources addressing the needs of parents are discussed in chapter 12.)

As with the rest of the collection, a variety of formats should be available. The opening-day scenario in chapter 1 identifies some professional demands upon the collection. Rodrigo, the guidance counselor, needed materials for his presentation to a community organization about the problems of teenagers. Teachers needed materials to help them prepare for specific units. If the collection does not have the appropriate materials, the media specialist will need to know where to obtain them or how to produce them.

Teachers and staff have other needs. The media specialist and school psychologist could use *The Best of Bookfinder: A Guide to Children's Literature About Interests and Concerns of Youth Ages 2-18* (American Guidance Service, 1992) to locate titles in a variety of formats to help students face situations. A kindergarten teacher may want ideas for activities. Those responsible for programs for preschoolers would will find Barbara J. Taylor's *A Child Goes Forth: A Curriculum Guide for Preschool Children* (7th ed., Macmillan, 1991) a helpful guide for selecting materials and activities for young children. Teachers interested in the selection and use of media will find *Instructional Media and the New Technologies of Instruction* by Robert Heinich, Michael Molenda, and James D. Russell (4th ed., Macmillan, 1993) a helpful guide. An eighth-grade English teacher may want to know about forthcoming television programs so that the students can analyze them. She may turn to *TV GUIDE* (Triangle Publications, 1953-); the newsletter of the local public broadcast station; or *C-SPAN Newsletter*, which includes programming schedules and articles of interest to teachers. A science teacher may seek information about how to obtain weather maps through the Internet by following the directions in *NorthWestNet's Guide to Our World Online* by Jonathan Kochmer and NorthWestNet (4th ed., NorthWestNet and Northwest Academic Computing Consortium, 1993) or Elizabeth Miller's *The Internet Resource Directory for K-12 Teachers and Librarians, 94-95 Edition* (Libraries Unlimited, 1994).

Some teachers may be interested in learning about free resources (books, magazines, newsletters, posters, and other materials). Carol Smallwood describes free materials for students and teachers in *Free Resource Builder for Librarians and Teachers* (2d ed., McFarland, 1992). Another source is *Vertical File Index: A Subject and Title Index to Selected Pamphlet Materials* (H. W. Wilson, 1955-), which is also available through Wilsonline. Other teachers may be interested in learning about the schedule of programs that will offer continuing education credit, as listed in announcements from a local university.

To meet these and other needs, the professional collection will need to include books, pamphlets, government documents, journals, films, videos, audiotapes, curriculum materials, bibliographic and selection tools, television and radio program guides, information about community resources, and program announcements of educational programs and teacher associations.

A major resource about current activities within schools are the documents in the ERIC (Educational Resources Information Center) databases. Manual searches can be done using *Resources in Education* (RIE) (Superintendent of Documents, 1975-) and *Current Index to Journals in Education: CIJE* (Oryx Press, 1969-). RIE and *CIJE* also can be accessed through the Internet using WAIS. A directory of libraries and organizations offering online services is available from the ERIC Processing and Reference Facility; the information also appears on the ERIC CD-ROM (DIALOG OnDisc). Paper copies or microfiche copies of ERIC documents may be ordered by mail from the ERIC Document Reproduction Service (EDRS). Journal articles can be obtained from other sources. Documents of particular interest to media specialists are described in *School Library Media Quarterly*.

Know what is available in the district media collection. These materials may be listed in the OPAC. If there is a separate list or catalog of these materials, obtain a copy. State education agencies and professional associations also provide a variety of information.

How does the media specialist keep up with all these sources of information? Professional journals in library science and education often publish articles or announcements. Appendixes A and B list materials, including journals with reviews in program areas, as well as agencies and associations that provide publications or offer other information services, such as clearinghouses or information networks.

Ask teachers or other media specialists in the district about the sources of information they find most useful. Teachers who are pursuing advanced degrees will make demands on the collection related to their course work. At the same time, they can offer suggestions of new materials.

IMPLICATIONS FOR THE COLLECTION

The media specialist must know the priorities and understand the constraints of the curriculum and teaching methods in the school if the collection is to meet the needs of the school's instructional programs. To support some of these programs, the collection must include materials that traditionally have been considered instructional or classroom materials. As curricula and teaching methods change, items in the collection must be reevaluated in terms of how effectively they contribute to the teaching and learning process.

Many teaching strategies require so-called library materials as major sources of information or instruction. Selection decisions based on instructional needs can only be achieved through cooperative efforts by teachers and media specialists. General selection tools do not include the type of analysis and evaluation of materials needed to match material and teaching strategies. However, they provide a starting point for the selection process. As teachers participate in selection decisions and use materials, record their evaluations. A sample form to using when working with teachers is provided in figure 10.1 on page 194.

UNIT RESOURCE RECORD

Subject/Unit: _____

Grade: _____ Teacher: _____

Special student needs:

Objectives:

Information skills required:

Resources required:	Call number or source:	Evaluative comments:

Fig. 10.1. Teacher use and evaluation form.

From *The Collection Program in Schools*. © 1995. Libraries Unlimited. 1-800/237-6124.

Janie Schomberg describes how her school's culture influences collection development. She identifies four factors:

- state guidelines for content;

- local learning outcomes based on state goals;

- the community in which the school is located and the geographical area from which the students come, whether they are one and the same or distinctly different; and

- the building culture, which includes such things as the way the building is organized and the teaching and learning styles that are part of that local school. The building in which I am the school library media specialist differs greatly from individual buildings in other districts and somewhat from the other buildings in the Urbana school district.[11]

Leal School is a K-5 elementary school with 457 students, serving the local and noncontiguous neighborhoods. The population is economically and culturally diverse. Each building determines what to teach in order to accomplish the learning outcomes provided by the Urbana school district curriculum. Consistent with the school's philosophy, the Leal Alternatives Program includes three environmental variations within one school, all designed to meet the needs of students. Kindergarten is a full-day, self-contained classroom instructional setting. In grades 1-4, a choice of instructional styles is offered, including a team-teaching environment of grades 1-2 or 3-4, a primarily self-contained environment of 1-2 or 3-4, and a single-grade classroom for grades 1-4.

> Students in grades 1-4 stay with the same teacher for two years in all environment choices. These classrooms offer an alternative-year curriculum, covering the learning outcomes and content for two grades over a two-year period. . . . Fifth grade is composed of a three-teacher team that departmentalizes instruction in major content areas. All choices and configurations strive to integrate the disciplines in a curriculum subscribing to a whole language philosophy. Throughout Leal School, there are no textbooks— all teaching and learning is resource based. This philosophy and teaching style place the focus of curriculum support on the school library media center, requiring a very different collection development process than, for instance, a school that has required textbooks throughout the district and a lock-step curriculum. . . . My collection development plan is always evolving.[12]

SUMMARY

Media specialists have a responsibility to ensure that the collection meets the curricular and instructional needs of the school. To carry out this responsibility, they must know the conditions for use of materials: who, how, and for what purposes. Trying to learn why materials are used is more difficult than finding out who uses them and how they are used. Curriculum plans may provide this information about conditions for use.

The challenge of meeting curricular needs is complicated by the different views of what education should be. Teachers and administrators may be unable to articulate their viewpoints; but if the media specialist sorts through what is seen and heard, the various approaches to education begin to become clear.

Needs for materials change. For one subject, a teacher may use a model that makes heavy uses of specified materials; but that teacher may later use a different model that makes no demands on the collection.

Learn more about teaching. Professional resources for teachers can provide helpful information. If media programs are to be integrated with the school's programs, the media specialist must understand the why and how of teaching. Professional reading should include literature on educational principles and methods. Take advantage of conversations, observation in classrooms, in-service programs, and other opportunities to further your knowledge of teaching. The knowledge gained will enhance your ability to work with teachers and result in more effective use of the collection. Involving teachers and administrators leads to their understanding of media center budget requests.

NOTES

[1]United States Department of Education, *National Goals for Education* (Washington, DC, 1990).

[2]United States Department of Education, *National Goals for Education*, 4-8.

[3]Barbara K. Stripling, *Libraries for the National Education Goals* (Syracuse, NY: ERIC Clearinghouse on Information Resources, 1992), 67.

[4]United States Department of Labor. Secretary's Commission on Achieving Necessary Skills, *What Work Requires of Schools: A SCANS Report for America 2000* (Washington, DC, 1991), vii.

[5]United States Department of Labor, *What Work Requires*, vii.

[6]Bruce Joyce, Marsha Weil, and Beverly Showers, *Models of Teaching*, 4th ed. (Boston: Allyn & Bacon, 1992), 15.

[7]Joyce, Weil, and Showers, *Models of Teaching*, 42.

[8]Joyce, Weil, and Showers, *Models of Teaching*, 48.

[9]Joyce, Weil, and Showers, *Models of Teaching*, 52.

[10]Joyce, Weil, and Showers, *Models of Teaching*, 49.

[11]Janie Schomberg, "Tools of the Trade: School Library Media Specialists, Reviews, and Collection Development," in *Evaluating Children's Books: A Critical Look: Aesthetic, Social, and Political Aspects of Analyzing and Using Children's Books*, ed. by Betsy Hearne and Roger Sutton (Urbana-Champaign: University of Illinois, Graduate School of Library and Information Science, 1993), 38.

[12]Schomberg, "Tools of the Trade," 39.

BIBLIOGRAPHY

Joyce, Bruce; Marsha Weil; and Beverly Showers. *Models of Teaching*, 4th ed. Boston: Allyn & Bacon, 1992.

Schomberg, Janie. "Tools of the Trade: School Library Media Specialists, Reviews, and Collection Development" in *Evaluating Children's Books: A Critical Look: Aesthetic, Social, and Political Aspects of Analyzing and Using Children's Books*, ed. by Betsy Hearne and Roger Sutton. Urbana-Champaign: University of Illinois, Graduate School of Library and Information Science, 1993, 37-46.

Stripling, Barbara K. *Libraries for the National Education Goals*. Syracuse, NY: ERIC Clearinghouse on Information Resources, 1992.

United States. Department of Education. *National Goals for Education*. Washington, DC, 1990.

United States. Department of Labor. Secretary's Commission on Achieving Necessary Skills. *What Work Requires of Schools: A SCANS Report for America 2000*. Washington, DC, 1991.

CHAPTER 11

Meeting Subject and Program Needs

Typical questions media specialists hear from students, teachers, and members of the community begin, "Do you have information on . . . ?" or "I am working with (a specific group), what can I use?" Many of the resources described elsewhere in this book help meet these demands. This chapter emphasizes resources designed to address subject and program needs, including preschoolers and kindergartners, inner-city programs, multicultural materials, and the reference collection. Entries in appendix B provide more information about the bibliographies and selection tools described in this chapter. For other subjects and programs, consult the catalogs, publications, and journals published by the associations listed in appendix A.

FACTORS INFLUENCING COLLECTION DEVELOPMENT

The School's Purpose

A look at the high school environment illustrates the complexity of trying to support subject-oriented needs. Some high schools serve a single, overriding purpose. Often this purpose is expressed in the name of the institution with adjectives such as *vocational-technical*, *preparatory*, or *alternative*. For these schools the purpose is obvious; the role of the media program may be narrow in scope.

More often a high school serves more than one purpose. A multipurpose, or comprehensive, high school exerts varied demands on the media center collection and presents added challenges to the media specialist. In some comprehensive high schools, the purposes are not clearly defined. This may present problems for budget allocations.

The media specialist will want to talk to administrators, teachers, and students to learn about the school's purposes and programs. Is the school a comprehensive high school with both academic and practical courses and departments? Is it a vocational-technical school emphasizing specific job-related courses? Is it a performing-arts or technical school offering special programs for talented students? Is there a nontraditional or alternative program? The school board's or principal's annual report to the community can offer additional insight into the purposes of the school and its place in the district's program.

A school's purpose has implications for the collection, some of which should be obvious. Each of the schools described above requires different titles in its collection. Some general materials, such as ready-reference works, may be in all of these collections. In the case of a relatively expensive multivolume work, such as Groves's *Dictionary of Music*, should all schools own a copy, or is there a way that schools can share? Will all schools need a specific tool? *University Press Books for Public and Secondary School Libraries* will be of more interest to students in a preparatory school than to those in a vocational-technical school.

The nature of the alternative school program and the characteristics of its student population strongly influence the proportion of traditional materials within the collection. These students may prefer visual, oral, and manipulative materials to ones in print. Educational comics and paperback books may be in evidence, but hardback books may be de-emphasized or not present. Software may appeal to the students and may be used to learn basic skills.

If the school has average students with many projects demanding current information, should the collection have an online database, a CD-ROM database, or increased periodicals subscriptions? If a school chooses a CD-ROM database with its coverage of more titles than *Readers' Guide to Periodical Literature*, should the number of subscriptions be increased? If not, will students become frustrated when they find citations to journals that are not readily available? Another concern is cost. The CD-ROM costs more than a print version of *Readers' Guide*. However, the media staff spend more time helping students learn to use the *Readers' Guide* than they do helping students learn a CD-ROM system, such as INFOTRAC II. Other concerns are the length of time needed to handle queries, the ease of using the materials, the availability of hardware to support the CD-ROM, and staff and administrative commitment.

Distribution of Learning Materials

Another factor influencing subject- and program-oriented materials is where they are housed. When departmental libraries or resource centers are established to support particular subject areas, the centers' relationships to the collection housed in the media center must be determined. Are the centers' materials purely instructional? Are textbooks, work books, and supplemental materials used with specific assignments? Or, are the materials considered part of the main collection and housed conveniently near the classrooms on that subject?

A visit to two schools illustrates the differences. In one, a room is set aside to store extra copies of textbooks, paperback copies of required readings, professional materials, and instructional magazines. The social studies department aide is responsible for maintaining the collection. Students use the materials as they work on specific assignments.

In another school, the social studies collection of books, maps, globes, trade books, transparencies, slides, and software is housed in a resource center near the social studies classrooms. Here, a member of the media center staff provides media instruction, gives reference service, and offers the other services associated with the media program. Teachers and students use this facility individually or in groups. At one carrel two students view a slide-tape program, at the next a teacher and a student conduct an online search, and at the third a student listens to a recording.

Another pattern of housing occurs when materials are stored in the classroom or teaching areas where they are used most frequently. For instance, cookbooks are in the home economics department and materials on auto repairs are in the shop. A tour of the school helps you identify the distribution pattern. If materials are not housed in the media center, who is responsible for them? Have they been entered on the OPAC? Are separate funds used to purchase these materials, or are they purchased with media center funds? The most important question is how convenient is access to materials.

Range of Course Offerings

To explore the school's unique demands on its collection, examine the range of courses offered. Compare the course offerings of a comprehensive high school and a vocational-technical one, as approved for schools in Florida.[1] A high school in Florida may offer basic courses in art, computer education, dance, drama, foreign languages, health, humanities, language arts, library media, mathematics, music, physical education, political science, research and critical thinking, Reserve Officer Training Corps and military training, safety and driver education, science, and social studies. The social studies department offers anthropology, economics, geography, history, multicultural studies and religion, philosophy, political science, psychology, social sciences, sociology, and interdisciplinary and applied social studies. History courses may include African, Asian, Bible, and world history. Additional courses are designed to meet the needs of exceptional students, including those with various disabilities and gifted students. On the other hand, a vocational education program may offer courses in agribusiness, natural resources, business, health occupations, home economics, industrial occupations, marketing, public service occupations, and technology.

The state department of education probably has a similar list of approved courses. If the collection is to support a wide variety of courses, it must provide some level of coverage for all of the subjects. The media specialist must be knowledgeable about the subjects taught, the teaching methods used, and the characteristics of the users to determine the breadth of coverage needed. Is the subject covered at an introductory, advanced, or remedial level? Are there honors courses? Do honors students have access to a nearby college collection? Has a shift in population created a need for materials that present concepts in simple English or bilingual formats?

How are the subjects organized or approached? For example, is art history taught as a separate course, or is it integrated into a study of humanities? As one high school moved to the integrated approach, the existing slide collection, which focused on specific artists and schools of art, was expanded. The new slides demonstrate an art medium, represent a particular technique or school of art, show the influence of philosophical thought upon art, or show the influence of technology upon the subject and medium. One can draw similar comparisons with programs in elementary schools or in middle schools.

Extracurricular groups and programs create demands for specific subject materials. A debate society needs timely information and opinions on issues. A drama club needs plays, information about and patterns for costumes, and ideas for set designs. After school programs call for information about crafts or sports.

New programs create new demands. In one district, a centrally located high school media center is open in the evening to serve students from all schools in the district. Media specialists from various schools take turns overseeing the media center. They find the reference collection needs to expand to meet the needs of students from diverse programs. In other communities, students in adult-education programs use the media center. They use some of the materials that the daytime students use but also need other subjects. Preschool and toddler programs present other demands on the collection. An inner-city school has unique demands on the collection.

MEETING PROGRAM NEEDS

Preschoolers and Kindergartners

Some programs for preschoolers orient both parent and child to the school before the child enrolls in kindergarten. Although your school may not sponsor such a program, anticipate questions from parents about materials recommended for preschoolers. High school students who are parents or who are taking courses in child care are another audience for this information.

During the early years, a child rapidly develops language skills, taking pleasure in words and rhymes. Interest in written language generally develops at age 4. Children are curious; they enjoy materials that encourage participation and involve naming, touching, and pointing. Manipulative materials, such as games, toys, and puzzles, prompt imaginative play. Active play is preferred to sitting or listening. The child is beginning to assert independence.

The following questions can guide you in selecting materials for this age group:

- Are the materials realistic and accurately reported?

- Does the story or book offer an element of surprise or suspense? Does the humor appeal to the child?

- Does the information build on a child's experiences?

- Is the length of the material designed for the interest and attention span of a young child?

- Are the words simple and descriptive, and can a child understand them?

- Can a child understand the ideas and concepts?

- Do illustrations closely represent the text?

- Are materials durable? Can parts be replaced?

Sources of information about materials for this age group include works for their parents and teachers. Barbara J. Taylor's *A Child Goes Forth* (7th ed., Macmillan, 1991),[2] offers guidelines on selection and use of materials. In *Play, Learn, and Grow: An Annotated Guide to the Best Books and Materials for the Very Young*, (R. R. Bowker, 1992), James L. Thomas provides criteria for selecting materials for children from infancy through age 5. This work recommends 1,074 titles (audiocassettes, books, compact discs, filmstrips, recordings, software, and videocassettes) for children and 97 titles for adults who work with children. In *Books, Babies, and Libraries: Serving Infants, Toddlers, Their Parents and Caregivers* (American Library Association, 1991), Ellin Greene identifies books, musical recordings, films, videos, and software for young children. Greene describes the young child's use of these materials and offers suggestions for ways adults can share these materials.

Inner-City Programs

As with schools in other settings, the collection in an inner-city school must be responsive to the philosophy, objectives, and curriculum of its school. Mary E. Oliver outlines the responsibility of a media specialist in this setting:

1. Bring the library media center of the inner-city school in line with the needs and equipment of today's educational mission and goals.

2. Learn about various methods and elements that will have a positive affect on the development of inner-city children.

3. Recognize the need for broadening, elaborating on, and extending selected services to inner-city school children.

4. Develop a library media program that serves the inner-city child.[3]

Given the range of available materials; limited resources; and concern for quality literature, materials, and equipment, the job of selection may appear difficult. The media specialist faces the challenge of justifying students' needs in requesting additional funding. One approach is to concentrate on a specific subject and work with teachers to develop programs to use the desired resources. In this way, the benefits to students can be documented and serve as justification for funds to develop other programs.

The story of Susan Hess, a middle school media specialist in Brooklyn, demonstrates what one individual can do. Her school has a culturally diverse population (60 percent Hispanic, 30 percent African American, 5 percent Asian, and 5 percent other). The community is economically disadvantaged. The budget was $1,500, but Hess's philosophy is that lack of money is no excuse for a poor collection. Seeking the support of her principal, Hess pursued grants and sought opportunities to serve as a test site for products and equipment. The program has moved from having its first computer in 1986 to being on the cutting edge of technology. Hess trains a few seventh-graders, who then train their peers to use laser videodiscs, conduct Boolean searches, obtain faxed materials from other sources, and use telecommunications in creative writing and joint research projects.[4]

Oliver suggests that the collection, including equipment, must also serve the home. Loaning equipment for home use has several advantages. Students learn about the care of equipment and how to do simple repairs, and their caregivers learn about available resources. This practice also helps families in rural areas where access to equipment is limited. Typically, smaller equipment, which students can handle, is loaned. For the inner-city school, Oliver recommends that the collection include

- Fiction works for leisure reading, including sport stories and stories of accomplished minorities.

- Materials on issues of the day: drugs, alcohol, family relationships, and early pregnancies for fourth grade and up.

- Some books on children living in and coping with problems of project living, and others showing children living in overcrowded apartment houses but striving to attain better housing or surroundings.

- Materials on mythology and religions.

- Career information, including occupations that do not necessarily require a college education.

- Other subjects of interest are gardening; care of small animals and fish; the body and general health care; cookbooks; books on beauty and skin care, hair styling, fashions; books on manners and dating; etiquette; and biographies about minorities.[5]

Oliver reports

An excellent way to foster good relations between the many ethnic groups of children is through exchange of language. There is no class activity more interesting than having a child who is a newcomer teach the class some simple words and phrases and even some short sentences in his or her own language. Students really enjoy this activity and the new student is made to feel comfortable.[6]

Children and their parents are resources for sharing information about ethnic and cultural backgrounds, including language, folklore, food, or holidays.

MULTICULTURAL MATERIALS

Multicultural materials support classes on that subject, present ethnic and cultural differences in other courses, and help students learn about individuals whose backgrounds differ from their own. Guidelines, criteria, and bibliographies come from school districts, state agencies, and commercial publishers.

The topic of multicultural materials can raise heated debate. Questions center on who is qualified to write about ethnic and cultural experiences. Are only members of the ethnic or cultural group qualified? Who is qualified to review such materials? By what standards should these materials be evaluated? Can members of a minority be presented with frailties, or must they always be represented as strong and good? Lillian N. Gerhardt, in an editorial tracing multiculturalism, wisely observes,

Good librarians exercising good sense have had to select their way with limited budgets through the production of books engendered by every "-ism." "Multiculturalism" will be no exception. Measures of literary and artistic merit will once again have to outweigh emotional or political commitments to a popular cause if a library collection for young readers is to be worthy of their reading time.[7]

To address these issues, the Dallas Independent School District's selection policy includes the following criteria:

1. Books and other materials should accurately portray the perspectives, attitudes, and feelings of ethnic groups.

2. Fictional works should have strong ethnic characters.

3. Books should describe settings and experiences with which all students can identify and yet accurately reflect ethnic cultures and lifestyles.

4. The protagonists in books with ethnic themes should have ethnic characteristics but should face conflicts and problems that are universal to all cultures and groups.

5. The illustrations in books should be accurate, ethnically sensitive, and technically well done.

6. Ethnic materials should not contain racist concepts, cliches, phrases, or words.

7. Factual materials should be historically accurate.

8. Multiethnic resources and basal textbooks should discuss major events and documents related to ethnic history.[8]

The following bibliographies and sources provide additional criteria: *Developing Library Collections for California's Emerging Majority: A Manual for Ethnic Collection Development*, edited by Katharine T. A. Scarborough (University of California, Berkeley, 1990), provides a wealth of information. The work identifies publishers, distributors, bookstores, organizations and agencies, resource specialists, holidays and celebrations, selected reference and professional literature, and selected periodicals. Barbara J. Kuipers's *American Indian Reference Resource Books for Children and Young Adults* (2d ed., Libraries Unlimited, 1995) is an annotated bibliography describing the strengths and weaknesses of more than 200 titles and their use in the curriculum. Kuipers identifies criteria for evaluating the treatment of American Indians in books and provides a checklist for evaluating such materials.

Articles about increasing awareness, as well as reviews, are found in *Interracial Books for Children Bulletin* (Council on Interracial Books for Children, 1967-) and *Multicultural Review* (Greenwood, 1992-). In *Against Borders: Promoting Books for a Multicultural World* (American Library Association, 1993), Hazel Rochman suggests curriculum units and other ways for adults working with students in grades 6-12 to promote reading using themes including outsiders, friends, and family. In *Our Family, Our Friends, Our World: An Annotated Guide to Significant Multicultural Books for Children and Teenagers* (R. R. Bowker, 1992), Lyn Miller-Lachmann critically compares works with other titles on the same subject, pointing out the strengths and weaknesses. In *Venture into Culture: A Resource Book of Multicultural Materials and Programs* (American Library Association, 1992), Carla D. Hayden recommends materials for elementary and middle school students about African American, Arabic, Asian, Hispanic, Jewish, Native American, and Persian cultures.

Isabel Schon writes regularly about materials relating to Hispanic students. *Books in Spanish for Children and Young Adults: An Annotated Guide, Series VI* (Scarecrow Press, 1992) and *A Hispanic Heritage, Series IV: A Guide to Juvenile Books About Hispanic People and Cultures* (Scarecrow Press, 1991) are two examples.

Books from other countries appeal to children, providing them with opportunities to experience different cultures or to use foreign language skills. If your school has a foreign language program, find out what kind of materials the teacher recommends and when they would be most helpful.

Bookbird, Journal of the International Institute for Children's Literature, contains articles and reviews. USBBY (United States Board on Books for Young People) is the U.S. affiliate of IBBY (International Board on Books for Young People). The USBBY newsletter talks about juvenile titles in the United States and abroad. Bibliographic essays in *School Library Journal* and the review columns in *Booklist* can be used as updates.

REFERENCE COLLECTION MATERIALS

Students' personal interests and classroom activities may necessitate the use of reference materials. Reference books are works, such as encyclopedias, that provide factual information and are intended for locating specific information. (This is not to say that a student will not read an encyclopedia from cover to cover; every school seems to have at least one child who does this, or at least tries.) Reference works may appear in traditional print format or on CD-ROM.

Certain reference titles, such as *Guinness Book of World Records*, are so popular that the collection will need a circulating copy as well as a reference copy. In schools where groups go on week-long camping trips or nature hikes, the media center should include several copies of nature handbooks. These works can be ordered in hardback or paperback, depending on how the books will be used.

Criteria used for adult reference materials—authority, scope, treatment of materials, arrangement, format, and special features—apply equally well to reference materials for students. Illustrations, cross-references, and pronunciation guides are important features in children's reference materials.

Basic selection tools include *Guide to Reference Books for School Media Centers*, by Margaret Irby Nichols (Libraries Unlimited, 1992); *Reference Books for Children*, by Carolyn Sue Peterson and Ann D. Fenton (Scarecrow Press, 1992); *Reference Books for Children's Collections* (New York Public Library, 1991); and *Guide to Reference Materials for Canadian Libraries* (University of Toronto Press, 1992). All recommend a wide range of titles on a variety of subjects. *Elementary School Library Collection* (Brodart, 1994), edited by Linda L. Homa, includes a section about recommended reference materials. Reviews of current titles are published in "Reference and Subscription Books Review" in *Booklist*. Other review sources include *Recommended Reference Books for Small and Medium-Sized Libraries and Media Centers* (Libraries Unlimited, annual), which includes titles selected from the more comprehensive *American Reference Books Annual* (Libraries Unlimited, 1970-); and Andrew L. March's *Recommended Reference Books in Paperback* (2d ed., Libraries Unlimited, 1992). The New York Public Library's Children's Reference Committee's *Reference Books for Children's Collections*, edited by Dolores Vogliiano (2d ed., New York Public Library, 1991), provides bibliographic and descriptive annotations for titles for younger readers and for adults working with children.

Kister's Best Dictionaries for Adults and Young People: A Comparative Guide, by Kenneth F. Kister (Oryx Press, 1992), discusses the selection of dictionaries and evaluates English-language dictionaries for audiences ranging from children to adult. Alphabet books and preschool dictionaries also are included. H. Robert Malinowsky's *Best Science and Technology Reference Books for Young People* (Oryx Press, 1991) recommends selected titles for students from third grade through high school. *Government Reference Books: A Biennial Guide to U.S. Government Publications* (Libraries Unlimited, 1970-) annotates and gives ordering information for pamphlets, folders, and multivolume sets. Leticia T. Ekhaml and Alice J. Wittig's *U.S. Government Publications for the School Library Media Center* (2d ed., Libraries Unlimited, 1991) covers the history of government publications, depository libraries, indexes and selection aids, and how to order. More than 500 publications are recommended. *Subject Bibliography Index* (U.S. Government Printing Office) is a free publication that lists free subject bibliographies. Melody S. Kelly's *Using Government Documents: A How-To-Do-It Manual for School Librarians* (Neal-Schuman, 1992) offers practical advice about how to locate specific documents and use the various catalogs, clearinghouses, and agencies.

SUBJECT-ORIENTED TOOLS

Media specialists acknowledge that no one individual can be knowledgeable about every subject or keep up with all developments. Media specialists consult with experts who are familiar with the collection and how it is used. Teachers, department chairpersons, and members of the community provide the expertise. People respond favorably when they know their opinions will be heeded.

This chapter makes no attempt to list all the bibliographies and selection tools media specialists could use to identify materials from a subject perspective. One of the difficult decisions media specialists face is what proportion of the budget to spend on bibliographic and selection tools. Given the wide range of subjects and the fact that each may have specialized tools, how can one decide which tools to buy? One consideration is whether teachers and students could use the bibliographies and selection tools. When they can, you are adding not only selection tools but reference works to the collection.

A sampling of professional sources in specific subject areas illustrates the type of information found in such tools. Carolyn W. Lima and John A. Lima's *A to Zoo: Subject Access to Children's Picture Books* (4th ed., R. R. Bowker, 1993) lists more than 15,000 fiction and nonfiction titles for preschoolers through second-graders.

Several sources suggest titles for exploring history. In *America as Story: Historical Fiction for Secondary Schools* (American Library Association, 1988), Elizabeth F. Howard recommends more than 150 novels to stimulate students' interest in history. Vandelia VanMeter's *World History for Children and Young Adults* (Libraries Unlimited, 1992) has separate author, title, subject, series, and grade-level indexes to help locate appropriate titles. In *Literature for Young People on War and Peace: An Annotated Bibliography* (Greenwood Press, 1989), Harry Eiss evaluates titles and comments about the various levels at which they can be read. He also identifies references for adults.

Several journals focus on science materials. *Appraisal* (Children's Science Books Review Committee, 1967-) provides reviews by librarians and science specialists for each of the 50-70 trade books and series covered per issue. *Science Books & Films* (American Association for the Advancement of Science, 1975-) offers reviews of books, films, filmstrips, discs, and software for preschool through professional use. Forthcoming programs on PBS (Public Broadcasting System) are listed. *Science and Children* (National Science Teachers Association, 1963-) reviews software, curriculum materials, and children's books. *The Science Teacher* (National Science Teachers Association, 1934-) reviews software, books for students, and professional books.

Other books focus on specific scientific subjects. Patti K. Sinclair identifies works for individuals between the ages of 3 and 14 in *E for Environment: An Annotated Bibliography of Children's Books with Environmental Themes* (R. R. Bowker, 1992). Jeffrey T. Huber's *How to Find Information About AIDS* (2d ed., Haworth Press, 1992) describes electronic and print sources. The work provides addresses and telephone numbers of organizational resources, health departments, research institutions, grant funding sources, federal agencies, hotlines, and audiovisual producers and distributors. Two companion works by DayAnn M. Kennedy, *Science & Technology in Fact and Fiction: A Guide to Children's Books* (R. R. Bowker, 1990) and *Science & Technology in Fact and Fiction: A Guide to Young Adult Books* (R. R. Bowker, 1990), provide evaluative comments about the titles listed. The author, title, subject, and readability indexes help readers locate appropriate works. Anthony L. Manna and Cynthia Wolford Symons's *Children's Literature for Health Awareness* (Scarecrow Press, 1992) identifies how various genres address health issues. The titles include folklore, fantasy, realistic fiction, historical fiction, poetry, informational books, biography, and plays.

Many professional associations publish journals, which carry reviews, and produce bibliographies. In the area of social studies, for example, there are the *Journal of Consumer Affairs* (American Council on Consumer Interest), *Journal of Geography* (National Council for Geographic Education), and *Social Education* (National Council for Social Studies). The Children's Book Council, working with professional associations, publishes lists of notable trade books in the subject areas of science and social science. The National Council of Teachers of English (NCTE) has many publications, including *Language Arts* (NCTE, 1975-), which reviews children's books and professional materials. Another source of reviews and bibliographies is the International Reading

Association, which publishes *Reading Teacher*. Some associations, like the Association for Supervision and Curriculum Development, have comprehensive memberships, so you can receive their journals and publications throughout the year. A list of these associations and others, along with information about national clearinghouses that provide information and bibliographies on many subject areas, is in appendix A.

COMMUNITY RESOURCES

The local community can be a rich resource for information on various subjects. Does the credit union have information about managing personal finances? Will a local businessperson or a representative of a state or federal agency help students understand how to set up and run a small business? Does the college or university have a speakers' bureau or list of consultants? Which state or local agencies have information packets or resource people? Will parent groups contribute time to projects?

Workers in the community can provide expert opinions about their expertise. They can help in the evaluation of materials and in identifying further sources of information. Surprise a dentist: Ask his opinion. Many professional people have access to career-related information appropriate for students. Media specialists realize that each new person and experience is an opportunity to help a student.

SUMMARY

Demands on the collection for coverage of specific subjects or to support programs come from a variety of sources and are always changing. Media specialists need to involve others in locating and evaluating the wide range of available materials. Bibliographies and other sources provide help in identifying appropriate materials. One of the decisions each media specialist faces is which source will help meet the needs of the school. Media specialists should make every effort to participate in the local planning and decision-making process in order to anticipate subject and program needs. If the collection is to be effective, all these factors—plus the curricular, instructional, and personal needs of users—must enter into the selection process.

NOTES

[1]Florida, Department of Education, *1993-94 Course Code Directory and Instructional Personnel Assignments* (Tallahassee, 1992).

[2]Eighth edition to be released in 1995.

[3]Mary E. Oliver, *The School Library Media Program: Extending Service to Inner-City Children* (New Haven, CT: In-Time Publications, 1990), 2.

[4]Nora Jane Natke, "Emerging Technologies in Resource Sharing and Document Delivery," *Journal of Youth Services in Libraries* 5, no. 2 (Winter 1992): 189-92.

[5]Oliver, *The School Library Media Program*, 7-10.

[6]Oliver, *The School Library Media Program*, 8.

[7]Lillian N. Gerhardt, "Multiculturalism," *School Library Journal* 37, no. 9 (September 1991): 154.

[8]Dallas Independent School District, Media Services Department, *Library Media Center Handbook* (Dallas, TX, 1993), 4.3.3.3.

BIBLIOGRAPHY

Cameron, Ann; Keiko Narahashi; Mildred Pitts Walter; and David Wisniewski. "The Many Faces in Children's Books." *School Library Journal* 38, no. 1 (January 1992): 28-33.

Dallas Independent School District. Media Services Department. *Library Media Center Handbook*. Dallas, TX, 1993.

Florida. Department of Education. *1993-94 Course Code Directory and Instructional Personnel Assignments*. Tallahassee, 1992.

Gerhardt, Lillian N. "Multiculturalism." *School Library Journal* 37, no. 9 (September 1991): 154.

Kruse, Ginny Moore. "No Single Season: Multicultural Literature for All Children." *Wilson Library Bulletin* 66, no. 6 (February 1992): 30-33.

Natke, Nora Jane. "Emerging Technologies in Resource Sharing and Document Delivery." *Journal of Youth Services in Libraries* 5, no. 2 (Winter 1992): 189-92.

Oliver, Mary E. *The School Library Media Program: Extending Service to Inner-City Children*. New Haven, CT: In-Time Publications, 1990.

Sutton, Roger. "What Mean We, White Man?" *VOYA: Voice of Youth Advocates* 15, no. 3 (August 1992): 155-58.

CHAPTER 12

Meeting the Needs of Individuals

One purpose of the school media collection is to meet informational and recreational needs of individuals. To fulfill this purpose, media specialists must know the individuals using the collection. This chapter focuses on materials and tools designed to help media specialists select materials that meet the typical needs of groups of individuals. (In appendix B, the notation "Chap. 12" indicates sources of more information about the bibliographies and selection tools cited in this chapter.) This chapter provides a starting point for getting to know users. When selecting materials for a collection, remember that individuals read, view, listen, and compute for different reasons: personal, informational, educational, cultural, and recreational. People use materials at various levels, seek various types of materials, and approach subjects in various fashions, depending on their immediate needs and interests. The school's staff will want books, journals, newsletters, and vertical file materials about special education.

In addition to format and content, criteria for selecting materials should consider who will use the materials and how. The range of human needs is endless, varying from person to person. The media specialist must know each user.

STUDENT DIVERSITY

To select materials to suit the range of needs and interests of students, media specialists use expertise about materials and knowledge of individual students. Familiarity with the school and community allows the media specialist to anticipate student interests. Is the school in a rural or urban setting? Do most students use public transportation or drive their own vehicles? How many hold full-time or part-time jobs? How many are preparing for college? At Fairmont Avenue High School, a comprehensive high school, 40 percent of the students are bound for college. Compare the implications of that fact with another school in the district where 75-80 percent of the students are college-bound. The primary interests of students at these two schools differ. Duplicate collections would not support these interests adequately. At Fairmont Avenue High School, students' reading levels range from fourth grade through college. This broad range created problems for Mary, the media specialist, when the school began to stress economic education. Materials presenting economic concepts for students with a fourth-grade vocabulary were difficult to locate.

Although the needs of groups of students are readily identified, each student has individual needs and interests. Sean, a serious stamp collector, is also a history buff. He and Nicole volunteer at the county historical museum as tour guides. Their motivation in history classes is strong, and they are aware of community resources that neither their history teacher nor Mary knows. Nicole and Sean are in a class of college-bound students who work on independent projects and make frequent use of the media center. These class members are comfortable using almost all the resources and equipment. Many of them also use a nearby college collection and the state archives. Mary checks bibliographies in their papers to see whether titles from the other libraries should be added to the Fairmont collection.

Sean, Nicole, and their college-bound classmates are the exceptions at Fairmont. Many of the other students do not feel comfortable in the media center. A failing student, Zachery, gets bored in classes he is repeating. When he disrupts class, he is sent to the media center. At the media center he listens to contemporary music. Through conversations with Zachery about music, Mary learned that he works at his brother's plant nursery. The nursery staff knows a great deal about growing houseplants but very little about orchids. When Zachery expressed an interest in expanding the business into orchids, Mary acquired a book on orchids and delivered it to Zachery to let him know the media center had materials he could borrow. Through this contact Zachery viewed the media center in an entirely new way. He learned that libraries are useful throughout a person's life.

Tetsya and Roshawn are computer techies; they profess to be nonreaders but eagerly devour computer magazines. They are reluctant to use the *Readers' Guide to Periodical Literature*, as they prefer to search for information on the Internet. Mary attracts other students to the media center by recognizing that students need recreational pauses in their busy days. To meet these needs, students find chess boards, checkers, jigsaw puzzles, crossword puzzles, and simulation games throughout the media center. These areas are particularly popular at the end of the semester.

This look at students illustrates differences among individuals. Regardless of how students are grouped or classified, one must never forget that each one is a unique individual. Coursework in child or adolescent psychology, communications, group dynamics, and human relations provides a background for understanding differences among people. But coursework alone is not enough; personal knowledge of each student is important in meeting each one's needs. Without concern for the individual, media specialists cannot know and meet students' needs.

RESOURCES FOR ADULTS
HELPING STUDENTS

General Sources

Many of the general works about children's literature, adolescent literature, and technology that media specialists take for granted are unfamiliar to parents and teachers. Each of the items identified in this section provides information that will help adults meet student needs described in the remaining sections of this chapter. General works should not be buried on the media specialist's desk but should be shared. The discussions and bibliographies in these works can serve as a basic introduction to the materials. The reader will quickly see that this list is only a sampling of the many resources that exist in this area.

Two classics in the area of children's literature are *Children and Books* (HarperCollins, 1991), by Zena Sutherland and others who carry on the tradition of May Hill Arbuthnot's sensitivity to quality, and *Children's Literature in the Elementary School*, by Charlotte Huck and others (Harcourt Brace Jovanovich College Publishers, 1993). A smaller work that focuses on literary aspects is Rebecca J. Lukens's *A Critical Handbook of Children's Literature* (Foresman/Little, Brown Higher Education, 1990). Carol Lynch-Brown and Carl M. Tomlinson's *Essentials of Children's Literature* (Allyn & Bacon, 1993) interweaves the history of each genre with the selection and evaluation of such materials. Their chapter on multicultural and international literature is the most extensive of any title mentioned here. An inexpensive, highly selective annual publication, *Children's Books of the Year* (Child Study Children's Book Committee, Bank Street College, annual) recommends high-quality books for children up to age 14. In *Picture Books for Children* (3d ed., American Library Association, 1990), Patricia J. Cianciolo discusses the value of illustration to titles for children from infancy through age 16. Virginia H. Richey and Katharyn E. Puckett's *Wordless/Almost Wordless Picture Books: A Guide* (Libraries Unlimited, 1992) identifies works in which the illustrations tell the story, identify a concept, or provide information.

For adolescent literature, parents and teachers can be directed to Arthea J. S. Reed's *Reaching Adolescents: The Young Adult Book and the School* (Macmillan, 1994), Reed's *Comics to Classics: A Parent's Guide to Books for Teens and Preteens* (International Reading Association, 1988), and Alleen Pace Nilsen and Kenneth L. Donelson's *Literature for Today's Young Adults* (HarperCollins, 1993) for discussions of specific titles and characteristics of young adult literature. The issues posed in these works provide topics for lively book discussions with parents.

Suggestions for the use of technology, bibliographies, and sources of materials can be found in *Instructional Media and the New Technologies of Instruction* by Robert Heinich, Michael Molenda, and James D. Russell (Macmillian, 1993). Additional sources can be found in general bibliographies, such as Dona J. Helmer's *Selecting Materials for School Library Media Centers* (2d ed., American Library Association, 1993).

Adults Sharing Literature with Students

Recently renewed interest in children's language development and in motivating all students to read may account for the number of sources designed to assist parents, teachers, and media specialists in sharing literature with students. Recommendations for listening levels and lengths of time (a few minutes to extended periods) can be found in Margaret Mary Kimmel and Elizabeth Segal's *For Reading Out Loud! A Guide to Sharing Books with Children* (Dell Publishing, 1991). Another approach is found in *Books Kids Will Sit Still For: The Complete Read-Aloud Guide* by Judy Freeman (R. R. Bowker, 1990). Freeman describes techniques for reading aloud, giving booktalks, leading creative dramatics, and storytelling. For older student audiences, see John T. Gillespie and Corinne J. Naden's *Juniorplots 4: A Book Talk Guide for use with Readers Ages 12-16* (Reed Reference Publishing, 1992). In *Booktalk! 5: More Booktalks for All Ages and Audiences* (H. W. Wilson, 1993), Joni Richards Bodart shares her enthusiasm for using booktalks to motivate readers. Classroom teachers and media specialist can use *Book Links: Connecting Books, Libraries, and Classrooms* (American Library Association, 1991-) to identify old and new titles about specific themes or topics.

Adults interested in motivating young people through film will use Joyce Moss and George Wilson's evaluative *From Page to Screen: Children's and Young Adult Books on Film and Video* (Gale Research, 1992), which identifies films for the hearing-impaired.

SOURCES FOR STUDENT NEEDS AND INTERESTS

Poor and Reluctant Readers

Those who encourage reading skills and literature appreciation have always been challenged by poor readers and reluctant readers. The poor reader reads below capacity but is not necessarily retarded. A reluctant reader is one who is capable but prefers not to read. Books with high appeal and appropriate reading levels can help these students. The phrases *high interest/low vocabulary* (hi-low) or *high interest/low reading level* (HILRL) are used to describe these works. Criteria for evaluating such books include:

- repetition of main points;

- repeating the main points in the summary;

- wide margins, extra space between lines, and short chapters with space between sections;

- direct and simple narrative;

- use of dialogue and action;

- well-organized, direct information;

- illustrations to explain the text; and

- simple vocabulary with sentences of varying lengths.

Three sources to consult are *High / Low Handbook: Encouraging Literacy in the 1990s*, compiled by Ellen V. LiBretto (R. R. Bowker, 1990); *The Best: High / Low Books for Reluctant Readers*, by Marianne Laino Pilla (Libraries Unlimited, 1990); and *High Interest-Easy Reading for Junior and Senior High School Students* (NCTE, 1990). *High / Low Handbook* includes an annotated list of titles recommended for reluctant readers and one for disabled readers. *The Best: High / Low Books for Reluctant Readers* describes 374 titles for recreational reading by third- to twelfth-graders. *High Interest-Easy Reading for Junior and Senior High School Students*, designed for student use, lists fiction and nonfiction titles with contemporary themes and issues that appeal to this age group. The annotations are brief booktalks.

Personal and Social Development

Media specialists are responsible for providing materials that promote self-awareness and understanding of others. A number of tools assist in this effort. Many of them provide or identify professional literature that will help heighten the media specialist's sensitivity to children's needs. The significance of promoting personal and social development is discussed by Sharon Spredemann Dreyer:

> Books have an important role in everyday life. Through well-chosen books, readers may increase their self-knowledge and self-esteem, gain relief from unconscious conflicts, clarify their values, and better understand other people. By identifying with characters in books, people may come to realize that they are part of humanity; that they are not alone in their struggles with reality. Reading increases personal knowledge and invites readers to consider themselves objectively.[1]

Dreyer's *The Best of Bookfinder: Selected Titles from Volumes 1-3: A Guide to Children's Literature About Interests and Concerns of Youth Ages 2-18* (American Guidance Services, 1992) recommends titles dealing with psychological, behavioral, and developmental topics of concern to children and adolescents. The entries include annotations, bibliographic information, main subject headings, synopses, analysis of strengths or limitations of presentation, and a list of works presenting the same content in other formats (films, tapes, paperbacks, braille, talking books, filmstrips, and recordings). Parents, teachers, counselors, psychologists, and psychiatrists will find this a helpful resource in working with students who are experiencing problems related to those in the recommended titles.

A sampling of resources to help teachers and media specialists in the selection of materials for these purposes illustrates possible approaches. *Books to Help Children Cope with Separation and Loss: An Annotated Bibliography*, by Marsha K. Rudman, Kathleen Duanne Gagne, and Joanne E. Berstein (R. R. Bowker, 1993), provides descriptive annotations and evaluations of books for children from age 3-16. Themes include the new sibling, the new school, death, divorce, desertion, serious illness, war, foster care, step-parents, adoption, and homelessness. Stephanie Zvirin's *The Best Years of Their Lives: A Resource Guide for Teenagers in Crisis* (American Library Association, 1992) reviews 200 nonfiction, fiction, and video titles on topics of interest to students 12-18 years old. In *Substance Abuse: A Resource Guide for Secondary Schools* (Libraries Unlimited, 1991), Sally Myers and Blanche Woolls identify books, audiovisual materials, free and inexpensive materials, and periodicals for students and teachers. They provide a sample evaluation form. The focus is on materials that trace the history of drug abuse or provide facts about the dangers of drugs.

Personal Interests

A number of bibliographies recommend materials that will appeal to specific age groups. Committees within the National Council of Teachers of English periodically revise *Adventuring with Books: A Booklist for Pre-School–Grade 6* (NCTE, 1989), *Your Reading: A Booklist for Junior High and Middle School Students* (NCTE, 1991), and *Books for You: A Booklist for Senior High Students* (NCTE, 1992). Recommended titles in *Your Reading* are grouped by subjects. The annotations in *Books for You* and *Your Reading* are written for students. In *Books for You*, the students are directed to other works by their favorite authors.

The coverage of the next work is evident in its appealing title: *More Exciting, Funny, Scary, Short, Different, and Sad Books Kids Like About Animals, Science, Sports, Families, Songs, and Other Things* (American Library Association, 1992), by Frances Laverne Carroll and Mary Meacham. The annotations are written for children. The Bowker series, *Best Books for Children: Preschool Through Grade 6* (4th ed., John T. Gillespie and Corinne J. Naden, R. R. Bowker, 1990); *Best Books for Junior High Readers* (John T. Gillespie, R. R. Bowker, 1991); and *Best Books for Senior High Readers* (John T. Gillespie, R. R. Bowker, 1991) identify fiction and nonfiction titles that have received favorable reviews. Another work designed to match a reader's interest with a book is Betty Rosenberg and Diana Tixier Herald's *Genreflecting: A Guide to Reading Interests in Genre Fiction* (3d ed., Libraries Unlimited, 1991), which covers westerns, thrillers, science fiction, supernatural, and romance.

Two bibliographies useful in identifying titles in series are Janet Husband and Jonathan Husband's *Sequels: An Annotated Guide to Novels in Series* (NCTE, 1990) and Judith K. Rosenberg's *Young People's Books in Series: Fiction and Non-Fiction 1975-1991* (Libraries Unlimited, 1992).

The following tools will assist in the selection of materials that appeal to teenage readers. *Books for the Teen Age* (New York Public Library, 1929-) annotates current popular fiction, current affairs titles, and nonfiction works enjoyed by this age group. Cosette Kies's *Supernatural Fiction for Teens: More Than 1300 Good Paperbacks to Read for Wonderment* (2d ed., Libraries Unlimited, 1992) includes notes on movie versions of the books. *Fiction for Youth: A Guide to Recommended Books* by Lillian L. Shapiro and Barbara L. Stein (Neal-Schuman, 1992) is designed to expose capable readers to exceptional twentieth-century fiction titles, including juvenile and adult works. *Reading Lists for College-Bound Students* by Doug Estell and others (Arco/Prentice Hall, 1990) reprints lists of books recommended by 103 colleges and a composite list of the 100 most often recommended works. In *Nonfiction for Young Adults from Delight to Wisdom* (Oryx Press, 1990), Betty Carter and Richard F. Abrahamson discuss the selection and use of nonfiction works and include conversations with popular nonfiction authors. The Young Adult Services Division of the American Library Association annually recommends *Best Books for Young Adults* and has other helpful publications, such as *Outstanding Books for the College Bound*. A different approach is found in *University Press Books for Public and Secondary School Libraries* (Association of American University Presses, 1991), which provides annotations for works from these presses that are recommended for high school honors students.

Two current reviewing sources focus on materials for the adolescent. *VOYA: Voice of Youth Advocates* (Scarecrow Press, 1978-) reviews books, reference titles, films, videotapes, and recordings in terms of quality and popularity. *KLIATT: An Annotated List of Current Paperbacks, Audio Books, and Educational Software* (The Guide, 1967-) recommends books for students ages 12-19. *KLIATT* includes codes for titles recommended for special groups of students, such as those with low reading abilities or those ready for mature subjects and themes.

INDIVIDUALS WITH DISABILITIES

Although each person is unique, he or she may be part of a group sharing characteristics that require special consideration in the collection. As you consider these special group characteristics, remember the message, "label cans, not people." Individuals with special needs may be students, teachers, or staff members. This discussion provides basic information and identifies resources that will help media specialists, teachers, other staff members, parents, and caregivers. A discussion of sources covering more than one disability is followed by sections on sources for the visually-impaired and for the deaf or hearing-impaired.

Background Information

Two pieces of national legislation of particular relevance for this discussion are the Education for All Handicapped Children Act of 1975 (Public Law 94-142), now called Individuals with Disabilities Education Act (IDEA), and the Americans with Disabilities Act (ADA; Public Law 101-336). The IDEA addresses the needs of the child and calls for an individualized educational program (IEP) based on each individual's needs. The media specialist will cooperate with teachers to learn about the methods being used in the IEP in order to offer support. A work that will help media specialists, parents, and teachers understand the process of ensuring the child's rights under IDEA is *Negotiating the Special Education Maze* by Winifred Anderson, Stephan Chitwood, and Deidre Hayden (Woodbine House, 1990).

The ADA has implications for addressing the needs of parents and caregivers. Marilyn H. Karrenbrock describes the impact of the IDEA and ADA, which

> encourage more students to stay in school, to seek vocational training and to enter postsecondary education. It has been suggested that the Individualized Educational Program or IEP should include recommendations "not only for vocational preparation but also to vocational awareness and vocational exploration." School library media centers usually assist students and vocation teachers and counselors by providing material about various vocations and their requirements, college and university catalogs and admission requirements, and other pertinent information which helps students in the transition to work or higher education. Parents and advocates for students with disabilities often want such materials also. Media centers will need to provide more information of this nature for students who have disabilities. Reference books, periodicals, catalogs, vertical file materials, computer programs, and audiovisual materials will all be needed to provide suitable materials in accessible formats.[2]

To better understand these students' needs, Karrenbrock suggests forming partnerships with people with disabilities. The community may have groups that address the needs and concerns of people with disabilities; members of these groups may be willing to form partnerships. Many local newspapers list such groups.

Remember that disabled students and staff members share the recreational interests and informational needs of their peers.

> They are individuals with unique personalities. There are important differences, however, that cannot be ignored. These differences can become barriers to information access. Some students lack the ability to use their bodies to retrieve materials from the shelves or to use the material once it is retrieved. Certain disabilities, notably

cerebral palsy, typically combine communication and physical disabilities. Because the degree of difficulty varies for individual students, library media specialists must be alert to individual differences.[3]

Children's interests, regardless of disabilities, usually are similar to that of their peers. One can anticipate the interests of a particular age group, but it is important to also know a particular child's individual interests. A general knowledge of the developmental characteristics of children and their interests is essential. This knowledge helps media specialists anticipate the recreational and informational needs of all children, including those with disabilities.

Information about the characteristics of disabilities and the materials recommended to meet the needs of the disabled can guide collection activities. The characteristics of a specific disability, however, may not apply to all individuals with that disability. And, many children with multiple disabilities have needs identified with more than one type of disability. According to Richard J. Sorennsen,

> The first step toward providing effective media and other services for EEN (exceptional educational needs) students is in acquiring a general knowledge of their special characteristics and needs. . . . Media specialists can serve students best if they have learned to recognize the signs of a disability, such as a slower learning rate, short attention span, restlessness, or other behavioral difficulties.[4]

School staff members can help. The teachers can describe students' behavior management programs, abilities, and learning styles. The media specialist can learn which disabilities call for modifications or adaptations and how they can be implemented. Specialists at the district or state level also can provide information and advice.

Sources About Multiple Disabilities

Students with special needs use the same range of formats other students use, but in some cases, alternatives or adaptations are necessary. Paperbacks are ideal for students with upper extremity weakness. Students with cognitive disabilities may find audio, video, toys, and multimedia formats useful. In *Adaptive Technologies for Learning & Work Environments* (American Library Association, 1993), Joseph J. Lazzaro describes available technologies and their sources. Table 12.1 lists the range of technologies Lazzaro covers. He also identifies other information sources, including organizations for persons with disabilities.

Table 12.1.
Adaptive Technologies

For vision-impaired

Internal and external speech synthesis hardware
Speech synthesis software
Screen readers for graphics
Magnification systems
Software-based magnification programs
Braille systems
Optical character recognition systems

For hearing-impaired

Text telephones
Braille text telephones
Facsimile communication
Computer-assisted access
Computer-aided transcription
Computerized sign language training
Signaling systems
Captioning systems
Electronic amplification systems
Telephone amplification systems

For motor- and speech-impaired

Adaptive keyboards
Keyboard guards
Keyboard modification software
Alternative input system
Morse code systems
Word-prediction software
Voice recognition systems
Alternative communications device
Environmental control system

Based on Joseph J. Lazzaro, *Adaptive Technologies for Learning & Work Environments* (American Library Association, 1993).

A variety of terms, such as *handicapped, disabled, exceptional, impaired,* and *special,* are used to describe individuals and their needs. Walling and Karrenbrock, in *Disabilities, Children, and Libraries: Mainstreaming Services in Pubic Libraries and School Library Media Centers* (Libraries Unlimited, 1993) address the issue by noting a change in their own approach. In an earlier work they used the phrase "the disabled child" as

> a step toward acknowledging the children's humanity, but we have come to realize that such phrases still place the disability first. In this book we speak of "the child with a disability" or "the child who is blind." This approach places the emphasis where it belongs—on the child.[5]

Walling and Karrenbrock provide information to help media specialists understand the characteristics of various disabilities: mobility and dexterity (amputation, spinal cord injury (SCI), spina bifida, cerebral palsy, juvenile rheumatoid arthritis, muscular dystrophy duchenne type); chronic health conditions (asthma-related allergic reactions, cystic fibrosis, sickle cell anemia, epilepsy, diabetes mellitus, HIV, AIDS); sensory disabilities (hearing, vision, speech, cognition, and perception); developmental disabilities; autism; Fetal Alcohol Syndrome (FAS); Traumatic Brain Injury (TBI); behavior disorders; and depression. This comprehensive resource guide recommends formats and assistive technologies for specific disabilities; identifies sources for these materials; and describes sources of information, including agencies and associations.

Walling and Karrenbrock offer many practical suggestions to help the media specialist help the child use resources and to ensure that their visits to the media center are a productive and pleasant experience. They identify three kinds of barriers: the disabilities, societal and individual attitudes, and environmental conditions. They conclude that though media specialists "are not in a position to eliminate disability barriers, . . . attitudinal and environmental barriers are within reach."[6]

One way media specialists can help change attitudes is through their selection of materials depicting disabled persons. Kieth C. Wright and Judith F. Davie offer the following guidelines:

- The work offers more than the mere inclusion of a disability or disabled person.

- Avoid work in which the disability is the primary focus. Individuals should be a natural part of the population.

- Avoid stereotypes, including dependent, pitiful, or supercapable characters.

- Avoid phrases that can demean individuals; avoid cliches or slang phrases to describe the disabled.

- Disabled persons should be shown as participants in society.

- Materials should present disabled persons interacting with others in mutually beneficial ways. Communication should be natural, without embarrassment or awkwardness.

- Disabled persons should be included as workers, community leaders, and participants in social and sports activities.

- Disabled persons should be included in materials for all levels of users (early childhood through adulthood).[7]

Ruth A. Velleman, who works with children with disabilities agrees. She observes, "Books about the disabled are purchased only when they have literary merit, since our students are quick to sense inaccuracies and insincerity in this sensitive area."[8]

Two works designed to help media specialists select materials are *Portraying Persons with Disabilities: An Annotated Bibliography of Fiction for Children and Teenagers* (3d ed., R. R. Bowker, 1992) by Debra Robertson, and *Portraying Persons with Disabilities: An Annotated Bibliography of Nonfiction for Children and Teenagers* (R. R. Bowker, 1992), by Joan Brest Friedberg, June B. Mullins, and Adelaide Weir Sukiennik. Both analyze and evaluate the strengths and weaknesses of the listed titles.

Not only do media specialists need to know the individuals and the materials appropriate for disabled children in the collection, they have a responsibility to know the resources available in the community. These may include rehabilitation agencies, information agencies, and other educational or recreational programs. For example, some communities have recreation areas designed to accommodate wheelchairs or to provide information that is learned through a variety of senses. In one recreational area, trails provide easy access to picnic areas, a fishing pier, and nature paths. Along the trails, information stations use models, large charts, printed information, and recorded messages to point out items of interest. Messages written in braille encourage people to feel the object or to smell it. Sheltered eating areas provide spaces for wheelchairs interspersed with picnic benches. The park is a beautiful spot all people can enjoy. The media specialist should make information about such facilities available and possibly suggest them as destinations for field trips.

Other sources of information are national clearinghouses and organizations. The National Center on Education Media and Materials for the Handicapped (NCEMMH), located at the Ohio State University College of Education, produces evaluation guidelines and forms for instructional materials. The Council for Exceptional Children (CEC) provides information about education for both disabled and gifted children. CEC hosts the ERIC Clearinghouse on Handicapped and Gifted Children, which distributes bibliographies, conference papers, curriculum guides, and other documents. The National Information Center for Children and Youth with Disabilities (NICCYD) provides free information to assist adults in helping children with disabilities become active members of their school and community. Journals of interest to adults working with exceptional children include: *Exceptional Children, The Exceptional Parent, Journal of Learning Disabilities*, and *Teaching the Exceptional Child.*

Visually Impaired

Children who have vision problems may require special types of materials. Some partially sighted individuals can use regular-print materials, while others need large-print materials. One cannot make the assumption that large-print materials are appropriate for all partially sighted children. Low-vision aids, handheld magnifiers, or closed-circuit televisions can magnify standard-print materials. Braille books, games, and outline maps can be used by trained children. A blind person can read printed materials by using optical machines that allow the user to feel sensation on his or her fingertips. For others, readers and taped materials may be most useful.

Visually disabled children can participate in all media center activities. Useful equipment includes: rear-projection screens, which permit children to get close to the screen without blocking images; tape recorders; speech compressors, which eliminate pauses between words and, thus, reduce the time needed to access recorded materials; and talking calculators.

Visually and physically disabled people can use talking books, which are tapes or records of books, textbooks, and magazines (available in English and other languages, including Spanish). Talking books are a free service of the National Library Service for the Blind and Physically Handicapped, part of the Library of Congress. Arrangements can be made through the local public library. *For Younger Readers: Braille and Talking Books* (Library of Congress, 1967-) is a biennial catalog of braille, disc, and cassette books announced in *Braille Book Review* (1933-) and *Talking Books Topics* (1935-) from the National Service for the Blind and Physically Handicapped. These titles are available free to the blind or disabled. Another type of material provided by the service is called twin-vision, a format in which printed text is interpaged with braille text in one volume. *Library Resources for the Blind and Physically Handicapped* (National Library Service for the Blind and Physically Handicapped, 1990) lists network libraries and machine-lending agencies that participate in the free service program.

Recordings for the Blind: Catalog of Recorded Books (Recording for the Blind, 1960-) features free taped books, including textbooks. Titles available in large type can be identified in *The Complete Directory of Large Print Books and Serials* (R. R. Bowker, 1992), which lists adult, juvenile, and textbook titles and indicates the type size and size of book. The American Foundation for the Blind publishes useful pamphlets, such as *Guidelines for Public School Programs Serving Visually Handicapped Children*, and the *Journal of Visual Impairment and Blindness*. The American Printing House for the Blind (APHB) publishes braille books and magazines as well as large-print texts, produces Talking Book records, and manufactures educational aids for the blind. The Instructional Materials Center for the Visually Handicapped at APHB serves as the National Reference Center for the Visually Handicapped and evaluates and disseminates instructional materials related to the education of the visually impaired.

Deaf or Hearing-Impaired

Hearing-impaired children have difficulty hearing spoken language and, as a result, often have difficulty understanding written and spoken language and abstract concepts. Visual formats are useful for these children. The visuals should be large and present a single, distinct concept or idea. Illustrations and print should be immediately recognizable. Language patterns and sentence structures need to be simple. Repetition and reinforcement are helpful.

Captioned films, filmstrips, and videotapes are useful for hearing-impaired children. Information about the captioned-film program can be obtained from Captioned Films and Telecommunications Branch, Division of Media Services, Bureau of Education for the Handicapped, United States Office of Education. This information also is available in *Captioned Films / Videos* (distributed by Modern Talking Picture Service), which lists free-loan educational and general-interest films and videos. Check with your local educational television station for information about captioned programming and the equipment necessary to receive it.

Children who have learned sign language will want signed books, films, filmstrips, and videotapes. Sources of professional materials and books in sign language are available from: Alexander Graham Bell Association for the Deaf, Gallaudet College Bookstore, and National Association of the Deaf. Reviews of games, kits, and learning materials designed for use with hearing- or speech-impaired children are found in *ASHA: A Journal of the American Speech-Language-Hearing Association*. Media specialists might take a course in sign language to increase rapport with these students.

SUMMARY

Students deserve to be known as individuals. When working with groups, it is easy to overlook individuals who seem to disappear into the crowd. Media specialists are involved with students during important years of development yet seldom realize how brief contact can affect children and their families.

This writer recalls a first-grader who came into the media center one day asking for information about logic and philosophy. He seemed to know what he wanted. With my fingers crossed, we went to the shelves. I knew we had only three titles about logic and wondered if he would be able to understand them. He did. Years later, as a woman was talking to me about media specialists' attitudes toward children, she mentioned that her young son proudly brought home a nonfiction book. His teacher had wanted him to read a picture book rather than a book about logic. As I listened, I wondered if this boy could have been the child I remembered. As it turned out, I had helped the boy in his early quest to study logic. He became a champion chess player in his early teens. Every day there are children or adults who are influenced by media specialists, but rarely do we get the opportunity to learn the results of our efforts.

NOTES

[1]Sharon Spredemann Dreyer, *The Best of Bookfinder: A Guide to Children's Literature About Interests and Concerns of Youth Aged 2-18* (Circle Pines, MN: American Guidance Service, 1992), xiii.

[2]Marilyn H. Karrenbrock, "The Impact of the ADA upon School Library Media Centers," in *How Libraries Must Comply with the Americans with Disabilities Act (ADA)*, ed. by Donald D. Foss and Nancy C. Pack (Phoenix, AZ: Oryx Press, 1992), 83.

[3]Linda Lucas Walling, "Granting Each Equal Access," *School Library Media Quarterly* 20, no. 4 (Summer 1992): 216.

[4]Richard J. Sorennsen, "Collaborative Efforts Can Create a Program That Meets Special Students' Needs," *Channel DLS: Wisconsin Division for Library Services* 29, no. 4 (December 1993): 10.

[5]Linda Lucas Walling and Marilyn H. Karrenbrock, *Disabilities, Children, and Libraries: Mainstreaming Services in Public Libraries and School Library Media Centers* (Englewood, CO: Libraries Unlimited, 1993), xi.

[6]Walling and Karrenbrock, *Disabilities, Children, and Libraries*, xvii.

[7]Kieth C. Wright, and Judith F. Davie, *Library Manager's Guide to Hiring and Serving Disabled Persons* (Jefferson, NC: McFarland, 1990), 38-40.

[8]Ruth A. Velleman, *Meeting the Needs of People with Disabilities: A Guide for Librarians, Educators, and Other Service Professionals* (Phoenix, AZ: Oryx Press, 1990), 174.

BIBLIOGRAPHY

Dreyer, Sharon Spredemann. *The Best of Bookfinder: A Guide to Children's Literature About Interests and Concerns of Youth Aged 2-18*. Circle Pines, MN: American Guidance Service, 1992.

Karrenbrock, Marilyn H. "The Impact of the ADA upon School Library Media Centers." In *How Libraries Must Comply with the Americans with Disabilities Act (ADA)*, ed. by Donald D. Foss and Nancy C. Pack. Phoenix, AZ: Oryx Press, 1992.

Sorennsen, Richard J. "Collaborative Efforts Can Create a Program That Meets Special Students' Needs," *Channel DLS: Wisconsin Division for Library Services* 29, no. 4 (December 1993): 10-11.

Velleman, Ruth A. *Meeting the Needs of People with Disabilities: A Guide for Librarians, Educators, and Other Service Professionals*. Phoenix, AZ: Oryx Press, 1990.

Walling, Linda Lucas. "Granting Each Equal Access." *School Library Media Quarterly* 20, no. 4 (Summer 1992): 216-22.

Walling, Linda Lucas, and Marilyn H. Karrenbrock. *Disabilities, Children, and Libraries: Mainstreaming Services in Public Libraries and School Library Media Centers*. Englewood, CO: Libraries Unlimited, 1993.

Wright, Kieth C., and Judith F. Davie. *Serving the Disabled: A How-To-Do-It Manual for Librarians*. New York: Neal-Schuman, 1991.

PART

III

ADMINISTRATIVE CONCERNS

Did you ever see a battered book in a media center? If you had a chance to glance at its title, you probably recognized it as a popular work that is rarely on the shelves. The media specialist has probably been trying for some time to rescue it to have it mended or replaced. Some books go from one student to the next with hardly a pause at the circulation desk.

Have you seen the edges of study prints crumbling from too many pin holes, games with missing pieces, or cassettes with loose tapes? Are the shelves of the media center overflowing in one section and bare in another? These situations happen in every collection. It is a challenge to ensure that they don't happen regularly.

The media specialist is the administrator of the collection. If the word *administrator* conjures images of pushing papers and filling out forms in triplicate, then you have overlooked important administrative roles. An administrator must be a planner, organizer, policy maker, businessperson, and evaluator. Through these roles, the media specialist shapes a collection and accesses resources that are responsive to the changing demands of the students, curriculum, and teachers. Making selection decisions, receiving new materials, and helping students use global resources through the Internet may be the more glamorous, exciting aspects of work with the collection. Administrative decisions, however, can ensure that students and teachers obtain the resources they need.

CHAPTER 13

Acquiring Materials

When the selection process is complete, it is time to obtain materials. Acquisition, the process of obtaining materials, includes confirming that materials are available, verifying order information, identifying and selecting the sources of the materials, arranging for order transmission and fulfillment, allocating funds, and keeping records. Of all the administrative activities, acquisitions is the one in which technology affects daily operations.

Materials may be acquired through purchase, rent, solicitation of free materials, gifts, or exchanges. Schools participating in resource-sharing programs may borrow and lend specific materials identified in coordinated collection-development plans or made available through interlibrary loan. The district processing center may handle the acquisition procedures and serve as the clearinghouse for resource-sharing transactions. This chapter focuses on the components of the acquisition process most likely to involve the building-level person directly (see fig. 13.1 on page 230). It also reviews the relationship of acquisition procedures to acquisition policy; describes procedures for acquiring materials; describes bibliographic tools and other sources of information indicating the availability of materials; identifies sources of materials; and discusses the relationship between media professionals and publishers/producers. Chapter 14 discusses other ways to acquire materials through resource sharing, coordinated collection development, and electronic means. Bibliographic information for acquisition tools, including those cited in this chapter, appear in appendix B. The bibliography for this chapter lists works that provide information outside the scope of this discussion.

RELATIONSHIP OF ACQUISITION PROCEDURES TO POLICIES

Policies state what will be done and why it will be done; procedures state how it will be done and who will do it. An acquisition policy may state that materials shall be purchased from the least expensive and most efficient source, for example, a jobber. The policy may go on to state that an item needed immediately may be purchased locally. A policy also could state that videotapes will be purchased rather than buying or renting 16-mm films.

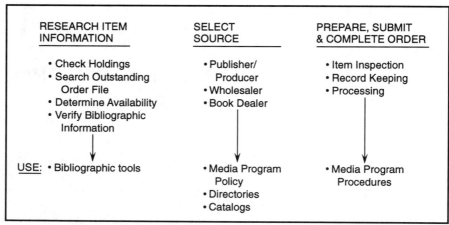

Fig. 13.1. Components of the acquisition process.

Acquisition policies are likely to be uniform throughout the school district. The school district may dictate the acquisition procedures. For example, the district purchasing agent may specify the order forms to be used. Other school districts may have agreements to use a jobber's online catalog. Procedures for accounting and recordkeeping are also frequently established at the district level. Ask the director of the district media program for a copy of the policies and procedures. Often this information is available in a handbook for all media specialists within the system.

ACQUISITION ACTIVITIES

The first stage of acquisition activities includes checking for the requested item in the present holdings and the file of outstanding orders, checking the availability of the item, and verifying the accuracy of bibliographic and purchase information. The second step is selecting the best source for the material. The third step is preparing and submitting the order. The fourth step is checking the received item against the original order and the invoice and checking the condition of the material. Are pages missing? Are all the elements in a kit? If the order is complete and in good condition, funds are disbursed and recordkeeping is completed.

Searching and Verifying

The first step in the acquisition process is to learn whether the item is already part of the collection. The requested item may be a new edition of a book recently acquired or a cassette, which is part of a kit already in the collection. If the item is in the collection, check with the requester to determine if the existing item is sufficient. If the collection does not have the item, find out whether it is on order or is being processed. In some media centers, a copy of the order slip is filed in the card catalog under title entry or is recorded in the online catalog. When a work is received, a note is added that it is being processed. This procedure simplifies the checking process.

If the media center has a standing order with a publisher, you will not need to initiate orders for titles that are delivered under the conditions of the standing order. For example, the American Library Association has categories of standing orders for materials relating to children and school libraries. You may have a comprehensive membership in an association, such as the Association for Supervision and Curriculum Development, that includes an automatic shipment of all pamphlets and books issued by the association during the year of membership. Your media center may belong to a book club. Check these agreements to identify titles you will be receiving under the plan. Pending titles could be ones you do not want to duplicate.

IMPACT OF TECHNOLOGY

Acquisition activities involve large amounts of detail work. Computers can simplify accessing information and generating records. Consideration files (the record of desired items) can be organized with a database management program, enabling one to print out a list of items to be ordered from a single publisher in priority order. Records are updated as materials are ordered and received. Some systems allow transfer of the information to a different file, such as outstanding orders or newly arrived acquisitions. Some systems also allow the administrator to create categories, such as a subject area, a specific format, back orders, or specified jobbers. Word processing programs can be used to create a template to print specific information on preprinted continuous forms, including purchase orders. A spreadsheet program can be used to keep track of budget reports and projections or for organizing batch orders. Schools use databases to combine orders from several schools and decide which schools should buy expensive works, such as reference books. If your school district is not using computer programs for management activities, learn what jobs can best be handled by them, what equipment resources are available, the staffing implications, and the capability of existing software packages before establishing a management system.

AVAILABILITY OF MATERIALS

To make wise selection decisions, the media specialist must know what materials are available in what formats, and what will be forthcoming. This involves being familiar with bibliographic tools and aware of sources of information about materials.

Bibliographic Tools

When checking the availability of materials, use sources of information that list currently available materials or forthcoming items. Two tools, *Books in Print* (R. R. Bowker, 1984-) and *Canadian Books in Print* (University of Toronto Press, 1975-), report what is available at the time of publication. This information can be updated using subsequent reviewing journals, publishers' catalogs, and supplements. Announcements of forthcoming publications, productions, and releases inform media specialists what materials will be available. Such announcements may appear in journals, such as *School Library Journal*, or in flyers from publishers and producers.

To learn whether an item is available, use a special type of bibliography called a trade bibliography. These tools provide ordering information for materials that are currently in print or otherwise available. Bibliographic tools that indicate availability also may state

- whether the item is available through purchase, rent, or loan, and the purchase or rental price;

- whether the item must be ordered directly from the publisher or producer or is available through a jobber or a distributor; and

- whether there are postage or delivery charges, the person(s) responsible for pick-up and return deliveries, the length of the loan, the notice required to ensure delivery on a needed date, and appropriate alternative arrangements.

The information included for each item varies from one tool to another. For print formats, the bibliographic entry usually includes author, title, edition, publisher, date of publication, series title and number, available bindings, price, and International Standard Book Number (ISBN) or International Standard Serial Number (ISSN). For audiovisual items, the bibliographic entry usually includes title; available formats; production and release dates; producer or distributor; physical characteristics (for example, color or black-and-white, captioned or sound, phonodisc or cassette, length or running time, and special equipment needed); number of pieces included (for example, four study prints and one teacher's guide); languages; price; and special conditions of availability.

Many bibliographies must be used. A few examples illustrate the process. To find the price of a particular book title, look under the title or author in *Books in Print* or on *Books in Print Plus* (R. R. Bowker), the CD-ROM version. For videotape rentals, check *Educational Film/Video Locator* (4th ed., R. R. Bowker, 1990). Information about equipment can be found in *Equipment Directory of Audio-Visual, Computer and Video Products* (International Communications Industries Association, 1984-). Use the latest edition for the most current information about price and availability. Other bibliographies are listed in table 13.1.

Table 13.1.
Bibliographic Tools for Selected Formats

Format	Sample Tools
Books and serials	*Alternative Press Publishers of Children's Books* *Books in Print* and related works *Canadian Books in Print* and related works *Children's Books in Print* and related works *The Complete Directory of Large Print Books and Serials* *El-Hi Textbooks and Serials in Print*
Software	*The Apple Software Directory* *Microcomputer Software Guide Online* *Microcomputer Software Sources* *Software Encyclopedia* *Software Information—for Apple II Computers* *Swift's Directory of Educational Software for the IBM PC*
Equipment	*Equipment Directory of Audio-visual, Computer and Video Products*
Films and videos	*Bowker's Complete Video Directory* *Educational Film & Video Locator* *Film and Video Finder* *The Video Source Book*
Free and inexpensive materials	*Captioned Films/Videos* *Educators Guides series* *Free Materials for Schools and Libraries* *Vertical File Index*
Recordings	*The Audio Store Catalog* (Wisconsin Public Radio) *Audiocassette & Compact Disc Finder* *Recordings for the Blind* *Schwann Spectrum* *Words on Cassette*
Other formats	*Filmstrip & Slide Set Finder* *Slide Buyer's Guide* *The University Prints Catalogue*

Note: Full citations for these tools are provided in appendix B.

The funds needed to buy these tools will strain even the strongest budget. While the cost may seem prohibitive for the CD-ROM formats, schools that can share them will find that option less expensive than purchasing print versions for each media center. In many districts, expensive bibliographies are available at the district media center or in a larger collection, such as that of a nearby college. Some media specialists ask local colleges or universities to share older editions as they are replaced.

These media specialists rely on current selection tools and jobber catalogs for current prices. Pamphlets and other materials can be located through use of *Vertical File Index* (H. W. Wilson, 1955-) or *Free Materials for Schools and Libraries* (Dyad Services, 1979-).

Other Information Sources

If your school does not receive advertisements from publishers and producers, write to request free catalogs. This approach has hidden costs, including clerical time, postage, filing, and storage of the materials. Although bibliographic tools provide quicker access, especially to materials on a given subject, catalogs have other advantages. They are up-to-date, and they provide full ordering information and other useful information, such as suggested grade level, a possible reading level, and curriculum application.

Catalogs provide price and availability information, but they should not be used for reviews. Remember that catalogs exist to sell materials, not to offer reviews. When catalogs do quote reviews, full citations to the reviews usually are not given, so the media specialist needs to consider the limitations of incomplete reviews, words taken out of context, and the absence of more critical comments, which reviews offer.

General catalogs are not the only form of advertising that media specialists find useful. Publishers, producers, wholesalers, distributors, and vendors may offer a subject catalog to draw attention to the uses of their materials within curriculum areas. Flyers and forthcoming announcements advertise new materials. Sales representatives may visit schools to present information about their publications or products.

Lists of publications and products can be found in catalogs from government agencies, manufacturers, professional associations, museums, and county extension services. These listings may include free and inexpensive materials used to promote or advertise products and services of the sponsoring producer.

Publications about the community may be found through announcements in the local newspapers or through local civic and social organizations. The local chamber of commerce may have pamphlets about the community, businesses, industries, recreation facilities, history, forthcoming events, and geography. The local historical society may have pamphlets or slides about historic buildings or events.

CHOOSING THE APPROPRIATE SOURCE

Tools that list available materials may show the original source (publisher or producer) but not the best source from which to obtain the material. Factors for choosing a particular source include which offers the best price for the item; how soon the item can be delivered; and other services, such as cataloging or processing.

Chief sources of materials include wholesalers, distributors, jobbers, publishers, producers, subscription agencies, dealers, remainders, vendors, and local sources. Wholesalers buy materials from publishers and producers and sell them to bookstores and libraries. For example, books and videocassettes can be brought directly from the publisher or producer; the same items are often available at lower cost from a jobber or distributor. The word *distributor* may refer to a wholesaler but more frequently means a vendor of magazines, paperbacks, or audiovisual materials. Distributors may serve a region of the country or the whole country. Jobbers and distributors may provide newsletter and product hotlines. The term *jobber* can be used interchangeably with the word *wholesaler*. Wholesalers, distributors, and jobbers are middlemen between publishers or producers and the buyer, the media specialist. *Remainders* handle materials at a discount price for items that usually are unavailable from other sources. A *book remainder* may handle titles a publisher is no longer keeping in stock.

Personnel at the district level may be responsible for selecting the wholesaler or other source. If that is not the situation, contact other media specialists in the area to learn which sources they use and whether they are satisfied with the service. There are many advantages to ordering materials through wholesalers:

- The cost and paperwork of ordering through many publishers is avoided.

- There is only one source to contact for follow-up on orders.

- Libraries receive better discounts from wholesalers than from publishers or producers.

- Some publishers refuse to deal directly with libraries or give poor service to small orders.

- Many wholesalers provide full processing, cataloging services, circulation materials, and plastic jackets for materials.

- Preselection plans—approval plans in which the library examines new titles at the usual discount rate with full return privileges—are frequently available.

- Some wholesalers offer online ordering services.

For videos, vendors offer leasing plans. Before leasing a video, learn whether the vendor

- offers a volume discount;

- provides a range of customer services, with clear billing and invoicing procedures and forms;

- has a toll-free telephone number;

- offers a full title line in terms of variety; and

- can handle backorders and returns in a timely, accurate, and acceptable manner.[1]

As you investigate these sources, ask about their pricing schedules. Some will have two discount plans: one a net title price, the other based on volume orders. Batch volume orders have lower per-item costs.

Disadvantages of using wholesalers include

- It usually takes one month for most orders to be filled, whereas publishers can deliver in one to two weeks.

- The availability of older titles depends on the inventory of the wholesaler.

- No wholesaler can supply every available title. Some titles, such as materials produced by professional organizations, can be purchased only through direct order.

- Policies on return of defective or damaged copies may say that credit or replacement is not granted until the returns have been received by the wholesaler.

Many schools have a policy that funds not spent within a specific time period must revert to the school's general fund. Changes in the book industry continually affect media programs. The Supreme Court's decision against the Thor Power Tool Company resulted in taxing warehoused goods. This led to a decrease in the number of back titles stored and delays in reprinting a title until there is a proven market. These changes affect retrospective purchases. Book titles only five years old may be difficult to obtain.

Libraries can expect wholesalers to have a large inventory of titles, to fill orders promptly and accurately at a reasonable cost, and to report on items not in stock. If you do not obtain satisfactory information about whether a book is out of print, out of stock indefinitely, or temporarily out of stock, "The first step is to let the publisher know . . . write letters to the editors, press the jobbers to search for a lost title, go to the right source in order to get the information. The need to communicate *directly* is another priority."[2]

The California Instructional Video Clearinghouse and the California Computer Software Clearinghouse encourage media specialists purchasing CD-ROMs and software to seek out producers and businesses who support the following policies:

- Provide for free preview of the CD-ROM.

- Provide a workstation for a limited time if needed at the site for preview of the CD-ROM.

- Provide dealer support and on-site training as appropriate.

- Maintain a toll-free telephone number to provide user support.

- Provide a full refund for a product that fails to operate as described in advertising or in the documentation.

- Provide licensing agreements that offer multiple copies at nominal cost.

- Provide a network-compatible version and licensing agreements that permit placing the CD-ROM on a network server.

- Provide free or inexpensive updates when a new CD-ROM or version of software is available.

- Replace lost or damaged disks at nominal or net cost.

- Label package and disks to identify clearly the operating platform, for example, MS-DOS or MAC.

- Do not require that the CD-ROM be returned when an update is received.

- Provide multiple sets of consumable support materials at a reasonable cost and/or grant permission for these materials to be reproduced at each site.

- State required hardware components in simple and explicit language.

- List all cables, extensions, controller cards, systems, and so forth required for program operation.

- Offer text-only CD-ROM for either color or monochrome monitors.

- Offer a subscription price for periodical indexes that is not more than twice the cost of an annual print subscription.

- Offer special pricing of a CD-ROM product when purchased in combination with the same product in print.[3]

A similar set of guidelines for software includes:

- Provide free preview of software and documentation.

- Recognize the need to provide free loan of lab packs or multiple copies of software for use in training sessions.

- For extensive multigrade programs, develop a preview disk with at least one complete interactive segment for each grade level; include sample documentation for each level.

- Provide a refund for any product that fails to operate as described in documentation.

- Provide a backup disk or a procedure for making one.

- Replace damaged disks at nominal or no cost.

- Provide free or inexpensive updates as new versions become available.

- Provide licensing agreements that permit users to make multiple copies of software or that provide multiple copies at a reduced cost.

- Provide an explicit statement of the publisher's policy regarding permission to load a single copy of the program on multiple computers for use at the same time.

- Provide a network-compatible version of software with a licensing agreement that permits placing the software on a hard disk for access by multiple computers.

- Provide adequate teacher support materials and training.

- Accommodate a minimum of 40 students in any record-keeping component included with the program, and protect the records from unauthorized access.

- Provide clear and adequate documentation for program operation.

- Provide multiple sets of consumable materials at reasonable cost or permission to reproduce masters included with the program.

- Make an explicit statement granting permission for students to take the software home, if this is the publisher's policy, and include a sample letter to parents that explains the copyright policy involved.

- Provide a method for soliciting recommendations for the improvement of a software package and offer incentives for suggestions that are incorporated into subsequent versions.[4]

Communication with publishers and producers need not be limited to complaints. If students become excited about a particular work, share that information with the publisher or producer. To obtain information about authors, extra book jackets, or other promotional materials, contact the people responsible for library services or library promotion at the appropriate publishing houses. Addresses of the publishers and the names of personnel can be found in *Literary Market Place* (R. R. Bowker, 1973-). Members of the Educational Paperback Association (paperback wholesalers) offer services, including book examination in their warehouses, annual or biennial open houses with special sales, book fairs, reading programs, and promotional materials. Similar types of information can be found in *Microcomputer Market Place* (R. R. Bowker, 1983-) and *Publishers and Distributors of Paperback Books for Young People* (American Library Association, 1987).

Media specialists share a bond with individuals responsible for promoting the use of materials. That bond that can only be strengthened by two-way communication. Marketing departments have services and products to share, such as posters; media specialists can share how students respond to materials and suggest needed materials, suggestions that can result in future products.

PROCESSING ACQUISITIONS

As each item is received, it is checked against the invoice for title match. In the case of videos, this step must take place before removing the shrink-wrap, because many jobbers and distributors will not accept returns of unwrapped materials. The item should be checked for damage or missing parts. Know the jobber's and distributor's policy on returns and whether credit will be given for damage which may occur in shipping.

The final stage in the acquisition process is preparing materials for use. This involves cataloging and classifying each item, entering it on the holdings record, identifying the media center as owner, adding security strips and circulation barcodes, adding needed labels, and providing protective cases or other packaging for circulating the materials. Copyright warnings and protection labels need to be placed on materials. Finally, how to market and display the new materials must be decided.

SUMMARY

Acquisition activities consume time and energy. Searching for accurate information may require travel to gain access to needed tools. Detailed record keeping and correspondence demand patience. Many routines cannot be slighted or handled in haste. A media specialist's organizational abilities, mathematical skills, and business sense frequently come into play. Errors or misjudgments can be costly. Using computer management systems can simplify procedures while controlling the information in a timely manner. While delays or inaccurate fulfillment of orders can try one's patience, it can all be worthwhile when a student or teacher declares that the materials they have found are precisely what they wanted.

NOTES

[1]James Scholtz, *Developing and Maintaining Video Collections in Libraries* (Santa Barbara, CA: ABC-Clio, 1989), 58.

[2]Judith R. Tennen, "Out-of-Prints Are Out of Order," *School Library Journal* 32, no. 7 (March 1986): 112-13.

[3]California Instructional Video Clearinghouse and California Computer Software Clearinghouse, *1991 Guidelines for CD-ROM in California Schools* (Long Beach, 1991), 13.

[4]California Instructional Video Clearinghouse and California Computer Software Clearinghouse, *1991 Guidelines for Computer Software in California Schools* (Long Beach, 1991), 11.

BIBLIOGRAPHY

Bosch, Stephen; Patricia Promis; and Chris Sugnet. *Guide to Selecting and Acquiring CD-ROMs, Software, and Other Electronic Publications*. Acquisition Guidelines no. 9. Chicago: American Library Association, 1994.

California Instructional Video Clearinghouse and California Computer Software Clearinghouse. *1991 Guidelines for CD-ROM in California Schools*. Long Beach, 1991.

———. *1991 Guidelines for Computer Software in California Schools*. Long Beach, 1991.

Scholtz, James. *Developing and Maintaining Video Collections in Libraries*. Santa Barbara, CA: ABC-Clio, 1989.

Tennen, Judith R. "Out-of-Prints Are Out of Order." *School Library Journal 32*, no. 7 (March 1986): 112-13.

CHAPTER 14

Accessing Information

This chapter describes ways media specialists can access information (acquire information upon demand from other sources) and expand the resources available to their users. The approaches described include formal and informal resource-sharing plans involving networks and coordinated collection-development programs. The chapter closes with a discussion about how technology is creating new ways to access information at the state and global level.

FACTORS INFLUENCING RESOURCE SHARING

With the increasing array of materials that are part of media center collections and the effort to meet both curricular and individual needs of users, media specialists are facing the reality that a single collection can not meet all the demands that will be made on it. This fact, combined with the increasing cost of materials and declining expenditures for resources, points to the increasing need for resource sharing.

Costs and Expenditures

Table 14.1, on page 242, lists average costs for materials in a variety of formats. To annually update the information, consult the April issue of *Publishers Weekly* or the latest edition of *The Bowker Annual Library and Book Trade Almanac* (R. R. Bowker, 1955-).

How do these costs compare to spending? According to Marilyn L. Miller and Marilyn Shontz, in 1991-1992, "schools were spending per pupil a median expenditure (the 'middle' number when all responses are ordered from lowest to highest) for books of $5.85, for audiovisual materials, $2.56;

Table 14.1.
Average Cost of Materials

Format		Average Cost Fiscal Year 1990	Average Cost Fiscal Year 1993
Paperbacks	Juvenile	$3.56	$3.68
Hardbacks	Juvenile	$13.01	$14.30
Filmstrips	(per set)	$121.76	$75.11
Videocassettes	(per minute)	$5.60	$2.35
Film, 16mm	(per minute)	$18.40	$22.14
Prerecorded cassette tapes		$10.47	$8.11

Based on *The Bowker Annual Library and Book Trade Almanac*, 39th ed. (New York: R. R. Bowker, 1994), 511, 518, 520.

for microforms, $1.16; for periodicals, $1.51; for software, $0.87; and CD-ROM, $1.00."[1] They observed a modest increase

in median pupil expenditures from local sources in FY 91-92 for all resources except AV materials. The 40 cents per pupil increase for books actually reflects a decline in allocations, since the inflation rate was 4.2 percent in 1990 and 3 percent in 1991. The average price for a hardcover children's book was $16.64 in 1992; the average price for an adult nonfiction book was $45.85. The average elementary media specialist could therefore purchase only about one-third of a book per child.[2]

Their figures are similar to those cited by Valerie Wilford in testimony to the U.S. Senate Labor and Human Resources Committee regarding S. 1040, Technology for Education Act of 1993. She reported preliminary findings from a study of expenditures of public and private school library media centers in the state of Illinois for materials.

Sixteen percent (N = 404) of the respondents reported that they spent less than $3 per student for library media resources in 1991-92. The average cost of a book in 1991 was $13.07 at the elementary level and $42.12 at the secondary level. Thus, a $3 per student expenditure in 1991 would buy less than one-fourth of an elementary book and less than one-tenth of a secondary level title.[3]

Distribution of Expenditures

Miller and Shontz report media specialists are spending increasingly larger portions of their funds for nonbook resources, such as CD-ROM, CD-ROM access, and CDs.[4] Additional funds are used for computer software, online services (bibliographic and technical processing), and to develop interactive video resources. They report, "10 percent of the library media specialists received additional funds to help develop interactive video resources. . . . Twenty-four percent received extra funds to purchase CD-ROMs."[5]

A growing number of schools have videodiscs, cable television, on-site access to databases, and fax machines. Also increasing is the number of respondents who have telephones in their media centers. In FY 1989-1990 less than 50 percent had telephones[6]; by FY 1991-1992 over two-thirds had telephones. As Miller and Shontz observe, these changes are taking place at a time when media specialists are recognizing that their collections are aging.[7]

State of Collections

Media specialists face difficult decisions as they move to include electronic formats while recognizing that book collections are becoming dated. Wilford, in her testimony about materials about astronomy, space science, the solar system, general biology, ecology, human anatomy, physiology, and hygiene, identifies three concerns:

- The Illinois survey data document the national trend that funding for school library media programs has eroded over the past decade.

- The data suggest that Illinois school library media center collections in the topical areas surveyed are old, reflecting funding of the late 1960s and early 1970s.

- Eight-one percent of the respondents reported that astronomy, space science, and the solar system is part of their school curriculum. But 45 percent have fewer than 20 titles on these topics. Forty-three percent have fewer than six books published between 1990 and 1993 on these subjects. Sixty-six percent responded that they have more than 20 titles published before 1970, 23 years ago.[8]

Similar concerns are expressed by Miller and Shontz.

The data reveal the emergence of electronic, or high-tech, library media centers. These centers, in technologically "smart" schools, are being developed with the requisite additional funds or, as noted above, at the expense of book collections. The high price of books, the popularity of video recordings for instructional purposes, inflation, the rapidity with which books go out-of-date, the addition of the cost of machines are combining to make many of our school library media centers obsolete.[9]

Alternative Funding

Media specialists are looking for ways to increase resources beyond those supported by local funds. This is done through grant proposals, serving as a Beta test site for developing technology, or forming partnerships with the private sector. A number of state networking projects require grant proposals as part of the application process. According to Miller and Shontz, "The schools that appear to have the most up-to-date collections are those that receive extra funding for online access, interactive video resources, and interlibrary loan resources."[10]

Sources about proposal writing include Peggy Barber and Linda D. Crowe's *Getting Your Grant* (Neal-Schuman, 1993), David G. Bauer's *The "How To" Grants Manual* (Oryx Press, 1988), and *Grants and Funding Sources*, available on the Internet through the AskERIC gopher site in the InfoGuide menu (see appendix A for the Internet address). A number of the resource-sharing examples described in this chapter were funded through the support of grants.

RESOURCE SHARING

The basic concept of sharing bibliographic information and collections is not new. Recognizing the demands of curricular and individual needs and faced with limited fiscal resources, schools are joining networks. The advent of telecommunications and other technologies has increased the opportunities to share resources. While location of information is an important aspect, delivery of the desired items is of greater concern. Changes in technological delivery systems make it possible to address the needs of individual learners more effectively regardless of geographic location. These multitype library organizations (that is, academic, public, school, and special libraries) establish formal cooperative organizations of independent and autonomous libraries or groups of libraries to work together for mutual benefit. Networks are not limited to regions—they can be found within a school system or at the community, county, state, national, and international levels.

The traditional library network was a cooperative in which participating members shared resources on formal and informal bases. These early consortia shared union lists of serials, provided loans through their interlibrary lending (ILL) network, or jointly owned a film collection. The current use of the term *networking* acknowledges the development of online infrastructures through which members are linked to resources by some type of telecommunications connection. The participants include multistate, multitype libraries. Examples include the state-level ACCESS PENNSYLVANIA and the national WLN. Frequently, the state and regional networks provide access to national databases. By the late 1980s "access to information not held locally via electronically-based lending has come to be the norm, expected by library users in even the most remote rural areas."[11]

Successful networks are characterized by a financial and organizational commitment from the members, who agree to perform specific tasks and adhere to specific guidelines. In return, the member library has immediate access through computer and communications technology to databases that originate in the public or private sector.

Commonly held beliefs about networks are:

- Opportunity to access information is the right of each individual.

- Networks do not replace individual collections; they enhance existing ones and expand their range of services.

- Participating libraries are responsible for meeting the daily needs of their users and for contributing to the network.

- Networking is not free. Costs include equipment, materials, and staff time.

- Effective communication among participants is essential.

- Commitment to participation is made at the district level.

- Local, district, and regional levels of service must be clearly defined.

- School-level personnel need to be notified early in the process and kept informed about plans.

- Decisions must be made as to which services—for example, bibliographic retrieval, cataloging, or interlibrary loan—will be provided by the network.

- Delivery systems for bibliographic data and information retrieval must be spelled out.

- Remuneration to or from systems must be mutually agreed upon.

- Legislative issues and governance must be agreed upon.

Schools planning to form or join a network can find guidance in the Association of Specialized and Cooperative Library Agencies' *Standards for Cooperative Multitype Library Organizations* (American Library Association, 1990), which addresses issues of governance, service program, financial support, accountability, and roles and responsibilities. The *PLA Handbook for Writers of Public Library Policies* by the Public Library Association Policy Manual Committee (Chicago: Public Library Association, American Library Association, 1993) offers additional guidelines.

One way to judge a cooperative multitype library organization is by the services it offers. Figure 14.1, on page 246, lists some such services.

Library Network Services

Access or referral to nonlibraries
Building and space planning
Consulting
Continuing education
Contracting for services
Contractual program administration
Cooperative acquisitions
Cooperative collection development
Cooperative programming
Database management
Delivery or courier system
Electronic bulletin board
Electronic mail
Grant writing
Graphics
Group purchasing
Handbook development
Hiring assistance
Information clearinghouse
Interlibrary loan
Loan of materials or equipment
    (temporary or permanent)
Materials examination center
Materials review
Meeting or conference planning
Newsletter

Policy development
Printing
Production facilities
Professional awareness
Professional collection
Program evaluation
Public information
Publications
Reciprocal access
Reciprocal borrowing
Reference center
Research and development
Retrospective conversion
Rotating collections
Serials cancellations
Shared licensing
Shared personnel
Shared system
    CD-ROM, microform,
    or online catalog/
    circulation
Software development
Technical services
Telefacsimile (fax)
    communications
Union list

Fig. 14.1. Sample services of multitype library organizations. Based on Association of Specialized and Cooperative Library Agencies, *Standards for Cooperative Multitype Library Organizations* (Chicago: American Library Association, 1990), 17; and Sally Drew and Kay Ihlenfeldt, comp., *School Library Media Centers in Cooperative Automation Projects* (Chicago: American Library Association, 1991), 112-13.

Example of a Statewide Network

A look at the State Library of Pennsylvania's ACCESS PENNSYLVANIA illustrates the potential of a statewide database. In 1986, the first edition of the compact disc union catalog represented the holdings of more than 100 libraries. By 1991, Doris M. Epler and Jean H. Tuzinski reported the bibliographic database had more than 12 million holdings in 626 libraries and agencies (academic, public, and special libraries; high schools, middle schools, and elementary schools; and instructional materials centers). Approximately 2.4 million unique titles are identified.[12] The database (four compact laser discs divided by date into two sets of two discs each) can be searched by title, author, subject, location, type of material, language, any word, or a combination of these. One keystroke automates printing of an interlibrary loan form on which the patron indicates the date when the material is needed.

The seven major goals for the database are "(1) improving each student's information-management skills; (2) increasing access to information by students and teachers; (3) improving the management of library media centers; (4) promoting effective use of resources in school, public, and academic libraries by developing machine-readable records of school catalogs; (5) creating a union catalog that contains information about the holdings of school, public, and academic libraries; (6) providing access to such a catalog in a cost-effective manner; and (7) establishing a network to share library resources."[13]

> Resource sharing is an important component of the ACCESS PENNSYLVANIA database program; it is not, however, a replacement for a strong local core collection. Resource sharing must be applied prudently so that it is used as efficiently and as cost-effectively as possible.[14]

Epler and Tuzinski claim student achievement is enhanced when students

- learn to determine the number of resources needed,

- generate bibliographies for class assignments, and

- can use the information found in the database to recommend items for their local library media center collection.[15]

Students need guidance to exercise discretion in requesting resources from those listed in the union catalog. Analysis of interlibrary loan requests can identify subjects and titles to consider for purchase.

Epler and Tuzinski warn that media specialists should plan budgets to provide for updating their equipment within five years of installation.[16]

Local Structure

Participation involves sharing resources within a consortium and making a specific commitment to statewide resource sharing. A local consortium, two or more libraries, shares through cooperative agreements made by the governing bodies of the libraries. This local network, with its proximity and librarians who are acquainted, is the primary lender. Periodic meetings of the involved librarians is a basic component for a successful interlibrary loan network.[17] When no local consortium is established, media specialists contact the closest public library, where the request is filled or forwarded to the district library center and processed as an interlibrary loan. Consortium members use electronic mail and fax machines to share copies of journal articles, send interlibrary loan materials, and to communicate. The materials may be requested or delivered by electronic mail, fax, U.S. mail, local truck delivery, Interlibrary Delivery Services, or telephone.

Online Links and Interlibrary Loan

Another Pennsylvania service is LIN-TEL (Linking Information Needs—Technology, Education, Libraries), an electronic network, designed to make

> online database searching available to students as another method of information retrieval and to make research or resource gathering an integral part of the school library media curriculum. Students are taught how to use microcomputers to search for information in commercial databases available through BRS Information Technologies, a database vendor located in McLean, VA. These online databases allow students to search through vast amounts of information in a matter of minutes.[18]

This increases the depth, breadth, and number of available resources and extends access to information found beyond the walls of the school's media center.

The LIN-TEL project's support services for members include (1) training for school librarians in online bibliographic searching; (2) document retrieval; (3) user meetings; (4) telephone support through toll-free telephone numbers for immediate assistance; and (5) quarterly newsletters.[19]

Four fundamentals guiding the interlibrary loan activities are:

1. All requests should be closely monitored to be certain that they are valid interlibrary loan requests. Materials may already be available in another part of a book or in a reference tool located in the borrower's library and, therefore, should not be requested via ILL.

2. Locally adopted interlibrary loan procedures, as well as the endorsed *Pennsylvania Interlibrary Loan Code*, must be followed.

3. Accurate records of items borrowed and loaned must be kept.

4. Interlibrary loan must be a two-way street . . . RECIPROCATE![20]

Reciprocating is a key factor in any resource-sharing plan.

OTHER TYPES OF
COOPERATIVE EFFORTS

Another approach to sharing resources is described by Virginia Miehe, the junior high school librarian for a consolidated rural Iowa school district. To encourage young adults to keep reading during the summer months, she says, "Let's promote the idea that books are as much a part of vacation as tennis balls, the beach, and sleeping late."[21] Students and faculty can sign books out for the summer. The school and public library share the school's collection of popular young adult literature during the summer. Miehe reports circulation continues to rise each summer, and "Loss has proved minimal (.5 percent), less than during the school year."[22] This practice seems to work efficiently in an area where people have access to paperbacks, magazines, and newspapers but not bookstores.

Other examples of cooperative efforts are coordinated collection-development projects, using fax as a delivery system for sharing resources, and using a dial-up system to remote databases on CD-ROM.

Coordinated Collection Development

Participants in networks and other cooperative efforts are practicing coordinated collection development. Each participating unit assumes responsibility for collecting specific subjects or materials. From a national study of media centers participating in multitype, multistate networks, the author and Adeline W. Wilkes report the wide range of materials and subjects assigned to their respondents' schools. Examples include video formats (including disc), films, career materials, professional materials, instructional equipment, ethnic materials, high interest/low vocabulary materials, children's materials, young adult materials, and materials for students with special needs.[23] The following example illustrates how this is practiced.

New York City Schools

In the New York City School Library System, the practice of coordinated collection development (CCD) began after the creation of the union catalog in 1984. Eleanor R. Kulleseid traces its development and describes the benefits. The system began with simultaneous development of special subject collections and creation of the bibliographic database. Initially, participating high school media specialists selected materials in subject areas based on their existing collection strengths, potential faculty interest, or professional expertise and personal interest. As more high schools and intermediate schools participated, the range of resources increased. The bibliography of the CCD holdings stimulated greater interlibrary loan activity. In the early 1990s, volunteer libraries collected in areas of new curriculum emphasis, such as African American history, Puerto Rican and Caribbean studies, and health sciences. Kulleseid observes that while the special collections were a matter of pride for some media specialists, others reported the selection and acquisition activities were extremely time-consuming and difficult. A telephone and modem in the library were tremendous morale boosters.[24] Kulleseid recognizes that the future success of coordinated collection development

> depends on the ability of participating libraries to describe and compare collection strengths using a common measure. The obvious model for such a measure is the conspectus approach developed by the Research Libraries Groups' Collections Inventory Project and later adapted by regional consortia to include pubic and school library systems.

> . . .

> CCD programs have already demonstrated that efforts to involve teachers and administrators in selection and collection assessment can lead to increased program visibility, greater librarian participation in curriculum development and greater use of shared resources.[25]

Conspectus Approach: WLN

Another example of a coordinated collection-development system based on the conspectus approach is WLN's program. (See pages 86-87 for a discussion of the conspectus approach.)[26] This private, nonprofit corporation has developed software for assessing a collection, for analyzing a subject in a library or group of libraries' collections, and comparing collections based on a variety of criteria. During the collection assessment phase, three aspects of collections are analyzed. The first, the present collection level (CL), describes the nature, quantity, and quality of the present collection in terms of the conspectus levels (identified in table 6.1 on page 87). The second, acquisition commitment (AC), describes the purchases and gifts for the last 3-5 years, budget allocations, and collection growth for each of the 24 divisions or 500 categories described in the CL analysis. The third, goal level (GL), identifies how and when the collection will be changed to meet priorities. The term *collection assessment* is used by WLN to describe

> an organized process for systematically analyzing and describing a library's collection, using both quantitative and qualitative measures. Collection assessment is based upon a descriptive approach to the subject information levels and formats available in the collection. It is

not judgmental of the collection, but descriptive of its extent age, scope, language, format, etc.[27]

This process provides information for the actual evaluation, or the process of judging the appropriateness of the collection for the mission of the collection and for the users.

Libraries forming cooperative collection arrangements identify shared needs or goals and exhibit a willingness to participate in collaborative efforts to meet those needs and to reach those goals. The policy or agreement that guides their efforts includes elements similar to those described for formation of networks. These elements include

- joint mission statement
- [delineation of the] audience & purpose of the policy
- definition of [the] client group (user needs)
- overview of collective collections
- cooperative scope and issues
- particulars about responsibilities for project and materials
- specific collection information (conspectus reports, comparative data, levels, and goals)
- enactment and implementation of evidence.[28]

Using the comparative data and the mission of each participating library, responsibilities can be assigned based on collection goals. The collection GL can alert participating members to areas in which they can suggest titles for purchase by the collecting library.

The CLEAR Project

The use of stand-alone computers with a modem, printer, and CD-ROM drive help the staffs of a group of small public and school libraries in eastern Washington overcome typical barriers to resource sharing. Jodi Reng, organizer of CLEAR (Coalition of Libraries to Expand Access to Resources) describes how the approach provides a "a system for resource sharing that includes document delivery, requires very little staff time, costs nothing extra to make available to multiple libraries, and provides instantaneous turnaround."[29]

The CLEAR project's unique features are:

- No network, the dial-up systems uses regular voice telephone lines.

- Each of the libraries is responsible for one computer and one CD-ROM application. If one computer is down, the rest of the system continues to operate.

- Only library administrators know the passwords, which are sent automatically and invisibly, avoiding staff time and vulnerability to hackers.

- There is no limit to the number of participating libraries, and busy signals for high demands for specific CD-ROMs products can be avoided by having the same product at more than one library.

- Cost is affordable; only slightly more than purchasing a stand-alone desktop computer.[30]

The system automatically logs all incoming and outgoing calls and disconnects after five minutes of inactivity if a remote user neglects to log off. Classes can schedule a particular database and can reserve their time by faxing an alert to the participating libraries. Criteria used to select the CD-ROM applications are:

> the database had to contain information that would be generally useful to all participants, the search mechanism had to be easily understood through on-screen directions, and users had to be able to print or download data without further intervention of the staff . . . the producer of the product had to permit it to be used in the project without additional cost beyond the usual single-user license.[31]

The system provides for a base on which decisions can be made about sharing databases and other resources. As is often the case, one of the high school students learned the various applications, taught them to his friends, and is a leader in introducing this new tool.

IMPACT OF TELECOMMUNICATIONS NETWORKS AND RESOURCES

The advent of telecommunications and the increasing availability of fax machines in media centers have increased access to resources outside of the school. As Barbara Swisher and others observe, "Students, faculty, and administrators do not want information tomorrow; they need it today. Fortunately, telecommunications technology can answer these needs through a variety of means."[32] Users can access remote CD-ROMs. These are gaining in popularity and are updated on a monthly or quarterly basis. For the users who need the latest information, online databases can be updated daily or even hourly. An increasing number have full-text capabilities, which saves time in the search process.

The Internet

Through telecommunication networks, students and teachers gain access to global information. Commonly used components of these systems are electronic mail, electronic bulletin boards, and electronic databases. Certainly the largest, and often the cheapest, electronic network is the Internet. A comprehensive discussion of the Internet is beyond the scope of this book. Resources at the end of this chapter provide background information about the Internet and explain how to locate the many resources available through it.

Schools make frequent and varied use of the Internet's resources, and this use has implications for collections. As Elizabeth Haynes advises

> Users should not succumb to the thinking that Internet access can serve as a substitute for acquiring resources locally. The Internet is intended to provide access to unique resources, but not to take the place of local resources that would be heavily used (such as periodical indexes).[33]

Range of Services

Electronic mail (e-mail) provides access to individuals and discussion or interest groups. Foreign language students practice writing skills through electronic correspondence with students in the country in which the language they are studying is spoken. Students also can find economic, geographic, and political information about the country.

Students, teachers, and researchers engage in global dialogues about specific issues. The number of collaborative and cooperative projects involving students throughout the world is increasing. Discussion groups, such as Kidsnet, carry information about global or national electronic projects in which students and teachers can participate. Students and teachers can learn through online tutorials in electronically delivered distance-education courses. Teachers can engage in electronic dialogue with colleagues and other experts. Science teachers can obtain NASA files from NASA Space Link.

Media specialists use LM_NET to exchange ideas and to learn how other media specialists are solving problems. Harriet A. Rood describes the professional benefits:

> I have subscribed to both LM_NET and a CD-ROM LAN network that have provided me with all sorts of material. We are building a new library and I hope to have it all networked. The CD-ROM LAN has had numerous messages that have been useful (not to mention the fact that I no longer feel alone in this quagmire of LANs, CD-ROMs, OPACs, etc.) I have also been in contact with the Library Science school I graduated from (East Carolina U.) which is extremely valuable.[34]

Bulletin Boards

Electronic bulletin board systems or (BBSs) may be community-based, subject-oriented, or institution-based. Some bulletin boards provide only read-only information, but others offer interactive communications and conferencing. Students facing decisions about which college they would like to attend can locate information through that institution's CWIS (campus-wide information system). They can learn about course offerings, financial aid, and student life. A local public library or community may offer an information system with news about the community and local events. Access may be direct or through the Internet.

Media specialists are using telecommunications in collection development, selection, ordering (from jobbers), and cataloging. According to Swisher, et al., "The cooperative undertaking of these tasks via telecommunications saves school library media programs time and money. It also fosters efficient use of personnel."[35]

The Oklahoma bulletin board system includes selection records provided by the Oklahoma Department of Education and provides

> the state's school library media specialists with semi-annual recommendations of new children's and young adult books, audiovisual materials, and special subject bibliographies. The program . . . assists schools in locating and selecting quality materials. Selection assistance is particularly critical to the many small school districts in Oklahoma that employ part-time library media specialists. Such media specialists not only face time limitations but also have limited access to reviewing sources due to budgetary considerations. . . . The bulletin board is accessed by library media specialists throughout the state, and selection records may be downloaded directly into a school's computer.[36]

This system results from the cooperative efforts of the Oklahoma Department of Education, Oklahoma Department of Libraries, the University of Oklahoma School of Library and Information Studies, libraries, and school districts.

Students will enjoy using discussion groups to meet others who share interests or hobbies, such as chess or computer games.

Databases

Accessing electronic databases can lead students to research data about agricultural markets, global climate simulations, or space missions. Teachers can access the ERIC (Educational Resources Information Center) database on topics of interest. They can subscribe to electronic journals, attend electronic conferences, or take students on electronic field trips. Teachers can communicate electronically with colleagues at other schools or with authorities in particular fields to obtain the most current information.

As schools expand use of these electronic resources, decisions will need to be made as to who can access what when. Some of the services are free. Some databases are available only at certain hours of the day or on weekends, when there is less demand for them by the original group for whom they were developed.

Other Resources

Other resources available through the Internet include commercial online databases, catalogs of hundreds of the world's libraries, free educational software, documents, and articles about how to use the Internet. For example, several of the resources cited at the end of this chapter are available in electronic form. Statewide telecommunications networks are being used for state reporting of educational information, financial management systems, instructional management tools, and teacher certification. Other examples include test scoring and analysis, educational data files, and legislative information.

Partnerships

Schools are forming partnerships with the private sector to support resource-sharing services. The Indiana Buddy System Project, created by a group of business and education leaders, began as pilot program in 1988 for fourth- and fifth-graders from five schools. Their goal is "to use technology and telecommunications as a catalyst for improving education and advancing economic opportunities for the state."[37] Another goal is to increase computer literacy. The Buddy Encyclopedia (the online database) is a compilation of student articles and reports. The database is accessed using Indiana Bell's public data network. Long-range plans call for making it accessible to the home computers of all students in grades 4 through 12.

Another joint effort involves Pacific Bell, Apple Computer, the University of California at Davis, and the Davis High School. This effort provides computers for student use in the library and computer lab. Through the Internet, the students can access the Bay Area Regional Research Network (BARR-Net). Students also use electronic mail and bulletin board exchanges to correspond with academicians and researchers around the world.

Bob Lee, Pacific Bell executive vice president for marketing, observes

Unfortunately, while businesses routinely invest in the latest applications in computers, lasers, robotics, and other technologies to remain competitive, our schools haven't kept pace. Projects like this one demonstrate what a potent force technology can be on the education of our young people.[38]

He shares the concern of Jonathan Kochmer, who sees the value of these experiences in helping students gain information literacy, a knowledge of how to navigate in and take full advantage of the networked world.[39]

Telefacsimile (Fax)

Telefacsimile, or fax, machines are effective for sharing periodicals, whether the media centers are urban or rural. The Periodicals by Fax project serves the Houston Area Independent School Library Network (HAISLN), which comprises local private schools. A similar facsimile network serves rural Skagit County, Washington. Libraries are using fax for interlibrary loan requests and fulfillment, reference, correspondence, book ordering, and even newsletters.

Houston Area Independent School Library Network

The Houston project began with the creation of a union list of holdings, which was compared to *Abridged Readers' Guide, Readers' Guide, Magazine Index,* and *INFOTRAC.* The participants agreed which titles would not be covered by the network. Each participating media specialist identified 5-10 periodicals from current collections and agreed to store back issues for at least five years to provide copies from them to other media centers in the network. The guidelines identify the procedures for initiating and fulfilling requests, specify rules of use—length of articles (10 pages or less), response time (24 hours), and cost (no charge to HAISLN members). The guidelines also specify which statistics to track, and they require that photocopies of faxed articles be retained for one year for copyright compliance records.[40]

Skagit County Network

Sally L. Jones reports the Skagit County, Washington, consortium sought funding through Title III of the Federal Library Services and Construction Act.[41] The consortium's goal was to provide patrons with access to all of the titles indexed in the unabridged *Readers' Guide to Periodical Literature.* Although most of the titles were owned by the 10 participating libraries, libraries agreed to purchase titles to fill the gaps. Titles uniquely held by school libraries are moved to the nearest public library each June so they may be accessed by libraries that remain open during the summer. Fax machines were programmed to automatically dial fax machines in member libraries. Student library aides use fax machines to send requests, so that a minimum of staff time is required. Jones observes that the student aides who send the faxes are learning a marketable skill while enjoying the novelty of using technology for interlibrary loan. This project has dramatically increased resources available to participating high school libraries, where fill rates have jumped from 15 percent to 95 percent. Jones reports positive client reaction and offers one reason why: "Valuable student time can be spent on research and writing rather than on trying to physically track down information from around this rural county where a 30 mile drive may be needed to reach a major library."[42]

SUMMARY

Media specialists are participating in resource-sharing plans to acquire information on demand. This movement addresses the problems raised by the increasing cost of materials, the decreasing levels of fiscal support, and the condition of collections. Resource-sharing plans do not replace local collections; they extend the resources available to students and teachers. Media specialists participating in coordinated collection development plans may be assigned responsibility for collecting materials on specific subjects or in specific formats. Use of telecommunication networks provides access to information from around the world. Fax machines provide speedy delivery systems. Today's media specialist has many resources available beyond those located in the media center.

NOTES

[1]Marilyn L. Miller and Marilyn Shontz, "Expenditures for Resources in School Library Media Centers, FY 1991-92," *School Library Journal* 39, no. 10 (October 1993): 29.

[2]Miller and Shontz, "Expenditures . . . FY 1991-92," 30.

[3]"AASL Member Testifies to Senate Committee Regarding Technology for Education Act," *School Library Media Quarterly* 22, no. 1 (Fall 1993): 65.

[4]Miller and Shontz, "Expenditures . . . FY 1991-92," 34.

[5]Miller and Shontz, "Expenditures . . . FY 1991-92," 34.

[6]Marilyn L. Miller and Marilyn Shontz, "Expenditures for Resources in School Library Media Centers, FY 1989-90," *School Library Journal* 37, no. 8 (August 1991): 40.

[7]Miller and Shontz, "Expenditures . . . FY 1991-92," 34.

[8]"AASL Member Testifies," 65-66.

[9]Miller and Shontz, "Expenditures . . . FY 1991-92," 27.

[10]Miller and Shontz, "Expenditures . . . FY 1991-92," 34.

[11]Association of Specialized and Cooperative Library Agencies, *Standards for Cooperative Multitype Library Organizations* (Chicago: American Library Association, 1990), 1.

[12]Doris M. Epler and Jean H. Tuzinski, "A System of Statewide Sharing of Resources: A Case Study of ACCESS PENNSYLVANIA," *School Library Media Quarterly* 20, no. 1 (Fall 1991): 19-23.

[13]Epler and Tuzinski, "ACCESS PENNSYLVANIA," 20.

[14]Epler and Tuzinski, "ACCESS PENNSYLVANIA," 23.

[15]Epler and Tuzinski, "ACCESS PENNSYLVANIA," 23.

[16]Epler and Tuzinski, "ACCESS PENNSYLVANIA," 23.

[17]State Library of Pennsylvania, *Pennsylvania Online: A Curriculum Guide for School Library Media Centers* (Harrisburg, 1990), 61.

[18]State Library of Pennsylvania, *Pennsylvania Online*, 61.

[19]State Library of Pennsylvania, *Pennsylvania Online*, 62.

[20]State Library of Pennsylvania, *Pennsylvania Online*, 63.

[21]Virginia Miehe, "Send Your Books on Vacation," *School Library Journal* 38, no. 5 (May 1992): 54.

[22]Miehe, "Send Your Books," 54.

[23]Phyllis J. Van Orden and Adeline W. Wilkes, "School Library Media Centers and Networks," *Library Resources & Technical Services* 37, no. 1 (January 1993): 10.

[24]Eleanor R. Kulleseid, "Cooperative Collection Development in the School Library Revolution," *The Bookmark* 50, no. 1 (Fall 1991): 21-23.

[25]Kulleseid, "Cooperative Collection Development," 22-23.

[26]See appendix A for address and phone number.

[27]Nancy Powell and Mary Bushing, *WLN Collection Assessment Manual*, 4th ed. (Lacey, WA: WLN, 1992), 13.

[28]Powell and Bushing, *WLN Collection*, 66.

[29]Jodi Reng, "Tying Small Libraries Together Through Remote Access," *Wilson Library Bulletin* 68, no. 8 (April 1994): 38.

[30]Reng, "Tying Small Libraries," 38-39.

[31]Reng, "Tying Small Libraries," 40.

[32]Barbara Swisher, et al., "Telecommunications for School Library Media Centers," *School Library Media Quarterly* 19, no. 3 (Spring 1991): 155.

[33]Elizabeth Haynes, "Using the Internet in the K-12 Environment," *School Library Media Quarterly* 21, no. 3 (Spring 1993): 189.

[34]Graceanne A. Decandido, "School Librarians on Internet: An Online Story," *School Library Journal* 39, no. 1 (January 1993): 11.

[35]Swisher, et al., "Telecommunications for School Library," 156.

[36]Swisher, et al., "Telecommunications for School Library," 157.

[37]Nancy A. Klinck, "Networking Projects Around the United States," *TechTrends* 35, no. 3 (April 1990): 34.

[38]Klinck, "Networking Projects," 35.

[39]Jonathan Kochmer and NorthWestNet, *NorthWestNet's Guide to Our World Online*, 4th ed. (Bellevue, WA: NorthWestNet and Northwest Academic Computing Consortium, 1993), 348.

[40]Dorcas Hand and Barbara Weathers, "Periodicals by Fax: A Houston Experience," *School Library Journal* 39, no. 3 (February 1993): 29-32.

[41]Sally L. Jones, "Just the FAX for High School Students," *School Library Journal* 37, no. 1 (January 1991): 42.

[42]Jones, "Just the FAX," 42.

BIBLIOGRAPHY

"AASL Member Testifies to Senate Committee Regarding Technology for Education Act." *School Library Media Quarterly* 22, no. 1 (Fall 1993): 65-66.

Association of Specialized and Cooperative Library Agencies. *Standards for Cooperative Multitype Library Organizations*. Chicago: American Library Association, 1990.

Decandido, Graceanne A. "School Librarians on Internet: An Online Story." *School Library Journal* 39, no. 1 (January 1993): 10-11.

Descy, Don E. "All Aboard the Internet." *TechTrends* 38, no. 1 (January/February 1993): 29-34.

Dewey, Patrick R. *FAX for Libraries*. Westport, CT: Meckler, 1990.

Dickinson, Gail K. *Selection and Evaluation of Electronic Resources*. Englewood, CO: Libraries Unlimited, 1994.

Drew, Sally, and Kay Ihlenfeldt, comps. *School Library Media Centers in Cooperative Automation Projects*. Chicago: American Library Association, 1991.

Epler, Doris M., and Jean H. Tuzinski. "A System of Statewide Sharing of Resources: A Case Study of ACCESS PENNSYLVANIA." *School Library Media Quarterly* 20, no. 1 (Fall 1991): 19-23.

Hand, Dorcas, and Barbara Weathers. "Periodicals by Fax: A Houston Experience." *School Library Journal* 39, no. 3 (February 1993): 29-32.

Haynes, Elizabeth. "Using the Internet in the K-12 Environment." *School Library Media Quarterly* 21, no. 3 (Spring 1993): 187-89.

Jones, Sally L. "Just the FAX for High School Students." *School Library Journal* 37, no. 1 (January 1991): 42.

Klinck, Nancy A. "Networking Projects Around the United States." *TechTrends* 35, no. 3 (April 1990): 30-36.

Kochmer, Jonathan, and NorthWestNet. *NorthWestNet's Guide to Our World Online*, 4th ed. Bellevue, WA: NorthWestNet and Northwest Academic Computing Consortium, 1993.

Kulleseid, Eleanor R. "Cooperative Collection Development in the School Library Revolution." *The Bookmark* 50, no. 1 (Fall 1991): 21-23.

Miehe, Virginia. "Send Your Books on Vacation." *School Library Journal* 38, no. 5 (May 1992): 54.

Miller, Marilyn L., and Marilyn Shontz. "Expenditures for Resources in School Library Media Centers, FY 1989-1990." *School Library Journal* 37, no. 8 (August 1991): 32-42.

———. "Expenditures for Resources in School Library Media Centers, FY 1991-92." *School Library Journal* 39, no. 10 (October 1993): 26-36.

Powell, Nancy, and Mary Bushing. *WLN Collection Assessment Manual*, 4th ed. Lacey, WA: WLN, 1992.

Reng, Jodi. "Tying Small Libraries Together through Remote Access." *Wilson Library Bulletin* 68, no. 8 (April 1994): 38-40, 140.

Spitzer, Kathleen L. "Fax for Library Services." *ERIC Digest* (December 1991). EDO-IR-91-10.

State Library of Pennsylvania. *Pennsylvania Online: A Curriculum Guide for School Library Media Centers*. Harrisburg, 1990.

Swisher, Barbara, et al. "Telecommunications for School Library Media Centers." *School Library Media Quarterly* 19, no. 3 (Spring 1991): 153-60.

Van Orden, Phyllis J., and Adeline W. Wilkes, "School Library Media Centers and Networks." *Library Resources & Technical Services* 37, no. 1 (January 1993): 7-17.

SELECTED RESOURCES ABOUT THE INTERNET

Engle, Mary E., et al. *Internet Connections: A Librarians' Guide to Dial-Up Access and Use*. LITA Monographs 3. Chicago: American Library Association, 1993.
    A practical guide to electronic service providers, including the concepts, terms, and overview.

Farley, Laine, ed. *Library Resources on the Internet: Strategies for Selection and Use*. RASD Occasional Papers, no. 12. Chicago: American Library Association, Reference and Adult Services Division, 1992.
    Also available through anonymous FTP: FTPDLA.UCOP.EDU, directory pub/Internet, filename libcat-guide. Provides basic information about the use of the Internet and identifies additional sources of help.

Kehoe, Brendan. *Zen and the Art of the Internet: A Beginner's Guide*, 2d ed. Englewood Cliffs, NJ: Prentice-Hall, 1993.
The first edition is available free from many FTP sites. To access via WAIS: zen-internet.src; ftp ftp.cs.widener.edu; login anonymous; cd pub/zen.

Kochmer, Jonathan, and NorthWestNet. *NorthWestNet's Guide to Our World Online*, 4th ed. Bellevue, WA: NorthWestNet and Northwest Academic Computing Consortium, 1993.
This straightforward guide describes step-by-step use of the Internet and suggests specific networks of interest to students and teachers. Like other guides, e-mail etiquette and proper use are emphasized.

Krol, Ed. *The Whole Internet User's Guide & Catalog*, 2d ed. Sebastopol, CA: O'Reilly and Associates, 1994.
This comprehensive guide covers how the network works, security, and other issues. Provides many examples of screens you may see and how to handle a variety of situations.

LaQuey, Tracey, and J. C. Ryer. *The Internet Companion: A Beginner's Guide to Global Networking*. Reading, MA: Addison-Wesley, 1992.
With a foreword by Vice President Al Gore, this step-by-step guide provides basic information and encourages use of the Internet. Covers using etiquette, using e-mail and finding e-mail addresses, locating online resources, and transferring information.

Machovec, George S. *Telecommunications, Networking and Internet Glossary*. LITA Monographs 4. Chicago: Library and Information Technology Association, 1994.
In a field where terminology is highly specialized and growing quickly, this glossary can help you understand terms relating to the Internet, TCP/IP, OSI, and other topics.

Miller, Elizabeth Bowden. *The Internet Resource Directory for K-12 Teachers and Librarians, 94/95 Edition*. Englewood, CO: Libraries Unlimited, 1994.
This book lists and describes hundreds of resources for students, teachers, and librarians, all available on the Internet. All curriculum areas are covered.

Polly, Jean Armour. *Surfing the Internet 2.0*.
Describes Internet resources, including electronic serials, listserv discussion groups, service providers, manuals, and guides. Available via anonymous FTP from NYSERNET.org (192.77.173.2) in the directory /pub/resources/guides surfing the.internet.2.0.txt.

Stoll, Clifford. *The Cuckoo's Egg: Tracking a Spy Through the Maze of Computer Espionage*, 1st ed. New York: Doubleday, 1989.
Do you like to read mysteries or spy stories? If yes, enjoy this work of fiction as you learn about global networking.

Tennant, Roy, et al. *Crossing the Internet Threshold: An Instructional Handbook*. Berkeley, CA: Library Solutions Press, 1992.
Recommended for its clear explanations, practical tips, easy-to-follow directions, and exercises from world examples. This handbook provides the basic information you need to get started.

CHAPTER 15

Maintaining the Collection

An effective collection maintenance program serves two purposes. A primary purpose is that materials and equipment are easily available and ready for use. Second, policies and procedures for preventive maintenance help ensure economical and efficient management of the collection. Maintenance activities include keeping accurate records of what is in the collection (an inventory); inspecting materials; and repairing, replacing, or removing items.

Policies, procedures, and reevaluation processes of the maintenance program are the focus of this chapter. The bibliography identifies works with more specific information about maintenance of the collection.

EQUIPMENT-MAINTENANCE POLICIES

Maintenance policies frequently exist at the district level. Policies related to equipment maintenance address

- when and why equipment will be traded in or discarded. The policy may guide replacement decisions by setting limitations on repair costs.

- the type of repairs that will be handled at the building level, the district level, and through repair contracts. Simple repairs, such as replacing light bulbs, may be done at the building level as a matter of policy, while major overhauls will be done by an external contractor.

- the records to be kept on equipment usage, repair, and maintenance. For example, the cost-effectiveness of a given item can be determined through analysis of data collected on equipment maintenance records.

Such a policy can address the quantity and type of usable pieces of equipment to be provided. To meet this level of access, the policy provides a replacement schedule, for example, a cycle of 7-10 years to replace video units. In preparing the budget, developmental items (those increasing the size of the collection) can be distinguished from replacement items (those maintaining the current level of service). Provision for replacement of materials and equipment can be based on the rates at which the items become unusable due to wear or dated content. Although the experience of the media center staff and the condition of the existing collection are the first guides to establishing renewal rates, table 15.1 provides some general guidelines.

Table 15.1.
Sample Replacement Rates

Type of Item	Average Years of Practical Usefulness
Materials	
Books	
hardback, K-8	6-8
hardback, 9-12	8-10
paperback	2
Software	6
Film formats	10
Recordings, audio and video	10
Transparencies	12-15
Equipment	
Computer terminals	8
Headphones	4-6
Library furniture	20-30
Microcomputers	8
Projectors	
filmstrip	10
opaque	12
overhead	8-10
16-mm	10
slide	10
sound filmstrip	8
sound slide	8
Players	
audio cassette	5
record	8
tape	8
video cassette	8
Television monitor or receiver	10
Video cameras	8

From *South Dakota Planning Guide for Building Library Media Programs*, 2d ed. (Pierre: South Dakota State Library and Archives, 1985), 42; Washington Library Media Association, Certification and Standards Committee, and Superintendent of Public Instruction, *Information Power for Washington: Guidelines for School Library Media Programs* (Olympia, WA: State Superintendent of Public Instruction, 1991), 22; and Charles W. Vlcek and Raymond V. Wiman, *Managing Media Services: Theory and Practice* (Englewood, CO: Libraries Unlimited, 1989), 118.

Another factor to consider is loss. A loss rate greater than 2 percent suggests a replacement-or-loss factor must be a budget item. See appendix B of *Information Power: Guidelines for School Library Media Programs*

(American Library Association, 1988) for two suggested budget formulas for materials and equipment.

Policies relating to the maintenance of materials appear as a section of the collection-program policy on evaluation of the collection (see page 88). That section of the policy describes criteria by which materials should be evaluated for replacement, repair, or removal from the collection. Provision for replacing specific kinds of materials, such as encyclopedias and CD-ROM materials, should be included.

ESTABLISHING PROCEDURES

Working within parameters of the district policies, the media specialist is responsible for establishing collection-maintenance procedures for systematic inspection of all materials and equipment. While technicians and aides can repair and clean materials and equipment, the media specialist identifies maintenance problems, diagnoses causes, establishes corrective measures, and monitors the quality of the work completed by media center staff or by an outside contractor.

Routine internal maintenance procedures include the following:

- Books and printed materials: replacing protective jackets, repairing torn pages, mounting pictures.
- Audio materials: splicing tapes, cleaning records.
- Equipment: cleaning areas of heavy use—playback heads, lenses.
- Monitors and screens: use antistatic wipes.

Other maintenance procedures relate to the identification and listing of holdings. Procedures should state how record-keeping activities and systematic inspection of materials will be accomplished. For materials, the holdings record serves this purpose, noting where an item should be stored and how many copies are owned. Often a similar list does not exist for equipment. If the district has an inventory control and maintenance form for equipment, establish a procedure for keeping those records up-to-date. If one does not exist, initiate a record. Devise a system for listing the purchase date for the equipment; its location; and dates for maintenance, cleaning, and repair.

Emergency Planning and Security

Provision should be made for fire, flood, leaky roof, tornado, or vandalism. Does the school district have a disaster plan or a cooperative agreement with the public library? If not, develop a disaster plan to answer the "what if" questions one faces in such situations. The plan can begin with attention to local conditions. Where are the fire extinguishers and smoke alarms? The plan can list their locations, how frequently and when they are to be checked, and the training scheduled for staff members. The local fire department will provide training. Emergency telephone numbers and people who can give advice on what to do with fire- or water-damaged materials should be readily available. Provision should be made for storing emergency supplies in the media center or knowing their location in the school. For instance, emergency supplies for water damage include paper towels, plastic drop cloths, and rolls of freezer wrap.

Procedures and information about what, where, and how records should be kept should be developed. Some relevant questions are: Which member of the school's staff has a copy of the insurance policy? What evidence will be needed to make a claim on the insurance policy? Is there a copy of the holdings record? How often should the copy be updated? Will pictures and negatives of furniture and equipment be kept?

The original pictures and negatives should be kept in separate locations, in the hope that damage will occur in only one location. One record—photograph or negative—and copy of the holding record should be maintained in a fireproof safe in the school's administrative offices or in the media center. At least one school administrator should know the location and nature of the records.

Security procedures should provide access to equipment while preventing loss. As a security precaution, permanently affix the school identification number assigned by the National Center for Educational Statistics (NCES) in Washington, D.C., to all equipment. The number can be obtained from the state department of education or public instruction. The first two digits of the number identify the state; the next five digits identify the school. With this number, your ownership of recovered stolen equipment can be easily verified.

Preventive Maintenance

With diminishing funds for media centers, developing protective practices are an important step in the collection program. The following discussion presents some basic steps to protect and preserve materials and equipment. General practices should include keeping the media center clean; storing materials properly—vertically, loosely, adequately supported; dusting materials regularly; controlling temperature and humidity; securing heavy equipment to a cart; purchasing books that will be heavily used in library binding or prebinding; and using CD formats for heavily used reference works.

Preventive measures for equipment include:

1. Keep warranties, manuals, and repair records in an accessible file.

2. Test each machine by operating it yourself.

3. Train media staff and students in the proper operation and care of equipment.

4. Offer faculty in-service sessions on proper use of the equipment.

5. During the yearly inventory, check equipment, including electrical cords, for problems.

6. Regularly schedule maintenance checks with vendors of computers and video equipment.

7. Cover machines not in use.

8. Keep a log of use, rotating the machines.

9. Keep equipment in a climate-controlled area.

10. Fasten televisions and VCRs to designated carts.

11. Do not allow students to move television equipment.

12. Clean the heads of VCRs and audiocassette players.

13. Create a maintenance area or a work space with the basic tools for minor repairs.

14. Attach "trouble-shooting" telephone numbers to equipment.[1]

To carry out these procedures, Jane E. Streiff recommends a tool box containing a 16-mm and 8-mm splicer; cotton swabs on 6-inch sticks; antistatic wipes; a drawer or box containing screwdrivers of assorted sizes, needle-nose pliers, wrenches, scissors, and a utility knife; head-cleaning tapes for VCRs and audiocassette players; and a computer disk for cleaning computer drives.[2] Streiff recommends affixing to each piece of equipment a sign bearing instructions for users (see fig. 15.1).

For the User of This Equipment

1. If machine does not function properly, check the instructions and the power source.

2. Have a problem? Call the media specialist before forcing parts or jamming the machine.

3. Rewind tapes after use.

4. Remove software materials from the machine after use.

5. Allow bulbs to cool before turning off the machine fan.

6. Secure reels, electrical cords, other movable components.

7. Replace covers on machines.

8. Inform the media specialist of any problems you have had with this machine.

9. Do not allow students to move televisions.

Fig. 15.1. Suggested instructions to be posted on media center equipment. From Jane E. Streiff, *The School Librarians' Book of Lists* (West Nyack, NY: Center for Applied Research in Education, 1992), 153-54.

INVENTORY AND
REEVALUATION OF MATERIALS

The reevaluation of the collection as a whole is discussed in chapter 17. The current discussion focuses on inventory and on reevaluating individual items to decide which items should be repaired, replaced, or removed from the collection. The maintenance policy should address criteria for evaluating and weeding the collection, including characteristics of materials to be permanently discarded. The policy must address concerns frequently voiced when proposing removal of items from a collection. What will occur when someone needs the materials that have been removed? How can we provide a replacement policy to assure that a decrease in numbers of items held will not lead to a budget cut? What will be the source of funding for the cost of the reevaluation, if additional personnel are needed? How will the transferring or disposal of materials and equipment be handled?

The policy also should address when reevaluation and inventory are to take place. The policy may recommend continuous, intermittent, or periodical weeding. The continuous plan, which takes place on a daily basis, may be difficult to handle without disrupting established routine. The intermittent plan calls for designating specific times for reevaluating and inventorying specific areas. The periodic plan makes use of days when the media center is not scheduled for use. Careful planning can avoid disrupting services to students and teachers. Carol L. Sitter points out that some materials, such as annual reports, newsletters, or college catalogs, should be discarded on receipt of new ones. Some policies suggest keeping them for two years.[3] The importance of establishing and holding to a designated time cannot be emphasized too heavily. Maintenance easily can be put off, resulting in neglect. Continuous weeding, once established in the daily routine, may be the most manageable, effective, and least disruptive plan. The school library media specialist, who knows the demands upon the collection, must take the initiative to start the task.

Inventory is the process that verifies holding records; during this process, the physical condition of the materials is assessed. In this context, inventory is more than the mere match of bar codes with records to obtain a count of the holdings. Inventory, as described here, is the process of checking each item physically and checking the records for accuracy. An album may be in the wrong cover, or a teacher's guide for a set of study prints may be missing. A detailed examination of materials can uncover problems overlooked during the routine checking of items at the circulation desk.

These activities take time but are beneficial because they

- assure that the collection contains accurate and current resource materials relevant to the curricular and recreational programs of the school;

- make more effective use of space;

- avoid the cost of cleaning, binding, mending, storing, and keeping records for unwanted items;

- remove dull and drab materials so that the collection catches the eye;

- maintain the reputation of the collection as a source of reliable information; and

- provide evidence of carefully treated materials to encourage students to handle them accordingly.

Carol Kroll describes the need to examine a collection before starting automation and retrospective conversion of records projects:

> As we begin to consider library automation, we need to re-examine our collection and how its records are maintained. Ideally this process takes place long before approval to automate has been received. Getting the collection ready for automation is usually part of a three- to five-year plan for library automation. Weeding, inventory, and standardization of the shelflist cards are significant steps in the automation process. Other important steps include retrospective conversion, selection of an online catalog and circulation system vendor, and the purchase of hardware.[4]

She points out that placing badly worn and unused titles in a database will not make them more attractive. "But previously hard-to-find materials might now be located by key word searching, thereby opening the collection to users."[5]

Some schools close collections for inventory, thus freeing the staff from other duties so they can review the collection in depth. However, closing the collection during the school year is in direct conflict with efforts to integrate the media program with the school's activities. Some school districts recognize this conflict and hire media personnel for a period when schools are not in session. Other districts rotate sections of the collection for inventory over a 3-year period. Inventory can take place, however, when items are in circulation. Through notation on the holdings and circulation records, media specialists can check to see whether unexamined materials are on the shelves or still circulating. Size of the staff, size of the collection, available time, and user demands influence the decision to evaluate the entire collection at once or one section at a time.

One school district appoints a team to inventory and weed various collections in the district during the summer months. This practice can prevent the emotional strain that removing items entails. The disadvantage is losing the insight of the individual who knows the needs of the school.

Case Study: Weeding a Collection

An example, Grant Senior High School, illustrates the problem. Since its beginning in 1934, this school's collection was a model for other schools. The previous media specialists and the principals prided themselves on the size of the collection in comparison to other schools.

By 1994, when Maria, the new media specialist, arrived, the scene was chaotic. Stuffed shelves, dusty boxes, and jammed closets held more than 30,000 items. One could see books with drab bindings. A typical example was a 1963 home-economics book still used by students doing assignments on average family income and expenses. Boxes were overflowing with old filmstrips and filmloops. Two closets held a complete run of *Life* magazine. Bibliographic records did not match holdings. Maria began by removing obsolete filmstrips, old filmloops, and warped recordings. Then she removed 10 sets of 20-year-old encyclopedias. The removal of these materials created space to work and to house other materials. Fortunately, the district hired the media center staff to do a badly needed inventory the week after school closed.

First, the collection was arranged according to the shelflist. Items that had been bar-coded were easy to check. Others had to be checked against the old shelflist. Missing items were noted. Second, equipment was checked against the inventory listing. Found items were noted with the date. Next it was time to decide where to begin re-evaluating the materials. When all the fiction titles were in the media center, the overflow items were left on the floor in front of the appropriate stacks. Many nonfiction titles, purchased with grant funds, had not circulated for more than 20 years. Maria asked two staff members to look at the publication dates of the nonfiction titles. They pulled old items using criteria related to age of information, last circulation date, and possible use in the curriculum. Meanwhile, Maria and another individual began examining the fiction section. Each team found books with small print, unattractive bindings, and missing pages. There were many unneeded duplicate copies, which made for easy withdrawal decisions. Of the 38 copies of John Bunyan's *Pilgrim's Progress*, Maria kept two illustrated copies. (Later, she would ask if anyone still needed that title.) Each team identified items to be mended, rebound, given to another media center, discarded, or recataloged. They considered the following questions in deciding whether to repair an item: Is the repair cost-effective? Is the title worth the time, supplies, and effort required to restore it? Is the title a unique item in the collection? Is it out of print, or readily available? Is it a duplicate copy? How useful has it been?

A work area was set aside for the repair jobs. Basic supplies included:

- Opaquing liquid (different shades) for pencil and ink marks
- Soft rubber erasers
- Fine-grade sandpaper for dirt and ink marks
- Rubber cement

- Scissors

- Ink eradicator for ink and marking pen

- Cleaning fluid for grease, dirt, and markings on the spine

- Soft rags

- Rice paper for holes and tears[6]

The inventory and weeding of this collection could not be accomplished in one week. However, the removal of 3,000 unattractive and out-of-date titles made an impression. Maria informed the teachers that their favorite titles were at the bindery or being replaced. Supporters admired the improved atmosphere created by less crowded shelves and the removal of worn and unattractive materials. However, the decrease in number count upset one assistant principal. This was the right moment for Maria to remind him about the value of usefulness over quantity.

Why Weed?

This example illustrates the time involved and the attitudes encountered when one weeds a collection. You may face similar situations; your conviction about the value of removing materials will be tested by others. You may have to overcome your own reluctance to discard materials. Avoiding this responsibility may be more comfortable than facing it. Carol Kroll suggests

> Peer support is particularly important for making decisions. A school library media specialist in a central high school district in New York State just discarded 6,000 books from her 18,000 volume library collection using a regional procedure as a guide. A high school and middle school media specialist organized a series of weeding workshops for the peers throughout Nassau County, New York, and are initiating "weeding parties." Teams of school library media specialists assist each other in developing standards for weeding and in making difficult discard decisions.[7]

People give many reasons and excuses for avoiding weeding. Typical attitudes include:

- Books are sacred objects; only vandals destroy books.

- Someone may need this in the future.

- I don't have enough time to examine every item in the collection.

- There will be a scene if teacher X wants this.

- We don't have time to remove the bibliographic and holding records for all these items. (What about the users' time and attitudes on finding useless materials?)

- Our policy doesn't justify the removal of materials bought with public funds.

- I cannot decide when a fiction title is out of date.

- This recording is scratched, but the students like the story.

- Kits are expensive to replace.

- These study prints are no longer available (even when the corners are torn and the explanatory text is missing).

- Someone may want to compare these editions.

- A class probably could use this 10-year-old set of encyclopedias. (Although we have the electronic version on our LAN.)

- I remember when Abdul made that model. (Abdul now holds a master's degree in engineering.)

- This software package has gone through several revisions, adding features we could learn to use, but many of us know how to use this version.

- I hate to admit I bought this shelf-sitter.

As you consider those statements, prepare to hear yourself thinking them as you make decisions. Remember, you are responsible for the collection. You can involve others in the process, but you lead the way by knowing the criteria for removing items. You may experience fatigue and doubt if you tackle a large-scale reevaluation project. To reassure yourself, refer to the policies.

Criteria for Weeding

You can make selection decisions about removing materials in the same way you make selection decisions about adding them. Find out what criteria were used for selecting the materials; these can apply to removing them. In addition, criteria related to the condition of materials can serve as a basis for judging when they should be removed. These criteria should be recorded as were the criteria for selection. Criteria for removal of materials can include:

- appearance and condition: unattractive covers or packaging, small print, dull or faded illustrations, missing pages or parts, garbled sound tracks, warped sound recordings, dirty beyond the state where they can be cleaned, dingy.

- poor content: out-of-date (see table 15.2, on page 272, for guidelines), mediocre writing or presentation, inaccurate or false information, materials not listed in standard works or indexes.

Table 15.2.
Age and Circulation Guidelines

Class	Subject or Format	Age	Last Circulated (Years)	Comments
000	General	5	NA	
030	Encyclopedia	5-10	NA	New edition every 5 years
100	Philosophy/ Psychology	10	3-5	
200	Religion	5-10	3-5	
290	Mythology	10-15	3-5	
300	Social science	10-15	5	Retain balance on controversial subjects
310	Almanacs and yearbooks	2-5	NA	Have latest
398	Folklore	10-15	5	Keep standard works
400	Language	10	3-5	
	Dictionaries	NA	NA	Keep basics
500	General	5	3	Closely examine anything over 5 years old, except botany and natural history
600	General	5	3	Most materials outdated after 5 years
620	Applied science	5-10	3-5	Retain car manuals
640	Home economics	5	3	Weed old patterns, keep cookbooks
700	General	NA	NA	Keep all basic, especially art history. Keep catalogs up-to-date
745	Crafts	NA	5	Keep well-illustrated items
770	Photography	5	3	Avoid dated techniques, equipment
800	Literature	NA	NA	Keep basic, especially criticism; discard minor, unassigned writers; check indexes
900	General	15	5	Evaluate demand, accuracy
920	Biography	NA	3-5	Keep until demand wanes, unless outstanding in content or style and still used
940	History	15	5	Keep outstanding broad histories
	Local history			Keep all books, local newspapers, local authors; consider oral history
F	Fiction/Easy	NA	2-5	Keep high demand; evaluate literary merit; classics should be replaced as new, more attractive editions become available
VF	Vertical file			Current information not found in other sources
	Government documents	5-10		

Class	Subject or Format	Age	Last Circulated (Years)	Comments
Ref	Reference			
	Indexes	3-5		As new annual or cumulations appear, discard old copies
	Atlases	5		
	Newspapers	1 week		For nonindexed
		2 years		For indexed
		Microform		If use requires
	Maps and globes			Check for accuracy
	Vocational files	2-5	2	Date items as added to collection to assist weeding
	College catalogs	2	NA	
	Periodicals	5	NA	Discard nonindexed
		5-8		Indexed
		10		Bound
Prof	Professional materials	8-10		
AV	Audiovisual and software			Weed worn or out-of-date items
	Films	8-12		
	Filmstrips	8-10		
	Transparencies	12-15		
	Records	8-12		
	Audiotapes	12-15		
	Videotapes	3-5		
	Software	6		

- inappropriate for the specific collection: neither circulated nor used for reference during the past five years, unneeded duplicates, interest or reading level inappropriate for students, works in languages not read by students or materials no longer needed in the curriculum (see table 15.2).

- age of materials (note any exceptions to these criteria): materials 10 years old and not listed in standard catalogs; out-of-date materials, for example, photographs or videos that show automobiles or fashions from 10 years ago (see table 15.2).

Exceptions

The policy also can identify materials that are not to be discarded. Examples include:

- classics, unless more attractive formats are available;

- local and state history, unless collected by another agency;

- major publications of the school, unless another department is responsible for the school's archives; and

- items incorrectly classified or poorly promoted, which might circulate under changed circumstances.

If you find materials published before 1900 which you think might be rare, ask an appraiser the value of the item. Be prepared to pay a fee for this service. Appraisers are listed in the yellow pages or business sections of telephone directories. If the item is indeed valuable, you might sell it or donate it to a special collection. If you decide to sell the item, contact a rare book dealer. The dealer will need the bibliographic information, including edition, printing, presence of an autograph, whether the author or illustrator is of local or state interest, and the condition of the work.

Involving Others

Members of the media center advisory committee can help formulate the reevaluation policy and participate in associated decisions. Teachers can provide subject-area expertise. Students in a high school science class can help spot inaccurate information in science materials. In one school district, the board of education's media center committee examined the collections, recognized the need to remove unusable materials, and offered specific suggestions for items to remove. For example, they found older titles—not classics—that their parents had used.

The *book slip* method can be used with titles when you are unsure of their current appeal and usefulness. Select duplicate or low-use titles and place a colored label that can be easily seen in each item. The slip should bear the call number and notice of the intent to remove the item from the collection. It should ask the user to remove the slip if the item should be kept. Slips remain in the items for a significant length of time (for example, six months or one year). Then the staff remove the materials that still contain slips.

An item should be removed if it does not meet the needs of the collection in which it is currently housed. However, removed materials may be of value to another collection. Removed items can be given to or exchanged with materials from other schools or agencies, sold (if district policy permits), or discarded.

Some large school districts establish exchange centers to provide temporary storage for materials no longer needed by schools. Check your school district's policy about withdrawing and discarding materials. Practices vary– some schools must burn discarded materials; others may sell them or give them away to other agencies. Schools that have lost materials to vandalism, fire, or tornado may need materials no longer useful to your collection. Before sharing unwanted materials, however, consider a comment made by a visitor from a developing country. He appreciated the generosity of Americans who had sent discarded books. However, he wondered about the books they sent, which were inaccurate and out-of-date. He asked, "Do they think my people don't know what is going on in the world?"

SUMMARY

Broken equipment, speakers that distort sound, puzzles with missing pieces, and books with missing pages are common in school collections. A user finding such items may lose interest in looking further. Collection maintenance is easy to delay. There is always someone who needs the media specialist's attention. Materials can wait, as they did at Grant High School, until the task is overwhelming. The chore of straightening out records can be boring and time-consuming. The amount of disposed materials and equipment can become excessive, resulting in emotional response and negative reactions.

Regularly maintaining materials and keeping records can help you avoid many of these problems. There always will be surprises and circumstances beyond your control. A brief story reveals how unusual maintenance problems can be. An odor pervaded the media center. It did not seem to come from the air ducts and, at first, it filled the entire room. As the sniffing investigators toured the room, they detected the strongest smell at the beginning of the fiction section. Books were removed; shelves were checked and moved. Nothing was found on or behind them. However, as the books were replaced, one of them felt damp. A recent bookmark was found– a juicy dill pickle.

NOTES

[1]Jane E. Streiff, *The School Librarians' Book of Lists* (West Nyack, NY: Center for Applied Research in Education, 1992), 152-53.

[2]Streiff, *School Librarians' Book of Lists*, 153.

[3]Carol L. Sitter, *The Vertical File and Its Alternatives: A Handbook* (Englewood, CO: Libraries Unlimited, 1992), 71.

[4]Carol Kroll, "Preparing the Collection for Retrospective Conversion," in *Online Catalogs in School Library Media Centers: A Planning Guide*, ed. by Catherine Murphy (Chicago: American Library Association, 1990), 7.

[5]Kroll, "Preparing the Collection," 7.

[6]Streiff, *School Librarians' Book of Lists*, 149, 150.

[7]Kroll, "Preparing the Collection," 6.

BIBLIOGRAPHY

American Association of School Librarians and Association of Educational Communications and Technology. *Information Power: Guidelines for School Library Media Programs.* Chicago: American Library Association; Washington, DC: Association for Educational Communications and Technology, 1988.

Clark, Lenore, ed. *Guide to Review of Library Collections: Preservation, Storage, and Withdrawal.* Collection Management and Development Guides, no. 5. Subcommittee on Review of Collections, Collection Management and Development Committee, Resources Section, Association for Library Collections and Technical Services. Chicago: American Library Association, 1991.

Johnson, Douglas A. "Weeding a Neglected Collection." *School Library Journal* 36, no. 11 (November 1990): 48.

Lankford, Mary D. "Some Observations on Book Preservation." *School Library Journal* 36, no. 11 (November 1990): 27-30.

Murphy, Catherine, ed. *Online Catalogs in School Library Media Centers: A Planning Guide.* Chicago: American Library Association, 1990.

Segal, Joseph P. *Evaluating and Weeding Collections in Small and Medium-Sized Public Libraries: The Crew Method.* Chicago: American Library Association, 1980.

Sitter, Carol L. *The Vertical File and Its Alternatives: A Handbook.* Englewood, CO: Libraries Unlimited, 1992.

Slote, Stanley J. *Weeding Library Collections: Library Weeding Methods*, 3d ed. Englewood, CO: Libraries Unlimited, 1989.

Streiff, Jane E. *The School Librarians' Book of Lists.* West Nyack, NY: Center for Applied Research in Education, 1992.

Vogel, Bruce. "The Adventures of Molly Keeper: A Cautionary Tale." *School Library Journal* 38 (September 1992): 136-42.

SELECTED SOURCES

Costa, Betty, and Marie Costa. *Micro Handbook for Small Libraries and Media Centers*, 3d ed. Englewood, CO: Libraries Unlimited, 1991.
    Describes and provides guidelines for various software for maintaining a collection, including acquisitions, cataloging, equipment inventory, and circulation.

DePew, John N. *A Library, Media and Archival Preservation Handbook.* Santa Barbara, CA: ABC-Clio, 1991.
    Covers care and handling of library materials; the environment; binding and in-house repair of books; care of photographic, audio, and magnetic media; disaster preparedness and recovery; preservation services; and suppliers.

Fortson, Judith. *Disaster Planning and Recovery: A How-To-Do-It-Manual for Librarians and Archivists.* New York: Neal-Schuman, 1992.
A practical approach to planning for disasters and recovery.

Greenfield, Jane. *Books: Their Care and Repair.* New York: H. W. Wilson, 1983.
Illustrated step-by-step guide covers repair and maintenance. Also available on videocassette: *Basic Book Repair with Jane Greenfield* (1987, 30 min.).

Lavender, Kenneth, and Scott Stockton. *Book Repair: A How-To-Do-It Manual for Librarians.* New York: Neal-Schuman, 1992.
A practical, carefully illustrated manual.

Morrow, Carolyn, and Carol Dyal. *Conservation Treatment Procedures: A Manual of Step-by-Step Procedures for the Maintenance and Repair of Library Materials,* 2d ed. Libraries Unlimited, 1986.
Another practical guide handy to have in the workroom.

Patrick, Gay D. *Building the Reference Collection: A How-To-Do-It Manual for School and Public Librarians.* How-To-Do-It Manuals for School and Public Librarians, number 7. Barbara L. Stein, series ed. New York: Neal-Schuman, 1992. ISBN 1-55570-105-1.
Recommends replacement intervals for specific titles and types of books found in reference sections of elementary, middle, and high school collections.

Schroeder, Don, and Gary Larc. *Audiovisual Equipment and Materials: A Basic Repair and Maintenance Manual.* vols. 1 and 2. Metuchen, NJ: Scarecrow Press, 1979, 1989.
Volume 1 covers 16-mm sound film, filmstrips, cassette tapes, and analog sound discs. Volume 2 covers videocassette, CDs, videodiscs, and software.

Sitter, Clara L. *The Vertical File and Its Alternatives: A Handbook.* Englewood, CO: Libraries Unlimited, 1992.
Includes conservation and preservation.

Sitts, Maxine K. *A Practical Guide to Preservation in School and Public Libraries.* Syracuse, NY: Syracuse University, ERIC Clearinghouse on Information Resources, 1990. Publication number IR-90. Available from Syracuse University Information Resources Publications, 030 Huntington Hall, Syracuse, NY 13244-2340. Cost is $6.50 plus $2.00 shipping and handling.
Covers national, state, regional, and cooperative initiatives; practical information regarding planning, environmental conditions, maintenance, repair, binding, local history, nonprint materials, disasters and emergencies.

Weihs, Jean Riddle. *The Integrated Library: Encouraging Access to Multimedia Materials.* Phoenix, AZ: Oryx Press, 1991.
Covers care, handling, and storage of analog sound discs, magnetic tapes, film media, two-dimensional opaque materials, three-dimensional and boxed materials, computer disks, and optical discs.

CHAPTER 16

Evaluating the Collection

How can the worth of a collection be determined? Several types of values can be derived from the concepts of collection discussed in chapter 2. You will recall that a collection (1) is a physical entity; (2) contains materials in a variety of formats; (3) meets the needs of the school's goals and programs and the informational, instructional, and personal needs of users; (4) provides access to human and material resources in the local and global community; (5) provides access to information and material from other library or information agencies; or (6) functions as an element within the media program. Each of these concepts of collection identifies something that can be measured or evaluated. Evaluation is the process of (1) identifying a problem; (2) establishing methods of measure; (3) collecting, analyzing, and interpreting data; and (4) reporting the information. This process, often a continual assessment of the collection, provides a basis for decision making. One can measure how well the collection meets the six defining concepts and how effectively each concept is addressed at any given time.

The *Guide to the Evaluation of Library Collections* (American Library Association, 1989) identifies three types of evaluative measures. Collection-centered measures include checking lists, catalogs, and bibliographies; examining the collection directly; compiling comparative statistics; and applying collection standards. Use-centered measures include circulation studies, in-house studies, surveys of user opinions, shelf-availability studies, and analysis of interlibrary loan statistics. Simulated use studies include citation studies and document-delivery tests. Each measure is described with a discussion of its advantages, disadvantages, and application in the school setting.

WHY EVALUATE?

Those who fund media programs need facts on which to base decisions regarding basic funding, shifts in financial resources, expansion of programs, and cutbacks. As managers, media specialists need information on which to base decisions about the collection and for communicating the needs of the collection to administrators. The evaluation process (see fig. 16.1) reveals answers to the following questions: Is the collection responsive to changes in the school's program? Is the collection integral to curricular and instructional needs? Is the collection meeting the needs of users? Does the collection provide access to materials from outside the school? Does the collection include formats preferred by users? Does the collection hinder or facilitate the media program? These questions identify general areas of investigation that are broad and complex. One cannot examine all these questions simultaneously; to do so would be an overwhelming task. Smaller issues, components of the larger questions, can be evaluated more readily.

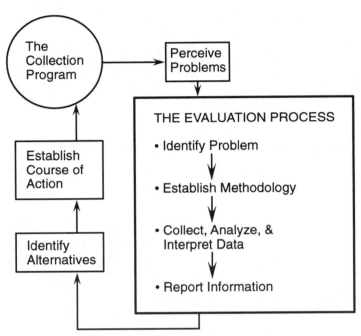

Fig. 16.1. The use of the evaluation process in the collection program.

Before beginning an evaluation project, one must identify what information will be collected, how it will be recorded, how it will be analyzed, how it will be used, and with whom and why it will be shared.

One school district that effectively used documentation to obtain increased funding is Lincoln, Nebraska. Marjorie J. Willeke and Donna L. Peterson describe a study of the size, age, and assessment of the collections' responsiveness to curricular demands.[1] They observe that although earlier principals, teachers, and media center staff had reported the outdated status of the collections, "It was the objective data, supporting subjective opinion, that resulted in the district's allocating additional monies for collection renewal."[2]

Further evidence of the power of objective data to gain support is reported in Carol A. Doll and Pamela Petrick Barron's *Collection Analysis for the School Library Media Center: A Practical Approach* (American Library Association, 1991). They emphasize that the length of the report is important. A single-page report is provided as an example of the amount of information an administrator can read briefly. They describe a number of situations in which media specialists use such reports to obtain internal and external funding and support. Directions and sample work forms are provided for analyzing collections in terms of (1) average age of the collection; (2) circulation patterns of collections; (3) comparing the collection to standard bibliographies, textbooks, and periodical indexes; (4) estimating updating costs and benefits; (5) estimating replacement costs; and (6) recording unmet teacher and curriculum needs. One media specialist can accomplish each of these techniques within a realistic time frame.

One South Carolina school district generated a news headline, "School Library Collections Have Outdated Books," to create publicity to influence votes to pass a bond referendum for books.[3]

EVALUATION AND MEASUREMENT

Evaluation is the process of deciding worth or value; measurement, a component of the evaluation process, is the process of identifying extent or quantity. We can count the number of items circulated in any given period, but that information is not evaluative; counting provides quantitative data, an objective measure. The count gives us information about the number of items that circulated; there is no information about whether the materials were used, by whom, under what set of circumstances, whether additional materials were used in other places, or even what materials were used within the media center. Merely counting the number of circulated science titles does not measure how adequately the collection supports the science curriculum. One must interpret additional quantitative data and perhaps consider some qualitative assessments before beginning to evaluate.

Although quantitative data gives an objective measure and lacks the element of judgment found in qualitative data, quantitative analysis does give us an objective basis for changing a collection policy.

Measurement can lead to meaningful evaluation. Professional judgment is used in deciding what to measure, whether it can be measured, and how the results are interpreted. The process can provide knowledge about alternatives, possible consequences, the effectiveness of operations, and insight into the managerial aspects of the collection program.

The reason for evaluation determines whether quantitative or qualitative techniques, or a combination of both, should be used.

Information produced by evaluation can be judged by four criteria: validity, reliability, timeliness, and credibility. If the information is essential to a decision, it has validity. If the information can be reproduced when repeating the same techniques, the evaluation has reliability. If the information reaches the decision maker when needed, it has timeliness. If decision makers trust the information, it has credibility. These criteria should be considered when planning how and when evaluation is to take place.

BARRIERS TO EVALUATION

As with weeding, media specialists can fall in the trap of finding reasons for putting off or avoiding evaluation. Sharon L. Baker and F. Wilfrid Lancaster identify five barriers to evaluation.[4] First, some people believe library services are intangible and library goals are impossible to measure objectively. However, media specialists who use the planning process recognize evaluation as a crucial component in the process. The cyclical planning process builds on the uniqueness of each media center. Assessment is made in the context of each collection's philosophy, mission statement, constraints, users, and environment. Long-range goals guide the direction of the organization. The process also involves short-term, measurable objectives to guide day-to-day activities. Strategies guide meeting the objectives and identifying measures for evaluating them. (Figure 3.2 on page 30 illustrates how evaluation is an integral part of the planning process, not an isolated event.)

A second barrier is concern about lack of staff time. Automation answers this argument. Automated circulation systems provide a means to easily obtain circulation figures and to analyze use of the collection. This information helps one see patterns in the media center. Online public access catalogs can be used to analyze other aspects of the collection. These analyses can lead to evaluation, which in turn can lead to more efficient and effective operations, thus saving staff time.

Third, media specialists may lack experience with or knowledge about collecting and analyzing empirical data. There are several ways to overcome this problem. For example, other members of the school's faculty can be called on to help with these operations. Courses and workshops on research methods provide opportunities to gain confidence in these activities. Resources listed at the end of this chapter include guides for evaluation activities.

Fourth, individuals unfamiliar with evaluation may fear the results. The results should be objective data identifying program strengths and weaknesses. The data can be used in making collection decisions. An informed manager can use documented weaknesses to gain additional support of funds.

Fifth is uncertainty about what to do with the results. Those responsible for the collection, including its funders, must be prepared to use the results to make the necessary changes. The results of evaluation need to be shared and used, not filed away.

TECHNIQUES FOR
MEASURING COLLECTIONS

There are many ways to measure the value of a collection. The most commonly used techniques for measuring collection value are described in the following sections. As you read about the techniques for measuring collections, think about their appropriateness for your purposes. How will the results help you present the media center program to others? What type of data will be collected? What effort is required to collect the data? How many people are needed? What costs are involved? How much time will it take? What will the instrument measure? What will it not measure? Once the information is obtained, how should it be organized? With whom can the information be shared? How can the information be used to communicate with others? Analyzing evaluation techniques with these questions in mind can help you select the most appropriate technique.

COLLECTION-CENTERED MEASURES

To determine the size, scope, or depth of a collection, one can use collection-centered techniques. These often are used in comparison with an external standard. They include checking lists, catalogs, bibliographies; examining the collection directly; compiling comparative statistics; and application of collection standards.

Checking Lists, Catalogs,
Bibliographies

In this procedure, the shelf list, catalog, or other holdings record is compared against a bibliography, list, or catalog of titles recommended for a certain purpose or type of collection. During the procedure, record the number of titles owned and not owned. The percent of recommended titles that the collection contains can be obtained from this data.

Lists that can be used in the technique include: standard catalogs; specialized bibliographies; basic subject lists; current lists; reference works; periodicals; lists designed to meet a specific objective; citations in textbooks or curriculum guides; or catalogs from jobbers, publishers, and producers. Examples of current lists include the Association for Library Service to Children's *Notable Children's Books*, *Notable Films and Videos for Children*, *Notable Computer Software*, and *Notable Children's Recordings*; or the Young Adult Library Services Association's *Selected Films and Videos for Young Adults* and *Outstanding Books for the College-Bound* series. Current lists of this nature identify highly recommended titles, but you must judge whether the collection needs those titles.

The purpose of an evaluation indicates which list is appropriate. If the purpose is to measure the general coverage of titles appropriate for the audience served, standard catalogs, such as *Children's Catalog* (H. W. Wilson, 1991), *Junior High School Library Catalog* (H. W. Wilson, 1990),

Elementary School Library Collection (Brodart, 1994), or *Senior High School Library Catalog* (H. W. Wilson, 1992), would be useful. If comparison reveals that the collection has many of the recommended titles, then, presumably, the collection is successful. The more closely the purpose of the tool matches the purpose of the collection, the more beneficial the comparison will be. The collection-development policy can provide a basis for judging the appropriateness of a specific list.

Advantages

1. A wide range of lists is available.

2. Many lists are selective and include informative annotations.

3. Lists of this nature are frequently updated and revised.

4. Lists can be compiled to meet the needs of a collection.

5. Searching lists is a comparatively easy way to evaluate a collection.

6. Most compilations have been prepared by competent professional media specialists or subject specialists.

Disadvantages

1. The only available lists may be those used as purchasing guides.

2. Some items may be out of print.

3. The cost of the list may outweigh the benefit of its use.

4. Not every subject or need can be covered by a single list.

5. Bibliographies cover materials for all ages and may have limited usefulness for evaluating a collection established to serve a specific age group.

6. This approach does not give credit to titles in the collection that may be equal to or better than those recommended in the list.

Application

This approach is especially helpful for identifying titles on a specific subject or checking certain sections of the collection. At Grant Senior High School, several teachers were so successful in motivating students to read short stories that that section of the stacks was often empty. Maria, the media specialist, compared the holdings with selection tools and indexes to short stories. In addition to identifying titles not in the collection, she recorded two items of information. First, on the pages of the index that list the works included, she recorded the call number of titles in the collection. This information helped students locate anthologies containing specific works. Second, on the holding record for each short-story collection, Maria recorded the name of the tool that indexed that particular work. This information was useful later, when she was weeding the short-story collections. If a particular work was in good condition and indexed, she kept the item for the collection.

In schools where teachers use textbooks or curriculum guides that include bibliographies of recommended materials, the collection can be measured against those titles. Teachers appreciate having a list of available titles with their call numbers. Creating such a list for teachers also can alert you to gaps in the collection and simultaneously provide teachers with an opportunity to suggest alternate materials. A limitation of this approach is that titles listed in textbooks and curriculum guides may be out of print. Newer materials may provide the same content.

Examining the Collection Directly

A physical examination of the materials can reveal the size, scope, and depth of a collection. An assessment of the timeliness of materials and their physical condition can help identify which items need to be mended, repaired, bound, replaced, removed, or discarded.

The examiner can be a member of the media center staff or an outsider. The latter is usually someone knowledgeable about materials on a specific subject. Fermi Middle School had a science consultant, who was knowledgeable about science materials for middle school students, examine the collection and recommend additional materials.

The collection can be examined by the media center staff at two levels. The more cursory approach is to examine only the shelves. Are there shelves that are consistently empty? Is that a sign of popularity or improper distribution? Are teachers giving assignments that call for those materials? Does the collection-development policy provide for adequate coverage in this area? Are there shelves where materials are seldom used? Have students turned to electronic forms for this information? This cursory approach can be done quickly and can indicate a section of the collection that should be studied more carefully.

A more in-depth approach is a systematic review of the collection. The materials are examined while considering the collection-development policy. If users' needs have changed, a policy change is imperative. For subjects that have low priority in a collection, infrequently used materials are probably not needed. Knowledge of the collection policy and the extent to which materials are added, withdrawn, or replaced can be used to establish goals for the review program.

Selection criteria, like those presented in chapter 7, can guide these decisions. Ideally, such a review is an ongoing process. It is easy to check the physical condition of books and periodicals when they are returned by users. More time is required to check damage to software. Other aspects of this process are described in chapter 15.

David V. Loertscher and May Lein Ho developed *Computerized Collection Development for School Library Media Centers* (Hi Willow Research and Publishing, 1986; distributed by Libraries Unlimited) as a way to do collection mapping. This computerized system allows one to analyze a collection in terms of curricular areas and numbers of students enrolled in courses. The resulting collection map provides a graphic presentation of the analysis of the collection.

The process involves four phases of activity. In phase 1 the media specialist identifies the collection's areas of strength, diversity of formats, publication dates, and duplicate titles. Phase 2 includes the analysis of the map in terms of meeting curriculum demands, identifying areas of the collection that need emphasis, remapping for proposed changes, and creating budget allocations to reflect the proposed changes. In phase 3, an automated acquisition system is designed to match the map. This is used to maintain the consideration file, create purchase orders, record received items, and track the budget. As these data are collected, the map is revised. Phase 4 provides ways to evaluate and monitor the collection's progress. For example, teachers are provided with an assessment form to evaluate how effectively the collection meets the needs of a specific unit. Media specialists using this technique report cases in which they were surprised at finding unexpected weaknesses in the collection. They also obtained objective data to support concerns about inadequacies in the collection.

Advantages

1. A cursory examination can be accomplished quickly.

2. Media specialists considering resource sharing can readily identify the weaknesses and strengths of a collection.

3. Reviewing a collection on a systematic and ongoing basis ensures that both the collection policy and the collection are responsive to school goals and user needs.

4. Establishing criteria for decisions about relegating, repairing, binding, replacing, and discarding materials facilitates and standardizes those processes.

Disadvantages

1. Materials being circulated during the examination study must be checked on the holdings record.

2. The process, unless computerized or focused on one aspect of the collection, is time-consuming and requires trained personnel.

3. If the collection-development policy and the rate of growth are not considered, individual items, rather than the collection as a whole, will be evaluated.

4. Resources available through cooperative efforts are not considered. If a media center is participating in a resource-sharing program where another collection is responsible for collecting on a specific subject, those materials will not appear in the examination.

5. People who are knowledgeable about the school program as well as a subject area may be difficult to locate and expensive.

Application

At Grant Senior High School, when Maria found materials that had not circulated in three years and were not recommended in standard catalogs, she placed the materials in the appropriate departmental areas. Department chairpersons provided assistance in deciding which items should be removed. When Maria found several titles relating to a specific course, she sought the aid of the teacher and used the occasion to suggest newer materials that would suit the same purpose as the items being considered for withdrawal. Teachers became more aware of the collection and their support increased.

The technique of collection mapping is used in the Los Angeles Unified School District for analyzing collections in terms of materials in languages other than English.[5] The October enrollment figures help identify the native languages of the student population. This information is translated into what percent of the students read each specific language and their reading level.

Another factor to consider is the percentage of Spanish readers at the given grade levels. In many schools, the majority of students in grades K-3 read in Spanish. However, the percentage drops off sharply in grades 4-6. Even if 90 percent of the children in grades K-3 are reading in Spanish, the collection should reflect a balance of English and Spanish books. It is important to provide high-quality English books at both the primary and the upper-grade levels. Easier English books are useful for teaching ESL and for giving older students who are transitioning into English reading books that they can easily read. As students become more proficient English readers, they need models of excellent English language use.[6]

For each language, the collection analysis work form used in Los Angeles includes the following categories: Dewey area; recommended percent of the collection, total recommended number of books (goal); the number of items in that language the library owns; the number of items the collection should have in that language; and the number of items in that language the collection needs. Media center staff complete the portion of the form that reports the actual count, and the district office staff calculates the columns for items the collection should have and needs. Table 16.1 is an example for an elementary school with 802 students. The example is for Spanish; similar analyses are done for Korean, Chinese, Vietnamese, Armenian, Farsi, Khmer, and Filipino titles. This information and the analysis of holdings by decade of publication can be displayed as graphs to visually present the information. The results guide the media specialist in removing out-of-date materials and selecting materials to meet the needs of non-English readers.

Table 16.1.
Analysis of Spanish-Language Titles

Dewey Area	Recommended Percent	Recommended Number of Books (Goal)	Spanish Holdings: Actual	Spanish Holdings: Should Have	Spanish Holdings: Needed
398.2	6%	481	92	121	29
500	10%	802	19	201	182
900	6%	481	7	121	114

Based on Bonnie O'Brian, *Collection Mapping* (Los Angeles: Instructional Media, Library Services, Office of Los Angeles Unified School District, n.d.).

Compiling Comparative Statistics

Although the limitations of quantitative methods have been discussed earlier in this chapter, there are reasons for collecting this type of data. For example, comparing data collected at various times of the year reveals patterns of use. Circulation statistics are typically requested by state and federal agencies, professional associations, and accrediting agencies.

Several writers have expressed concern about the lack of comparative national statistics that could document the contributions of media centers or the status of their collections. This information would be useful for policy makers. Kathleen Garland found that a majority of state agencies collect three types of statistics from media centers: expenditures, holdings, and personnel.[7] Comparing statistics among states is impossible because no single statistic is collected uniformly by all states, nor are terms or time periods standard. Garland found that elementary and middle school media specialists collect circulation statistics for a variety of reasons, including reports to principals, superintendents, and boards of education. Viewing the importance of statistics as documentation of the contributions media programs make to education, Garland points out the need to share this information with policy makers at the state and national levels. She observes

Unfortunately, statistics describing the condition of library media centers and assessing their performance are rarely published. Library media specialists must make policymakers aware of the contributions of library media programs to the schools they support, and they must have supporting data.[8]

Lillian N. Gerhardt addresses the consequences of not providing this information at the local level.

If your position is not a quantifiable part of the full plan for improving local education, then school librarians can remain a fringe benefit—to be added, divided, or subtracted according to the whims and worries of the local taxpayers.[9]

Miller and Shontz call for data to document the deterioration of collections by calling for

state-collected data, data from regional accrediting associations, and national data collected by the National Center for Education Statistics to provide the information needed by the states, the U.S. Department of Education, and Congress.

There seems to be one avenue left to us, and that is for state associations to become militant on the issue of sinking school library media centers. We are talking about rural children, inner-city children, the children of migrant workers, and the parents of tomorrow. Local control, local autonomy, local decision-making means local exposure of conditions that are crippling and will continue to cripple the learning possibilities for our children. Local leadership has to be developed, organized, motivated, and led by state associations. These may be our last hope.[10]

There are several types of statistics to use with local, state, and national policy makers. Statistics can be collected about

- Size: total number of volumes or titles, number of titles in various formats, subjects, or classification.

- Growth rate: volumes added within a given period of time; number of volumes by format, subject, or classification; cataloging statistics; or volumes compared to circulation.

- Expenditures for materials: by format, classification, or genre; percentage of total budget; or amount per user or category of user.

- Collection overlap: how many individual titles are held in common among two or more collections. This information is helpful in assigning areas of collection responsibility for resource sharing.

Advantages

1. Easy to compile if records have been kept.

2. If application is clearly defined, easy to understand and compare.

3. Relates directly to the users in the case of requests filled or not filled.

Disadvantages

1. Lack of standard definitions of the content or quantity of a unit.

2. Difficulty in counting nonprint items and sets of materials.

3. Significance may be difficult to interpret.

4. Possible inaccuracy or inconsistency in data collection and recording.

5. Statistics are usually inapplicable to a media center's goals and objectives.

Application

The gathering of statistics is commonly used to compare one collection with another, examine subject balance within a collection, decide whether resources should be shared, or allocate monies. Media specialists lack a universally accepted set of definitions. When data are being used for comparative purposes, the participating agencies need to agree on the definition of each statistical component and use identical measurement methods. Learn what is considered a statistical component and which data collecting methods are used in your district or state.

If the collections in your district or state are being compared, data must be gathered in the same way. Check for the district's or state's guidelines. Are you to use a volume or title count? If each volume of an encyclopedia set or each record in an album is counted, the total size of the collection may be distorted. Some districts with centralized processing may count an item as it appears in its main entry. For example, since each school may have a separate main entry, a school owning a kit containing two filmstrips, five books, and a teacher's guide might record one kit; another school with only one of the filmstrips and one of the books might record two items—a book and a filmstrip. An encyclopedia set cataloged as one item would count as one title. A multivolume set in which each volume is separately cataloged would be recorded as the number of individual titles.

When information is to be used for allocating funds, there is an advantage to having uniform data about the quantity of materials accessible to each student. One could argue that several students can use the encyclopedia set; however, circulating materials, such as kits, are usually checked out to one individual at a time. Data that include both a title and a volume count reveal more about the accessibility of materials than a volume count alone. This dual procedure accounts for duplicate titles that can serve more people for a specific item but records the limit of the total resources available.

Statistics about unfilled requests can be used to determine what materials should be added to a collection. Record requests by students and teachers for information or specific items not in the collection. These records can be used when making selection decisions.

Applying Standards

In this procedure, the collection is compared to quantitative and qualitative recommendations listed in standards, guidelines, or similar publications. The issuing body may be professional associations, such as the American Association of School Librarians and the Association for Educational Communications and Technology, who jointly published *Information Power: Guidelines for School Library Media Programs* (American Library Association, 1988). The guidelines, which focus on qualitative standards and a planning approach based on the needs of individual media centers, note that

> Quantitative descriptions are limited in value because the quantitative characteristics of programs vary in relation to needs and program activities. They are, by no means, the sole criteria by which individual programs should be evaluated.[11]

The guidelines provide qualitative and quantitative descriptions of state-of-the-art schools, which provide a basis for comparison of performance standards. (The information about the schools is from a 1985-1986 national survey.)[12] Media specialists can compare their schools with others at the same level of service and with similar student populations.

A standard produced by a state association and state agency is *Information Power for Washington: Guidelines for School Library Media Programs* (Washington Library Media Association and Superintendent of Public Instruction, 1991). These guidelines include a survey of media centers in the state of Washington using categories from the national survey reported in *Information Power*. Accreditation agencies, for example, the Southern Association of Colleges and Schools, are another source of standards. Typically such standards include basic criteria for evaluation of materials, level of financial support, size and condition of the collection, and access to materials. Listings of regional accrediting bodies are provided in appendix A.

Accreditation agency standards are based on resources or inputs, such as the amount of money spent per student. Another approach to standards is to consider both quantity and quality in terms of direct service output. *Output Measures for Public Library Service to Children: A Manual of Standardized Procedures*, by Virginia A. Walter (American Library Association, 1992), is a practical guide to quantifying and measuring outputs of service. Many of the suggestions can be adopted for use in the media center environment. The output measures include (1) library use, such as equipment use by children; (2) materials use: circulation per child, in-library use per child, and turnover rate of materials; (3) materials availability:

children's fill rate, homework fill rate; (4) information service: completion rate, transactions per child; and (5) community relations, such as the annual number of community contacts. The manual also describes how to conduct focus groups and user surveys.

Advantages

1. The guidelines generally are relevant to media center and school goals and objectives.
2. Standards and guidelines are usually widely accepted by educators and considered authoritative.
3. They can be used in persuasive ways to solicit support.

Disadvantages

1. The recommendations may be stated so generally that a high degree of professional knowledge and judgment may be needed to interpret the statements.
2. Knowledgeable people may disagree about the application and interpretation of the statements.
3. Minimum standards may be perceived as sufficient.

Application

Judge the appropriateness of standards and guidelines for your purpose by considering the following questions: Who (people, associations, or agencies) created the document? What was their purpose? How and by whom were the standards approved, accepted, or endorsed? Are the recommendations rigid, or are alternative approaches suggested? Do the guidelines represent the long-range goals of your program, or has it developed beyond the scope of the recommendations? Are the philosophy and rationale of the guidelines acceptable? On what basis would you recommend these guidelines to others? These questions imply some of the uses of standards.

Standards and guidelines allow media specialists to compare the collection to accepted measures or goals so that weaknesses in the collection can be identified. However, standards represent only an opinion of the collection level needed to support a program; accreditation agencies use them in this way. The quantitative descriptions in *Information Power* are based on research findings.

Be familiar with state and national guidelines. These documents can be used with administrators, teachers, and others to interpret the concept of the media program, articulate needs, and formulate goals and objectives. Some media specialists obtain copies of such documents for their administrators, highlighting sections applicable to the media program.

USE-CENTERED MEASURES

Use-centered measures can be used to determine whether, how often, and by whom materials are used. Circulation studies, in-house studies, surveys of user opinions, shelf-availability studies, and analysis of interlibrary-loan studies focus on the users and the use of materials.

Circulation Studies

Analysis of circulation data can be used to examine the collection as a whole, or any part of it, in terms of publication data, subject, or user group. This information can be used to identify (1) low-usage materials, which may be ready to be removed from the collection; (2) high-usage materials, which may be titles to duplicate; (3) patterns of use in selected subject areas or by format, for example, if filmstrips are no longer being used, future purchases of videos might be increased; and (4) materials used by specific user groups.

Advantages

1. Data are easily arranged into categories for analysis.
2. Allows great flexibility in duration of study and sample size.
3. Units of information are easily compiled.
4. Information is objective.
5. Data can be readily available with automated circulation systems.
6. Can correlate type of user with type of material used.

Disadvantages

1. Excludes in-house use, thus under-representing actual use.
2. Reflects only materials found by users and does not record if the user did not locate what was wanted or if the collection did not have what was wanted.
3. May be biased because of inaccessibility of heavily used materials.
4. Not suitable for noncirculating collections, such as periodicals.

Application

Kathleen Garland compares the results of sampling circulation activity over short periods of time with activity over the period of one school year.[13] The results of her study of an elementary school showed a high correlation between a typical week's activities and that of the whole year. The evidence from such studies can be used to show how well the collection supports the curriculum. Increased circulation of reading for pleasure may result from whole-language or sustained-silent-reading programs. Through documenting this increase, a media specialist could justify an increased budget allocation for fiction. New media specialists can use this technique to identify which courses and teachers make extensive use of which sections of the collection. By identifying weak areas of the collection, teachers and media specialists can work together to identify materials to fill those gaps. Garland offers practical advice for elementary school media specialists who want to try this technique.

Acknowledging the limitations of circulation analysis, Linda H. Bertland used an automated circulation system to analyze use of materials.[14] She notes that the analysis can indicate which materials probably will not circulate again, show how a collection is used, and help one evaluate past acquisitions decisions. In turn, these results can provide justification for future expenditures or other management decisions. Bertland describes locating fiction paperbacks in several locations in the media center. Regardless of location, even when intershelved with hardback copies of the same titles, her students prefer paperbacks. This information helped her make a collection-development decision. Paperback fiction books became a selection priority.[15]

In-House Use Studies

In-house studies can focus on either the use of noncirculating materials, or on the users of materials within the media center. During these studies, users are asked not to shelve materials. This allows the media center staff to record use of the materials as they reshelve them. Other examples include keeping logs of computerized database use.

Advantages

1. Can be used to correlate type of user with type of material used.

2. Can be used with a circulation study about the same part of the collection to provide more information about the use of that section.

3. Is appropriate for noncirculating materials.

4. Can be used to determine which journals to keep and for how long, which databases meet students' needs, areas in which students need help in developing search strategies, and gaps in the collection.

Disadvantages

1. Users' cooperation is needed.

2. If conducted during a high- or low-use period, results may be biased.

3. Circulating items will not be included, and this could create bias.

4. Does not reflect a student's failure to locate and find desired information.

Applications

This analysis can be used to study the amount of use of the reference collection. During the period of the study, students are asked not to shelve the reference materials they use but to leave them on the tables. At designated time periods, a staff member collects, counts, and reshelves the reference materials.

Another example is recording which materials are used by particular classes as they use the media center. This could involve counting the various formats or types of materials by classification number. When compared with the characteristics of the learners or the teaching methods used, this information could be used to anticipate future needs.

Yet another example is the analysis of automated logs or logs kept by students as they conduct searches online or on CD-ROMs. The logs can be analyzed in terms of (1) the database used, (2) the search terms used, (3) the number of items retrieved, (4) the number of retrieved items meeting the user's need, (5) types of formats retrieved, and (6) whether the user found the material in the collection or borrowed it through an interlibrary loan or other resource-sharing plan. Sample logs are described in Elizabeth S. Aversa and Jacqueline C. Mancall, *Managing Online Search Services in Schools* (ABC-Clio, 1989).

Survey of User Opinions

A survey of users and user groups requires soliciting verbal or written responses through interviews, questionnaires, or a combination of methods. User opinions can be gathered informally, leading the media specialist to think that users' needs have been identified. Examples of informal surveys include asking students as they check out materials whether they found what they wanted and recording their answers.

A formal survey is more systematic and thorough. The formal approach involves a series of steps: identifying the objectives, selecting and designing the data-collection technique, developing and testing the instrument, selecting the sample (the subgroup of the population), collecting the data, analyzing the data, and interpreting the results.

Whether using a written questionnaire or conducting interviews, one can use carefully worded questions to identify the strengths and weaknesses of the collection as perceived by the users. The questions should be directed to specific goals, which may or may not be of significance to the user. Formulating questions that solicit the type of information you need can be time-consuming. Interviews, which take longer to administer, can provide more in-depth information. However, the length of time involved may mean that fewer individuals participate in the process. The results of either type of survey can provide the basis for making changes in the collection-development policy.

Advantages

1. The survey can be developed to relate directly to the needs of users and to the goals and objectives of the collection.

2. The information collected may reflect current interests.

3. A survey can be used for most types of users.

Disadvantages

1. The method requires aggressive seeking of opinions.

2. Those polled may be passive about participating or lack a point of comparison.

3. Users' interests may be narrower than the collection-development policy.

4. Designing written questionnaires for young children may be difficult.

Application

Users' needs can be assessed formally and informally. At one level a student may ask for a specific title that a cousin recommended, while another may ask for the latest recording by a favorite singer. These requests reveal students' interests. A busy media specialist may forget to write down the request or be unable to obtain sufficient information on which to initiate an order. Individual requests may not reflect priorities established in the collection-development policy. Through a more formal approach, one can obtain a consensus of opinion and direct the inquiry in accordance with the goals of the school. Resources listed at the end of this chapter include a number of works that provide further information about designing surveys. Examples of questionnaires can be found in guides used for preparing self-studies when seeking accreditation.

Shelf-Availability Studies

To determine whether users are finding specific works they seek, users can be interviewed or handed a brief questionnaire that asks them to identify titles they could not find. This data can help identify titles not owned, titles for which duplicate copies are needed, items that have been improperly shelved, and lack of directions for locating materials. One also may learn that the user had an incomplete or inaccurate citation, copied the call number incorrectly, or did not know where to locate the materials.

This information about the collection and the user identifies areas in which corrective action and changes are needed.

Advantages

1. Identifies failures users face in trying to find materials.
2. Provides data on which changes in library policies and procedures may be based.
3. Can be easily repeated to measure changes in library performance.

Disadvantages

1. Requires user cooperation.
2. Involves staff time in planning and collecting data.
3. Does not identify the needs of nonusers.
4. Users may not remember the titles.

Application

A media specialist, using a simple questionnaire, could have students indicate what they were looking for and whether they found it. The results can indicate areas of the collection that need strengthening or areas where circulation is high and duplicate copies may be needed. Staff members may need to follow-up on the survey by checking to determine whether students had the wrong call number or whether materials were shelved incorrectly.

Analysis of Interlibrary Loan Statistics

Interlibrary loan requests represent materials people did not find in the collection and sought to obtain from other sources. Analyzing these requests can identify subject or format weaknesses in the collection, identify specific titles needed, and monitor resource-sharing agreements. Analyses of subject areas should be compared with similar analyses of acquisition and circulation data to identify areas of heavy use or lack of materials. The results must be evaluated in terms of the collection-development policy and existing resource-sharing agreements involving interlibrary loan.

Advantages

1. The data are often readily available. For example, statistics on requests for periodical titles are usually kept to avoid copyright infringement.

2. The items are needed by at least one person.

3. Requests may indicate weaknesses in the collection.

Disadvantages

1. The significance of the data may be difficult to interpret, as it represents the request of only one person.

2. Does not identify needs of users who personally go to other collections and skip making interlibrary loan requests.

Application

Records of interlibrary loan requests can be analyzed to identify titles being requested. The results can be analyzed in terms of frequently sought subjects for which the collection needs additional materials. Analysis of requests for articles can reveal heavily used periodicals that may be needed in the collection. Joann, a high school media specialist, uses this type of evaluation to identify which magazines were used most frequently. Then she checks whether the magazines in the collection cover the same subjects and whether they have the same appeal as the loaned items. This information indicates which titles to add and which should not be renewed.

When John, an elementary school media specialist, receives materials that teachers have requested through interlibrary loan, he asks them to fill out a brief questionnaire. He enters the bibliographic information describing the item and asks, "Was the item useful?" and "Will you need it again?" If teachers indicate they will need the material in the future, John adds the item to the "to be purchased" list.

Simulated Use Studies

Information about the use of the collection can be gathered without directly involving the user. These simulated situations include citation studies and document-delivery tests.

Citation Studies

This method can be used if the users of the collection also use other libraries. If students write term papers or do independent projects, media specialists can check the bibliographies of student papers or projects to identify titles cited that are not holdings of the school collection.

Advantages

1. Lists are easily obtained from the students' project bibliographies.

2. The method relates directly to the user.

3. The procedure is easy to apply.

4. Study identifies works not in the collection.

Disadvantages

1. The value is limited if students use only the collection being evaluated.

2. Citations are limited to the subject of the paper, a small portion of the total collection.

3. The method is limited by the number of students who write papers.

Application

One example of how this technique can be used is from Fermi Middle School's program for students gifted in the area of science. These students' projects were judged outstanding at the district science fair. One of their assignments was to write term papers on a recent advance in science. They were encouraged to use resources at other libraries, including the nearby university and industrial libraries. When the students completed their projects, the media specialist checked their citations to see which titles were not in the school's collection. Titles cited by several students were considered for addition to the school's collection.

Document Delivery Tests

This technique is similar to the shelf-availability study, but searching is done by library staff rather than users. It also carries the citation study a step further. It is used to determine if the collection includes a specific title, whether the item can be located, and how long it takes to do so. The purpose of document-delivery tests is to assess the capability of a library to provide users with the items they need at the time they need them. A typical approach is to compile a list of citations that reflects users' needs and test the time it takes to locate each item.

Advantages

1. Provides objective measurements of the capability of the collection to satisfy user needs.

2. Data can be compared between libraries if identical citation lists are used.

Disadvantages

1. A representative list may be difficult to create.

2. Because library staff perform the searches, the test understates the problems encountered by users.

3. To be meaningful, tests need to be repeated or compared with studies conducted in other libraries.

Application

Logs can be kept of interlibrary loan requests to record the requested item, the date of the request, the date the item was available to the requestor, and the response time (days between request and availability). The same type of information can be recorded about the response time for a teacher requesting a title for purchase. Further information can be gained by asking if the requestor still needs the item.

When Lisa, an English teacher, complained that the students at Rolling Hills High School could not find the materials they needed for their term papers, Gisella, the media specialist, took action. She checked the reading list against the holdings and compared this information with the titles that were in circulation during the assignment. Later she repeated the comparison and realized that she needed to either add more titles or establish a reserve system.

COMBINATION OF MEASURES STUDIES

In 1990-1991 the Birmingham, Alabama, schools surveyed the status of their collections through a study of the availability of materials, the age of the collections, and the number of unfulfilled requests due to lack of materials, combined with an assessment of circulation statistics. They found that 66 percent of the books in the collection were 10 years old or older. In a two-week period in January, they documented 4,000 unfilled requests due to lack of materials or lack of current ones. Using these figures and the average costs of books, they projected a three-year budget to purchase the needed materials. Geraldine Watts Bell reports the study.[16] Her article includes copies of the directions and work forms used, which demonstrate that the planners adhered to the dictum that for comparative statistics data, all participants must follow the same procedures and use the same formulas. Graphs presenting the findings show how visuals can impart information for administrators.

SUMMARY

Techniques for measuring and evaluating collections are not limited to those described in this chapter. References in the bibliography can serve as a starting point for learning more about the techniques described here and about other techniques.

The techniques described in this chapter included qualitative and quantitative measures. Often two or more techniques are used together to obtain more meaningful results. The evaluation process provides an opportunity to work with students, teachers, and administrators to ensure that the collection meets their needs. Their involvement can lead to understanding of why certain decisions are made.

NOTES

[1]Marjorie J. Willeke and Donna L. Peterson, "Improving the Library Media Program: A School District's Successful Experience with Change," *School Library Media Quarterly* 21, no. 2 (Winter 1993): 101-5.

[2]Willeke and Peterson, "Improving the Library Media Program," 105.

[3]Carol A. Doll and Pamela Petrick Barron, *Collection Analysis for the School Library Media Center: A Practical Approach* (Chicago: American Library Association, 1991), 8.

[4]Sharon L. Baker and F. Wilfrid Lancaster, *The Measurement and Evaluation of Library Services*, 2d ed. Arlington, VA: Information Resources Press, 1991: 4-7.

[5]Bonnie O'Brian, *Collection Mapping* (Los Angeles: Los Angeles Unified School District, Office of Instructional Media, Library Services, n.d.).

[6]O'Brian, *Collection Mapping*, 3.

[7]Kathleen Garland, "An Analysis of School Library Media Center Statistics Collected by State Agencies and Individual Library Media Specialists," *School Library Media Quarterly* 21, no. 2 (Winter 1993): 108.

[8]Garland, "An Analysis," 107.

[9]Lillian N. Gerhardt, "News in Contrast," *School Library Journal* 37 (June 1991): 4.

[10]Marilyn L. Miller and Marilyn Shontz, "Expenditures for Resources in School Library Media Centers, FY 1991-1992," *School Library Journal* 39, no. 10 (October 1993): 36.

[11]American Association of School Librarians and Association for Educational Communications and Technology, *Information Power: Guidelines for School Library Media Programs* (Chicago: American Library Association; Washington, DC: Association for Educational Communications and Technology, 1988), 115.

[12]For further analysis of the findings, see Howard D. White, "School Library Collections and Services: Ranking the States," *School Library Media Quarterly* 19, no. 1 (Fall 1990): 13-26.

[13]Kathleen Garland, "Circulation Sampling as a Technique for Library Media Program Management," *School Library Media Quarterly* 21, no. 2 (Winter 1992): 73-78.

[14]Linda H. Bertland, "Usage Patterns in a Middle School Library: A Circulation Analysis," *School Library Media Quarterly* 19, no. 2 (Winter 1991): 73-78.

[15]Linda H. Bertland, "Circulation Analysis as a Tool for Collection Development," *School Library Media Quarterly* 19, no. 2 (Winter 1991): 90-97.

[16]Geraldine Watts Bell, "Systemwide Collection Assessment Survey," in *School Library Media Annual 1992*, vol. 10, ed. by Jane Bandy Smith and J. Gordon Coleman, Jr., (Englewood, CO: Libraries Unlimited, 1992), 135-47.

BIBLIOGRAPHY

American Association of School Librarians and Association for Educational Communications and Technology. *Information Power: Guidelines for School Library Media Programs*. Chicago: American Library Association; Washington, DC: Association for Educational Communications and Technology, 1988.

American Library Association. Resources and Technical Services Division. Resources Section. Collection Management and Development Committee. Subcommittee on Guidelines for Collection Development. *Guide to the Evaluation of Library Collections*, ed. by Barbara Lockett. Collection Management and Development Guides, no. 2. Chicago: American Library Association, 1989.

Baker, Sharon L., and F. Wilfrid Lancaster. *The Measurement and Evaluation of Library Services*, 2d ed. Arlington, VA: Information Resources Press, 1991.

Bell, Geraldine Watts. "Systemwide Collection Assessment Survey" in *School Library Media Annual 1992*, vol. 10, ed. by Jane Bandy Smith and J. Gordon Coleman, Jr. Englewood, CO: Libraries Unlimited, 1992, 135-47.

Bertland, Linda H. "Circulation Analysis As a Tool for Collection Development." *School Library Media Quarterly* 19, no. 2 (Winter 1991): 90-97.

——. "Usage Patterns in a Middle School Library: A Circulation Analysis." *School Library Media Quarterly* 16 (Spring 1988): 200-203.

Doll, Carol A., and Pamela Petrick Barron. *Collection Analysis for the School Library Media Center: A Practical Approach*. Chicago: American Library Association, 1991.

Garland, Kathleen. "An Analysis of School Library Media Center Statistics Collected by State Agencies and Individual Library Media Specialists." *School Library Media Quarterly* 21, no. 2 (Winter 1993): 108.

——. "Circulation Sampling as a Technique for Library Media Program Management." *School Library Media Quarterly* 20, no. 2 (Winter 1992): 73-78.

Gerhardt, Lillian N. "News in Contrast." *School Library Journal* 37 (June 1991): 4.

Lockett, Barbara, ed. *Guide to the Evaluation of Library Collections*. Collection Management and Development Guides, no. 2. Chicago: American Library Association, 1989.

Loertscher, David V., and May Lein Ho. *Computerized Collection Development for School Library Media Centers*. Fayetteville, AR: Hi Willow Research and Publishing, 1986.

Miller, Marilyn L. and Marilyn Shontz. "Expenditures for Resources in School Library Media Centers, FY 1991-92." *School Library Journal* 39, no. 10 (October 1993): 26-36.

O'Brian, Bonnie. *Collection Mapping*. Los Angles: Los Angeles Unified School District, Office of Instructional Media, Library Services, n.d.

Willeke, Marjorie J., and Donna L. Peterson. "Improving the Library Media Program: A School District's Successful Experience with Change." *School Library Media Quarterly* 21, no. 2 (Winter 1993): 101-5.

SELECTED STANDARDS AND GUIDELINES

Hopkins, Dianne McAfee. *School Library Media Programs: A Resource and Planning Guide*. Bulletin no. 7368. Madison: Wisconsin Department of Public Instruction, 1987.

Library Media Master Plan Steering Committee. *A Master Plan for Utah's School Library Media Programs: Empowering Students to Function Effectively in an Information World*. Salt Lake City: Utah State Office of Education, 1991.

Maryland. Department of Education. *Standards for School Library Media Programs in Maryland*. Baltimore, 1986.

National Study of School Evaluation. *Evaluative Criteria for Middle Level Schools*. Falls Church, VA, 1990.

North Carolina. Department of Public Instruction. Division of Media and Technology Services. *Learning Connections: Guidelines for Media and Technology Programs*. Raleigh, 1992.

Northwest Association of Schools and Colleges. *Standards for Accreditation*. Boise, ID, 1990.

Southern Association of Colleges and Schools. Commission on Elementary Schools. *Policies, Principles, and Standards for the Accreditation of Elementary and Middle Schools for Use as a Checklist During the 1990-1991 School Year*. Decatur, GA, 1990.

Southern Association of Colleges and Schools. Commission on Secondary Schools. *Standards of the Commission on Secondary Schools*, 1986 ed. Atlanta, 1986.

State Library of Pennsylvania. *Pennsylvania Guidelines for School Library Media Programs*. Harrisburg, 1989.

Texas Education Agency. *School Library Media Centers*. Austin, n.d.

Utah. Office of Education. *A Master Plan for Utah's School Library Media Programs: Empowering Students to Function Effectively in an Information World*. Salt Lake City, 1991.

Washington Library Media Association Certification and Standards Committee and State of Washington Office of Superintendent of Public Instruction. *Information Power for Washington: Guidelines for School Library Media Programs*. Olympia, WA: Office of Superintendent of Public Instruction, 1991.

SELECTED RESOURCES

Doll, Carol A., and Pamela Petrick Barron. *Collection Analysis for the School Library Media Center: A Practical Approach*. Chicago: American Library Association, 1991.
   Provides directions, examples, and forms for measuring and reporting evaluation of the collection.

Hafner, Arthur W. *Descriptive Statistical Techniques for Librarians*. Chicago: American Library Association, 1989.
   Describes and applies descriptive statistics in a number of problem-solving situations in libraries.

Katzer, Jeffrey; Kenneth H. Cook; and Wayne W. Crouch. *Evaluating Information: A Guide for Users of Social Science Research*, 3d ed. New York: McGraw-Hill, 1991.
   Clearly written text and glossary provide basic information for conducting or evaluating research.

Powell, Ronald R. *Basic Research Methods for Librarians*, 2d ed. Norwood, NJ: Ablex Publishing, 1991.
   Describes library uses of the processes of planning, collecting, analyzing, and writing research projects and proposals.

Walter, Virginia A. *Output Measures for Public Library Service to Children: A Manual of Standardized Procedures*. Public Library Development Program. Chicago: American Library Association, Public Library Association, Association for Library Service to Children, 1992.
   Describes how to collect, interpret, and use data. Includes sample forms in English and Spanish.

CHAPTER 17

CREATING, SHIFTING, AND Closing Collections

When student populations shift or there is a change in grade levels served by the school, media specialists respond by creating an initial collection, combining collections, or closing a collection. Each situation presents different demands upon media specialists' knowledge and skill. A media specialist's human relations skills may be tested in the tensions of these stimulating experiences. Emotions can run high when a school is closed or a favorite group or grade level is lost.

INITIAL COLLECTION

The opening of a new school calls for creation of an initial collection. When a new building is being planned, various patterns of preparation for the initial collection can occur. The optimal time to begin planning is when the building contract is awarded. In this ideal situation, the media specialist and faculty are hired to plan during the year preceding the opening of the building. This procedure has definite advantages. The media specialist can benefit from participating with the faculty members as they identify philosophy and goals, create the curriculum, and develop plans. The media specialist's major responsibility during the year is to ensure that the desired types of learning environments will be ready on opening day. Orders must be placed early enough to allow for delivery, processing, and time to make any necessary substitutions. Admittedly, school districts rarely have the financial resources or educational foresight to provide a whole year of planning.

Whether or not the entire faculty is engaged in planning during the year prior to opening the school, the collection needs to be ready on opening day. If the school's staff has not been appointed, the responsibility often rests with district-level staff. Those planning the new facility need to be aware of the long-range goals and objectives of the district's educational program and the equipment and materials needed for an initial collection. Planners should design flexibility into the plans to accommodate changes that may occur in teaching styles, subjects taught, and the needs of unknown users.

Districts follow various patterns for handling orders for a new building. In some districts, one-third of the initial collection budget is used to purchase materials to have on opening day. One-third is reserved for recommendations by the principal and professional staff. The remaining third is reserved for orders generated by the media specialist, who works with teachers and students to make selections. Other districts spend the entire first year's budget prior to the opening of the school.

School districts with recent student population growth patterns often have lists of recommendations for the initial collection or have automated holdings records for such collections. In some cases, such districts are willing to share or sell their lists. This type of list is designed to cover the broad scope needed by teachers and students in widely varying school communities and is frequently revised on an annual basis.

Major book jobbers also offer prepackaged opening-day collections. While this package, or any list developed by other school districts, may not address the unique needs of your school, there are some advantages: current costs are known, out-of-print titles are excluded, time and effort is saved by not having to consider unavailable items, the media specialist can add additional materials, and the printout or online order saves time. Such a list has the following disadvantages: direct order items will not be covered, standing order items will not be included, and the unique needs of the school may not be met.

General guidelines about the number of items that should be in an initial collection may be available from the state's school library media consultant or state association. An example is *Standards for School Library Media Programs in Maryland* (Maryland State Department of Education, 1986), which recommends:

1. Each school should have an initial collection of a variety of media, fully cataloged and processed to serve as a base for an adequate collection.

2. An analysis of the special needs of the school population should determine the composition of the initial collection.

3. The acquisition of an initial collection in a new school should begin at the time the building contract is awarded. This plan will provide time for sound selection procedures necessary to have the materials ready for use on the opening day of school.

4. Funds for initial collections should be included in capital budgets. Otherwise, funds especially designed for equipping new buildings should be provided.[1]

The recommended size of the basic collection for schools with enrollments of more than 600 students is: for elementary schools, 12,000 items or at least 20 items per pupil; for junior high or middle schools, 15,000 items or at least 25 items per pupil; and for high schools, 18,000 items or at least 30 items per student. For schools with 200 pupils or less, the recommendations are for elementary schools, 20 items per pupil or no less than a total of 1,000 items; for junior high or middle schools, 25 items per pupil or no less than a total than 1,250; and for high schools, 30 items per pupil or no less than 1,500.[2]

State and association guidelines outline the range of formats and number of items on which a collection can be built. Some of the guidelines outline several stages of development, from the initial collection to one considered to be excellent.

Specific titles for the collection can be identified through selection tools. Useful sources include *Children's Catalog* (H. W. Wilson, 1991), *Elementary School Library Collection* (Brodart, 1994), *Junior High School Library Collection* (H. W. Wilson, 1990), and *Senior High School Library Collection* (H. W. Wilson, 1992). The broad scope and coverage of these tools helps the media specialist identify titles to match the wide range of information needs that will be experienced during the opening days of the collection.

CLOSING COLLECTIONS

When schools are closed, consolidated, or have attendance districts reorganized, the full impact may not be felt until the formal announcement is made. An individual should be assigned the responsibility for determining procedures for removing materials. Media specialists must be involved in the planning to avoid confusion and inefficiency.

Consolidation and reorganization of attendance districts can be "hot" issues calling for special handling by the media specialist. A sense of standards, diplomacy, and tact, along with a sensitivity to the politics of the situation, will help. Perhaps the loss can be turned into a gain for other schools in the district. Planning is a key factor in retaining items the collection needs while preparing for the transfer of other items. If several schools are involved in the reorganization plan, Dale L. White, a supervisor in such a situation, recommends using the selective withdrawal approach between paired schools. The following example involves elementary schools currently serving grades K-6. A school designated to serve K-3 will be paired with a school for kindergarten and grades 4-6. The first school will keep its materials for the kindergarten classes and those for the lower fourth-graders but will selectively withdraw materials appropriate for older children who will attend the second school.[3]

This illustration points up the need for communication of anticipated needs. Information about the available items, with plans for their transfer, should be sent to the receiving school. Each of the newly formed collections will need to be assessed in terms of their weaknesses and strengths to meet the new demands.

When schools close, answers to the following questions can guide the planning process: What will be the disposition of the materials? Equipment? Furniture? What legal guidelines are there for the disposition of materials and equipment? Are there local constraints? What are the closing deadlines? Will extra help be provided?[4]

Once the target date is known, create a timeline with specific goals. Post this information to alert the users and staff and to remind yourself. Notifying students and teachers is especially important when services are being curtailed. This public relations move will have future implications for relations with your clientele.

Teachers who are being moved to other schools can help by indicating titles they want available. These items should be the first materials reallocated so they can be processed into those collections.

Criteria for weeding materials described in chapter 15 should be applied. Does the policy on gift materials provide for transferring the materials to another school? Are there other materials covered by other regulations or agreements? Check such policies before considering how to dispose of the items.

A list of the remaining materials can be distributed throughout the system so other media specialists can request specific titles. Unclaimed items must be stored, distributed, or discarded. Distribution possibilities include storing materials at an exchange center, where they can be examined, or donating the materials to other agencies serving children, such as hospitals or institutions. The materials could be advertised for sale to beginning collections. Policies within the district will govern how materials can be dispersed; they may grant approval for sale to individuals for fund-raising.

NOTES

[1]Maryland, Department of Education, *Standards for School Library Media Programs in Maryland* (Baltimore, 1986), 19.

[2]Maryland, Department of Education, *Standards*, 19.

[3]Dale L. White, "Closing/Reorganizing Library Media Centers (And Living To Tell About It!)," *Ohio Media Spectrum* 37, no. 2 (Spring 1985): 36.

[4]Ann Hanes, "Close, Closing, Closed—Your School Library Media Center," *Indiana Media Journal* 5, no. 2 (Winter 1983): 2-9.

BIBLIOGRAPHY

Hanes, Ann. "Close, Closing, Closed—Your School Library Media Center." *Indiana Media Journal* 5, no. 2 (Winter 1983): 2-9.

Maryland. Department of Education. *Standards for School Library Media Programs in Maryland*. Baltimore, 1986.

White, Dale L. "Closing/Reorganizing Library Media Centers (And Living To Tell About It!)." *Ohio Media Spectrum* 37, no. 2 (Spring 1985): 35-37.

POSTSCRIPT

There may be days when you feel you are operating in a vacuum, isolated from anyone who shares your enthusiasm for what a media program can be. This is not unusual, particularly for the media specialist who works alone at the building level. Remember that through electronic mail, a telephone call, or a letter you can contact someone who shares your concerns. You can contact media specialists you meet at professional meetings, staff members of professional associations, and former professors. Like the media program, you are part of a larger circle of people who share common interests.

Information and dialogue are available, if you initiate the contact. You will find others who welcome you.

Appendix A
Agencies, Associations, and Suppliers

Agency for Instructional Technology (AIT)
Box A
Bloomington, IN 47402-0120
812-339-2203 or 800-457-4509
FAX 812-333-4218

Alexander Graham Bell Association for the Deaf
3417 Volta Place, NW
Washington, DC 20007-2778
202-337-5220
Publishes *Volta Review* (ISSN 0042-8639; seven issues per year); includes reviews of books for parents and teachers of deaf children. Also publishes books and audiovisual materials.

American Alliance for Health, Physical Education, Recreation, and Dance
1900 Association Drive
Reston, VA 22091
703-476-3400
Journals include *Health Education* (ISSN 0097-0050, bimonthly) and *Journal of Physical Education, Recreation and Dance* (ISSN 0730-3084, monthly August-May); each has information about professional resources and occasionally includes reviews or features on materials for students.

American Association for the Advancement of Science (AAAS)
1333 H Street, NW
Washington, DC 20005
202-326-6446
FAX 202-843-0159
Publishes *Science Books and Films* (ISSN 0098-324X, five issues per year) (sometimes listed as *AAAS Science Books and Films*). Includes reviews of books, films, and filmstrips on mathematics and the sciences (social, physical, and life).

American Association of School Administrators (AASA)
1801 North Moore
Arlington, VA 22209-9988
Order department: 703-875-0730
FAX 703-841-1543
Publishes *School Administrator* (ISSN 0036-6439, 11 issues per year), pamphlets, filmstrips, and books; sponsors conferences, conventions, and other information services.

American Association of School Librarians (AASL)
50 E. Huron Street
Chicago, IL 60611
312-280-4386 or 800-545-2386
Illinois residents, 800-545-2433
FAX 312-664-7495
Publishes *School Library Media Quarterly*, bibliographies, and other materials. The free annual *AASL Checklist of Materials* lists publications that can be ordered directly from AASL.
See also **American Library Association**.

American Association of University Women
2210 Wilshire Boulevard, Suite 174
Santa Monica, CA 90403
310-395-0244
FAX 310-394-6470

American Civil Liberties Union
132 West 43rd Street
New York, NY 10036
212-944-9800
Has affiliates in all 50 states. Publishes materials on intellectual freedom and student's rights.

American Council on Consumer Interests
240 Stanley Hall
University of Missouri-Columbia
Columbia, MO 65211
FAX 314-884-4807
Publishes *Journal of Consumer Affairs* (ISSN 0022-0087, two issues per year); contains reviews of books and articles on consumer matters.

American Federation of Teachers
555 New Jersey Avenue, NW
Washington, DC 20001
202-879-4400
Publications include the periodicals *American Teacher* (ISSN 0003-1380, monthly), *American Educator* (ISSN 0148-432X, monthly), newsletters, pamphlets, books, films, and videotapes.

American Foundation for the Blind
15 West 16th Street
New York, NY 10011
212-620-2000
Publishes *Journal of Visual Impairment and Blindness* (ISSN 0145-482X, monthly September-June); includes reviews of books, films, etc. The Foundation's publications include books, films, pamphlets, and bibliographies.

American Library Association (ALA)
50 E. Huron Street
Chicago, IL 60611
312-944-6780 or 800-545-2433
Illinois residents: 800-545-2433
FAX 312-440-9374
TDD 312-944-7928

Publications, such as books or journals (e.g., *Booklist*), can be purchased through the order department. Inexpensive and specialized materials can be ordered directly from the issuing division or office at the above address. See separate entries for the **American Association of School Librarians (AASL)**, **Association for Library Service to Children (ALSC)**, and **Young Adult Library Services Association (YALSA)**.

— **Headquarters Library & Information Center**
312-280-2153 or 800-545-2433, ext. 2153
FAX 312-440-9374
E-mail: U58959@uicvm.uic.edu

— **Office for Intellectual Freedom**
312-280-4223 or 800-545-2433, ext. 4223
Publishes interpretations of the *Library Bill of Rights* and other materials dealing with intellectual freedom.

— **Publishing Services (ALA Books and Production Services)**
312-280-5416 or 800-545-2433, ext. 5416

— **Washington Office**
202-547-4440
FAX 202-547-7363
Publishes the *ALA Washington Newsletter* (ISSN 0001-1746, at least 12 issues per year); communicates legislative activities and issues.

American Printing House for the Blind (APHB)
1839 Frankfort Avenue
P.O. Box 6085
Louisville, KY 40206
502-895-2405
FAX 502-895-2405
Publishes braille books, magazines, and Talking Book records; manufactures educational aids for the blind. The Instructional Materials Center for the Visually Handicapped at APHB evaluates and disseminates instructional materials and serves as the National Reference Center for the Visually Handicapped.

American Speech-Language-Hearing Association
10801 Rockville Pike
Rockville, MD 20852-3294
301-897-5600, ext. 294
FAX 301-571-0457
Produces audiocassettes and videotapes; publishes *ASHA: A Journal of the American Speech-Language-Hearing Association* (ISSN 0001-2475, monthly), which reviews games, kits, and learning materials designed for use with hearing- or speech-impaired children.

American Vocational Association
1410 King Street
Dept. 93B
Alexandria, VA 22314
703-683-3111
Order department: 800-826-9972
FAX 703-683-7424
Publishes *Vocational Education Journal* (ISSN 0164-9175, monthly); includes announcements and reviews for professional materials and media for students.

Association for Educational Communications and Technology (AECT)
1025 Vermont Avenue, NW, Suite 820
Washington, DC 20005
202-347-7834
Publishes *TechTrends* (ISSN 8756-3894, six issues per year), books, pamphlets, and audiovisual materials of interest to media specialists. Provides information about copyright questions.

Association for Library Service to Children (ALSC)
50 E. Huron Street
Chicago, IL 60611
312-280-2163
800-545-2433, ext. 2163
Publishes *Journal of Youth Services in Libraries* (ISSN 0040-9286) with **YALSA**. This division's publications, *Caldecott Calendar*, and bibliographies can be ordered directly from ALSC.

Association for Supervision and Curriculum Development (ASCD)
225 North Washington Street
Alexandria, VA 22314
703-549-9110
Publishes *Educational Leadership* (ISSN 0013-1784, monthly), which contains reviews of professional books. ASCD publishes books, pamphlets, videotapes, and audiocassettes.

Association of American Publishers
2005 Massachusetts Avenue, NW
Washington, DC 20036
202-232-3335
Frequently publishes or co-sponsors activities related to freedom to read and related collection matters.

California Computer Software Clearinghouse
California State University, Long Beach
1250 Bellflower Boulevard
Long Beach, CA 90840-1402
213-985-1764
FAX 213-985-1753
Published *1991 Guidelines for CD-ROM in California Schools* and *1991 Guidelines for Computer Software in California Schools*.

California Instructional Video Clearinghouse
Stanislaus County Office of Education
801 County Center Three Court
Modesto, CA 95355-4490
209-525-4993
FAX 209-525-4984
Published *1991 Guidelines for Computer-Interactive Videodiscs in California Schools*.

Canadian Library Association
200 Elgin Street, Suite 602
Ottawa, ONT K2P 1L5
Canada
613-232-9625 or 800-267-6566
FAX 613-563-9895
Publishes the annotated critical bibliography, *CM: Canadian Materials for Schools and Libraries* (ISSN 0363-9479, six issues per year).

Captioned Films for the Deaf Distribution Center
5034 Wisconsin Avenue, NW
Washington, DC 20016
202-363-1308
This branch of the U.S. Department of Education, Bureau of Education for the Handicapped provides educational and full-length entertainment subtitled films to deaf persons free of charge.

Children's Book Council, Inc.
568 Broadway, Suite 404
New York, NY 10012
212-966-1990
Publishes *CBC Features* and other informational packets about children's books. Provides an examination center and information about new titles for children.

Children's Television Workshop
1 Lincoln Plaza
New York, NY 10023
212-595-3456

Comics Magazine Association of America, Inc.
355 Lexington Avenue, 17th Floor
New York, NY 10017
Publishes *Code of the Comics Magazine Association of America.*

Consumer Education Resource Network (CERN)
1500 Wilson Boulevard, Suite 800
Rosslyn, VA 22209
800-336-0223
A resource and service network in the consumer-education field.

Consumer Products Safety Commission
4330 East-West Highway
Washington, DC 20207
301-504-0580

Council for Exceptional Children (CEC)
1920 Association Drive
Reston, VA 22091-1589
703-620-3660
Publishes *Teaching Exceptional Children* (ISSN 0040-0599, quarterly), which includes articles on instructional methods and materials. Other publications include newsletters, books, and media. CEC is the ERIC Clearinghouse on Handicapped and Gifted Children and publishes *Exceptional Child Education Resources* (ECER) (ISSN 0160-4309, quarterly), a print presentation of all citations in the ECER database.

C-SPAN
Department of Educational Services
400 N. Capitol Street, NW
Washington, DC 20001
800-523-7586
Publishes *C-SPAN Newsletter*, which includes programming schedules and articles of interest to teachers.

Denoyer-Geppert Scientific Co.
5225-T N. Ravenswood Avenue
Chicago, IL 60640
312-561-9200
FAX 312-561-4160

Educational Paperback Association
P.O. Box 1399
East Hampton, NY 11937
Trade organization of paperback distributors who specialize in work with schools and libraries in the United States and Canada. They offer services including book fairs and examination opportunities.

Educational Resources Information Center (ERIC)
Office of Educational Research and Improvement (OERI)
U.S. Department of Education
555 New Jersey Avenue, NW
Washington, DC 20208-5720
202-219-2290
FAX 202-219-1817
Internet: eric@inet.ed.gov
The ERIC Program staff manages the ERIC System, which consists of clearinghouses, adjunct clearinghouses, and support components. Basic ERIC reference tools are *Resource in Education (RIE)*, a monthly journal of abstracts of current education-related documents, published by the Superintendent of Documents, Washington, DC 20402; *Current Index to Journals in Education (CIJE)*, a monthly journal of abstracts of education-related articles, published by Oryx Press, 4041 North Central Avenue, Phoenix, AZ 85012, 800-279-ORYX; *Thesaurus of ERIC Descriptors*, a master list of subject headings used in indexing and searching, available from Oryx Press.

ERIC Clearinghouses

Each publishes research summaries, bibliographies, information analysis papers, and other products. They offer free reference and referral services for their subject area. Clearinghouses not listed here include Higher Education (HE) and Community Colleges (CC).

Adult, Career, and Vocational Education (CE)
The Ohio State University
Center on Education and Training for Employment
1900 Kenny Road
Columbus, OH 43210-1090
614-292-4353 or 800-848-4815
FAX 614-292-1260
Internet: ericacve@magnus.acs.ohio-state.edu

Counseling and Personnel Services (CG)
ERIC/CASS
University of North Carolina at Greensboro
School of Education
1000 Spring Garden Street
Greensboro, NC 27412-9001
919-334-4114 or 800-414-9769
FAX 919-334-4116
Internet: bleuerj@iris.uncg.edu

Disabilities and Gifted Education
Council for Exceptional Children
1920 Association Drive
Reston, VA 22091-1589
703-264-9474 or 800-328-0272
FAX 703-264-9494
Internet: krnclanc@inet.ed.gov

Educational Management (EA)
University of Oregon
1787 Agate Street
Eugene, OR 97403-5207
503-346-5034
FAX 503-346-5890
Internet: ppicle@oregon.uoregon.edu

Elementary and Early Childhood Education (PS)
University of Illinois
College of Education
805 West Pennsylvania Avenue
Urbana, IL 61801-4897
217-333-1386
FAX 217-244-4572
Internet: ericeece@uc1.cso.uiuc.edu

Information & Technology
Syracuse University
4-194 Center for Science and Technology
Syracuse, NY 13244-4100
315-443-3640 or 800-464-9107
FAX 315-443-5448
Internet: eric@ericir.syr.edu
AskERIC (Internet-based question-answering service): askeric@ericir.syr.edu

Languages and Linguistics (FL)
Center for Applied Linguistics
1118 22nd Street, NW
Washington, DC 20037-0037
202-429-9551
FAX 202-429-9766
Internet: cal@guvax.georgetown.edu

Reading and Communication Skills (CS)
Indiana University
Smith Research Center, Suite 150
2805 East 10th Street
Bloomington, IN 47408-2698
812-855-5847 or 800-759-4723
FAX 812-855-4220
Internet: ericcs@ucs.indiana.edu

Rural Education and Small Schools (RC)
Appalachia Educational Laboratory
1031 Quarrier Street
P.O. Box 1348
Charleston, WV 25325-1348
304-347-0400, Charleston area, or 800-759-4123
Internet: u56d9@wvnvm.wvnet.edu

Science, Mathematics, and Environmental Education (SE)
The Ohio State University
1929 Kenny Road
Columbus, OH 43210-1080
614-292-6717
FAX 614-292-0263
Internet: ericse.@osu.edu

Social Studies/Social Science Education (SO)
Indiana University
Social Studies Development Center
2805 East 10th Street, Suite 120
Bloomington, IN 47408-2698
812-855-3838
FAX 812-855-0455
Internet: ericso@ucs.indiana.edu

Teaching and Teacher Education (SP)
American Association of Colleges for Teacher Education
One Dupont Circle, NW, Suite 610
Washington, DC 20036-2412
202-293-2450
FAX 202-457-8095
Internet: jback@inet.ed.gov

Urban Education (UD)
Teachers College, Columbia University
Institute for Urban and Minority Education
Main Hall, Room 303, Box 40
525 West 120th Street
New York, NY 10027-9998
212-678-3433 or 800-601-4868
FAX 212-678-4048
Internet: ef29@columbia.edu

ERIC Adjunct Clearinghouses

New clearinghouses with narrower scopes are called adjunct clearinghouses. The broader based clearinghouse with whom the adjunct is affiliated handles the cataloging, indexing, and abstracting of the documents. Like the clearinghouses, the adjuncts provide free reference and referral services, as well as research summaries, bibliographies, information analysis papers, and other products.

Adjunct ERIC Clearinghouse for Consumer Education
National Institute for Consumer Education
207 Rackham Building, West Circle Drive
Eastern Michigan University
Ypsilanti, MI 48107-2237
313-487-2292 or 800-336-6423
FAX 313-487-7153
Internet: cse_bonner@emunix.emich.edu

Adjunct ERIC Clearinghouse for ESL Literacy Education
Center for Applied Linguistics
1118 22nd Street, NW
Washington, DC 20037
202-429-9292, ext. 200
FAX 202-659-5641
Internet: cat@guvax.georgetown.edu

National Clearinghouse for US-Japan Studies
Indiana University
Social Studies Development Center
2805 East 10th Street, Suite 120
Bloomington, IN 47408-2698
812-855-3838
FAX 812-855-0455
Internet: cabrooks@ucs.indiana.edu

Adjunct ERIC Clearinghouse on Chapter 1
Chapter 1 Teaching Assistance Center
PRC Inc.
2601 Fortune Circle East
One Park Fletcher Building, Suite 300-A
Indianapolis, IN 46241-2237
317-244-8160 or 800-456-2380
FAX 317-244-7386

Adjunct ERIC Clearinghouse on Clinical Schools
ERIC Clearinghouse on Teaching and Teacher Education
American Association of Colleges for Teacher Education
One Dupont Circle, NW, Suite 610
Washington, DC 20036-2412
202-293-2450
FAX 202-457-8095
Internet: labdalha@inet.ed.gov

ERIC Support Components

Production, publication, and dissemination of ERIC documents and services are handled by:

ACCESS ERIC
1600 Research Boulevard
Rockville, MD 20850-3172
301-251-5264 or 800-LET-ERIC (538-3742)
FAX 301-251-5767
Internet: acceric@inet.ed.gov
ACCESS ERIC's publications include *A Pocket Guide to ERIC*, *All About ERIC*, *The ERIC Review*, *ERIC User's Interchange*, *The Catalog of ERIC Clearinghouse Publications*, and the following reference directories: *ERIC Information Service Providers*, *Education-Related Information Centers*, and *ERIC Calendar of Education-Related Conferences*.

ERIC Document Reproduction Service (EDRS)
CBIS Federal Inc.
7420 Fullerton Road, Suite 110
Springfield, VA 22153-2852
703-440-1400 or 800-442-ERIC (3742)
FAX 703-440-1408
Internet: edrs@gwuvm.gwu.edu
EDRS produces and sells microfiche and paper copies of documents announced in *Resources in Education* (RIE). EDRS products can be ordered online through BRS, DIALOG, OCLC, or by FAX.

ERIC Processing and Reference Facility
ARC Professional and Reference Facility
1301 Piccard Drive, Suite 300
Rockville, MD 20850-4305
301-258-5500
FAX 301-948-3695
Internet: ericfac@inet.ed.gov
This facility serves as the central editorial and computer-processing agency and prepares *Resources in Education* (RIE). To order *Resources in Education*, contact:

U.S. Government Printing Office
Superintendent of Documents
P.O. Box 371954
Pittsburgh, PA 15250-7954
202-783-3238
FAX 202-512-2250

Oryx Press
4041 North Central Avenue, Suite 700
Phoenix, AZ 85012-3399
602-265-2651 or 800-279-ORYX (6799)
FAX 800-279-4663
FAX 602-265-6250
Internet: arhjb@asuvm.inre.asu.edu
Publishes *Current Index to Journals in Education (CIJE)*, the *Thesaurus of ERIC Descriptors*, and other ERIC publications.

Freedom to Read Foundation
50 E. Huron Street
Chicago, IL 60611
312-280-4226 or 800-545-2433, ext. 4226
FAX 312-440-9374

Gallaudet University
800 Florida Avenue
Washington, DC 20002-3699
202-651-5051
FAX 202-651-5054
TDD 202-651-5052
Write to Gallaudet College Bookstore for the catalog of their materials for the deaf. Site of the National Information Center on Deafness, which provides specific answers to questions through fact sheets and bibliographies.

Handicapped Learner Materials-Special Materials Project (HLM-SMP)
624 East Walnut Street, 2nd Floor
Indianapolis, IN 46204
317-636-1902
A small fee covers usage of captioned films and other materials for children or teachers.

Hubbard Scientific
1952-T Raymond Drive
Northbrook, IL 60062
708-272-7810
FAX 708-272-9894

Information Center on Children's Culture
U.S. Committee for UNICEF
331 East 38th Street
New York, NY 10016
212-686-5522
Provides names and addresses of domestic and foreign book dealers, as well as publications about different countries.

International Communications Industries Association
3150 Spring Street
Fairfax, VA 22031-2399
703-273-7200
Provides information about the copyright law. As the trade association for the communications-technologies industries, has publications, products, and services relating to use of this technology.

International Reading Association

800 Barksdale Road
P.O. Box 8139
Newark, DE 19714-8139
302-731-1600 or 800-336-READ, ext. 266
FAX 302-731-1057

Publishes *Reading Teacher* (ISSN 0034-0561, nine issues per year) on reading instruction at the elementary school level and *Journal of Reading* (ISSN 0022-4103, eight issues per year) on teaching reading at the high school through adult level. Both journals include reviews and articles of interest. Also publishes books, bibliographies, and audio recordings.

International Technology Education Association

1914 Association Drive
Reston, VA 22091-1502
703-869-2100
FAX 703-860-0353

Publishes *The Technology Teacher* (ISSN 0746-3537, eight issues per year), which has a review column for professional materials. Produces videos and publishes other professional materials.

Metropolitan Museum of Art

Fifth Avenue and 82nd Street
New York, NY 10028
212-535-7710

Middle States Association of Colleges and Schools

3624 Market Street
Philadelphia, PA 19104
215-662-5600
FAX 215-622-5950

Music Educators National Conference

1902 Association Drive
Reston, VA 22091
703-860-4000

Publications include *Music Educators Journal* (ISSN 0027-4321, nine issues per year); includes reviews.

National Association of Elementary Principals

1615 Duke Street
Alexandria, VA 22314-3483
703-684-3345

Publishes *Principal* (ISSN 0271-6062, five issues per year), books, pamphlets, and films.

National Association of Independent Schools

75 Federal Street
Boston, MA 02110
617-451-2444
FAX 617-482-3913

Publishes *Independent School* (ISSN 0145-9635, quarterly), books, reports, and curricular materials.

National Association of Partners in Education (NAPE)
209 Madison Street, Suite 401
Alexandria, VA 22314
703-836-4880
Formed by the merging of the National School Volunteers Program (NSVP) and the National Symposium in Partnership in Education. Publishes *The Partners in Education* (nine issues per year).

National Association of Secondary School Principals
1904 Association Drive
Reston, VA 22091-1537
703-860-0200 or 800-253-7746
Publications include *NASSP Bulletin* (ISSN 0192-6365, nine issues per year), *Curriculum Report* (ISSN 0547-4205, bimonthly), and *The Practitioner* (ISSN 0192-6160, quarterly) (sometimes listed as *The NASSP Practitioner*).

National Association of the Deaf
814 Thayer Avenue
Silver Spring, MD 20910-4500
Bookstore: 301-587-6282 TDD/V
FAX 301-587-1791
Publications include children's books and materials for parents and teachers; some are in sign language and some are about sign language.

National Audiovisual Center
Office of Public Programs
National Archives and Records Administration
8700 Edgeworth Drive
Capitol Heights, MD 20743-3701
301-763-1896

National Catholic Educational Association
1077 30th Street, NW, Suite 100
Washington, DC 20007-3852
202-337-6232
FAX 202-333-6706
Publications include journals, books, pamphlets, and audiocassettes. The Association offers workshops, seminars, and consulting services.

National Center for Audio Tapes (NCAT)
c/o Academic Media Services, Campus Box 379
University of Colorado
Boulder, CO 80309
303-492-7341
Associated cooperatively with Association for Educational Communications and Technology (AECT); reproduces audiotapes on direct order from educational institutions.

National Center for Educational Statistics
555 New Jersey Avenue, NW
Washington, DC 20208
202-219-1839 or 800-424-1616

National Center for Health Education

72 Spring Street, Suite 208
New York, NY 10012
212-334-9470
FAX 212-334-9845

Provides information to schools interested in developing or redesigning health curriculum. Will direct individuals to programs and contacts within the Center's School Health Education Project (SHEP).

National Clearinghouse for Bilingual Education

1555 Wilson Boulevard
Arlington, VA 22209
703-522-0710
Hotline: 800-336-4560

Offers information about organizations involved in bilingual education, publishes information analysis products, offers a computerized information database with limited online search services, and provides field representatives.

National Coalition Against Censorship (NCAC)

275 7th Avenue, 20th floor
New York, NY 10001
212-807-6222
FAX 212-807-6245

Publishes *Censorship News* (ISSN 0749-6001, quarterly). Provides technical help to individuals and groups on how to fight censorship. NCAC's Clearinghouse on Book-Banning Litigation helps lawyers and educators keep current on library and school issues.

National Conference of Christians and Jews

71 Fifth Avenue, Suite 1100
New York, NY 10003-3095
212-206-0006
FAX 212-225-6177

National Council for Geographic Education

16A Leonard Hall
Indiana University of Pennsylvania
Indiana, PA 15705
412-357-6290
FAX 412-357-7708

Publishes *Journal of Geography* (ISSN 0022-134, seven issues per year); reviews textbooks and other books of interest to teachers.

National Council for the Social Studies (NCSS)

3501 Newark Street, NW
Washington, DC 20016
Order department: 800-683-0812
FAX 212-563-5703

Publishes *Social Education* (ISSN 0037-7724, seven issues per year); includes reviews of books and professional materials as well as articles dealing with selection and use of materials.

National Council of Teachers of English (NCTE)
1111 Kenyon Road
Urbana, IL 61801
217-328-3870
Order department: 800-369-NCTE
FAX 217-328-9645

Publications include *Language Arts* (elementary) (ISSN 0360-9170) and *English Journal* (middle school and junior and senior high school) (ISSN 0013-8274), each is eight issues per year; plus a wide range of materials: professional topics, literary maps, cassettes, and booklists. NCTE has a Committee on Censorship and offers resources, aid, and support.

Within the NCTE structure, two assemblies publish items of interest. The *ALAN Review* (ISSN 0882-2840, three issues per year); by the Assembly on Literature for Adolescents; reviews hardbacks and paperbacks. *The Bulletin of the Children's Literature Assembly* provides in-depth discussion on specific topics in this subject area.

National Council of Teachers of Mathematics
1906 Association Drive
Reston, VA 22091-1593
703-620-9840, ext. 135
Order department: 800-235-7566
FAX 703-476-2970

Publishes *Arithmetic Teacher* (elementary) (ISSN 0004-136X) and *Mathematics Teacher* (junior high school through teacher education) (ISSN 0025-5769), each is nine issues per year; both include reviews and articles of interest.

National Education Association
For orders: Professional Library
P.O. Box 509
West Haven, CT 06516
800-229-4200

Publishes *Today's Education: General Edition* (ISSN 0272-3573, monthly during the school year), plus books, pamphlets, curricular resource materials, and audiovisual materials.

National Gallery of Art
6th Street & Constitution Avenue, NW
Washington, DC 20565
202-737-4215

National Information Center for Special Education Materials (NICSEM)
University of Southern California
University Park
Los Angles, CA 90007
800-421-8711

National Library Service for the Blind and Physically Handicapped
Library of Congress
1291 Taylor Street, NW
Washington, DC 20540
202-287-5100

Publications include *Talking Books Topics* (large-print edition, ISSN 0039-9183) and *Braille Book Review* (large-print edition, ISSN 0006-873X), bimonthly magazines that announce books and magazines available in these formats. The agency also provides information about equipment, bibliographies, and information about blindness and physical handicaps.

National PTA, National Council of Parents and Teachers
700 N. Rush Street
Chicago, IL 60611
312-787-0977
FAX 312-787-8342
Publications include *PTA Today* (ISSN 0195-2781, seven issues per year) and pamphlets.

National Public Radio Educational Cassette Programs
National Public Radio
2025 M Street, NW
Washington, DC 20036
202-414-2000

National School Boards Association
1680 Duke Street
Alexandria, VA 22314
703-838-6722
FAX 703-683-7590

National Science Teachers Association
1742 Connecticut Avenue, NW
Washington, DC 20009-1171
Customer service: 202-328-5800
Telephone orders: 800-722-NSTA
FAX 202-328-5840
Publishes *Science and Children* (elementary) (ISSN 04240-8767, eight times a year) and *Science Teacher* (ISSN 0036-8555, nine issues per year); both include reviews of materials for teachers and students.

National Study of School Evaluation
5201 Leesburg Pike
Falls Church, VA 22041
703-820-2727
FAX 703-820-0749
Publishes evaluation instruments.

New England Association of Colleges and Schools
The Snagborn House
15 High Street
Winchester, MA 01890
617-729-6762
FAX 617-729-0924

Northwest Association of Schools and Colleges
Boise State University
Education Building #528
1910 University Drive
Boise, ID 83725
208-385-1596

People for the American Way
2000 M Street, NW, Suite 400
Washington, DC 20036
202-467-4994
FAX 202-293-2672

Public Broadcasting Service
1320 Braddock Place
Alexandria, VA 22314
703-739-5000

Recording for the Blind, Inc.
20 Roszel Road
Princeton, NJ 08540
609-452-0606 or 800-221-4792 or 800-221-4793
FAX 609-987-8116

Southern Association of Colleges and Schools
Commission on Elementary Schools
Commission on Secondary Schools
1866 Southern Lane
Decatur, GA 30033-4097
404-679-4500
Publishes *Guide to Evaluation and Accreditation of Schools*.

Speech Communication Association
5105 Backlick Road, Bldg. E
Annandale, VA 22003
703-750-0533
FAX 703-914-9471
Publishes *Communication Education* (ISSN 0363-4523, quarterly); includes
reviews of books and nonbook materials useful to teachers of speech. The Association publishes books, pamphlets, and audiocassettes.

United States Board on Books for Young People (USBBY)
c/o International Reading Association
800 Barksdale Road
P.O. Box 8139
Newark, DE 19714-8139
302-731-1600
Encourages interest in international children's literature through the *United
States Board on Books for Young People Newsletter* and meetings.

U.S. Copyright Office
Public Information Office
Library of Congress
202-707-3000
Information specialists are available from 8:30 a.m. to 5:00 p.m. eastern time,
Monday through Friday. Recorded information is available 24 hours a day. The
hotline number for copyright forms is 202-707-9100.

Ward's Natural Science Establishment, Inc.
5100-T N. Henrietta Road
P.O. Box 92912
Rochester, NY 14692-9012
716-359-2502
FAX 716-334-6174

Western Association of Schools and Colleges, Inc.
3060 Valencia Avenue
Aptos, CA 95003
408-688-7701
FAX 408-688-1841

Young Adult Library Services Association (YALSA)
50 E. Huron Street
Chicago, IL 60611
312-280-4391 or 800-545-2433, ext. 4391
FAX 312-664-7450
Publishes *Journal of Youth Services in Libraries* (ISSN 0040-9286) with the **Association for Library Service to Children**. The division's publications and bibliographies can be ordered directly from YALSA.

Appendix B
Bibliographic and Selection Tools

The chapter number at the end of the entry indicate the chapter(s) of this book in which the title is specifically mentioned or the chapter(s) that discusses activities for which the reference would be helpful. Use the index to find page numbers. Addresses are provided for journals; see appendix A for associations' addresses.

A to Zoo: Subject Access to Children's Picture Books. 4th ed. Carolyn W. Lima and
    John A. Lima. New York: R. R. Bowker, 1993. ISBN 0-8352-3201-8. Chap. 11.
    Identifies more than 15,000 titles (fiction and nonfiction) for preschoolers
through second-graders. Author, title, and illustrator indexes provide access.

Adaptive Technologies for Learning & Work Environments. Joseph J. Lazzaro.
    Chicago: American Library Association, 1993. ISBN 0-8389-0615-X. Chap. 12.

*Adoptable Copyright Policy: Copyright Policy and Manuals Designed for Adoption
    by Schools, Colleges, & Universities.* Charles W. Vlcek. Washington, DC:
    Copyright Information Services, 1992. ISBN 0-8924-0064-1. Chap. 6.
    Provides copyright policy; adoptable faculty copyright manual consisting of
an overview, application of the law to specific media, copyright management,
copyright quick guide, and instructions on how to obtain permission; adoptable
student copyright manual; and addresses that may be needed in seeking copyright
permission. Available from the Association for Educational Communications and
Technology, 1025 Vermont Avenue NW, Suite 820, Washington, DC 20005.

Adventuring with Books: A Booklist for Pre-K-Grade 6. 9th ed. Ed. by Mary
    Jett-Simpson and the Committee on the Elementary School Booklist of the
    National Council of Teachers of English. Urbana, IL: National Council of
    Teachers of English, 1989. ISBN 0-8141-0078-3. Chap. 12.
    Recommends titles of interest to ages pre-K through grade 6. Provides bibliographic
information, age, and grade level. Indexed by author, title, subject, and illustrator.

Against Borders: Promoting Books for a Multicultural World. Hazel Rochman.
    Chicago: American Library Association, 1993. ISBN 0-8389-0601-X. Chap. 11.
    Suggests curriculum units and activities for adults to use with students in
grades 6-12 on themes such as outsiders, friends, and family.

ALAN Review. Athens, GA: Assembly on Literature for Adolescents, National
    Council of Teachers of English, 1979- . ISSN 0882-2840. Chap. 7, 9.
    Published three times per year. Available on microfiche. Reviews new hard-
back and paperback titles for adolescents. To order: ALAN/NCTE, 1111 Kenyon
Rd., Urbana, IL 61801.

America as Story: Historical Fiction for Secondary Schools. Elizabeth F. Howard.
    Chicago: American Library Association, 1988. ISBN 0-8389-0492-0. Chap. 11.
    Recommends over 150 novels to stimulate students' interest in history.

American Book Publishing Record. New Providence, NJ: R. R. Bowker, 1960- . ISSN 0002-7707. Chap. 9, 13.

Published monthly. Related work: *American Book Publishing Record Cumulative* (published annually). *ABPR* is a monthly compilation of titles cataloged by the Library of Congress. Arranged by Dewey classification with special sections for fiction, juvenile fiction, and mass-market paperbacks. Entries provide full cataloging data, LC and DDC numbers, subject headings, and price. Indexed by author.

American History for Children and Young Adults: An Annotated Bibliographic Index. Vandelia VanMeter. Englewood, CO: Libraries Unlimited, 1990. ISBN 0-87287-773-1. Chap. 11.

Also available in disc formats: Apple, ISBN 0-87287-768-X; Mac, ISBN 0-87287-769-8; IBM, ISBN 0-87287-770-1. Arranged by time period. Provides 2,000 citations for nonfiction and fiction books (for K-12) with complete bibliographic information, physical description, review citations (1980-1988), and a brief annotation.

American Indian Reference Books for Children and Young Adults. Barbara J. Kuipers. Englewood, CO: Libraries Unlimited, 1991. ISBN 0-87287-745-0. Chap. 11.

Recommends more than 200 titles for grades 3-12. Discusses strengths and weaknesses of each title and describes its use in the curriculum. Includes criteria for selection and provides a checklist for evaluating materials. Second edition to be published in 1995. ISBN 1-56308-258-6.

American Music Teacher. Baldwin, NY: Music Teachers' Association, 1951- . ISSN 0003-0112. Chap. 11.

Published bimonthly. Feature articles. To order: Music Teachers National Association, Inc., 617 Vine St, Suite 1432, Cincinnati, OH 45202-2434.

American Reference Books Annual. Englewood, CO: Libraries Unlimited, 1970- . ISSN 0065-9959. Chap. 11.

Apple Library Users Group Newsletter. Cupertino, CA: Apple Computer, Inc. ISSN 0887-2716. Chap. 9.

Published four times per year. Available free of charge to those interested in using Apple computers in libraries or information centers. Subscription address: Monica Ertel, Apple Computer, Inc., 10381 Bandley Drive, Cupertino, CA 95014.

Appraisal: Science Books for Young People. Boston: Children's Science Books Review Committee, 1967- . ISSN 0003-7052. Chap. 7, 9, 11.

Published quarterly. Includes reviews of trade books and series by librarians and science specialists for 50-70 titles per issue. Entries provide bibliographic and ordering information, grade level, and rating code. Index in each issue; cumulated annually. Subscription address: Appraisal, 605 Commonwealth Avenue, Boston, MA 02215.

Arithmetic Teacher. Reston, VA: National Council of Teachers of Mathematics, 1954- . ISSN 0004-136X. Chap. 11.

Published monthly (September-May). Available in microform. The column "Reviewing and Viewing" covers teaching materials, including games, videotapes, workbooks, software, and books for teachers. Subscription address: NCTM, 1906 Association Drive, Reston, VA 22091.

Audio Store Catalog. Madison, WI: Wisconsin Public Radio. Chap. 9.

Published quarterly. Lists cassettes, student guides, and faculty guides for radio programs offered by Wisconsin Public Radio. For a free copy of the catalog: The Audio Store, 821 University Ave., Madison, WI 53706; 1-800-972-8346.

Audiocassette & Compact Disc Finder. 3d. ed. Medford, NJ: Plexus Publishing Co., 1993. ISBN 0-8375-548-22-7. Chap. 13.

NICEM (National Information Center for Educational Media) indexes. Subject guide to educational and literary materials on audiocassettes and compact discs. Covers 40,000 items. Entries, arranged alphabetically by title, include content description, audience level, format, running time, date of release, and the purchase or rental source. Also available through Learned Information, Inc., 143 Old Marion Pike, Medford, NJ 08055-8750.

AV Guide. Des Plaines, IL: Scranton Gillette Communications, 1922- . ISSN 0091-360X. Chap. 7.

Published monthly. Available on microfilm. Reviews software programs, videos, and equipment.

AV Market Place: The Complete Business Directory of Audio, Audio Visual, Computer Systems, Film, Video, Programming with Industry Yellow Pages. New York: R. R. Bowker, 1980- . ISBN 0-8352-3155-0. Chap. 14.

Published annually. Continues *Audio Video Market Place: AVMP.* Lists the addresses and services of producers, distributors, production services, manufacturers, and equipment dealers.

The Best: High/Low Books for Reluctant Readers. Marianne Laino Pilla. Englewood, CO: Libraries Unlimited, 1990. ISBN 0-87287-532-6. Chap. 12.

Disk versions: Apple (Appleworks), ISBN 0-87287-532-6; Mac (Microsoft Works), ISBN 0-87287-780-9; and IBM (ASCII comma delimited files), ISBN 0-87287-775-2. Describes 374 titles for recreational reading for grades 3-12. Entries provide bibliographic information, subject headings, reading/interest levels, and availability in library binding and paperback editions. Indexed by reading level and subject.

Best Books for Children: Preschool Through Grade 6. 4th ed. John T. Gillespie and Corinne J. Naden. New York: R. R. Bowker, 1990. ISBN 0-8352-2668-9. Chap. 12.

Includes brief annotations for 11,299 titles, which had two or three recommendations from leading journals. Entries provide bibliographic and order information and citations to reviews. Indexes for author, title, illustrator, and subject.

Best Books for Junior High Readers. John T. Gillespie. New York: R. R. Bowker, 1991. ISBN 0-8352-3020-1. Chap. 12.

Organized by subject, identifies 5,600 books recommended by *School Library Journal, Booklist, Voice of Youth Advocates,* and other journals for grades 7-9.

Best Books for Senior High Readers. John T. Gillespie. New York: R. R. Bowker, 1991. ISBN 0-8352-3021-X. Chap. 12.

Describes over 10,000 titles recommended in journals such as *School Library Journal, Booklist, Voice of Youth Advocates,* and *The Book Report.* Arranged by subject with indexes for subject/grade level, author, and title.

The Best of Bookfinder: A Guide to Children's Literature About Interests and Concerns of Youth Ages 2-18. Sharon Spredemann Dreyer. Circle Pines, MN: American Guidance Service, 1992. Chap. 10, 12.

Includes 676 selected titles from volumes 1-3 (1977, 1981, 1985). Entries include bibliographic information, description, recommended age of audience, and availability in other formats. Extensive subject index identifies primary and secondary themes for the title.

Best Science and Technology Reference Books for Young People. H. Robert Malinowsky.
Phoenix, AZ: Oryx Press, 1991. ISBN 0-89774-580-9. Chap. 11.
Recommends titles for third grade through high school. Entries include
bibliographic information, grade level, and source of reviews. Indexes for title,
name, subject, and grade level.

Best Videos for Children and Young Adults: A Core Collection for Libraries.
Jennifer Jung Gallant. Santa Barbara, CA: ABC-Clio, 1990. ISBN 0-87436-
561-9. Chap. 9.
Arranged by title; annotated list of approximately 350 of the most notable
VHS video titles includes director; producer; distributor; release date; running
time; description; price; suggested audience level; recommendation for classroom,
discussion, or recreational use; annotation covering plot/story line, themes, possible
uses, technical qualities, and strengths and weaknesses. Provides list of video
distributors. Indexed by audience/usage and subject/title.

The Best Years of Their Lives: A Resource Guide for Teenagers in Crisis. Stephanie
Zvirin. Chicago: American Library Association, 1992. ISBN 0-8389-0586-2.
Chap. 12.
Reviews 200 nonfiction, fiction, and video titles on timely topics of interest to
students 12-18 years old. Entries include bibliographic information, age level, and
critical annotations. Includes interviews with authors, author-title index, and
subject index.

Beyond Picture Books: A Guide to First Readers. Barbara Barstow and Judith
Riggle. New York: R. R. Bowker, 1989. ISBN 0-8352-2515-1. Chap. 12.
Provides brief plot synopsis, critical evaluations, publishers series, and bib-
liographic information for 1,600 titles.

Book Links: Connecting Books, Libraries, and Classrooms. Chicago: American
Library Association, 1991- . Chap. 12.
Published six times per year. Reviews old and new books. Includes these
columns: "Book Strategies" (book about a theme or topic), "Classroom Connec-
tions" (book with similar theme), "Visual Links" (illustrations in picture books),
"The Inside Story" (one work), and "Poetry." Subscription address: ALA, 50 E.
Huron Street, Chicago, IL 60611.

The Book Report: The Journal for Junior and Senior High School Libraries.
Worthington, OH: Linworth, 1982- . ISSN 0524-0581. Chap. 7.
Published bimonthly during the school year. Reviews books, films, filmstrips,
videocassettes, and software for junior and senior high school use. Subscription
address: Linworth Publishing, 5701 North High Street, Suite 1, Worthington, OH
43214.

Book Review Digest. New York: H. W. Wilson, 1905- . ISSN 0006-7326. Chap. 7, 9.
Published monthly, with quarterly and annual cummulations. Also available
on CD-ROM (WilsonDisc) and online through BRS Online Products and Wilsonline
(File BRD).

Book Review Index. Detroit, MI: Gale Research, 1965- . ISSN 0524-0581. Chap. 7, 9.
Available as an annual cumulation or on a subscription basis of six bimonthly
issues. Indexes over 500 publications for reviews of books, periodicals, and books
on tape. Also available online as DIALOG File No. 137.

Bookbird. Aabenráa, Denmark: Forlaget ARNIS, 1963- . ISSN 0006-7377. Chap. 9, 11.
  Published quarterly. Available on microfilm. Issued by International Institute for Children's Literature and Reading Research and International Board on Books for Young People. Features articles about books of international interest and reviews selection tools. Subscription address: Publishing Finn ARNIS, Jakob Gormsen, powtbopks 130, Toenderveg 197, DK-6200, Aabenráa, Denmark.

Booklist: Includes Reference Books Bulletin. Chicago: American Library Association:
  1905- . ISSN 0006-7385. Chap. 7, 9, 11.
  Published semimonthly. Available in microform. Reviews current books, videos, and software. Special columns review foreign language materials and materials on special topics. Provides monthly author/title index and semiannual cumulative indexes. Subscription address: ALA, 50 E. Huron Street, Chicago, IL 60611.

*Books, Babies, and Libraries: Serving Infants, Toddlers, Their Parents and
  Caregivers.* Ellin Greene. Chicago: American Library Association, 1991. ISBN 0-8389-0572-2. Chap. 11.
  Discusses library's role in early learning, offering theoretical concepts of child development and learning. Recommends books, records, and toys.

Books for the Teen Age. New York: New York Public Library, Committee on Books
  for Young Adults: 1929- . ISSN 0068-0192. Chap. 12.
  Published annually. Approximately 1,250 titles chosen on the basis of their appeal to teenagers. Indexed by title. Order from: Office of Branch Libraries, New York Public Library, 455 Fifth Avenue, New York, NY 10016.

Books for You: A Booklist for Senior High School Students. 11th ed. Shirley Wurth,
  ed. Urbana, IL: National Council of Teachers of English, 1992. ISBN 0-8141-0365-0. Chap. 12.
  Recommends 850 fiction and nonfiction titles of interest to young people and for curricular areas. Provides full bibliographic information. Access by author, subject, and title indexes.

Books in Canada. Toronto: Canadian Review of Books Ltd., 1971- . ISSN 0045-
  2564. Chap. 7.
  Published nine times per year. Available in microform. Reviews Canadian hard cover and paperback books for grades K-12. Subscription address: Canadian Review of Books Ltd., 130 Spadina Ave., Suite 603, Toronto, Ontario M5V 2L4 Canada.

Books in Print. New York: R. R. Bowker, 1948- . ISSN 0068-0214. Chap. 9, 13.
  Published annually. Related works includes *Subject Guide to Books in Print*, ISBN 0-8352-3251-4; *Books in Print Supplement*, ISSN 0000-0310; *Forthcoming Books*, ISSN 0015-8119; *Books in Print with Book Reviews Plus*, CD-ROM; *Books in Print Plus*, CD-ROM; *Publishers Trade List Annual*, ISBN 0-8352-3241-7. *Paperbound Books in Print*; *Books in Print Supplement*; *Subject Guide to Books in Print*; and *Forthcoming Books* are available in print, CD-ROM, fiche, online, and data tapes formats. Related entry: See *Children's Books in Print*.

Books in Spanish for Children and Young Adults: An Annotated Guide, Series VI
  (*Libros Infantiles y Juveniles en Español: Una Guida Anotada, Serie No. VI*).
  Isabel Schon. Metuchen, NJ: Scarecrow Press, 1992. ISBN 0-8108-2662-4. Chap. 11.
  A basic guide to Spanish literature for children and young adults.

Books Kids Will Sit Still For: The Complete Read-Aloud Guide. 2d ed. Judy Freeman. New York: R. R. Bowker, 1990. ISBN 0-8352-3010-4. Chap. 12.
  Describes techniques for reading aloud, booktalks, creative dramatics, and storytelling. Recommends 2,184 titles with notes regarding potential audience and number of chapters. Provides author, title, illustrator, and subject indexes.

Books to Help Children Cope with Separation and Loss: An Annotated Bibliography. Marsha K. Rudman, Kathleen Dunne Gagne, and Joanne E. Berstein. New York: R. R. Bowker, 1993. ISBN 0-8352-3412-6. Chap. 12.
  Reviews 750 fiction and nonfiction titles for ages 3-16. Grouped by topic; each annotated entry covers plot, theme, interest/reading level, suggestions for use, and bibliographic information.

Booktalk 5! More Booktalks for All Ages and Audiences. Joni Bodart-Talbot, ed. New York: H. W. Wilson, 1993. ISBN 0-8242-0836-6. Chap. 12.
  Provides techniques and field-tested talks, ranging from 2 to 7 minutes, for stimulating interest in reading.

The Bowker Annual Library and Book Trade Alamanac. New York: R. R. Bowker, 1955- . ISSN 0068-0540. Chap. 14.
  Available in print and CD-ROM (*Library Reference Plus*).

Bowker's Complete Video Directory. New York: R. R. Bowker, 1994. ISBN 0-8352-3391-X. Chap. 9.
  Published annually. Identifies videos (Entertainment, Volume I; Education, Volume II) available in online and tape formats.

Braille Book Review. Washington, DC: National Library Service for the Blind and Physically Handicapped, 1933- . Chap. 12.
  Published bimonthly. Describes books for children and adults. Provides title, order code, author, number of volumes, and date of original print edition. Indexed monthly and annually. Address: National Library Service for the Blind and Physically Handicapped, 1291 NW Taylor St., Washington, DC 20542.

Building the Reference Collection: A How-To-Do-It Manual for School and Public Librarians. Gay D. Patrick. New York: Neal-Schuman, 1992. ISBN 1-55570-105-1. Chap. 11.

Bulletin of the Center for Children's Books. Champaign, IL: University of Illinois Press, 1945- . ISSN 0008-9036. Chap. 7, 9.
  Published monthly (except August). Reviews include description of content, characters, theme, development level, curricular use, grade or age. Codes of recommendations given, including special distinction and not recommended. Author-title index in each volume. Subscription address: University of Illinois Press, BCCB, 54 E. Gregory Dr., Champaign, IL 61820.

Canadian Books in Print: Author and Title Index. Toronto: University of Toronto Press, 1975- . ISSN 0702-0201. Chap. 13.
  Published annually. Supplemented quarterly by *Canadian Books in Print: Update on Fiche,* 1979- . Includes English- and French-language titles published by predominantly English-language Canadian publishers.

Canadian Books in Print: Subject Index. Toronto: University of Toronto Press, 1975- . ISSN 0315-1999. Chap. 13.

Published annually. Text in English or French. Covers French-language titles published by predominantly English-language Canadian publishers.

Canadian Children's Literature. Guelph, Ontario: Canadian Children's Press, 1975- . ISSN 0319-0080. Chap. 7.
Published quarterly. Bilingual journal with articles and reviews of books for grades K-12. Subscription address: Canadian Children's Literature Association, University of Guelph, Department of English, Guelph, Ontario N1G 2W1 Canada.

Captioned Films/Videos. Distributed by Modern Talking Picture Service Inc., 5000 Park Street North, St. Petersberg, FL 33709-9989. Chap. 12.
Published annually with fall supplement. Lists free-loan educational, general-interest films, videos, and other teaching materials. Users pay postage for the films. Videos have prepaid return postage labels. Write for *Catalog of Free-Loan Videos/16mm Films and Teaching Materials* or call 800-237-6213 (Voice/TDD).

The Catholic Library World. Haverford, PA: Catholic Library Association, 1929- . ISSN 0008-820-X. Chap. 7.
Reviews audiovisual materials (videocassettes, software, filmstrips, audio-cassettes, 16-mm film), reference books, children's books, professional books. Subscription address: *Catholic Library World*, 461 West Lancaster Avenue, Haverford, PA 19041.

CD-ROM Collection Builder's Toolkit: The Complete Handbook of Tools for Evaluating CD-ROMs. Paul T. Nichols. Weston, CT: Pemberton Press, 1990. ISBN 910965-01-3. Chap. 9.
Evaluates CD-ROM products and offers guidelines for evaluation and selection. Entries provide publisher, hardware requirements, software, frequency of update, price, order information, evaluative description, rating, and citations to other reviews. Address: Pemberton Press, 11 Tannery Lane, Weston, CT 06883.

CD-ROM Software, Dataware, and Hardware: Evaluation, Selection, and Installation. Péter Jacsó. Database Searching series. Ed. by Carol Tenopir. Englewood, CO: Libraries Unlimited, 1991. ISBN 0-87287-907-0. Chap. 9.
Identifies criteria for CD-ROM databases, their search software, and CD-ROM drives. Provides guidelines for decision making. Includes comparative charts, tables, templates, and screen samples.

Changing Times. Washington, DC: Kiplinger Washington Agency, 1941- . ISSN 0009-143X. Chap. 9.
Published monthly. Available in microform. Reviews some software and equipment. Subscription address: *Changing Times*, Editor's Park, MD 20782.

A Child Goes Forth: A Curriculum Guide for Preschool Children. 7th ed. Barbara J. Taylor. New York: Macmillan, 1991. ISBN 0-0241-9711-4. Chap. 10, 11.
Eighth edition set to be released in 1995. Taylor, Barbara J. *A Child Goes Forth: A Curriculum Guide for Preschool Children.* 8th ed. New York: Merrill, 1995. ISBN 0-0241-9282-1. Describes criteria for selecting materials for young children.

Children and Books. 8th ed. Zena Sutherland and May Hill Arbuthnot (chapters contributed by Dianne L. Monson). New York: HarperCollins, 1991. ISBN 0-6734-6357-5. Chap. 12.
A standard work on children's literature, including sources of information for teachers and media specialists.

Children's Book Review Index. Detroit, MI: Gale Research, 1976- . ISSN 0147-5681. Chap. 9.

Published annually. Master cumulation 1965-1984 in volume 5; master cumulation 1969-1981 in volume 4.

Children's Books in Print. New York: R. R. Bowker, 1969- . ISSN 0000-0965. Chap. 9.

Published annually. Related works: *Subject Guide to Children's Books in Print*, ISSN 0000-0167; *Forthcoming Children's Books*, ISSN 0000-965. Provides bibliographic and ordering information. *Subject Guide to Children's Books in Print* provides access under Sears subject headings, supplemented by LC headings. Excludes textbooks. Available online or on data tapes.

Children's Books of the Year. New York: Child Study, Children's Book Committee, Bank Street College. Chap. 12.

Recommends books for children up to age 14. Notes outstanding titles. Indexed by author/illustrator. Address: Bank Street College, 610 W. 112th St., New York, NY 10025.

Children's Catalog. 16th ed. Juliette Yaakov, ed., with the assistance of Anne Price. Standard Catalog series. New York: H. W. Wilson, 1991. ISBN 0-8242-0805-6. Chap. 7, 9, 16.

Includes four supplements. Preschool through grade 6. Arranged by *Abridged Dewey Decimal Classification*, with separate sections for fiction, story collections, and easy books. Entries provide bibliographic and order information, recommended grade level, subject headings, and descriptive/critical annotations. Index lists authors, subjects, titles, and analytical references to composite works.

Children's Literature for Health Awareness. Anthony L. Manna and Cynthia Wolford Symons. Metuchen, NJ: Scarecrow, 1992. ISBN 0-8108-2582-1. Chap. 11.

Discusses the selection of books and describes how different genre (folklore, fantasy, realistic fiction, historical fiction, poetry, informational, biography, and plays) address health issues.

Children's Literature in the Elementary School. 5th ed. Charlotte S. Huck, Susan Hepler, and Janel Hickman. Fort Worth: Harcourt Brace Jovanovich College Publishers, 1993. ISBN 0-0304-7528-7. Chap. 9, 12.

For teachers and media specialists when selecting and using literature with children.

Children's Reference Plus. R. R. Bowker. CD-ROM. Chap. 9, 14.

Includes *Children's Books in Print* series, children's serials from *Ulrich's International Periodical Directory*, children's audiocassettes from *Words on Cassette*, children's videos from *Bowker's Complete Video Directory*, titles from *El-Hi-Textbooks and Serials in Print*, full-text from juvenile and YA reviewing journals, and complete bibliographic contents of numerous Bowker publications. Updated annuals.

Choice. Middletown, CT: Association of College and Research Libraries, 1963- . ISSN 0009-4978. Chap. 7.

Published monthly (except bimonthly July/August). Available on microfilm. Related work: *Choice Reviews on Cards*. Reviews periodicals, books, nonprint media (film, audio, video, slide, microform, software, and filmstrip). Annual cumulated index published separately. Subscription address: *Choice*, 100 Riverview Center, Middletown, CT 06457.

Choosing Books for Children: A Commonsense Guide. Betsy Hearne. New York: Delacorte Press, 1990. Chap. 12.
Written to help parents and other adults select and use literature with children.

CM: A Reviewing Journal of Canadian Materials for Young People. Ottawa, Ontario: Canadian Library Association, 1971- . ISSN 0821-1450. Chap. 7.
Six issues per year. Reviews books and videos for young people and professional titles. Index in each issue with annual cumulations. Address: CLA, 200 Elgin St., Suite 602, Ottawa, Ontario, K1P 1L5 Canada.

Comics to Classics: A Parent's Guide to Books for Teens and Preteens. Arthea J. S. Reed. Newark, DE: International Reading Association, 1988. Chap. 12.
Describes the reading habits and interests of children and teenagers aged 10-18; recommends specific titles; offers suggestions for sharing and ideas for locating books.

The Complete Directory of Large Print Books and Serials. New Providence, NJ: R. R. Bowker, 1992. ISBN 0-8352-3176-3. Chap. 12.
Includes children's books. Access by subject, author, and title. Also available in large print.

The Computing Teacher: Journal of the International Society for Technology in Education. Eugene, OR: International Council for Computers in Education, 1979- . ISSN 0278-9175. Chap. 9.
Eight issues per year (August through May, including combined issues August/September and December/January). Reviews software and includes a column on free and inexpensive resources for computers. Subscription address: International Council for Computers in Education, 1787 Agate, University of Oregon, Eugene, OR 97403-1923.

The Consumer Information Catalog. Washington, DC: Consumer Information Center, General Services Administration, 1977- . Chap. 9.
Published quarterly. Free. Subscription address: Consumer Information Center-R, P.O. Box 100, Pueblo, CO 81002.

Consumer Reports. Mt. Vernon, NY: Consumers Union, 1942- . ISSN 0010-7174. Chap. 8.
Published monthly (December issue is annual buying guide issue). Available in microform. Available online. Subscription address: *Consumer Reports*, P.O. Box 2480, Boulder, CO 80322.

A Critical Handbook of Children's Literature. 5th ed. Rebecca J. Lukens. New York: HarperCollins, 1994. ISBN 0-6734-6937-9. Chap. 12.
Discusses the literary elements of children's literature.

Current Index to Journal in Education: CIJE. Phoenix, AZ: Oryx Press, 1969- . ISSN 0011-3565. Chap. 10.
Published monthly. Also available as part of the ERIC online database. Subscription address: Allen Press, 1041 New Hampshire Street, P.O. Box 368, Lawrence, KS 66044.

Curriculum Materials Digest. Alexandria, VA: Association for Supervision and Curriculum, 1985- . Chap. 10.
Published annually. Bibliography of materials created by school districts and other educational units.

Curriculum Review. Chicago: Curriculum Advisory Service, 1960- . ISSN 0147-2453. Chap. 9, 10.

Published monthly except June-August. Also available in microform. Reviews textbooks, supplementary materials, professional books, microcomputer software, videocassettes, films and filmstrips. Includes close to 360 reviews annually. Address: Curriculum Advisory Service, 407 S. Dearborn St., Suite 1360, Chicago, IL 60605.

Database: The Magazine of Database Reference and Review. Wilton, CT: Online, Inc., 1978- . ISSN 0162-4105. Chap. 9.

Published bimonthly. Articles include information about database search aids and provide in-depth evaluative reviews. Subscription address: Online, Inc., 462 Danbury Rd., Wilton, CT 06897.

Dealing with Selection and Censorship: A Brief Handbook for Wisconsin Schools. Bulletin No. 92152. Carolyn Winters Folke. Madison, WI: Bureau of Instructional Media and Technology, Wisconsin Department of Public Instruction, 1991. Chap. 6.

Available from: Bureau of Instructional Media and Technology, Wisconsin Department of Public Instruction, P.O. Box 7841, Madison, WI 53707.

Developing Library Collections for California's Emerging Majority: A Manual for Ethnic Collection Development. Katherine T. A. Scarborough, ed. Berkeley, CA: Bay Area Library and Information System, University Extension and School of Library and Information Studies, University of California-Berkeley, 1990. Chap. 11.

Digest of Software Reviews: Education. Ann Lathrop, ed. Fresno, CA: School and Home Courseware, 1983- . Chap. 9.

Published monthly. Looseleaf. Reviews 300 instructional software programs for students in grades K-12. Entries provide title, author, producer and address, copyright, price, system requirements, contents, suggested grade level, instructional mode, DDC number, and Sears subject heading. Address: School and Home Courseware, 3999 N. Chestnut, Suite 333, Fresno, CA 93726-4797.

E for Environment: An Annotated Bibliography of Children's Books with Environmental Themes. Patti K. Sinclair. New York: R. R. Bowker, 1992. ISBN 0-8352-3028-7. Chap. 11.

For work with children ages 3-14.

Educational Film & Video Locator of the Consortium of College & University Film Centers and R. R. Bowker. 4th ed. New York: R. R. Bowker, 1990. ISSN 0000-135X. Chap. 13.

Updated triennially. Union list of some 52,000 films and videos available for rent from the members of the Consortium of University Film Center (CUFC). Entries provide running time, video film format, color, production date, former title, series notation, subjects, audience levels, and rental sources. Index for subject, title, and audience level.

Educational Leadership: Journal of the Association for Supervision and Curriculum Development. Washington, DC: The Association, 1943- . ISSN 0013-1784. Chap. 10.

Published monthly (September-May, except bimonthly December/January). Available in microform. Reviews professional books. Subscription address: ASCD, 1250 North Pitt Street, Alexandria, VA 22314-1453.

Educational Media and Technology Yearbook. Littleton, CO: Libraries Unlimited, 1973- . ISSN 8755-2094. Chap. 14.
Published annually. Published in cooperation with and cosponsored by the Association for Educational Communications and Technology. Covers expenditures for educational media and lists pertinent organizations.

Educational Technology. Saddle Brook, NJ: Educational News Service, 1961- . ISSN 0013-1962. Chap. 10.
Published semimonthly. Reviews software and professional literature. Subscription address: Educational Technology Publications, Inc., 140 Sylvan Avenue, Englewood Cliffs, NJ 07632.

Educators Guides (annuals). Available from Educators Progress Service, 214 Center Street, Randolph, WI 53956. Chap. 13. Titles include
Educators Grade Guide to Free Teaching Aids.
Educators Guide to Free Audio and Video Materials.
Educators Guide to Free Films.
Educators Guide to Free Filmstrips and Slides.
Educators Guide to Free Guidance Materials.
Educators Guide to Free Health, Physical Education and Recreation Materials.
Educators Guide to Free Home Economics Materials.
Educators Guide to Free Science Materials.
Educators Guide to Free Social Studies Materials.
Educators Index of Free Materials.
Elementary Teachers' Guide to Free Curriculum Materials.
Guide to Free Computer Materials.

The Elementary School Journal. Chicago: University of Chicago Press, 1900- . ISSN 0013-5984. Chap. 10.
Published bimonthly (September-May). Available in microform. Subscription address: University of Chicago Press, P.O. Box 37005, Chicago, IL 60637.

The Elementary School Library Collection: A Guide to Books and Other Media, Phases 1-2-3. 19th ed. Lauren K. Lee, ed. Williamsport, PA: Brodart, 1994. ISBN 0-8727-2096-9. Chap. 4, 7, 11, 16, 17.

El-Hi Textbooks and Serials in Print: Including Related Teaching Materials K-12. New Providence, NJ: R. R. Bowker, 1969- . ISSN 0000-0825. Chap. 9, 13.
Published annually. Identifies textbooks (K-12), periodicals, maps, and teaching aids. Arranged by subject, entries provide bibliographic and order information, and grade and reading level. Includes author, title, and series indexes.

Electronic Learning. New York: Scholastic, 1981- . ISSN 0278-3258. Chap. 9.
Eight issues per year. Reviews hardware, classroom software, and books about computers. Subscription address: Electronic Learning, P.O. Box 3024, Southeast, PA 19398.

Emergency Librarian. Vancouver, BC: Rockland Press, 1973- . ISSN 0315-8888. Chap. 7.
Published bimonthly (five per year). Available in microform. Reviews professional reading, children's recordings, magazines, and paperbacks. Subscription address: Rockland Press, Department 284, Box C34069, Seattle, WA 98124-1069.

English Journal. Urbana, IL: National Council of Teachers of English, 1912- . ISSN 0013-8274. Chap. 11.

Published monthly (September-April). Available in microform. Reviews young adult literature, films, videos, software, and professional publications. Subscription address: NCTE Subscription Service, 1111 W. Kenyon Road, Urbana, IL 61801-1086.

The Equipment Directory of Audio-Visual, Computer and Video Products. Fairfax, VA: International Communications Industries Association, 1953- . ISSN 0884-2124. Chap. 8, 13.
Published annually. Subscription address: ICIA, 3150 Spring St., Fairfax, VA 22031-2399.

Essentials of Children's Literature by Carol Lynch-Brown and Carl M. Tomlinson. Boston: Allyn & Bacon, 1993. ISBN 0-205-13937-X. Chap. 12.
A concise and comprehensive survey of children's literature, featuring genres, authors within the genre, and recommended titles. Includes a chapter on multicultural and international literature.

Exceptional Children. Reston, VA: Council for Exceptional Children, 1934- . ISSN 0014-4029. Chap. 12.
Published bimonthly. Available in microform. Subscription address: CEC, 1920 Association Drive, Reston, VA 22091.

The Exceptional Parent: Parenting Your Child with a Disability. Boston: Psy-Ed, 1971- . ISSN 0046-9157. Chap. 12.
Eight issues per year. Available in microform. Subscription address: Dept. Exceptional Parent, Box 3000, Denville, NJ 07834.

Fiction for Youth: A Guide to Recommended Books. 3d ed. Lillian L. Shapiro and Barbara L. Stein. New York: Neal-Schuman, 1992. ISBN 1-55570-113-2. Chap. 12.
Intended to encourage and motivate capable readers. Includes adult works published in the twentieth century, subjects of interest to adolescents, and juvenile titles of more than passing value. Arranged by author, entries can be accessed through the title and subject indexes.

Film & Video Finder. 3d ed. Medford, NJ: National Information Center for Educational Media, 1991. 3 vols. ISBN 0-9375-4820-0 (set). Chap. 13.
Related works: *Index to AV Producers & Distributors, Audiocassette Finder* (2d ed., 1991), and *Filmstrip & Slide Set Finder* (1991). Available from Plexus Publishing Co., 143 Old Marlton Pike, Medford, NJ 08055-8750. *Film & Video Finder'* entries for 92,000 films and videos include description of content, audience level, format, running time, date of release, purchase/rental cost, and source. Also available from DIALOG as A-V Online (File 46) and on CD-ROM (SliverPlatter).

Filmstrip & Slide Set Finder. 1st ed. Medford, NJ: National Information Center for Educational Media, 1990. ISBN 0-937548-15-4. Chap. 13.
NICEM (National Information Center for Educational Media) Indexes. Plexus Publishing Co., publisher and distributor. Also available through Learned Information, Inc., 143 Old Marion Pike, Medford, NJ 08055-8750. Indexes 35-mm educational filmstrips and slide sets by title, producer, and distributor. Provides subject heading outline and index, directory of producers and distributors, and title section listings.

For Reading Out Loud! A Guide to Sharing Books with Children. Margaret Mary Kimmel and Elizabeth Segal. New York: Dell Publications, 1991. ISBN 0-4405-0400-7. Chap. 12.

Suggests listening levels and provides the length of time needed to read the work aloud.

For Younger Readers: Braille and Talking Books. Washington, DC: National Library Service for the Blind and Physically Handicapped, The Library of Congress, 1967- . ISSN 0093-2825. Chap. 12.
Published biennially. Annotates braille, disc, and cassette books announced in *Braille Book Review* and *Talking Books Topics*. Available in braille, sound recording, and large type. Free.

Free Materials for Schools and Libraries. Vancouver, BC: Dyad Services, 1979- . ISSN 0836-0073. Chap. 7, 9, 13.
Published five times per year. Order from: Dyad Services, Box C34069, Dept. 284, Seattle, WA 98124-1069.

Free Resource Builder for Librarians and Teachers. 2d ed. Comp. by Carol Smallwood. Jefferson, NC: McFarland, 1992. ISBN 0-89950-685-2. Chap. 10.
Identifies free materials for students and teachers and provides ordering information, including telephone numbers.

From Page to Screen: Children's and Young Adult Books on Film and Video. Joyce Moss and George Wilson, eds. Detroit: Gale Research, 1992. ISBN 0-8103-7893-0. Chap. 12.
Provides book title, author, bibliographic information, genre, summary, production information, evaluative comments, review citations, awards, audience, and distributor. Identifies film, adaptation, and cinematic ratings. Appendix identifies films for the hearing-impaired. Separate indexes for awards, age level, and subject. Combined index for author and film title.

Genreflecting: A Guide to Reading Interests in Genre Fiction. 3d ed. Betty Rosenberg and Diana Tixler Herald. Englewood, CO: Libraries Unlimited, 1991. ISBN 0-87287-930-5. Chap. 12.
Covers westerns, thrillers, science fiction, fantasy, supernatural/horror fiction, and romance. Provides annotated bibliography.

Getting Your Grant. Peggy Barber and Linda Crowe. How-To-Do-It Manuals for Libraries, Number 28. New York: Neal-Schuman, 1993. ISBN 1-55570-038-1. Chap. 14.
Identifies sources of funding (government, foundation, corporate) and provides directions and samples of proposal writing.

Good Housekeeping. New York: Hearst Corporation, 1885- . ISSN 0017-209X. Chap. 9.
Published monthly. Subscription address: Good Housekeeping, 7186 Red Oak, IA 51591-0186.

Government Periodical and Subscription Services. Washington, DC: Superintendent of Documents, 1960- . Chap. 9.
Published quarterly.

Government Reference Books: A Biennial Guide to U.S. Publications. Littleton, CO: Libraries Unlimited, 1970- . ISSN 0072-5188. Chap. 9, 11.
Covers pamphlets, folders, and multivolume sets. Entries include bibliographic citations, LC card number, ISBNs and ISSNs, OCLC numbers, *Monthly Catalog* numbers, GPO stock numbers, price, annotations, and SuDocs classification numbers.

Guide to Microforms in Print: Author/Title. Munich, Germany: K.G. Saur, 1975- . ISSN 0164-0747. Chap. 9.
Published annually.

Guide to Popular U.S. Government Publications. 3d ed. William G. Bailey. Englewood, CO: Libraries Unlimited, 1993. ISBN 1-56308-031-1. Chap. 9.
Covers 2,500 publications (June 1989-January 1993). Entries provide bibliographic information, illustrative material, stock number, price, SuDocs classification number, and annotation.

Guide to Reference Books for School Media Centers. Margaret Irby Nichols. 4th ed. Englewood, CO: Libraries Unlimited, 1992. ISBN 0-87287-833-3. Chap. 11.
Covers more than 2,000 titles with age and reading levels, presentation styles, strengths and weaknesses, comparison with other titles, and citations to reviews.

Guide to Reference Materials for Canadian Libraries. 8th ed. Toronto: University of Toronto Press, 1992. ISBN 0-8020-6004-8. Chap. 11.

Guide to Selecting and Acquiring CD-ROMs, Software, and Other Electronic Publications. Stephen Bosch, Patricia Promis, and Chris Sugnet. Acquisition Guidelines No. 9. Chicago: American Library Assocation, 1994. ISBN 0-8389-0629-X. Chap. 9.
Describes the characteristics of these types of materials; identifies criteria, discusses acquisitions issues, and provides a glossary.

High Interest-Easy Reading: A Booklist for Junior and Senior High School Students. 6th ed. William G. McBride, ed., and the Committee to Revise High Interest-Easy Reading of the National Council of Teachers of English. Urbana, IL: The Council, 1990. ISBN 0-8141-2097-0. Chap. 12.
Annotations arranged alphabetically by category with index by author, title, and subject.

High/Low Handbook: Encouraging Literacy in the 1990s. 3d ed. Ellen V. LiBretto, comp. and ed. New York: R. R. Bowker, 1990. ISBN 0-8352-2804-5. Chap. 12.
Annotates titles for the disabled reader (lower than a fourth-grade level) and for reluctant junior and senior high school students. Discusses selection of these materials.

The High School Journal. Chapel Hill, NC: University of North Carolina Press, 1918- . ISSN 0018-1498. Chap. 10.
Published four times per year. Available in microform. Subscription address: University of North Carolina Press, Box 2288, Chapel Hill, NC 27515-2288.

A Hispanic Heritage, Series IV: A Guide to Juvenile Books about Hispanic People and Cultures. Isabel Schon. Metuchen, NJ: Scarecrow Press, 1991. ISSN 2636-2723. Chap. 11.
Identifies titles for kindergarten through high school about the people, history, and art, as well as political, social, and economic conditions for the following: Argentina, Bolivia, Chile, Colombia, Costa Rica, Cuba, Dominican Republic, Ecuador, El Salvador, Guatemala, Honduras, Mexico, Nicaragua, Panama, Paraguay, Peru, Puerto Rico, Spain, Uruguay, Venezuela, and Hispanic-heritage people in the United States. Includes evaluative comments. Indexes for author, title, and subject with references and cross-references.

The History Teacher. Long Beach, CA: Society for History Education, 1967- . ISSN 0018-2745. Chap. 11.

Published quarterly. Available on microfilm. Subscription address: Society for History Education, Department of History, California State University, 1250 Bellflower Blvd., Long Beach, CA 90840. Reviews audiovisual materials, videos, textbooks, supplementary readers, and tradebooks.

The Horn Book Magazine. Boston: Horn Book, 1924- . ISSN 0018-5078. Chap. 7.

Six issues per year. Available in microform. Related work: *The Horn Book Guide to Children's and Young Adult Books*, 1990- , ISSN 1044-405X. Reviews hardback and paperback books. Entries provide bibliographic and order information, size, age level, summary of content, characterizations, themes, and comments on writing and illustrating. New editions and reissues. Books in Spanish. Column on out-of-print books that may be found in libraries. Subscription address: Circulation Department, Park Square Building, 31 James Avenue, Boston, MA 02116.

How to Find Information about AIDS. 2d ed. Jeffrey T. Huber, ed. Haworth Medical Information Sources series. Binghamton, NY: Haworth Press, 1992. ISBN 1-56024-140-3. Chap. 11.

Provides addresses and telephone numbers for organizational resources, health departments, research institutions, grant funding sources, federal agencies, hotlines, and audiovisual producers and distributors. Describes electronic and print sources of information. Access is through the general index (author, title, subject) and the geographical index.

Index to AV Producers & Distributors. 8th ed. 1991. ISBN 0-937548-21-9. Chap. 14.

NICEM (National Information Center for Educational Media) Indexes. Medford, NJ: Plexus Publishing Co., publisher and distributor. Also available through Learned Information, Inc., 143 Old Marion Pike, Medford, NJ 08055-8750. Provides addresses, telephone numbers, and type of media produced and/or distributed for over 20,000 producers and distributors.

Instructional Media and the New Technologies of Instruction. 4th ed. Robert Heinich, Michael Molenda, and James D. Russell. New York: Macmillan, 1993. ISBN 0-0235-3060-X. Chap. 10, 12.

Standard work on the selection and use of media.

Instructor and Teacher. Dansville, NY: Instructor Publications, 1981- . ISSN 0020-4285. Chap. 11.

Intellectual Freedom and the School Library Media Program: Documents and Resources. Intellectual Freedom Committee, American Association of School Librarians. Chicago: American Library Association, 1989. ISBN 0-8389-7357-4.

Interracial Books for Children Bulletin. New York: Council on Interracial Books for Children, 1975- . ISSN 0146-5562. Chap. 7, 11.

Subscription address: Council on Interracial Books for Children, Box 1263, New York, NY 10023.

Journal of Consumer Affairs. Columbia, MO: American Council of Consumer Interest, 1967- . ISSN 0022-0078. Chap. 11.

Published semiannually. Available in microform and computer laser optical discs. Reviews professional materials. Subscription address: American Council of Consumer Interest, 240 Stanley Hall, University of Missouri, Columbia, MO 65211.

Journal of Geography. Macomb, IL: National Council for Geographic Education, 1902- . ISSN 0022-1341. Chap. 11.
 Published bimonthly. Reviews textbooks and professional materials; has a column on free and inexpensive materials. Subscription address: National Council for Geographic Education, Western Illinois University, Macomb, IL 61455.

Journal of Health Education. Reston, VA: American Alliance for Health, Physical Education, Recreation & Dance, 1991- . Chap. 11.
 Published bimonthly. Available in microform. Subscription address: American Alliance for Health, Physical Education, Recreation & Dance, 1900 Association Dr., Reston, VA 22091.

Journal of Home Economics. Washington, DC: American Home Economics Association, 1909- . ISSN 0022-1570. Chap. 11.
 Published quarterly. Available in microform. Reviews trade and professional books. Subscription address: American Home Economics Association, 2010 Massachusetts Avenue, NW, Washington, DC 20036.

Journal of Learning Disabilities. Chicago: Professional Press, 1968- . ISSN 0022-2194. Chap. 12.
 Published monthly (bimonthly June-September). Available in microform. Reviews professional materials. Subscription address: 8700 Shoal Creek Blvd., Austin, TX 78757-6897. (512) 451-3246.

Journal of Visual Impairment and Blindness. New York: American Foundation for the Blind, 1977- . ISSN 0145-482X. Chap. 12.
 Published monthly (except July and August). Text in regular print or in braille. Available in microform and on audiocassette.

Journal of Youth Services in Libraries. Chicago: Association for Library Service to Children and the Young Adult Library Services Association, divisions of the American Library Association, 1987- . Chap. 11.
 Published quarterly. Reviews professional materials. Subscription address: American Library Association, 50 East Huron Street, Chicago, IL 60611.

The Junior High School Library Catalog. 6th ed. Juliette Yaakov, ed. Bronx, NY: H. W. Wilson, 1990. ISBN 0-8242-0799-8. Chap. 7, 9, 16, 17.
 Four supplements. Main section arranged by *Abridged Dewey Decimal Classification*, followed by fiction and story collections. Entries provide bibliographic and order information, suggested Sears subject headings, and annotations. Author, title, subject, and analytical indexing.

Juniorplots 4: A Book Talk Guide for Use with Readers Ages 12-16. John T Gillespie, and Corinne J. Naden. New Providence, NJ: Reed Reference Publishing, 1992. ISBN 0-8352-3167-4. Chap. 12.

Kirkus Reviews. New York: Kirkus Service, 1933- . ISSN 0042-6598. Chap. 9.
 Published semimonthly. Available in microform. Reviews trade books. Entries provide bibliographic/order information, paging, month and day of release, type of book, and grade level. Subscription address: Kirkus Service, 200 Park Avenue South, New York, NY 10003.

Kister's Best Dictionaries for Adults and Young People: A Comparative Guide. Kenneth F. Kister. Phoenix, AZ: Oryx Press, 1992. ISBN 0-89774-191-9. Chap. 11.

Presents general discussions about dictionaries and their selection. Evaluates English-language dictionaries for children through adults, including alphabet books and preschool dictionaries. Access by author, title, and subject index.

KLIATT Young Adult Paperback Book Guide. Newton, MA: The Guide, 1978- . ISSN 0199-2376. Chap. 9, 12.
Eight issues per year. Available in microform. Reviews software, paperbacks, and audiobooks for ages 12-19. Subscription address: The Guide, 425 Watertown St., Newton, MA 02158.

Language Arts. Urbana, IL: National Council of Teachers of English, 1975- . ISSN 0360-9170. Chap. 11.
Published monthly (September through May). Available in microform. Reviews children's books and professional materials. Subscription address: National Council of Teachers of English, 1111 Kenyon Rd., Urbana, IL 61801.

Library Hi Tech Journal. Ann Arbor, MI: Pierian Press, 1983- . ISSN 0737-8831. Chap. 14.
Published quarterly. Includes professional articles, reviews, and notices of vendors' workshops and training sessions.

Library Journal. New York: Cahners/R. R. Bowker, 1876- . ISSN 0363-0277. Chap. 7.
Published semimonthly (monthly January, July, August, and December). Available in microform. Reviews books, magazines, videocassettes, and audiocassettes. Includes annual buyer's guide to hardware and equipment. Subscription address: P.O. Box 1977, Marion, OH 43305-1977.

Library Resources for the Blind and Physically Handicapped. Washington, DC: National Library Services for the Blind and Physically Handicapped, 1990. Chap. 12.
Lists network libraries and machine-lending agencies that participate in the free service program. Provides directory information (fax number, hours of service, formats of materials in the collection, special collections, services, assistance devices, and publications) for each facility. Free. Address: National Library Services for the Blind and Physically Handicapped, 1291 NW Taylor St., Washington, DC 20542.

Library Talk: The Magazine for Elementary School Librarians. Carolyn Hamilton, ed. Worthington, OH: Linworth Publishing, 1988- . ISSN 1043-237X. Chap. 7.
Five issues per year. Reviews tradebooks, including Spanish and professional books, films, filmstrips, videocassettes, and software. Identifies free and inexpensive materials. Order address: 5701 N. High St., Suite 1, Worthington, OH 43085.

Library Technology Reports. Chicago: American Library Association, 1976- . ISSN 0024-2586. Chap. 8.
Published bimonthly. Evaluates library systems, equipment, and supplies. Subscription address: American Library Association, 50 E. Huron Street, Chicago, IL 60611.

Literary Market Place with Names and Numbers. New York: R. R. Bowker, 1973- . ISSN 0161-2905. Chap. 13.
Published annually. Available in print or CD-ROM (*Library Reference Plus*).

Literature for Today's Young Adult. Alleen Pace Nilsen and Kenneth L. Donelson. New York: HarperCollins College Publishers, 1993. ISBN 0-6734-6652-3. Chap. 12.

Literature of Delight: A Critical Guide to Humorous Books for Children. Kimberly Olson Fakih. R. R. Bowker, 1993. ISBN 0-8352-3027-9. Chap. 12.

Magazines for Children: A Guide for Parents, Teachers, and Librarians. 2d ed. Selma K. Richardson. Chicago: American Library Association, 1991. ISBN 0-8389-0552-8. Chap. 9.
 Reviews magazines for children under 14 years old, describes typical issues, and indicates which are indexed in *Children's Magazine Guide*.

Magazines for Libraries. 7th ed. Bill Katz and Linda Sternberg Katz. New Providence, NJ: R. R. Bowker, 1992. ISBN 0-8352-3166-6. Chap. 9.
 New index by subject. Provides full bibliographic data: frequency, cost, size of circulation, where indexed, intended audience, and availability of microform, microfiche, or online.

Magazines for Young People: A Children's Magazine Guide. Companion Volume. 2d ed. New Providence, NJ: R. R. Bowker, 1991. ISBN 0-8352-3009-0. Chap. 9.
 Formerly *Magazines for School Libraries*. Evaluates over 1,100 magazines. Entries provide beginning year of publication, frequency, cost, address, presence of illustrations, advertising, and library level.

The Mathematics Teacher. Reston, VA: National Council of Teachers of Mathematics, 1908- . ISSN 0025-5769. Chap. 12.
 Published monthly (except June-September). Available in microform. Reviews software, text materials, and professional books. Subscription address: National Council of Teachers of Mathematics, 1906 Association Drive, Reston, VA 22091.

Media and Methods. Philadelphia, PA: American Society of Educators, 1969- . ISSN 0025-6897. Chap. 7.
 Published monthly (except June-August). Available in microform. Reviews trade books, textbooks, films, videos, filmstrips, software, databases, recordings, cassettes, and equipment. Has videodisc updates. Announces new software and audiovisual products. Subscription address: American Society of Educators, 1511 Walnut Street, Philadelphia, PA 19102.

Media Resource Catalog. Capitol Heights, MD: National Archives and Records Administration, National Audiovisual Center. Chap. 7.
 Published annually. Identifies 16-mm films, videos, filmstrips, slide sets, and multimedia kits produced by federal agencies. Provides title, format, color or black-and-white, running time, producing agency, description of content, and price or rental cost. Indexed by title. Free. Address: National Audiovisual Center, 8700 Edgeworth Dr., Capitol Heights, MD 20743-3701.

Media Review Digest. Ann Arbor, MI: Pierian Press, 1970- . ISSN 0363-7778. Chap. 7.
 Guide to reviews of educational and feature films, videocassettes, videodiscs, filmstrips, educational spoken-word records, tapes, compact discs, slides, transparencies, kits, maps, globes, charts, and games.

Microcomputer Market Place. New York: R. R. Bowker, 1983- . ISSN 0735-1925. Chap. 13.
 Published annually.

Microcomputer Software Guide Online. Vendor DIALOG Information Services,
Inc. Chap. 10.
File 278 on DIALOG provides information on 15,000 software programs from
over 4,000 producers. Provides full ordering information and description.

*Microcomputer Software Sources: A Guide for Buyers, Librarians, Programmers,
Businesspeople, and Educators.* Englewood, CO: Libraries Unlimited, 1990.
ISBN 0-87287-560-1. Chap. 9.
Describes the software industry, applications, machine-specific software,
guides to inexpensive and free software. Includes evaluation forms to use before
purchasing software packages.

Microform Review. Westport, CT: Microform Review, 1972- . ISSN 0002-6530. Chap. 9.
Published quarterly. Available in microform. Subscription address: Meeker
Publishing, 11 Perry Lane West, Westport, CT 06880. Reviews professional books
and microforms.

Monthly Catalog of United States Government Publications. Superintendent of
Documents. Washington, DC: U.S. Government Printing Office, 1895- . Chap. 9.
Published monthly. Lists the publications of major branches, departments,
and bureaus of the U.S. government. Provides depository and order information.
Also available online through DIALOG and BRS.

*More Exciting, Funny, Scary, Short, Different, and Sad Books Kids Like About
Animals, Science, Sports, Families, Songs, and Other Things.* Ed. by Frances
Laverne Carroll and Mary Meacham. Chicago: American Library Association,
1992. ISBN 0-8389-0585-4. Chap. 12.
Designed for use by children, the recommended titles cover a wide range of
interests. The author/illustrator index and subject index help readers find old
favorites and meet new works with similar appeal.

*Multicultural Review: Dedicated to a Better Understanding of Ethnic, Racial and
Religious Diversity.* Westport, CT: Greenwood Publishing, 1992. ISSN 1058-
9236. Chap. 11, 13.
Published quarterly. Includes article, often bibliographic essays, and reviews
of materials for juvenile and adult audiences. Contact: *Multicultural Review*,
Greenwood Publishing Group, Inc., 88 Post Road W., Box 5007, Westport, CT
06881-5007.

Negotiating the Special Education Maze. 2d ed. Winifred Anderson, Stephan
Chitwood, and Deidre Hayden. Rockville, MD: Woodbine House, 1990. ISBN
0-9331-4930-1. Chap. 12.
Provides a guide to legislation for parents and teachers.

New Books: Publications for Sale by the Government Printing Office. Superintendent
of Documents. Washington, DC: U.S. Government Printing Office, 1982- .
Chap. 9.
Published quarterly. Lists title, issuing agency and date, paging, SuDocs
number, stock number, and price. Provides no annotations or index. Free. Address:
Government Printing Office, Washington, DC 20402.

The New Booktalker. Ed. by Joni Richards Bodart. 2 vols. Englewood, CO: Libraries
Unlimited, 1992. ISSN 1064-7511. Chap. 13.
Each volume covers 150-200 titles.

The New York Times Book Review. New York: New York Times Company, 1896- . ISSN 0028-7806. Chap. 7.

Published every Sunday. Subscription address: New York Times Company, Box 5792 GPO, New York, NY 10087.

Newsletter on Intellectual Freedom. Chicago: Intellectual Freedom Committee of the American Library Association, 1952- . ISSN 0028-9485. Chap. 4.

Published bimonthly. Available in microform. Reports events relating to intellectual freedom and censorship. Subscription address: American Library Association Committee on Intellectual Freedom, 50 E. Huron St., Chicago, IL 60611.

Nonfiction for Young Adults from Delight to Wisdom. Betty Carter and Richard F. Abrahamson. Phoenix, AZ: Oryx Press, 1990. ISBN 0-89774-555-8. Chap. 12.

Discusses interest, accuracy, content, style, organization, format, and uses of nonfiction works; accompanied by conversations with Lee J. Ames, Milton Meltzer, Laurence Pringle, Brent Ashabranner, James Cross Giblin, and Daniel and Susan Cohen. Bibliography includes background sources and citations to the works mentioned in the text. Author, title, and subject indexes provided.

Northwest's Guide to Our World Online. 4th ed. Jonathan Kochmer and North-WestNet. Seattle, WA: NorthWestNet and Northwest Academic Computing Consortium, 1993. Chap. 14.

Online: The Magazine of Online Information Systems. Wilton, CT: Online, Inc., 1970. ISSN 0146-5422. Chap. 9.

Published six times per year. Provides articles about online applications and in-depth evaluative reviews. Subscription address: Online Inc., 462 Danbury Rd., Wilton, CT 06897.

Online & CD-ROM Review. Medford, NJ: Learned Information Inc., 1977- . ISSN 0309-314X. Chap. 9.

Published bimonthly. Includes articles listing new databases, development of search aids, and the use and management of online and optical information retrieval systems. Subscription address: Learned Information Inc., 143 Old Marion Pike, Medford, NJ 08055-8750.

Online Searching Goes to School. Doris M. Epler. Phoenix, AZ: Oryx Press, 1989. ISBN 0-89774-546-9. Chap. 9.

Provides a practical guide to the selection, use, and management of online databases.

Only the Best: The Annual Guide to Highest-Rated Educational Software, Preschool-Grade 12. Shirley Boes Neill and George W. Neill. New Providence, NJ: R. R. Bowker, 1989- . Chap. 10.

Describes system compatibility, subject areas, grade level, order information, annotation, and citations of reviews.

Our Family, Our Friends, Our World: An Annotated Guide to Significant Multicultural Books for Children and Teenagers. Lyn Miller-Lachmann. Providence, NJ: R. R. Bowker, 1992. ISBN 0-8352-3025-2. Chap. 11.

Compares works with other titles on same subject pointing out strengths and weaknesses. Appendixes include professional sources and series titles. Access by author, title/series, and subject indexes.

Paperbound Books in Print. New York: R. R. Bowker, 1955- . ISSN 0031-1235.
Chap. 9, 14.
Available in microform.

Picture Books for Children. 3d ed. Patricia J. Cianciolo. Chicago: American Library
Association, 1990. ISBN 0-389-0527-7. Chap. 12.
Recommends titles for children from infancy through 16 years old. Describes
each of the 464 illustrated titles in terms of the contributions of the illustration
to the work. Index is by author, title, and illustrator.

*Play, Learn, and Grow: An Annotated Guide to the Best Books and Materials for
Very Young Children.* James L. Thomas. New Providence, NJ: R. R. Bowker,
1992. ISBN 0-8352-3019-8. Chap. 11.

*Portraying Persons with Disabilities: An Annotated Bibliography of Fiction for
Children and Teenagers.* Debra Robertson. New Providence, NJ: R. R.
Bowker, 1992. ISBN 0-8352-3023-6. Chap. 12.
Evaluates the strengths and weaknesses of fiction works for readers ages
5-18.

*Portraying Persons with Disabilities: An Annotated Bibliography of Nonfiction for
Children and Teenagers.* Joan Brest Friedberg, June B. Mullins, and Adelaide
Weir Sukiennik. New Providence, NJ: R. R. Bowker, 1992. ISBN 0-8352-3022-
8. Chap. 12.
Evaluates the strengths and weaknesses of nonfiction works for readers ages
5-18.

Publishers, Distributors, and Wholesalers of the United States. New Providence,
NJ: R. R. Bowker, 1979- . ISSN 0000-0671. Chap. 13.
Published annually. Lists more than 50,000 publishers, wholesalers, distributors,
software firms, and museum and association imprints. Access by name, imprint,
subsidiaries, divisions, state, firms with toll-free numbers, ISBN prefix, and
publisher's field of activity.

Publishers Weekly: The Journal of the Book Industry. New York: R. R. Bowker,
1872- . ISSN 0000-0019. Chap. 14.
Published weekly. Available in microform. Reviews books and audiovisual
materials. Subscription address: P.O. Box 1979, Marion, OH 43302.

Quill and Quire. Toronto: Key Publishers, 1935- . ISSN 0033-6491. Chap. 7.
Published monthly. Available in microform. Special supplement: *Forthcoming
Books = Livres a Paraitre.* Reviews books and advertisements for tapes and
records. Subscription address: Customer Service, 35 Riviera Drive, Unit 17,
Markham, Ontario L3R 8N4 Canada.

Reaching Adolescents: The Young Adult Book and the School. Arthea J. S. Reed.
Macmillan, 1994. ISBN 0-02-398861-4. Chap. 12.
Covers history, selection, use in the curriculum, and censorship related to
young adult literature.

Reading Lists for College-Bound Students. Doug Estell, et al. New York:
Arco/Prentice Hall, 1990. ISBN 0-13-635251-0. Chap. 12.
Reprints lists of books recommended by 103 colleges and a composite anno-
tated list of the 100 most frequently recommended works.

The Reading Teacher. Newark, DE: International Reading Association, 1950- . ISSN 0034-0561. Chap. 11.

Nine issues per year. Available in microform. Subscription address: International Reading Association, P.O. Box 8137, Newark, DE 19714.

Recommended Reference Books for Small and Medium-Sized Libraries. Littleton, CO: Libraries Unlimited, 1982- . ISSN 0277-5948. Chap. 11.

Published annually. Selected from *American Reference Books Annual.* Lengthy reviews are coded to identify titles of interest to school libraries.

Recommended Reference Books in Paperback. 2d ed. Andrew L. March. Englewood, CO: Libraries Unlimited, 1992. ISBN 1-56308-967-1. Chap. 11.

Evaluates 1,000 titles.

Recommended Videos for Schools. Beth Blenz-Clucas and Gloria Gribble, eds. Santa Barbara, CA: ABC-Clio, 1991. ISBN 0-87436-644-5. Chap. 9.

Arranged by subject, the 400 reviews of videos for grades K-12 are from the 1990 publications of *Video Rating Guide for Libraries.* Each entry includes the rating, entry number, full title, bibliographic/imprint information, ISBN, Library of Congress number, suggested Dewey classification number, Library of Congress subject headings, recommended audience, awards received, review of 300-400 words, and number of reviewers. Entries are accessed through title, subject, and price indexes (under $50 to $200 and over). Addresses and telephone numbers are provided for producers and distributors.

Recordings for the Blind, Catalog of Recorded Books. Princeton, NJ: Recording for the Blind, 1960- . Chap. 12.

Published irregularly. Lists free taped educational books, including textbooks, available in cassette format. Address: Recording for the Blind, 20 Roszel Rd., Princeton, NJ 08540.

Reference Books for Children. 4th ed. Carolyn Sue Peterson and Ann D. Fenton. Metuchen, NJ: Scarecrow Press, 1992. ISBN 0-8108-2543-0. Chap. 12.

Evaluates reference works and selection tools. Discusses criteria for selecting such works. Author/title index and subject index provided.

Reference Books for Children's Collections. 2d ed. Compiled by the Children's Reference Committee, Dolores Vogliano, ed. New York: New York Public Library, 1991. Chap. 11.

Provides bibliographic and descriptive annotations for over 420 titles, including those for younger readers and for adults working with children. Arranged by subject with an author and title index.

The Reviewing Librarian. Toronto: Ontario School Library Association, 1974- . ISSN 0318-0948. Chap. 7.

Published quarterly. Reviews books, audiovisual materials, government publications, and magazines. Subscription address: Ontario Library Association, 73 Richmond Street West, Toronto, Ontario M5H 1Z4 Canada.

School Libraries in Canada. Ottawa, Ontario: Canadian School Library Association, 1980- . ISSN 0227-3780. Chap. 7.

Published quarterly. Available in microform. Reviews books, films, videos, and CDs for grades K-12. Subscription address: SLIC Subscriptions, Canadian Library Association, 200 Elgin St., Suite 602, Ottawa, Ontario K2P 1L5 Canada.

School Library Journal: The Magazine of Children's, Young Adult, and School Libraries. New York: R. R. Bowker, 1954- . ISSN 0000-0035. Chaps. 4, 7, 9, 11, 13.

Twelve issues per year. Available in microform. Reviews books (preschool through adult titles for young people), films, videocassettes, filmstrips, slides, recordings, and software. Includes checklists of pamphlets, posters, and free materials. Includes monthly index, annual author/title book review index, and audiovisual index. Subscription address: P.O. Box 1978, Marion, Ohio 43305-1978.

School Library Media Quarterly. Chicago: American Library Association, 1954- . ISSN 0278-4823. Chap. 6, 10, 13.

Published quarterly. Available in microform. Reviews professional literature and software. Subscription address: American Library Association, 50 E. Huron St., Chicago, IL 60611.

Schwann Opus. Santa Fe, NM: Stereophile, 1949- . ISSN 1066-2138. Chap. 9.

Schwann Spectrum. Santa Fe, NM: Stereophile, Inc., 1990- . Chap. 9.

Four issues per year. Formerly *Spectrum.* Lists rock, pop, jazz, gospel, Christmas, and religious music; children's recordings; and spoken records. Covers musicals, soundtracks, and New Age music. Address: 21625 Prairie St., Chatsworth, CA 91311.

Science and Children. Washington, DC: National Science Teachers Association, 1963- . ISSN 0036-8148. Chap. 9, 11.

Published eight times per year (September through May). Available in microform. Reviews software, curriculum materials, and children's books. Subscription address: National Science Teachers Association, 1742 Connecticut Ave., Washington, DC 20009-1171.

Science & Technology in Fact and Fiction: A Guide to Children's Books. Day Ann Kennsy, Stella S. Spangler, and Mary Ann Vanderwerf. New York: R. R. Bowker, 1990. ISBN 0-8352-2708-1. Chap. 11.

Provides evaluative comments accessed by separate author, title, subject, and readability indexes.

Science & Technology in Fact and Fiction: A Guide to Young Adult Books. Day Ann Kennedy, Stella S. Spangler, and Mary Ann Vanderwerf. New York: R. R. Bowker, 1990. ISBN 0-8352-2710-3. Chap. 11.

Provides evaluative comments accessed by separate author, title, subject, and readability indexes.

Science Books & Films. Washington, DC: American Association for the Advancement of Science, 1965- . ISSN 0098-342X. Chap. 11.

Nine issues per year. Available in microform. Reviews books, films, filmstrips, videos, and software and lists what is on Public Broadcasting System. Covers preschool through professional materials. Subscription address: American Association for the Advancement of Science, 1333 H St. NW, Washington, DC 20005.

The Science Teacher. Washington, DC: National Science Teachers Association, 1934- . ISSN 0036-8555. Chap. 11.

Published monthly (September-May). Available in microform. Reviews software, books for students, and professional books. Subscription address: National Science Teachers Association, 1742 Connecticut Ave. NW, Washington, DC 20009.

Selection and Evaluation of Electronic Resources. Gail K. Dickinson. Englewood, CO: Libraries Unlimited, 1994. ISBN 1-56308-098-2. Chap. 9.

Discusses hardware requirements, criteria, selection of CD encyclopedia, and magazine indexes and provides a glossary.

Selection Policies and Reevaluation Procedures: A Workbook. Minnesota Coalition Against Censorship. Stillwater, MN: Minnesota Educational Media Organization, 1991. Chap. 6.

Includes sample wording for various sections of the policy, using wording from existing policies. Identifies and reprints professional association documents supporting intellectual freedom. Order from: Minnesota Educational Media Organization, 408 Quarry Lane, Stillwater, MN 55082.

Selecting Materials for School Library Media Centers. 2d ed. Dona J. Helmer, comp. and ed. Chicago: American Library Association, 1993. ISBN 0-8389-7693-X. Chap. 12.

Senior High School Library Catalog. 14th ed. New York: H. W. Wilson, 1992. Chap. 7, 9, 16, 17.

Four annual supplements. Arranged by DDC with separate sections for fiction and story collections. Entries provide bibliographic and order information, availability of paperback editions, Sears subject headings, and descriptive/critical annotations. Author, title, subject, and analytical indexing provided.

Sequels: An Annotated Guide to Novels in Series. 2d ed. Janet Husband and Jonathan F. Husband. Chicago: American Library Association, 1990. ISBN 0-8389-0533-1. Chap. 12.

Serials Review. Ann Arbor, MI: Pierian Press, 1975- . ISSN 0098-7913. Chap. 9.

Published quarterly. Available in microform. Subscription address: Pierian Press, P.O. Box 1808, Ann Arbor, MI 48106.

Slide Buyer's Guide: An International Directory of Slide Sources for Art and Architecture. 6th ed. Norine D. Cashman, ed. Englewood, CO: Libraries Unlimited, 1990. ISBN 0-87287-787-3. Chap. 9.

Identifies slide sources in United States, Canada, and foreign countries. Lists companies, museums, and institutions with slides to sell, rent, or exchange.

Social Education. Arlington, VA: National Council for the Social Studies, 1937- . ISSN 0037-7724. Chap. 11.

Seven issues per year. Reviews books for children and young adults. Subscription address: National Council for the Social Studies, 3501 Newark St. NW, Washington, DC 20016.

Software Encyclopedia. New Providence, NJ: R. R. Bowker, 1985- . Chap. 9.

Published annually. Provides annotated listings for over 21,000 software programs. Indexed by title, compatible system, and application. *Microcomputer Software Guide Online* is available through DIALOG File No. 278.

Software Information—for Apple II Computers. Pittsburgh, PA: Black Box Corporation, 1990. ISBN 0-942821-18-1. Chap. 9.

Lists 12,000 programs with name, address, system, disk medium, RAM requirements, description, ISBN (International Standard Program Number), and price. Available online through DIALOG and Applelink.

Software Reviews on File. New York: Facts on File, 1985- . ISSN 8755-7169. Chap. 9.
Published monthly. Reviews over 600 software programs per year. Indexed by subject and company. Entries provide publisher, address, price, and publisher's description. Condenses and cites reviews.

Standard Periodical Directory. 16th ed. Matthew Manning, ed. New York: Oxbridge Communications; distr., Detroit: Gale Research, 1993. ISBN 0-917460-30-8. Chap. 14.
Published annually. Identifies 70,000 U.S. and Canadian periodicals with bibliographies and order information. Includes title index.

Subject Bibliography Index. Superintendent of Documents. Washington, DC: U.S. Government Printing Office. Chap. 11.
Free. Lists free subject bibliographies. Index also serves as the order form. Address: Government Printing Office, Washington, DC 20402.

Subject Guide to Children's Books in Print. See *Children's Books in Print*.

Substance Abuse: A Resource Guide for Secondary Schools. Sally L. Myers and Blanche Woolls. Englewood, CO: Libraries Unlimited, 1991. ISBN: 0-87287-805-8. Chap. 12.

Successful Field Trips. Mary D. Lankford. Santa Barbara, CA: ABC-Clio, 1992. ISBN 0-87436-638-0. Chap. 5.
Provides guidance for arranging, conducting, and evaluating field trip experiences.

Suggested Copyright Policy and Guidelines for California's School Districts. California Department of Education. Sacramento: California Department of Education, 1991. Chap. 6.
Provides a model policy, identifies guidelines for use of specific types of copyrighted materials, and includes sample forms for requesting to use copyrighted materials. Available from: Bureau of Publications, Sales Unit, California Department of Education, P.O. Box 271, Sacramento, CA 95812-0271.

Supernatural Fiction for Teens: More Than 1300 Good Paperbacks to Read for Wonderment. 2d ed. Cosette Kies. Englewood, CO: Libraries Unlimited, 1992. ISBN 0-87287-940-2. Chap. 12.
Provides bibliographic information with a brief annotation, reading level, notes on movie versions, and category of book. Indexed by movie, title, and subject.

Swift's Directory of Educational Software for the IBM PC. Austin, TX: Sterling Swift, 1982- . Chap. 9.
Annual and semi-annual updates provided. Subscription address: DC Health & Co., 125 Spring Street, Lexington, MA 02713.

Talking Books Topics. Washington, DC: National Library Services for the Blind and Physically Handicapped, 1935- . Chap. 12.
Published bimonthly. Available in large print, cassette, and disc formats. Includes annotated list of recorded books and magazines available through cooperating libraries. Includes juvenile titles and foreign languages books. Free. Address: National Library Services for the Blind and Physically Handicapped, 1291 NW Taylor St., Washington, DC 20542.

Technology & Learning. Dayton, OH: Peter Li, Inc., 1980- . ISSN 1053-6728. Chap. 10.
  Eight issues per year. Formerly *Classroom Computer Learning.* Reviews computer software and multimedia for elementary and secondary students. Entries provide hardware requirements, emphasis, grade level, publisher, description of software manuals and guides, rating, strengths, and weaknesses. Address: Peter Li, Inc., 2451 E. River Rd., Dayton, OH 45439.

TechTrends. Washington, DC: Association for Educational Communications and
  Technology, 1985- . ISSN 8756-3894. Chap. 8.
  Eight issues per year. Available in microform. Announces new products. Subscription address: Association for Educational Communications and Technology, 1126 16th St. NW, Washington, DC 20036.

T.E.S.S.: The Educational Software Selector. Hampton Bay, NY: EPIE Institute.
  Published annually. Describes software in terms of educational philosophy, subject, grade level, instruction methods, and hardware requirements. Available through CompuServe. Updated bimonthly. Address: EPIE Institute, 103-3 W. Montauk Highway, Hampton Bay, NY 11946.

Through Indian Eyes: The Native Experience in Books for Children. Beverly Slapin
  and Doris Seale. Philadelphia: New Society Publishers/New Society Educational Foundation, 1992. ISBN 0-86571-212-3. Chap. 13.
  Expands on earlier editions of *Books Without Bias: Through Indian Eyes.* Critically evaluates and offers guidelines for selection of books on Native Americans.

TV Guide. Radnor, PA: Murdoch Magazines, 1953- . ISSN 0039-8543. Chap. 9, 10.
  Published weekly. Subscription address: Radnor Corporate Center, 100 Matsonford Rd., Box 500, Radnor, PA 19088.

*Understanding Abilities, Disabilities, and Capabilities: A Guide to Children's
  Literature.* Margaret F. Carlin, Jeannine L. Laughlin, and Richard D. Saniga. Englewood, CO: Libraries Unlimited, 1991. ISBN: 0-87287-717-5. Chap. 12.
  Provides evaluative summaries and ratings of books and films. Three indexes: title, author/illustrator/photographer, and subject.

U.S. Government Books. Superintendent of Documents. Washington, DC: U.S.
  Government Printing Office, 1982- . Chap. 9.
  Published quarterly. Annotates 1,000 government publications. Provides order information, including stock number and SuDocs classification number. Free. Address: Government Printing Office, Washington, DC 20402.

U.S. Government Publications for the School Library Media Center, 2d ed. Leticia
  T. Ekhaml and Alice J. Wittig. Englewood, CO: Libraries Unlimited, 1991. ISBN 0-87287-822-8. Chap. 9, 11.
  Describes depository libraries, indexes, and selection aids for U.S. government publications, along with ordering information. Recommends selected titles on a wide range of topics from aeronautics to wildlife management.

University Press Books for Public and Secondary School Libraries. New York:
  Association of American University Presses, 1991- . ISSN 1055-4173. Chap. 12.
  Published annually. Free. Annotates more than 500 titles with bibliographic information, reading level, and appeal.

The University Prints Catalogue. Address: University Prints, 21 East Street, P. O.
  Box 485, Winchester, Massachusetts 01890 (617-729-8006)

Using Government Documents: A How-To-Do-It Manual for School Librarians. Melody S. Kelly. No. 5. Neal-Schuman, 1992. ISBN 1-55570-106-X. Chap. 9, 11.
Describes catalogs, clearinghouses, and agencies, and recommends special documents. Lists regional depository libraries, U.S. government book stores, and commercial vendors.

Venture into Cultures: A Resources Book of Multicultural Materials and Programs. Carla D. Hayden, ed. Chicago: American Library Association, 1992. ISBN 0-8389-0579-1. Chap. 11.
Provides recommendations for elementary and middle school levels on African American, Arabic, Asian, Hispanic, Jewish, Native American, and Persian culture. Provides background information; availability of materials; ideas for programs, crafts, celebrations, and food preparation; and annotated bibliography.

The Vertical File and Its Alternatives: A Handbook. Clara L. Sitter. Englewood, CO: Libraries Unlimited, 1992. ISBN 0-87287-910-0. Chap. 9.
Describes the acquisition, processing, and management of materials for the vertical file. Provides information about the acquisition, processing, and management of a wide range of materials, including college catalogs, postcards, local history collections, sheet music, and music scripts. Lists the addresses and telephone numbers for the vendors.

Vertical File Index: A Subject and Title Index to Selected Pamphlet Materials. New York: H. W. Wilson, 1955- . ISSN 0042-4493. Chap. 9, 10, 13.
Published monthly (except August). Available online (Wilsonline). Provides order information for free and inexpensive publications (e.g., pamphlets, maps, charts, posters). Arranged by subject with title index. Subscription address: H. W. Wilson, 950 University Avenue, Bronx, NY 10452.

The Video Librarian. Bremerton, WA: Randy Pitman, 1986- . ISSN 9887-6851. Chap. 9.
Published monthly. Subscription address: Randy Pitman, 2219 East View Avenue, NE, Bremerton, WA 98310.

Video Policies and Procedures for Libraries. James C. Scholtz. Santa Barbara, CA: ABC-Clio, 1991. ISBN 0-8743-6582-1. Chap. 6.
Includes guidelines and sample wording for policies and sample forms for reconsideration.

The Video Rating Guide for Libraries. Beth Blenz-Clucas, ed. Santa Barbara, CA: ABC-Clio, 1990- . ISSN 1045-3393. Chap. 9.
Published quarterly. Provides rating, bibliographic, ordering, and cataloging information. Indexed by subject, title, price, audience, and the best videos of the issue. The index is cumulated in the fourth quarterly issue.

The Video Source Book. Syosset, NY: National Video Clearinghouse, 1979- . ISSN 0277-2217. Chap. 9.
Published annually. Information on prerecorded video programs currently available on videocassette, videodisc, and videotape. Provides date of release, running time, major plot, theme, closed captions or signing for hearing impaired, and availability. Order from: Gale Research, Book Tower, Detroit, MI 48226.

VOYA: Voice of Youth Advocates. Metuchen, NJ: Scarecrow Press, 1978- . ISSN
0160-4201. Chap. 7, 12.
Published bimonthly. Available in microform. Reviews books (trade, paperbacks, reprints, professional), reference titles, films, videotapes, and recordings.
Evaluates for quality and popularity.

Wilson Library Bulletin. New York: H. W. Wilson, 1939- . ISSN 0043-5651. Chap. 7.
Published monthly (except July and August). Available in microform. Reviews books (picture, middle school and young adult, adult, reference), software,
CD-ROM/online, references on discs, recordings, videos, and other audiovisual
materials. Subscription address: H. W. Wilson, 950 University Avenue, Bronx, NY
10452.

Wordless/Almost Wordless Picture Books: A Guide. Virginia H. Richey and
Katharyn E. Puckett. Englewood, CO: Libraries Unlimited, 1992. ISBN 0-
87287-878-3. Chap. 12.
Provides information about works in which illustrations carry the meaning.
Indexed by title, format, series, illustrator, and subject.

Words on Cassette, 1994. New Providence, NJ: R. R. Bowker, 1994. ISBN 0-8352-
2343-0. Chap. 9.
Published annually. Merge of *On Cassette* and *Words on Tape*. Provides reader's
name, author, title, playing time, number of cassettes, purchase/rental price, order
number, and publisher. Indexed by title, subject, author, producer/distributor, and
reader.

World History for Children and Young Adults: An Annotated Bibliographic Index.
Vandelia VanMeter. Englewood, CO: Libraries Unlimited, 1992. ISBN 0-
87287-732-9. Chap. 11.
Identifies titles with bibliographic information, reviews, and brief notes.
Separate indexes by author, title, subject, series, and grade level provided.

Young People's Books in Series: Fiction and Non-Fiction 1975-1991. Judith K.
Rosenberg, Englewood, CO: Libraries Unlimited, 1992. Chap. 12.
Briefly describes series. Indexed by fiction series title, nonfiction series title,
nonfiction series subjects, and combined author/title.

Your Reading: A Booklist for Junior High and Middle School Students. Alleen Pace
Nilsen, ed. 8th ed. Urbana, IL: National Council of Teachers of English, 1991.
ISBN 0-8141-5940-0. Chap. 12.
Recommends 3,000 fiction and nonfiction titles for grades 5-9 with interest
and reading levels. Designed for student use. Includes a best books list.

APPENDIX C

Statements on People's Rights

This appendix includes three statements regarding intellectual freedom. As you read these statements, consider the rationale for, and the meanings and interpretations of, the words used. Do you share the beliefs expressed in these statements? Are they ones you will recommend for adoption by your school board?

LIBRARY BILL OF RIGHTS*

The American Library Association affirms that all libraries are forums for information and ideas, and that the following basic policies should guide their services.

1. Books and other library resources should be provided for the interest, information, and enlightenment of all people of the community the library serves. Materials should not be excluded because of the origin, background, or views of those contributing to their creation.

2. Libraries should provide materials and information presenting all points of view on current and historical issues. Materials should not be proscribed or removed because of partisan or doctrinal disapproval.

3. Libraries should challenge censorship in the fulfillment of their responsibility to provide information and enlightenment.

4. Libraries should cooperate with all persons and groups concerned with resisting abridgment of free expression and free access to ideas.

---

*Adopted June 18, 1948, by the ALA Council. Amended February 2, 1961; June 27, 1967; and January 23, 1980. The history of this statement with interpretative documents appears in *Intellectual Freedom Manual* (4th ed., American Library Association, 1992).

Reprinted with permission of the American Library Association and the Office for Intellectual Freedom (50 E. Huron St., Chicago, IL 60611) from *Intellectual Freedom Manual*, 4th ed., copyright © 1992.

5. A person's right to use a library should not be denied or abridged because of origin, age, background, or views.

6. Libraries which make exhibit spaces and meeting rooms available to the public they serve should make such facilities available on an equitable basis, regardless of the beliefs or affiliations of individuals or groups requesting their use.

ACCESS TO RESOURCES AND SERVICES IN THE SCHOOL LIBRARY MEDIA PROGRAM: AN INTERPRETATION OF THE LIBRARY BILL OF RIGHTS*

The school library media program plays a unique role in promoting intellectual freedom. It serves as a point of voluntary access to information and ideas and as a learning laboratory for students as they acquire critical thinking and problem solving skills needed in a pluralistic society. Although the educational level and program of the school necessarily shape the resources and services of a school library media program, the principles of the Library Bill of Rights apply equally to all libraries, including school library media programs.

School library media professionals assume a leadership role in promoting the principles of intellectual freedom within the school by providing resources and services that create and sustain an atmosphere of free inquiry. School library media professionals work closely with teachers to integrate instructional activities in classroom units designed to equip students to locate, evaluate, and use a broad range of ideas effectively. Through resources, programming, and educational processes, students and teachers experience the free and robust debate characteristic of a democratic society.

School library media professional cooperate with other individuals in building collections of resources appropriate to the developmental and maturity levels of students. These collections provide resources which support the curriculum and are consistent with the philosophy, goals, and objectives of the school district. Resources in school library media collections represent diverse points of view and current as well as historical issues.

---

*Originally presented by the American Association of School Librarian's Committee on Intellectual Freedom to, and adopted by, AASL's directors on June 26, 1986. Adopted July 2, 1986; amended January 10, 1990, by the ALA Council. The history of this interpretation appears in *Intellectual Freedom Manual* (4th ed., American Library Association, 1992).

Reprinted with permission of the American Library Association and the Office for Intellectual Freedom (50 E. Huron St., Chicago, IL 60611) from *Intellectual Freedom Manual*, 4th ed., copyright © 1992.

While English is, by history and tradition, the customary language of the United States, the languages in use in any given community may vary. Schools serving communities in which other languages are used make efforts to accommodate the needs of students for whom English is a second language. To support these efforts, and to ensure equal access to resources and services, the school library media program provides resources which reflect the linguistic pluralism of the community.

Members of the school community involved in the collection development process employ educational criteria to select resources unfettered by their personal, political, social, or religious views. Students and educators served by the school library media program have access to resources and services free of constraints resulting from personal, partisan, or doctrinal disapproval. School library media professionals resist efforts by individuals to define what is appropriate for all students or teachers to read, view, or hear.

Major barriers between students and resources include: imposing age or grade level restrictions on the use of resources, limiting the use of interlibrary loan and access to electronic information, charging fees for information in specific formats, requiring permissions from parents or teachers, establishing restricted shelves or closed collections, and labeling. Policies, procedures, and rules related to the use of resources and services support free and open access to information.

The school board adopts policies that guarantee students access to a broad range of ideas. These include policies on collection development and procedures for the review of resources about which concerns have been raised. Such policies, developed by persons in the school community, provide for a timely and fair hearing and assure that procedures are applied equitable to all expressions of concern. School library media professionals implement district policies and procedures in the school.

STATEMENT ON INTELLECTUAL FREEDOM*

The First Amendment to the Constitution of the United States is a cornerstone of our liberty, supporting our rights and responsibilities regarding free speech both written and oral.

The Association for Educational Communications and Technology believes this same protection applies also to the use of sound and image in our society.

---

*Adopted by the AECT's board of directors on April 21, 1978. The basic assumptions underlying this statement can be found in *Media, the Learner, and Intellectual Freedom: A Handbook.*

Reproduced with the permission of the Association for Educational Communications and Technology, from *Media, the Learner, and Intellectual Freedom: A Handbook* (1979), 1025 Vermont Ave., N.W., #820, Washington, DC 20005.

Therefore, we affirm that:

Freedom of inquiry and access to information—regardless of the format or viewpoints of the presentation—are fundamental to the development of our society. These rights must not be denied or abridged because of age, sex, race, religion, national origin, or social or political views.

Children have the right to freedom of inquiry and access to information; responsibility for abridgement of that right is solely between an individual child and the parent(s) of that child.

The need for information and the interests, growth, and enlightenment of the user should govern the selection and development of educational media, not the age, sex, race, nationality, politics, or religious doctrine of the author, producer, or publisher.

Attempts to restrict or deprive a learner's access to information representing a variety of viewpoints must be resisted as a threat to learning in a free and democratic society. Recognizing that within a pluralistic society efforts to censor may exist, such challenges should be met calmly with proper respect for the beliefs of the challengers. Further, since attempts to censor sound and image material frequently arise out of misunderstanding of the rationale for using these formats, we shall attempt to help both user and censor to recognize the purpose and dynamics of communication in modern times regardless of the format.

The Association for Educational Communications and Technology is ready to cooperate with other persons or groups committed to resisting censorship or abridgement of free expression and free access to ideas and information.

Index